Legal Resistance under Authoritarianism

Legal Resistance under Authoritarianism

The Struggle for the Rule of Law in Hong Kong

Yan-ho Lai

Routledge
Taylor & Francis Group
LONDON AND NEW YORK

First published in 2025 by Amsterdam University Press Ltd.

Published 2025 by Routledge
4 Park Square, Milton Park, Abingdon, Oxon OX14 4RN
605 Third Avenue, New York, NY 10158

Routledge is an imprint of the Taylor & Francis Group, an informa business

ISBN: 9789048558438 (hbk)
ISBN: 9781041182108 (pbk)
ISBN: 9781003698869 (ebk)
NUR 697

Cover illustration: Miss B
Cover design: Coördesign, Leiden

DOI: 10.5117/9789048558438

Table of Contents

Acknowledgements

This book marks the culmination of my seven years of research on Hong Kong's Rule of Law. Since 2017, when Carrie Lam became the fourth Chief Executive of Hong Kong, the city has undergone a tumultuous yet profoundly inspiring period for scholars and practitioners examining legal and political developments in Hong Kong and China.

Throughout this challenging period, I have been fortunate to receive immense academic and personal support during my fieldwork. I wish to express my heartfelt gratitude to Tim Pringle, Carol Tan, and Michael Palmer for their unwavering commitment, guidance, and assistance during my years as a research student.

My academic journey would not have begun without the inspiration and enlightenment from Hsin-Chi Kuan, Ngok Ma, and Ming Sing, who were my academic mentors and supervisors at the Chinese University of Hong Kong and the Hong Kong University of Science and Technology respectively. I am grateful to Benny Yiu-ting Tai, who is currently serving a ten-year prison sentence following his conviction for the so-called "conspiracy to subversion" under China's National Security Law imposed on Hong Kong. I remain deeply indebted to his insightful guidance on my research design. My thanks also extend to Kin-man Chan, Yu-Jie Chen, Edmund Cheng, Ching-Fang Hsu, Jen-Shuo Hsu, Carol Jones, Wing-sang Law, Ching Kwan Lee, Karen Lee, Michael Ng, Jothie Rajah, Max Wai Lun Wong, as well as many other legal scholars, social scientists, and lawyers for their invaluable feedback on my work.

I could not have completed my fieldwork without the generous support and hospitality of the Rule of Law Education Project and the Centre for Comparative and Public Law at the Faculty of Law, the University of Hong Kong. I am particularly grateful for the visiting fellowship they offered me between 2018 and 2020. My deepest thanks go to all interviewees who candidly shared their thoughts and experiences with me. For reasons that are all too clear, I will refrain from naming others who supported and aided my research over the years, but I hope they continue to thrive in their intellectual and professional pursuits, both in Hong Kong and elsewhere.

I extend my gratitude to James V. Feinerman and Thomas E. Kellogg, directors of the Center for Asian Law at Georgetown University Law Center, where I have served as a research fellow since 2021. Their boundless support has sharpened my skills in interdisciplinary legal research on Hong Kong and China, as well as in knowledge transfer and public engagement. I also thank Eva Pils, formerly at King's College London's Dickson Poon School of Law, and Malte Kaeding of the University of Surrey, for their endorsements of my visiting appointments in their departments.

In 2023, as I neared the completion of this manuscript, I had the privilege of sharing my preliminary findings at the Richard Charles Lee Canada-Hong Kong Library at the University of Toronto, the University of Tokyo and the Institutum Iurisprudentiae Academia Sinica in Taiwan. I am grateful for their warm hospitality and the thoughtful feedback from the audience.

Over the past seven years, I have also been fortunate to engage in public dialogues as a public intellectual. I owe much to the editors of The Conversation, The Diplomat, East Asian Forum, Hong Kong Free Press, Initium Media, Lawfare, Ming Pao, as well as the now-defunct Citizen News and Stand News. I must also express my gratitude to two publishers in Taiwan, namely Showwe Information and SpringHill Publishing. They edited and published my Chinese monographs, *Unravelling Authoritarian Rule of Law* (2021) and *Resistance Through the Cracks* (2024). The feedback from these works has deepened my reflections on Hong Kong's Rule of Law and legal activism, which are central to this book.

My experience with Amsterdam University Press—from the initial submission through peer reviews and revisions to the final publication—has been admirable. I am grateful to everyone involved for their patience and support throughout the process. I sincerely appreciate the hard work the press invests in bringing authors' ideas to life.

Last but certainly not least, I owe an immeasurable debt of gratitude to my dear friends and comrades around the world. Their unwavering encouragement and support have sustained me throughout this long and often difficult research and writing journey. Our friendships have been a source of renewal during times of personal struggle amidst the shifting political landscape of the past seven years. I also extend my heartfelt thanks to my Jesuit friends and the community at Newman House Catholic Chaplaincy in London. Their spiritual companionship helped me flourish, offering prayers, advice, and invaluable wisdom that enabled me to learn from failure, adopt new perspectives, and cultivate the virtues of joy, perseverance, fortitude, and prudence.

This book is dedicated to my family and to those who have sacrificed their personal liberty in the fight for the Rule of Law and democracy in Hong Kong.

Any errors that remain are mine alone.

List of Figures and Tables

Figures

Tables

1. Introduction: Defending the Rule of Law in the Rise of Authoritarianism

Abstract: This introductory chapter briefly explains how Hong Kong's legal community navigates the challenges posed by authoritarianism under the "One Country, Two Systems" framework. It introduces the concept of "authoritarian legal transplantation," outlining how China's legal and political interventions have reshaped Hong Kong's Rule of Law, merging colonial legal legacies with authoritarian statecraft. The chapter opens the discussion of the tensions between legal professionalism and activism, emphasising lawyers' pivotal role in defending the Rule of Law amidst increasing state encroachment. This chapter presents the main ways of lawyers' resistance, namely civil society empowerment, legal assistance, and leadership contestation, and then the methodology, originality and organisation of the monograph.

Keywords: Rule of Law, Authoritarianism, Legal Transplantation, Hong Kong, Judicial Independence, Legal Profession

The blazing sun hung high in the sky, and few were willing to stroll under the scorching heat dressed in heavy formal attire. For lawyers, regarded as the social elite, it was natural to present themselves with dignity in air-conditioned offices or courtrooms, but under the glaring daylight, who would willingly endure profuse sweating?

Yet, I caught sight of an exceptional scene. It was on 6 June 2019, when I was outside Timar Park in Central Hong Kong. I joined a rally where there were estimated 2,500 lawyers marching outdoors in their suits. People around me included lawmakers, barristers, law students, solicitors, legal scholars, as well as journalists who were live streaming the event. We were asked to march in silence, expressing their disapproval of the Hong Kong government's attempt to pass a legislative amendment that allowed extradition

Lai, Y. *Legal Resistance under Authoritarianism: The Struggle for the Rule of Law in Hong Kong.* Taylor & Francis Group, 2025
DOI: 10.5117/9789048558438_CH01

between Hong Kong and its sovereign state, the People's Republic of China (hereafter China).

This protest, known as the "black-clad march" of the legal profession, began in silence and concluded in the same quiet manner. This form of demonstration is not new in Hong Kong. Since Hong Kong's transfer of sovereignty from Britain to China, some members of Hong Kong's legal community have repeatedly used silent black-clad marches to express their strong dissatisfaction with what they perceive as the erosion of the Rule of Law and judicial independence in the city. These grievances often point to China, accusing it of undermining "One Country, Two Systems," known as the legal firewall between the two systems, through the exercise of sovereign power, interfering with Hong Kong's internal autonomy and judicial independence.

The silent black-clad march was just one of the many protest actions against the extradition amendment bill in the final six months of 2019. While there were citizens adopting militant and violent tactics when confronting law enforcement in street protests, and being eventually labelled as rioters by the government and the court, hundreds and thousands of individual citizens, civil society groups, international advocates, the Bar Association and many legal professionals had engaged in different forms of non-violent mobilisations in order to resist the bill, and broadly the authoritarian rule from China towards Hong Kong. Yet, the city-wide protests were disrupted by the pandemic in early 2020, and then suffered from a total swept by China's imposition of a national security law in the eve of Hong Kong's anniversary of sovereignty transfer in the same year. Many scholars in law and political science, including myself, argue that since then, Hong Kong has entered an era of autocratisation via the enforcement of security legislations and established an "authoritarian Rule of Law" under the shadow of China (Cody 2020; Tai 2021; Lee and Chan 2023; Chan 2023; Lai 2023 and 2024a; Rajah 2024).

China's autocratic agenda, initiated over four years ago with the introduction of the national security law in Hong Kong, remains ongoing, with developments continuing to unfold dynamically. However, the city's resistance to authoritarian rule began long before 2020. This book examines one of the key forces of resistance in Hong Kong, the legal community, which upholds one of the fundamental pillars of the city's exceptional system and values: The Rule of Law. At its core, this book seeks to address a critical question: How can lawyers safeguard the Rule of Law within authoritarian and semi-authoritarian regimes?

Lawyering is a professional occupation that provides clients and societal goods by settling interpersonal and inter-organisational disputes, facilitating economic activities, protecting cliental interests in trials and defending the Rule of Law in courts and society. In many jurisdictions, lawyers are governed by professional bodies and have to follow a series of professional code and practice to maintain their career. However, establishing legal professionalism can also be considered as an ideology that justifies the state's institutional settings of controlling the legal professionals and their privileged position in the social division of labour (Ghai, Luckham and Snyder 1987, 649). Hence, understanding the dynamics between the state, the legal profession and society is of paramount importance for studying how lawyers contest with the state. While conventional lawyering serves the best interests of clients with legal expertise, cause lawyering is a set of "social, professional, political, and cultural practices in which lawyers and other social actors mobilise the law to promote or resist changes" (Marshall and Hale 2014, 301). Cause lawyering, as well as other labels such as "political lawyering," "activist lawyering," or "legal activism," are often seen as creating tensions with some principles of legal professionalism, such as political impartiality, respects for the existing legal system and prohibition of discriminating clients (best known as cab-rank rule).

This book serves to examine how lawyers in hybrid or semi-authoritarian regimes operating a common law system have managed the tensions between legal activism and legal professionalism to resist authoritarian rules beyond the courtroom. This book examines whether and how lawyers can effectively carry out various strategies and tactics to resist authoritarian rules as ways of defending the Rule of Law. Based on my findings, despite the strong statecraft of legal transplantation that tamed the legal environment in the post-Umbrella era of Hong Kong, the local legal profession developed a greater political sensitivity beyond the technical character of law. They also deployed creative and diverse tactics to resist state encroachment on the legal profession itself, including the significant increase in cause lawyering in response to the limitations imposed on the legal system.

In this book, I use the concept of authoritarian legal transplantation to explain why the Rule of Law is at stake in Hong Kong. I also innovate the idea of legal resistance to explain how lawyers defend the Rule of Law in this context. I argue that Hong Kong's Rule of Law, inherited from British colonialism, is a form of authoritarian legality due to China's authoritarian legal transplantation into Hong Kong's legal system and its professional legal culture. China is regarded as an authoritarian regime by academic lawyers and political scientists, given its minimal safeguards of the Rule of Law and its political system that centralises all power to the single Chinese Communist Party (CCP).

As for Hong Kong, it had long been a hybrid or semi-authoritarian regime under the British colonial administration and China's sovereignty respectively. Combined with the colonial legal legacy, China's strategy towards the legal sector in post-colonial Hong Kong and the impacts of economic globalisation, the domestic legal profession has become more politicised than before. As a result, the legal professionals in Hong Kong have become more divergent, consolidating the power imbalance between the state and the legal profession. Additionally, China also expanded its united front strategy in Hong Kong, where local legal elites are recruited and co-opted by the state, which provides economic and political opportunities to facilitate the process of authoritarian legal transplantation. The united front strategy also succeeded in consolidating "comprador professionalism," referring to lawyers being "compradors" of the state for economic interests, serving as leverage for the authoritarian state to continue its "rule by law" project, namely, the operationalisation of an "authoritarian legal transplantation" into Hong Kong, which eventually became an authoritarian regime under the Chinese sovereign.

Lawyers in this context can only defend the inevitable assault on the Rule of Law by exercising their political agency, going beyond a form of legal professionalism that covers all tensions between the state, professional bodies and individual lawyers. At the same time, both the governments of China and Hong Kong politicise the legal environment comprehensively by encroaching on the constitutional and legal orders of Hong Kong, creating a sense of threat among legal professionals and civil society. In response, a number of liberal, critical lawyers carried out different strategies to resist the deterioration of the Rule of Law institutions and culture in civil society, social movements and legal professional bodies that govern them. Lawyer's resistance to authoritarianism is thus a process of politicising the legal profession for liberal political ideals and enhancing the resilience of the Rule of Law in Hong Kong against authoritarian legal transplants. In this introductory chapter, I provide key theoretical framework, analytical overview of the case study, methodology and contributions of this book, alongside the organisation of chapters.

Realising the Rule of Law Ideal under Authoritarianism

Conventionally, law is defined as a set of codes and norms regulating relationships between individuals, communities and the governing authority. Chinese philosopher, Han Feizi, defined law in the third century as merely "statutes and commands [publicly] published by the government, which people know to be backed by the threat of punishments, following them will be rewarded and violation of them will be punished" (Chen 2016, 11). In modern times, legal order and legal authority were also regarded as the most common way for the state to establish legitimacy, but they are also seen as instruments of the capitalist class to exercise domination over society (Weber 1946 and 1978; Marx and Engel 1848; Cain 1974; Turk 1976; Stone 1985, cited in Liu 2015, 4). With the emergence of the modern state as the primary form of polity, law has become a key instrument for the political authority to exercise social control, regulate social relationships and maintain social order with coercive force (Vago 2017). In other words, law is a means for powerholders in political and economic spheres to sustain domination.

The idea of the Rule of Law departs from the view that law is just functional to powerholders. As suggested by A. V. Dicey, the Rule of Law is about "equality before the law" (Dicey 1915, 114). It means that, "government officials and citizens are bound by and abide by the law" (Tamanaha 2007, 3–7; 2012, 233). This notion draws a significant difference between the Rule of Law and rules or governing by law, in which the latter does not imply the public authority being checked and constrained by laws and regulations.

Nevertheless, the definition of the Rule of Law above only provides a minimalist understanding of the matter. Such thin conception of the Rule of Law is contrasted by a more comprehensive interpretation. As Tamanaha suggested, the development of the idea of the Rule of Law has evolved from being conceptualised by its legal characteristics to non-legal values such as political and social justice. He argued that the Rule of Law can be thought of in "formal" and "substantive" terms. A formal understanding of the Rule of Law focuses on the features of the form of law and the design of legal institutions (Fallon Jr. 1997, 1). A substantive understanding that emphasises law's intrinsic values and purposes as tools of rights protection and limiting government power and duties (Raz 1994, 370). A spectrum of the rule of law shall be illustrated from a "thin" definition to a "thicker" one. Such interpretations demonstrate that different conceptions of the Rule of Law are not mutually exclusive, when the understandings and components were evolved over political, economic and social transformation; they can be stretched to achieve higher political ideals (Tamanaha 2004; 2017, 3). It helps us pay attention to a comprehensive ideal of the Rule of Law: in addition to the principles of legality and equality, the Rule of Law should protect individual rights and freedoms, as well as realisation of political and economic justice. To achieve such ideal, understanding the political dynamics and process of constructing and destroying the Rule of Law institutions, including laws and courts, is of paramount importance.

This understanding also explains why the Rule of Law and democracy are mutually constitutive. As Fukuyama argues, the rule is a constitutive element in checking the exercise of the power of bureaucratic government and lays the foundation for the formation of a state (2011 and 2014). The notions of the Rule of Law are often embedded as a core principle in constitutions and judicial systems of sovereign states. Defended by an independent judiciary, a state is made democratic if it asserts practical functions of electoral accountability, protects the political rights of citizens and warrants democratic procedures (O'Donnell 2004, 32). The Rule of Law is also regarded as one of the "indispensable conditions" of consolidated democracy, according to Linz and Stepan, since it embraces constitutionalism, it can ensure the government commits to self-binding rules and the civil and political society is autonomous and independent (1996, 10). Diamond and Morlino further position the Rule of Law as "the base upon which every other dimension of democratic quality rests" (2015, 36). While the rule itself constitutes democracy, it needs to be realised by other conditions as well. Consolidating the Rule of Law in society requires an institutional setting, a shared cultural belief, and a general commitment that recognises, embraces and internalises core elements (Tamanaha 2012, 246). Stromseth et al suggest that,

> The "Rule of Law" describes a state of affairs in which the state successfully monopolises the means of violence, and in which most people, most of the time, choose to resolve disputes in a manner consistent with procedurally fair, neutral, and universally applicable rules, and in a manner that respects fundamental human rights norms. In the context of today's globally interconnected world, this requires modern and effective legal institutions and codes, and it also requires a widely shared cultural and political commitment to the values underlying these institutions and codes (Stromseth et al 2006, 328).

Their argument stresses that the Rule of Law is not merely about internalising the normative characters of law in codified rules and legal institutions following procedural justice and international human rights law, but also about building a cultural norm that constitutes an appreciation of democracy and universal human rights in society. Nevertheless, the optimism of advancing the Rule of Law culture and institutions following democratic and human rights norms is challenged by the global resurgence of democratic backsliding and autocratisation in contemporary world (Lai 2023, 9–10).

Today, the notion of the Rule of Law is no longer a franchise of liberal democracies. Authoritarian regimes can also employ the label of the Rule of Law to justify their practices of "rule by law." Here, rule by law is defined as rule-based governance to maintain social order, emphasising obedience to the law over limiting government by statute, masking the repressive rule before the international community by law-based governance in private and commercial spheres, and deploying legal instruments that violate civil liberties.

Authoritarian regimes generally refer to political regimes in which the executive gains power without free and fair elections or with leaders achieving power through democratic means but change the rules of the game late on (Schmitter and Karl 1991, 75; Geddes, Wright and Frantz 2014, 313; Frantz 2018). Hybrid or semi-authoritarian regimes are distinguished from authoritarian regimes by the degree of competitiveness of the opposition to contest in lawful elections for executive power, alongside the extent of state manipulations of civil liberties and periodic elections (Levitsky and Way 2010). Such manipulations are mainly deployed by coercive use of force, legal instruments and the courts, which legitimise the state's arbitrary use of power.

One typical example of rule by law is colonialism. Under colonialism, indigenous people were not regarded as agents protected by the Rule of Law. A.V. Dicey, though famed as an advocate of Rule of Law, was enthusiastic about the "imperial unity" of the British Empire and justified racial discrimination and abandoning the Rule of Law principles in colonies that attempted to advance decolonisation for independence (Lino 2018, 739). Historians also discovered that the British Empire could undermine the Rule of Law in colonies if national interests were affected (Wiener 2012, 277–291). Throughout history, the "law and order" was implemented by British colonial administrations in many African colonies through partially transplanting the common law and codified statutes to legalise repressive rule in the name of "public order" or a "state of emergency" (Hussain 2003; Killingray 1986; Wong 2011).

Authoritarian regimes commonly rely on laws and courts to achieve their political agenda under the legitimising cover of upholding "the Rule of Law" and "judicial independence." Authoritarian governments can take advantage of the courts to consolidate a given regime while allowing a certain degree of autonomy of the judicial system to present an image of the Rule of Law (Ginsburg and Moustafa 2008). Quite often, the idea of the Rule of Law is undermined or reshaped as political rhetoric by authoritarian regimes, veiling a governance of rule by law, as law and constitution are merely instruments of the ruling party (Whiting 2017, 1907). Alternatively, authoritarian and hybrid regimes can preserve the practice of the Rule of Law only in private and economic aspects while simultaneously being repressive against the opposition through legal measures (Rajah 2012). One critical example was Germany in 1930s. As Frankel highlighted, the Nazi state developed a duality of legal system: while the normative state ensured the nation-building process in economic front, the prerogative state enabled the political authorities with unlimited arbitrary powers to punish their political enemies without judicial checks (Frankel 2017).

Authoritarian legal transplantation is a process of the movement of authoritarian legal norms, laws, statutes, and practices from an authoritarian regime to another political regime, in order to resist the norms and practices of a democratic Rule of Law. This concept emphasises why and how political regimes play a significant role in "legal transplantation," or the "transplantation of law" as interchangeably used by some legal scholars (Schauer 2000; Zhuang 2005; Garoupa and Ogus 2006; Dai 2009; Spamann 2009; Mertus 2011; Cairns 2013; Wang 2013; Ogbonnaya and Iteshi 2016).

Legal transplants have been well studied and debated in comparative law and public policy. Alan Watson defines legal transplantation as "the moving of a rule or a system from one country to another, or from one people to another" and suggests such "legal borrowing" is the "most fruitful source of legal change" (Watson 1993, 21; 1996, 335; Zhou 2011). However, his notion of legal transplantation received criticism for disregarding the socio-cultural surroundings of law, and therefore making legal transplantation impossible (Zhou 2011). Today, studies of legal transplants have evolved to be more inclusive of the broader understanding of law and the legal system to help transplant legal rules and norms into a particular social and cultural context. Legal transplantation expands to underlying policies, general legal ideas and other components of a jurisdiction's legal culture, such as human rights protections and legal education (McBarnet 2002, 100; Chiu 2010; Farran 2013; Siem 2018, 232). Still, legal transplantation generally points to achieving legal modernisation or globalisation and advancing local legal reform and economic development by improving the regulatory framework; legal transplants can be welcomed by developing countries such as China (Chen 2007; 2015). The concept of authoritarian legal transplantation in this book captures the broadening understanding of legal transplants in spheres of law, public policy and cultural values.

For a country that deliberately borrows legal rules from another legal system, they can enjoy the benefits of saving the costs of innovating new legal rules, generating legitimacy from adopting modern legal models and receiving more economic loans or aids alongside foreign investments as international organisations and global corporations would appreciate the transplantation of modern and neoliberal legal norms (Eörsi 1979, 564; Markesinis 2000, 61; Mattei and Nader 2008, 19–20 and 142; Milhaupt and Pistor 2008, 209; Miller

2003, 845; Nelkin 2001, 20; Pirie 2013, 183; Siem 2018, 233–235). These benefits for transplant countries are resulted from 'semi-voluntary transplantation" or "voluntary transplantation" of laws (Müller-Chen et al. 2015, 103–105). Yet, they lack perspective on involuntary legal transplants, which can be seen as an imposition of legal rules only for the origin (donor) country's interests.

On the other hand, the originating countries of legal transplants can benefit from legal transplantation two-fold. Economically, the businesses of the origin country can do business with corporations in the transplanted country that share a familiar legal system. Politically and legally, the origin country can also expand its influence on other countries and thus raise the prestige of its own legal model in which foreign investors are more eager to invest and purchase in jurisdictions that adopt such systems (Siem 2018, 235). Furthermore, the origin country can impose "externally-dictated" transplants, in which case the appropriate term becomes interchangeable with "legal imposition" or "legal imperialism," enabling it to institutionalise its influence over other jurisdictions. Such practices were common in times of colonialism and are highlighted by scholars critical of the Cold War and globalisation today (Mattei 2003; Mattei, Ruskola and Gidi. 2009, 241–242; Miller 2003, 847; Siem 2018, 235).

The concept of authoritarian legal transplantation fits into this strand of literature by highlighting the important association between the process of legal transplantation and political regimes, which is under-researched by scholars of legal transplants. This is because legal transplantation theories rarely consider whether they originate from a liberal democratic or an authoritarian regime. Authoritarian legal transplantation is specific in how it treats legal transplantation as one of the strategies that authoritarian regimes use to expand their influence through the substances and process of legal transplantation. The substance refers to the legal ideology, values, norms, rules and institutions that are illiberal and contradict the fundamental principle of the Rule of Law: limiting government power. The process can be authoritarian if consultation or democratic procedures are absent and if the authoritarian governments controls the process.

Hong Kong's Rule of Law: Decolonisation, Autocratisation and Resistance

Authoritarian Legal Transplantation: From Colonial Rule to "One Country, Two Systems"

I choose Hong Kong as a case study for several reasons. In the first place, Hong Kong serves as a textbook case of how external-dictated legal transplant works. Hong Kong underwent authoritarian legal transplantation twice. The first stage refers to the transplantation of legal rules, such as the public order laws and the common law system, to Hong Kong from other former British colonies, such as India and Malawi (Halpérin 2010; Menski 2006, 242; Mommsen 1992, 10). The second stage is the post-colonial era of Hong Kong, when the legal environment became more hybridised: on the one hand, colonial laws and the old legal system continued to work in Hong Kong as part of the agreement of the sovereign transfer from Britain to China; on the other hand, a process of involuntary legal transplantation continues to be carried out by China, the new sovereign of Hong Kong. Hong Kong's experience resembles an "externally-dictated transplant" or "legally imposed" transplant. Furthermore, the lessons of legal resistance in Hong Kong help us to understand the dynamics of law, politics and social protests amid the intersection between a semi-authoritarian regime and a common law legal system.

During the era of colonial administration (1842–1997), Hong Kong was transplanted with a common law system like other British colonies, and customary law was kept in some areas. After occupying the land since 1842, while keeping a few Chinese laws and customs in effect, the colonial government gradually transplanted the common law system of judicial bodies, criminal justice system, laws and statutes from its home jurisdiction and that of other British colonies (Norton-Kyshe 1971, 16–17; J. Wong 2020). The laws of England were fully in force in 1843, and a Supreme Court with a Chief Justice in Hong Kong was established in 1844, but the power of final appeal remained with London's Judicial Committee of Privy Council (Munn 2019: 2–3). However, the administration of justice at that time was accused of arbitrariness and serious deficiencies, and Chinese residents were excluded from the British-installed legal system (Tsang 2004). In addition, the British transplantation of the English legal system did not include establishing a democratic rule in Hong Kong (Choi and Lee 2017, 187). Rather, many draconian laws that practised deportation, repressed anti-colonial activism, censored the press and empowered the governor with emergency powers were brought to Hong Kong to reinforce censorship and social control (Munn 2009 and 2017; Ng 2016 and 2017). One example was the 1967 Public Order Bill, in which the provisions of unlawful assembly and rioting were transplanted from the penal code of Nyasaland, a former British protectorate and now the Republic of Malawi (Hong Kong Legislative Council Official Report of Proceeding 1967; *Hong Kong Special Administrative Region v Mok Ka To* 2018). Only from the 1970s onwards, the colonial government has made infrequent use of such draconian laws, and the Bill of Rights Ordinance (BORO) was introduced in 1991 to incorporate international human rights law, i.e., the International Covenant on Civil and Political Rights, into domestic legal and judicial practices (Tai 2012; Wong 2017).

The second wave of authoritarian legal transplantation came after Hong Kong's sovereignty transfer to China in 1997. It was a gradual process, and the climax of such transplantation project commenced in 2020 when the National Security Law was imposed by China. After the Second World War, Hong Kong did not immediately enjoy self-determination like other former colonies. On the contrary, when China was allowed to join the United Nations, Hong Kong and Macau, a Portuguese colony on Chinese territory at that time, were removed from the United Nations List of Non-Self-Governing Territories in 1972. Hence Hong Kong was unable to follow internationally recognised mechanisms to declare self-determination and independence. The only destination of Hong Kong's political future would be reunification with China. Twelve years later, under the Sino-British Joint Declaration signed by China and the United Kingdom, China resumed Hong Kong's sovereignty by setting up a Special Administrative Region on 1 July 1997. In sum, Hong Kong remained subordinate to the Chinese sovereign instead of becoming independent after the so-called decolonisation process commenced (Lau 1987).

To stabilise Hong Kong's society and maintain the confidence of both local capitalists and foreign investors, China agreed to keep Hong Kong's existing institutions unchanged, including the common law system, capitalist economy, and public administrative structure. China decided it would not impose single-party rule, a centralised economy, or a socialist legal system (United Nations 1994). These arrangements were considered as the "One Country, Two Systems" formula, and were inserted into the Basic Law of Hong Kong as a mini-constitutional document of the semi-autonomous city. As scholars including Hung and myself argue, the formula of "One Country, Two Systems" is not originated from China's Hong Kong policy. It was inherited from the Qing Dynasty's strategy of governing the multi-ethnic empire's minorities in the periphery and was later on adapted by the Chinese Community Parties as a policy tool to gradually absorb the different governing systems of peripheral communities into the single political economic system. Such policy commenced as early as 1950s, including Xinjiang, Tibet, and then Hong Kong and Macau (Lai 2021c, 45; Hung 2022, 105–107). Evidence can be found in China's agreement with Tibet in 1950s and the Sino-British Joint Declaration in 1984, as there are many parallel provisions between the two documents, such as promises of not altering existing systems and recognition of Chins" sovereignty and its jurisdiction on external affairs (Harris 2008, cited by Hung 2022, 106; Lai 2021c, 46–47).

Hong Kong's version of "One Country, Two Systems" is an experiment in which a socialist state allows practices of a British common law system, separations of powers, protections of individual freedoms and a capitalist economy to co-exist within its territory. The "Two systems" design distinguishes Hong Kong's institutions from the socialist ones in mainland China. The former arrangement warrants basic freedoms and rights for citizens according to international human rights standards, safeguards the economic and legal systems inherited from the British colonial administration and grants Hong Kong a distinctive identity to participate in various international and regional platforms (Chen 2020, 19). However, the "One country" principle only keeps Hong Kong as a special administrative region under the Chinese sovereign state for 50 years. The Basic Law allows the sovereign state to intervene in the "Two systems" by legal and political decisions in several circumstances. After all, Hong Kong has no ultimate authority to decide on its political reform (Kuan 1991, 774).

Hong Kong is thus a city undergoing autocratisation since its sovereignty transfer to China. The "One Country, Two Systems" formula and underlying philosophy, as I highlighted above, characterise Hong Kong as a hybrid or semi-authoritarian regime moving towards full authoritarianism. While China is recognised as an authoritarian regime, post–1997 Hong Kong has often been conceptualised in various ways ranging from "liberal oligarchy," "electoral autocracy" and 'semi-authoritarian regime," all of which stresses the institutional hybridity of protections of civil liberties, civic space for social mobilisations, checks and balances by civil society and the press, alongside partial elections (Allan 1998; Lau and Kuan 2002; Cheng 2005; Ma 2005 and 2007; Bush 2016; Fong 2016 and 2017b; Wong, Ma and Lam 2018; Tai 2021). However, these analyses do not fully address the distinctive nature of Hong Kong, which is not a sovereign state and is subordinate to China's authoritarian governance from British colonial rule. Apart from the absence of a genuinely competitive democratic system, the substantive laws, legal institutions and legal ideology inherited from the colonial administration are transplanted to constitute a governance of rule by law, which elevates the executive power over other branches of government alongside civil society, and which undermines fundamental freedoms and rights of individuals. The Chinese and Hong Kong authorities have used the local legal system, including laws, courts and lawyers, to marginalise political opposition and limit civic space as well as individual freedoms through transplanting authoritarian legal rules, ideology and practices from the mainland to

Hong Kong. Court decisions influenced by the sovereign state's actions have expanded political control in the city while continuing to provide legitimacy to the existing governing system. Official discourse concerning the Rule of Law and judicial independence in Hong Kong is robustly maintained to preserve Hong Kong's positive reputation in the international business community. Such logic adheres to Rajah's and Frankel's notions of how authoritarian regimes aim to create a "duality of law" that, for regime legitimacy and security purposes, divides the politically driven enforcement of law and the economic law that warrants stability and prosperity.

In this book, the process of authoritarian legal transplantation has been carried out directly and indirectly. Direct transplantation is implemented by the Basic Law of Hong Kong and its legal system, whereas indirect transplantation targets the legal profession in Hong Kong, which plays a significant role in supporting the existing legal system. Dezalay and Garth observe in a comparative historical analysis that lawyers can act as pragmatic "double agents" who defend and challenge the state when the state threatens lawyers' interests (2010, 3). In many instances, legal transplants are unfavourable to the recipient legal systems as the transplanted legal rules or values either disrupt the domestic legal order or are irreconcilable with the context of the transplanted jurisdiction (Foster 2007, 273–274; Gutteridge 1949, 25; Siem 2018, 256–258; Teubner 1998). In response, the Chinese state can suppress the liberal norms and establish an alliance with the key stakeholders of law in support of the imposition of authoritarian legal rules and values. Lawyers are an obvious target for such an alliance or become "enemies" of authoritarian legal transplantation. Thus, co-optation and encroachment of the legal profession are essential.

Wu's model of the influencing mechanisms of the "China factor" is here adapted to theorise the encroachment of the legal profession and authoritarian legal transplantation in Hong Kong (2016). He distinguished between "direct" and "indirect" mechanisms of transplantation. The direct influencing mechanism refers to military or political intimidation against another state by China. The indirect mechanism indicates China's establishment of local agents in another state by "cultivating government-business relations." Both mechanisms aim to increase China's political significance in that territory (Wu 2016, 432).

In Hong Kong, the concept of the China factor has been used by political scientists and sociologists to explain the increasing influences of the Chinese state in the city (Fong 2017b, 1; Kwong 2015; Ma 2017, 17). I modify the idea of the China factor to explain the direct and indirect mechanisms of authoritarian legal transplantation in Hong Kong. Direct intervention by China's

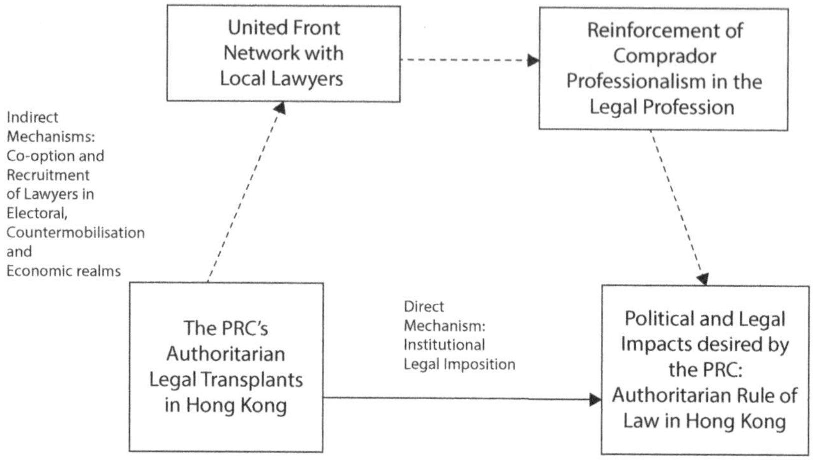

Figure 1. Theoretical Framework of Authoritarian Legal Transplantation in Hong Kong by China

Standing Committee of the National People's Congress entails institutional dimensions of the China factor. This is expressed by legal imposition in the context of authoritarian discourse and constitutional practices that promote the norms of rule by law while keeping with the colonial legal heritage to increase the sovereign's interests in Hong Kong (solid line in figure 1). The other three dimensions constitute indirect mechanisms of authoritarian legal transplantation, and they are operationalised by the famous strategy of the CCP, i.e., the United Front. This is a form of corporatism that maintains the state's hegemony by developing a high degree of political encroachment and infiltration in society for national interests, which encompass national integration, economic growth, social stability without responding to the popular demands for democratisation (Foreweaker 1987, 57; Unger and Chan 1995, 29; Wiarda 1996; Spalding 2003, 139). The United Front Work in China has meant implementing state corporatism by building a temporary alliance between the CCP and one or more non-CCP parties in Hong Kong (Armstrong 1977, 11; Cheng 2020, 1).

The United Front work serves as a strategy of co-optation, a common tactic for authoritarian regimes, to enhance regime legitimacy, stabilise the political order and deploy counter-mobilisation against dissent (Frantz 2018, 111–15). In Hong Kong, United Front work can be found in the remaining three dimensions of indirect authoritarian legal transplantation. The electoral dimension lies in the increase in pro-government lawmakers with a professional background in law. The economic dimension is demonstrated in expanding a cross-border economic partnership between Hong Kong lawyers, the Hong Kong government and the Chinese authorities. The counter-mobilisational dimension refers to infiltrating the legal sector by creating parallel organisations and recruiting pro-government lawyers in state-sponsored counter-mobilisation (dotted line in figure 1). This four-dimensional model of the China factor helps us understand holistically the nature, characteristics, and mechanisms of authoritarian legal transplantation.

One obvious outcome of implementing the direct mechanism of authoritarian legal transplantation is reinforcing the ideology of "authoritarian rule of law". In Hong Kong, lawyers who collaborate with the authoritarian state support such an ideological foundation. While the commercial and economic sides of the legal system in Hong Kong remain effective and stable, the constitutional order and legal rules inherited from the colonial past that suppress political opposition and the liberal legal norms are either reinforced or imposed by the exercises of the sovereign's power to interpret and influence the applications of the Basic Law in Hong Kong. Regarding the indirect mechanisms, they have strengthened the state's encroachment on the legal profession and reinforced a form of comprador professionalism that induces some more outspoken legal professionals and even professional legal bodies to publicly support authoritarian legal rhetoric, consolidating the state's authoritarian rule in Hong Kong.

Comprador professionalism describes a group of state-adjacent lawyers who collaborate with political authorities for advancing economic interests. According to Encyclopaedia Britannica, the word "comprador" originated from the Portuguese, meaning "buyer." In Hong Kong, comprador refers to members of the Chinese merchant class who have helped foreign traders invest in China since the late eighteenth century (Encyclopaedia Britannica 1998). Carol Jones proposed the concept of "comprador lawyers" to describe legal professionals who serve the transnational capitalist class conducting business with China (Jones 2010). For authoritarian states, inculcating a political ideology is more than just imposing "ruling ideas" or rhetoric of the ruling class (Marx and Engels 1848; Scott 1985, 315). As Gramsci highlighted, the dominant relationships between the ruling class and subordinate class extend to the cultural and symbolic domains to dissimilate the values of the dominant class and reinforce its position (Gramsci, translated by Hoare and Smith 1971; Scott 1985, 315). The implementation of ideology needs both symbolic and material support to form a hegemony in society. The legal system thus serves as an instrument to maintain the hegemonic position of the dominant class. Indirect legal transplantation thus supports the direct transplantation of authoritarian legal ideology and norms by encroaching on the domestic legal profession, endorsing the newly transplanted system in the process. In short, comprador professionalism tells us how the organised legal profession tends to collaborate, legitimise and aid the state for lawyers' economic interests by concentrating on the economic and technical characters of legal practices and with the repeated emphasis of political neutrality and non-partisanship. Yet, neither of these attributes is value-free.

China's authoritarian legal transplantation has worked together with a continuing colonial legal legacy on the one hand and a new ideology and a new set of norms and practices on the other. The internal tensions of "One Country, Two Systems" formula are no more apparent than in the ideological struggle over the Rule of Law when China commenced to transplant its legal rules and norms in Hong Kong, which itself inherited a common law system from its British colonial legacy. It has long enjoyed a high reputation for judicial independence in terms of its protection of fundamental freedoms and rights along with common law principles, shared with at least some commonwealth jurisdictions that uphold the integrity of law (Wacks 1989, 127). In contrast, China as a state interprets and advocates the Rule of Law as "rule-based governance" (*yī fǎ zhì guó*), while at the same time 'socialist rule of law" and "party leadership" are emphasised as complementary to each other to achieve "*yī fǎ zhì guó*" (Trevaskes 2019, 251). Instead of an independent judiciary, the mainland's juridical institutions are supervised by the CCP's Central Political and Legal Affairs Commission (Li 2019, 19). It means law and courts are subject to the CCP rather than the party being subject to the checks and balances of the courts.

One important note is that such authoritarian legal transplantation process should not be seen as Hong Kong's decolonisation process. But rather, China's autocratisation project on Hong Kong via the "One Country, Two Systems" formula is an approach to consolidate the British colonial legacies and China's empire-building project. As Hung suggested,

> Though the Communist party-state always claim it is building a modern nation-state, the incorporation and governing of the vast and diverse geographical space inherited from the Qing empire necessitate that it adopts ruling strategies overlapping with those of Qing times. This makes the PRC an empire pretending to be a nation-state (Hung 2022, 108).

Hung's notion on China's empire-building project is based on the fact as aforementioned, the Communist's policy formula of "One Country, Two/multiple Systems" in Tibet, Hong Kong and Macau has been designed as a transitional arrangement, which eventually enabled the ruling regime to assimilate and absorb the peripheral communities into the party-state.

Furthermore, many outstanding Chinese scholars appreciated and appointed by the Chinese authorities expressed positive connotations to describe China as an empire nowadays. One prominent example is JIANG Shigong. He was a fellow at China's Liaison Office in Hong Kong and was reported as the main contributor to the 2014 State Council's White Paper on Hong Kong's implementation of "One Country, Two Systems." He authored a number of pieces that endorsed China's imperial legacies as applicable and imperative to the Communist rule today (Hung 2022, 139).

China's empire-building statecraft works oppositely with the general notion of decolonisation, which is often conceptualised as a process of liberating people from different forms of repression and violence, ranging from physical violence, dehumanising racism, land dispossession, economic exploitations, warfare to domination of hegemonic ideology as well as knowledge (Fanon 1963; Bourdieu and Sayad 2004; Mignolo and Walsh 2018: 136, cited by Lee 2025). China's empire-building project aims to consolidate the long-standing patterns of power that defines the power structure and inequalities, labour relations, culture and knowledge that are not only inherited from Marxism, but also Chinese imperial legacies (Zēng 2014). Such performance is very similar to operating colonisation instead of decolonisation (Maldonado-Torres 2007, 243, cited by Adébísí 2023).

Hong Kong is a textbook case of how China carries out an empire-building project pretends to be a nation-state by preserving colonial legacies. Once Hong Kong was removed from the United Nations List of Non-Self-Governing Territories in 1972, it lost the entitlement of self-determination from both British and Chinese rules. The Sino-British Joint Declaration between British and Chinese authorities in 1984 only warranted that Hong Kong's sovereignty would be transferred from one sovereign power to another. Some scholars described this design as "deep freezing" Hong Kong as most pre-existing systems remained intact under the "One Country, Two Systems" formula and the Basic Law, the mini-constitutional document for post-colonial Hong Kong (Lui and Fong 2014). In short, Hong Kong's sovereignty transfer was an unfinished decolonisation. It ironically froze non-democratic institutions and upheld draconian laws that are able to suppress basic liberties of local residents, and to enable the new sovereign power to combine colonial repressive means with authoritarian legal transplants for regime consolidation (Lai 2024c). Despite the autonomy that "One Country, Two Systems" offers on face value, Hong Kong does not have the final say in in its political reform (Kuan, 1991, 774). And after all, the formula was set as a temporal arrangement that is expected to expire in 2047. After that, full assimilation of Hong Kong into China appears to be the most possible result.

Hong Kong's autonomy is conditionally and unavoidably subject to the Chinese sovereign state. China's authoritarian legal transplantation in Hong Kong, as I will discuss in the following chapters, only serves to converge hegemonic legal ideology between Hong Kong and China, and to strengthen social and political control with the aid of the Communist's co-optation strategy with domestic, state-adjacent legal professionals.

An examination of the interactions between the sovereign power of China and the legal community in Hong Kong can enhance our understanding of how the Rule of Law can be developed under a co-existence of the common law and the socialist law between a subnational polity and a sovereign state, and how authoritarian legal transplants have facilitated Hong Kong's autocratic rule driven by China. It is often argued that the power relations between China and Hong Kong under "One Country, Two Systems" can only remain harmonious and stable if the sovereign state and different parties in Hong Kong can exercise self-restraint by not provoking one another (Chan 2019, 85; Chan and Londras 2020, 1). Once the state, the main designer of the games' rules break the equilibrium, other parties can only choose to adapt or resist. If China does not practice self-restraint in exercising its power over Hong Kong but rather implements a governance of integration and convergence that engenders conflicts between state and society, are there ways for Hong Kong civil society to resist and preserve "One Country, Two Systems?"

Contesting the Rule of Law: Civil Society and Lawyers

Defence of Hong Kong's civil society often lies in their contestation against the state actors over the understanding, values and actions that support a liberal notion of the Rule of Law, including protections of fundamental rights and freedoms, universal suffrage, and democratic citizenship. In colonial times, the government branded Hong Kong as establishing the Rule of Law and the court was a substitute for any opening of formal public political participation. At the same time, however, democracy was absent, and draconian laws were remaining in force (Jones 1999; Ho 2004). Since the sovereignty transfer, the Hong Kong government has been trying to continue an official discourse on "law and order" as a ruling framework over a rights-based discourse of the Rule of Law (Ku 2004, 647). Such contestation was also escalated into mass mobilisation against state actions that were perceived as damaging the city's Rule of Law and the constitutional order as a whole.

Another conventional strategy for civil society to resist government's authoritarian and anti-rights agenda is judicial review. As democratisation failed to materialise, activists and marginalised groups have turned to both constitutional and administrative reviews as possible avenues for correcting government's wrongdoings, defending constitutional rights, checking the excesses of state administration and striving for policy change, leading to "the politicisation of the judiciary" and "the judicialisation of politics and public policy" (Cheung and Wong 2006, 117; Chan 2007, 407; Kapai 2011, 49; Kong 2012, 588; Tam 2012). Pro-government lawmakers have criticised pursuing judicial review as a misuse of the law (*Legislative Council of the HKSAR,* 8 June 2011). These criticisms were revealed in famous cases on the constitutionality of government policies that violated human rights of individual residents (*The Director of Immigration v. Master Chong Fung Yuen 2001*; *Chu Yee Wah v Director of Environmental Protection 2011*; *Vallejos Evangeline Banao, also known as Vallejos, Evangeline B. and Daniel Domingo L. v. Commissioner of Registration and Registration of Persons Tribunal 2013*).

However, judicial reviews are only applicable to challenge the acts of the Hong Kong government, while many instances of the authoritarian encroachments came from the sovereign state, China. Rulings in Hong Kong's court also made clear that they have no jurisdictions to challenge the acts of China even if the acts impact the city's political and legal systems at all. This is the reason why this book pays more attention to lawyers' resistance strategies beyond the courtroom. As my study reveals, lawyers' engagement in civil society, social movements and even council elections within the legal professional bodies, engendered strong capacities and a support base for the people to resist authoritarian legal transplantations from China.

The contest over Hong Kong's Rule of Law has been heavily tied with the city's anti-authoritarian protests since 2003. The first happened in 2002 when the government introduced a national security bill following the imperative prescribed in Article 23 of the Basic Law. The bill was perceived by lawmakers, journalists and religious leaders as a fundamental challenge to safeguarding civil liberties and the Rule of Law (Cheng, ed 2005; M. Ng 2017). The controversy over the bill and the reluctance of the government to expand consultation led to more than half a million citizens protesting on 1 July 2003. The bill was eventually withdrawn under this public pressure (Fu, Petersen and Young 2005). In return, since then, Beijing has become more directly involved in the local legal and judicial affairs of Hong Kong (Cheng 2009).

The second contest over the idea and practice of Rule of Law in Hong Kong refers to Professor Benny Yiu-ting Tai's call for acts of civil disobedience in the struggle for universal suffrage in 2013. He launched an Occupy Central with Love and Peace campaign with sociologist Kin-man Chan and an evangelical pastor Yiu-Ming Chu, aiming to promote the idea of civil disobedience, also known as "achieving justice by breaking the law" (*wéi fǎ dá* yì), and to organise a public deliberation forum to reach a consensus on a concrete proposal of constitutional reform for the 2017 Chief Executive elections (Lee and Chan 2018). The campaign, unsurprisingly, was heavily attacked by government officials and its allies as inciting the public to break the law and disrupt law and order. One year later, the Occupy campaign evolved into the Umbrella Movement, when student activists took over the campaign's leadership and thousands of protestors occupied three city hubs for 79 days to oppose Beijing's rejection of genuine universal suffrage by setting a tight screening mechanism for candidates. The movement was a contestation between the liberal conception of the Rule of Law that places political liberalism as the basis of legal order and the rhetoric of law and order that emphasises obedience to the law (Pang 2020, 175). The court became a contentious platform when pro-government groups filed civil injunctions against the occupations, and when the court ordered the clearance of occupied sites, drawing the movement to an end (Fu 2018a, 83).

The latest citywide protests contesting the Rule of Law in Hong Kong was the 2019 Anti-extradition Law Amendment Bill (Anti-ELAB) Movement. In February 2019, the Hong Kong government introduced amendments to the Fugitive Offenders Ordinance, which allowed for the extradition of fugitive offenders between Hong Kong and China. Fearing the passage of the Extradition Law Amendment Bill (ELAB) would undermine the role of Hong Kong's legal system as a firewall against China's legal apparatus, the Hong Kong Bar Association (the Bar), civil society organisations, foreign governments and expatriate commercial chambers publicly expressed opposition to the amendments (Hong Kong Bar Association 2019; Meick 2019; Pomfret 2019; The American Chamber of Commerce in Hong Kong, 2019). On 9 June 2019, more than a million local citizens protested on the streets against the bill. A violent clash between riot police and protestors occurred on 12 June 2019 outside the Legislative Council (LegCo) building before the scheduled second reading of the bill. The mass mobilisations are in part explained by China's notoriety for its lack of fair trials and for its "global kidnapping campaign" of those it accuses of having violated the law (Dorfman 2018; Rifkind 2019; Hui 2019). Although the government withdrew the bill a few months after, peaceful mass rallies and militant protest actions continued when both radical demonstrators and law enforcement escalated their use of force in street protests. Moreover, the Anti-ELAB Movement also led to a revival of the enforcement of draconian laws, including the Public Order Ordinance and the Emergency Regulation Ordinance, that the colonial administration used to suppress anti-colonial labour strikes and protests (Hong Kong Watch 2019). As of 2023, more than 10,000 Hong Kong residents got arrested for allegedly involving in the Anti-ELAB protests, nearly 3,000 prosecuted, and more than 1,300 incarcerated (Chan, Lai and Kellogg 2023). Prosecutions and trials regarding the 2019 protests are still going on in Hong Kong. The Anti-ELAB movement came to an end in mid–2020, when Beijing decided to impose a new National Security Law (NSL), as well as to set up a new national security agency in May 2020 (Beattie and Walker 2020; Wong and Cheung 2020). Since the imposition of the NSL, the Rule of Law again has become the nexus of clashes between the state and society of Hong Kong.

Local legal professionals played a pivotal role in civil society and protest movements in defence of the rule above. Being a lawyer in Hong Kong has been a privilege in professional and economic terms. Since British colonial rule, lawyering in Hong Kong is a self-regulated profession overseen by two professional bodies: the Bar and the Law Society of Hong Kong (the Law Society). The former body governs barristers and the latter for solicitors. Both bodies own legal monopoly from government's statutes and support. As a city of over 7 million residents, Hong Kong is served by more than 10,000 solicitors and over 1,500 barristers (HKTDC Research 2019). The legal profession in Hong Kong is a powerful group in Hong Kong's political, economic and cultural development. The exports of legal services amounted to US$386 million (HK$3 billion) in 2018 (HKTDC Research 2020b). Law schools in Hong Kong continue to maintain their academic reputation and nurture hundreds of legal professionals for the city's legal service market. In addition, the local political system also gives privileges to the legal profession and other professional sectors. Before 2021, half of the seats in LegCo were dedicated to functional constituencies, which consisted of selected industrial, commercial and professional sectors in Hong Kong. The legal industry was thus given one seat in the legislature. Before the election overhaul in 2021, the legal profession also had 30 out of 1,200 seats on the Election Committee that selects the Chief Executive of Hong Kong.

However, these privileges do not necessarily make all lawyers loyal to the state. Lawyers' allegiance to defending the Rule of Law and judicial independence sometimes clashes with political allegiance to the state. Lawyers mobilised for silent "black-clad" marches six times against China's re-interpretation of the Basic Law and against the PRC's political demand in the 2014 official White Paper for judicial officials to show patriotic commitment. Until 2020, seats of delegates of the legal profession in LegCo and the Election Committee that selects the Chief Executive of Hong Kong have always been given to liberal and pro-democracy lawyers through periodic elections. Tensions between the legal profession and the state over constitutional matters and legal ideology have never ceased since the handover. The politicisation of the legal profession in Hong Kong can also be found in the professional bodies, which identify themselves as defenders of the Rule of Law. Yet sometimes the Bar and the Law Society were also criticised for being politicised by actively challenging the state, or by publicly condemning anti-government protestors. Such politicisation of the legal community could be perceived as creating conflicts with the understanding of the appropriate role of legal professionals (Sarat and Scheingold, eds. 1998, 8; Cummings 2011, 25–27).

While lawyering is an occupation, sometimes practitioners, in light of lawyers' ethical code and professional spirit, go beyond profit-making by providing pro bono legal services or cause lawyering, meaning engaging in litigation and legal assistance to address a moral cause. Unlike lawyers in the legal aid system or duty lawyer schemes that provide professional legal services to individual clients, cause lawyering or activist lawyering demonstrates the resilience of the legal profession against undesirable legal, political and social structures by both activist-like advocacy and professional practices. In Hong Kong, apart from joining silent black-clad marches, hundreds of barristers and solicitors provided public legal education for rally participants, arrested protestors, and formed networks of pro bono legal visitors to assist arrestees and represent them in trials later. When lawyers are active in social movements, the tension between upholding professional identity and exercising political agency appears. The boundary of lawyering between achieving a professional project in building the Rule of Law and realising a democratic project in society is blurred. Although the number of lawyers publicly engaging in the movement was not a majority within the profession, it is puzzling to examine why those who participated in the political movement as legal professionals did so and the extent to which they were conscious of the tension between conventional lawyering and cause lawyering as well as how they negotiated that tension.

This book focuses on Hong Kong's legal and political developments between 2014 and 2020. This is the period between the aftermath of the Umbrella Movement and the collapse of the Anti-ELAB Movement by China's imposition of the NSL in Hong Kong on 30 June 2020. I label this temporality as "Post-Umbrella Hong Kong". Considering the drastic change of Hong Kong's laws and courts after the NSL was enforced, the post–2020 development of Hong Kong's legal system remains uncertain and unpredictable to a certain extent. Hence, this book mainly focuses on how lawyers resist the authoritarian rule of the Chinese and Hong Kong authorities before the enactment of the NSL. As I argue here, while many scholars and analysts regard the NSL as indicating the beginning of the end of Hong Kong's Rule of Law, the latter has already been at stake since the sovereign state commenced encroaching on Hong Kong's legal system through "authoritarian legal transplantation" in 1997. As this book reveals, Hong Kong's legal community has generated synergy with civil society to resist such statecraft in different ways, and some of them remain crucial in defending the city's legal system and generally the equilibrium of "One Country, Two Systems" in post-NSL times. The next section explains the role of lawyers in defending the Rule of Law in authoritarian contexts, and how lawyers' strategies and tactics in Hong Kong shed light on the ongoing academic debate.

Legal Resistance under Authoritarianism

While the state can wield monopolised violence and ultimate authority to institutionalise the legal institutions, personnel, culture and values for its interests, there are still potential avenues for resistance against the transplantation of an authoritarian Rule of Law. Resistance lies not only in legal institutions but also in the legal profession and civil society organisations that are potential parties to developing a cultural commitment to the Rule of Law.

In colonial studies of law, scholars write of how the colonialists often perceived the imposition of law as a civilising mission; the scholars themselves see it as a means of exploitation (Chanock 1985, 4; Fitzpatrick 1992, 107–11; Merry 1995, 890; 2000, 572; Choi and Lee 2017,190). Colonial legal transplants and their imposition were considered instruments justifying the domination and economic exploitation of the colonised. Ultimately, the exploitation benefited Western capitalism, although in some cases colonial legal transplants did aid the economic development of recipient colonies (Schmidhauser 1989, 862; Stoler and Cooper 1997, 1–3; Merry 2000, 890; Comaroff 2001, 307–11; Benton 2002, 19, Choi and Lee 2017, 191–192). That said, the colonised people could enjoy political agency to resist or support colonial rule. While local elites facilitated the colonisers' civilising mission in complex and diverse colonised societies, anti-colonial forces disrupted legal exploitation in various ways (Brown 1995, 104; Comaroff 2001, 307–308; Merry 2000, 917; Stoler and Cooper 1997, 5–7, Choi and Lee 2017, 192–193).

This book uses the term "legal resistance" to describe how bottom-up resistance to authoritarian legal transplantation evolved in Hong Kong in several ways; in particular, the concept covers strategies and tactics of lawyers responding to and resisting the process and consequences of authoritarian legal transplants, in order to build institutional strengths of the legal system and promote a Rule of Law culture in society. As suggested by Stromseth et al (2006, 340–345), such processes of building credible legal institutions and developing cultural norms and beliefs regarding the Rule of Law are integral to consolidating a just political culture and the legitimacy of the political regime.

Professions have a "monopolistic character in the labour market" and play the role of "privileged private governments" (Cairnes 1887, 66–67; Friedman 1962, 137–160; Gilb 1966; Freidson 1983, 19). It means that the political authority endorses their professional qualifications and statuses. The legal profession was one of the learned "status professions" recognised by the universities of Europe in the medieval period. When the Industrial Revolution fostered the development of capitalism and the middle class in the nineteenth century, newly formed middle-class occupations also sought the title of profession for a secure and privileged place, the professional project shielded from competition in the labour market. To do so, they needed state approval to enjoy an exclusive identity and status. Such privileges were given by the state's recognition of professional qualifications issued by the occupations' corporate organisations or higher education (Freidson 1983, 23-5). Today, lawyers provide individual and collective services in court representation, commercial trade, litigation, and alternative dispute resolutions; in some liberal democratic jurisdictions, lawyers even provide knowledge transfer of law and engagements in law reform at local and global levels. They have an enormous economic and political impact on society (Rostain 2008, 163). In short, the legal profession is a "socio-political" artefact endorsed by the state's power to occupy a distinctive position in the labour market (Freidson 1983, 34). The strong professionalism of lawyers in some societies may help them to acquire economic, social, and political power collectively, depending on the extent of their collaboration with the political authority (Rostain 2008, 163).

On face value, lawyers' contestation with the state in authoritarian regimes is full of tensions, as they struggle with the authority that approves their professional licences. Quite often, the power to grant licence to lawyers is centralised to political authorities in authoritarian regimes. But on the other hand, lawyers' moral commitment to defending the Rule of Law can be a strong incentive to challenge the power abuses or *ultra vires* of political authorities. Even in repressive contexts, lawyers would risk their professional careers or even personal safety to challenge the state. Examples can be found in China when some prominent human rights lawyers suffer from criminal prosecutions and long jail sentences (Fu 2018b).

In this book, the experience of lawyers resisting the process of authoritarian legal transplantation in Hong Kong reveals that the collective agency of lawyers is illustrated in institutional, collective and individual forms of activist lawyering. I use the idea of "legal resistance" rather than directly apply the concept of cause lawyering to highlight the point that even if lawyers or the organised professions do not identify themselves as cause lawyers, the intentions and motivations underpinning such lawyering, as well as their conventional and dutiful legal practices and advocacy for the Rule of Law can and shall be counted as strategies to resist authoritarian legal transplants. Moreover, legal resistance is not limited to legal mobilisation in court. Legal mobilisation mainly studies how lawyers are mobilised to promote or resist social change through litigation alongside formal and quasi-formal dispute resolution mechanisms (Chua 2019; Tam 2012). Non-litigation and even activist-like strategies and tactics are counted in this book because the site of contestation lies in the more comprehensive state-building project. Such reactions reflect the political dynamics between the state, legal profession and society that influence the production and development of the Rule of Law in Hong Kong, affirming the fundamental assumption of this book: the Rule of Law is a sociological and historical construct that has resulted in part from power struggles between stakeholders in the legal system.

Legal resistance results from the awakening of the political agency of lawyers and their public spirit to defend the Rule of Law from authoritarian legal transplantation. This book examines three strategies of resistance one by one. They are "civil society empowerment," "legal assistance for protestors" and "leadership contestation."

Civil Society empowerment refers to the efforts of lawyers to utilise their legal expertise, including legal knowledge, skills and professional identity, to connect and work with civil society actors for defending the principles and institutions of a rights-based Rule of Law, and enhancing a liberal Rule of Law culture in the public sphere. Lawyers adopting this strategy in Hong Kong acted like cause lawyers and activist lawyers, since they provide their legal expertise not for their own interests, nor individual clients, but for a political or human rights cause. Cause lawyers are generally regarded as "morally activist lawyers' for the public good (Sarat and Scheingold 1998, 3). Cause lawyering also goes beyond taking legal cases; cause lawyers are eager to organise civil society activities and engage in political mobilisation at local and international levels (Sarat and Scheingold 1998, 4–7; 2001,4; 2004).

That said, cause lawyers must always negotiate the tension between promoting a fundamental liberal rights and broader democratic values against the state's abuse of power as activist lawyers and being policed by the organised profession that upholds legal professionalism (Sarat and Scheingold 1998, 8–11). While critics would interpret professionalism as a "top-down project of social control" to protect lawyers' privileged status against outsiders, the discourse of professionalism can also be used by cause lawyers to "counterpoise their professional vision of lawyering for a cause against the conventional commitment to client service" (Sarat and Scheingold 1998, 11).

In authoritarian regimes, the tensions between activist lawyering and professional lawyering escalated when the authorities repress the legal profession to marginalise opposition, produce pro-government lawyers in order to consolidate the political rule. One example is China's "709 Crackdown," in which more than a hundred human rights lawyers were arrested for their legal advocacy (Fu 2018b, 554).

In the face of such repression of lawyers, scholars have identified at least four tactics for sustaining cause lawyering under authoritarian regimes. Firstly, lawyers can engage in political mobilisation, even under risky circumstances, to uphold professional autonomy (Ahmed and Stephan 2010, 492; Liu and Halliday 2011; Marshall and Hale 2014, 316). Secondly, lawyers can be involved in transnational human rights networks that support cause lawyering and domestic activism to generate international political pressure on the regimes (Meili 1998, 487; 2001, 307; Marshall and Hale 2014, 316). Thirdly, lawyers can continue to protect the legal rights of clients from the threats of state power by focusing on issues of due process in legal proceedings (Bisharat 1998, 453; Hajjar 2001, 68; Liu and Halliday 2011, 831; Tam 2010; Marshall and Hale 2014, 316). Fourthly, lawyers can participate in regime transition by designing constitutions and political reform (Klug 2001, 264).

The strategy of civil society empowerment intersects the first and the second modes. I argue that promoting public legal education to empower citizens with rights-based legal consciousness and disseminating a democratic culture within the legal profession are ways for lawyers to engage in political mobilisation and earn support from transnational human rights networks. In practice, lawyers collaborated with civil society actors and individual citizens to decentralise legal knowledge and legal arguments to "enhance and enable broader public engagement and deliberation about major social issues inside and outside professional domains" (Dzur 2008, 129–130). Throughout the process of empowerment, lawyers serve as an intermediary between citizens and democratic institutions, constructing a realm of "middle democracy" (Dzur 2008, 130). One specific tactic to achieve this goal is promoting public legal education from the bottom. This is treated as legal mobilisation, as educating the public is an essential social movement tactic (Barclay and Marshall 2005; Katuna and Holzer 2016, 81; McCann and Silverstein 1998; Pedriana and Stryker 1997, 636). Lawyers engaging in civil society empowerment reinterpret the Rule of Law, judicial independence and human rights defence as goals of pursuit in the local democratisation movement. They provide legal justifications and a legal framework for civil society organisations as well as activists to deploy in their struggle with the political authority and to develop liberal legal consciousness against authoritarian legal transplantation (Blackstone, Uggen and McLaughlin 2009; Hilson 2002; Katuna and Holzer 2016, 82; Leachman 2013; Marshall 2001; Pedriana 2006; Turner 2006; Yazdiha 2014). During such processes, activist lawyers also influence the legal socialisation of the public. The legal profession is also politicised and democratised by political liberalism, which interprets the Rule of Law as an essential element of democratisation (Donnelly 2009; Henry and Gordon 2003; Katuna and Holzer 2016, 83).

Another strategy happens in protest movement settings. Social movement is a valuable space for cause lawyers to promote a democratic notion of professionalism in civil society and to extend the political struggles of the movement into both criminal and civil legal proceedings. Charles Tilly defines a social movement as a series of interactions between power holders and persons representing those who lack formal representation, demanding changes in power distribution by mass mobilisation (1984, 15; cited in Sarat and Scheingold 2006, 2). Cause lawyers engage in social movements, advocating demands by supporting the social movement organisers and participating in the legal mobilisation against state power. Their actions in movement space include: (1) associating a collective sense of grievance with a discourse for constitutional and legal rights; (2) strategising litigation to widespread rights consciousness and to seek public attention for movement goals; (3) struggling over policy or legislation with the political authority in the courtroom; (4) empowering citizens by levering the outcome of litigation (McCann 2004, 506). These characteristics, however, are usually found in democratic regimes, or more specifically, in the American context, where legal mobilisation for advancing equal citizenship had been a prominent phenomenon during the American civil rights movement since the 1950s and the critical legal studies movement in the 1970s (Unger 2015, 79–82; Liu 2015, 4). In authoritarian regimes, lawyers usually exercise their professional role in social movements by performing legal representation in criminal trials instead, when the state authorities weaponise laws and courts to prosecute activists and protestors.

In this sense, lawyers engaging in the strategy of *legal assistance for protestors* do not choose to confront the authority through professional bodies or advocacy in civil society. Instead, they provide legal expertise to protestors facing criminal sanctions. However, by providing legal support for activists, those lawyers would be seen as antagonistic to authoritarian governments, which regard such political lawyering (or activist lawyering) as enriching the legal capital of the opposition movement. Thus, lawyering for protest groups is highly contentious, as it already constitutes resistance against legal repression by the state.

Lawyers defending activists in such a context are supposed to treat the activist defendants as clients. Yet, at the same time, lawyers often share the beliefs in legal and political justice with the defendants or commit to the values of the Rule of Law, due process and protection of human rights for individual citizens; otherwise, they would have less motivation to act. Such legal representation is not limited to the courtroom: even before prosecution, these lawyers can advocate for political rights or provide pro bono legal support for activists under police arrest (Pils 2014; Stern 2017; Wilson 2017; Winn and Yeh 1995). In this book, legal assistance consists of lawyers, paralegals and law students who collaborate with or work in social movement organisations to provide legal assistance to those who resist authoritarian rule at the frontline; these lawyers are rear-guards and defenders of protestors in the legal sphere (Glick 2017; Jones 2001). At the same time, local crowdfunding platforms sustain interested law firms to represent protestors in trial processes. Legal assistance for protestors also enhances the resilience and capacities of the "critical minority" of lawyers in resisting authoritarian legal transplantation, when lawyers and social movement actors are organically tied to defend access to justice for arrested protestors suffered from authoritarian policing and legal repression.

Last but not the least, the interactive complex between the state and lawyers is always reflected in the relationship between bar associations and the government that sponsors the legal profession's monopoly and the bar associations' regulatory autonomy in market control and qualifying lawyers. Whether bar associations are regarded as competitors, consultants or partners in policymaking depends on the degree of state incorporation in the legal profession. In hybrid and authoritarian regimes, the bargaining power between professional bodies and the state varies, depending on the degree of state control over the legal profession, its tolerance over the autonomy of professional bodies, or the mobilisation power of professional bodies in times of struggle with the state (Solomon Jr. 2010; Ahmed and Stephan 2010; Shafqat 2018; Liu and Stern 2020; Stern and Liu 2020; Winn and Yeh 1995). For instance, Turkey's newly passed bar associations law allows multiple bar associations in the provinces to diminish the influence of significant bar associations critical of the government, thus dividing the Turkish legal profession (Butler and Toksabay 2020). Nevertheless, Bar associations can find ways to play the role of opposing the government when the former's normative interests (say, the Rule of Law) and substantive interests (monopoly in the labour market) are threatened (Gobe and Salaymeh 2016; Halliday 2005, 375).

The strategy of *leadership contestation* refers to lawyers' engagement in elections of legal professional bodies. They get involved in elections for seizing the institutional powers of the Hong Kong Bar Association and the Law Society of Hong Kong to legitimately challenge the state's authoritarian agenda and defend the professional interests, i.e., mainly upholding professional autonomy from state's interference. With the mandate of lawyers, legal professional bodies often publish public statements to address fundamental legal principles and opine for government's legislative and policy agendas. It means that organised profession can publicly opposes and criticises the state in legal and constitutional matters. However, legal professional bodies are also bounded by their statutory nature. As this book reveals, although legal professional bodies could be confrontational against the state in legal and constitutional matters, their expression of opposition or resistance were mainly discursive due to their formal ties with the institutional structure of the state. That said, getting into the councils of the Bar and Law Society via leadership contestation serve as an important strategy for liberal lawyers to develop a Rule of Law culture within the legal profession, and to earn support from the public by their statements and support for an anti-authoritarian agenda as independent bodies. Above all, winning seats in the councils of the two legal professional bodies are direct ways of minimising the state's influence and infiltration of the legal community through the United Front Work.

Civil society empowerment, legal assistance for protestors and leadership contestation are mutually constitutive. The organised efforts of liberal and activist lawyers in empowering civil society actors offered many law students and junior lawyers to get involved in civil society development of Hong Kong. They became more sympathetic in the pro-democracy activists, and eventually turned to committed supporters for the pro-democracy movement. Many of them called on their peer lawyers to provide legal assistance for anti-authoritarian protestors in police custody and the criminal court. The Bar, which consisted of barristers sharing concerns of authoritarian legal transplantation in the city, also promoted public education on the Rule of Law, and even appreciated legal assistance for protestors. After experiencing and witnessing legal assistance and civil society empowerment, some solicitors further committed themselves to leadership contestation against state-adjacent lawyers, generating a greater solidarity among liberal and activist lawyers, expanding a critical minority within the legal profession of Hong Kong.

One remark is that I choose not to use the concept of "legal complex" in my study. This concept has been used by socio-legal scholars to explain political lawyering in pursuit of political liberalism (Halliday, Kapik and Feeley 2007, 1). The legal complex refers to "a cluster of legal actors related to each other in dynamic structures and constituted and reconstituted through various processes" (Kapik and Halliday 2011, 220). Lawyers often constitute the mobilisation of legal actors in such ties, such as judges, legal academics and even prosecutors, especially the relationship between lawyers and judges (Halliday, Kapik and Feeley 2007, 2; Kapik and Halliday 2011, 221–222 – italics added by the authors). This book does not focus on judicial responses to the struggle for the Rule of Law in Hong Kong, and my units of analysis do not include judges but rather the interactions between lawyers and civil society. Hence, this book does not apply legal complex in analysing the subject matter.

About this Book

At the heart of this book is the question of how China installs authoritarian rule in Hong Kong through strategies of "authoritarian legal transplantation," and how liberal and activist lawyers in Hong Kong resist such processes in civil society, anti-authoritarian protests and the professional bodies that govern them. This book uses socio-legal methods to study the dynamics between authoritarian legal transplantation and legal resistance in Hong Kong, rather than employing the methods of doctrinal legal studies, which is seen as not helpful to understand "law in context" (Cownie and Bradney 2013, 35). Research on the legal profession, legal culture and cause lawyering is often conducted by mixed methods, such as combining survey research, in-depth interviews, archival research, discourse analysis and even ethnography (Guinier et al. 1994, 1; Merry 2010, 48-52; Mertz 2007, 32; Dezalay and Garth 2010; Wilson 2011,459).

Ostensibly, the quantitative method has emerged to be a famous approach in empirical legal studies and policy analysis of the performance of judicial institutions worldwide (Sherr and Webb 1989, 225; Kuan 1997; Tai 2007; Barclay and Silbey 2008, 666–667; Wu 2016, 2; the World Bank 2019; World Economic Forum 2019; Freedom House 2020; Lee and Lo 2020; World Justice

Project 2020) But qualitative research has a more significant potential to provide a causal explanation of legal and judicial phenomenon. It enables a thorough description of the mechanisms that sustain the interactions of different actors in a socio-legal phenomenon.

To study the interactions and dynamics between the state, legal professionals and civil society, I use three qualitative research methods to collect data and analyse the findings of my fieldwork research: archival research, in-depth interviews and participant observation.

In terms of *archival research*, two clusters of archives were examined. The first cluster is the documentary records in Hong Kong, including those archived in LegCo, the judiciary, the Department of Justice, the Bar, the Law Society, various statutory committees related to Hong Kong law, and the special collections in the libraries of Hong Kong University (HKU) and the Chinese University of Hong Kong (CUHK). The second cluster deals with media documentary records from different media outlets in Hong Kong, including Apple Daily and Stand News, which shut down in 2021 as the Hong Kong government charged their editors and entities with national security crimes. I also studied news reports from two local-based state media, *Wen Wei Po* and *Tai Kung Pao*, and press reports from *Xinhua News Agency* in my archival research. Chinese state media in Hong Kong demonstrated solid support for upholding Hong Kong's status quo, including preserving pre-existing judicial bodies, for the city's prosperity and stability (Wong 2022). Such discourse, though remaining as the principal narrative, commenced diverging when these state-sponsored media outlets criticised the top court's performance on the right of abode case in 1999 (Jiang 2015). After that, Chinese state media continued to be critical of Hong Kong courts" liberal judgements and promoted many state-adjacent lawyers as "true defenders of the Rule of Law" (Zhu 2019, 30; Lee and Yu 2020). These records provide detailed descriptions of the development and dynamics of the domestic legal profession and reflect different interpretations of and debates on the Rule of Law, the legal profession, state-lawyer relations, professional bodies and activist lawyering since the handover.

In-depth interviews help researchers and readers "[learn] about people's meanings and meaning-making" by listening to "people talk about their experiences in their ways and their words" (Magnusson and Marecek 2015, 2). During my visiting fellowship in the Centre of Comparative and Public Law (CCPL) at the University of Hong Kong (HKU) from 2018 to 2020, I conducted 86 in-depth interviews with 77 interviewees through multi-source snowball sampling in Hong Kong. Among the interviewees, 68 were legal personnel, including 27 barristers, Senior Counsel and 17 solicitors.

Interviewed legal personnel also included legal academics, in-house lawyers, paralegals, legal executives, solicitor trainees and law students; some of them are simultaneously academic and practising lawyers. 55 out of 68 interviewees from the legal sector had received professional qualifications to practice law locally. The remaining nine were activists with experience in criminal defence work and former or current NGO workers who engaged in pro bono legal services; lastly, there was a court journalist. For security reasons, all interviewees are anonymised.

During my fieldwork in Hong Kong, I exercised *participant observations* to witness several lawyer-only activities, law school seminars and court trials related to the local legal profession. I also observed how some lawyers engaged in civil society alongside social movements when the Anti-ELAB Movement began in mid–2019. Having no professional practising experience, I positioned myself as an outsider of the subject matter, i.e., the legal community, and made use of both my detachment from legal professionals and trained capacity as an academic researcher to "know how to assemble and assess the evidence without regard for what the analysis seems to imply about the worth of one's group" (Merton 1972, 41). My civil society track record and academic background also encouraged my interviewees, mainly barristers and solicitors, to speak freely, as I have no conflict of interest with their business in the legal sector.

My experience in Hong Kong's social movement also helped my research on the relationship between legal professionals and civil society and social movement organisations in the city. I have been engaged in social activism in Hong Kong to advocate for the realisation of citizens' right to universal suffrage, as well as the rights of migrants and foreign domestic helpers in Hong Kong, for more than a decade. Starting in 2010, I have been in touch with overseas and local activists, civil society organisations, lawmakers and lawyers. I have also collaborated with some barristers and solicitors in appeals against decisions by Hong Kong's police commissioner that banned public rallies and assemblies in 2012 when I was the convenor of the Civil Human Rights Front (CHRF). It was a flagship coalition to promote human rights protections in Hong Kong by organising mass mobilisations, including the annual 1 July rally and the most significant rallies in the Anti-ELAB Movement of 2019. During the Anti-ELAB Movement, I was a (pro bono) vice convenor of the CHRF. Before my appointment, the CHRF has already formed a hotline for pro bono legal visits for arrested protesters. I had a chance to directly observe how activist or cause lawyering was carried out on the street, in law firms and barristers' chambers, and how they collaborated with other local organisations to aid arrested protestors. The CHRF was disbanded on 15 August 2021 due to the political pressure from pro-Beijing media and law enforcement, who alleged CHRF for organising an unauthorised society and endangering national security (Chau 2021c). Under such politically sensitive circumstances, I have not included my personal engagement in or the operational details of the CHRF in this book.

Despite my apparent social movement background, I succeeded in collecting the best possible data from lawyers of diverse backgrounds and even opposite political orientations to present a more comprehensive picture. Hence, the composition of the dataset is more comprehensive than lawyers supporting or sympathetic to local social movements. The list of interviewees can be found in the Appendix. While benefiting from my experience and engagement in Hong Kong's social movement organisations, I remained distant from those groups formed by activist lawyers. I did not operate any pro bono legal visit teams for arrested protestors during the Anti-ELAB Movement. Those lawyers worked independently of the CHRF. While participating in the Anti-ELAB Movement as a non-violent rally organiser, I observed, rather than intervened, lawyers' engagement in the movement, with reference to some existing works of ethnography and activist scholars (Lee 2017; Terwindt 2019; Stott et al. 2020).

In their latest edited volume *Out of Place: Fieldwork and Positionality in Law and Society*, Chua and Massoud suggest that the declaration of researchers' positionality in academic works, which refers to the "disclosure of how an author's self-identifications, experiences, and privileges influence research methods, has several benefits, especially for those living in an out-of-place or marginalised position." The benefits include establishing connection and credibility, challenging structures of oppression, opening up social science, empowering communities, and communicating privileges (2024, 8). As a former activist and an out-of-place researcher in Hong Kong's legal community, I see the importance of disclosing my identity not only as a non-conventional legal researcher and a former social activist, but also a Hong-Konger as well. Although Hong Kong has gained wide attention from media outlets and policymakers worldwide, it is inevitably a marginal community in realpolitik and academic scholarship. Hong Kong is not a sovereign state, making it less influential in the existing international order that is mainly driven by national sovereign states. Hong Kong can be independently and comparatively studied in disciplinary fields, but it is far from gaining an equivalent position in area studies like China, Russia or the United States. I believe my personal background, including my academic, activist and ethnic self-identification, have more benefits than drawbacks in presenting my research in this book. Studying Hong Kong's Rule of Law from the perspective of agents, especially activist lawyers, rather than statutes and case law, would not happen if I were not a social scientist nor an activist in the city. My academic training, experiences and track records in local activism, enabled me to build trust with interviewees, and to be more sympathetic to their words and deeds in resisting the authoritarian power structures in Hong Kong. Conventional studies of law and social science, such as the mainstream Hong Kong law scholarship, stressed objectivity and neutrality, but my methods demonstrate the need to challenge the overemphasis on studying law, statutes and institutions than behaviours and subjectivities of stakeholders in the legal system (Yam and Yap 2023). As Massoud suggests, "putting people first in legal studies increases empathy for research subjects and other researchers." (Chua and Massoud 2024, 4). I, as a researcher from Hong Kong, also hope to be an "impassioned interlocutor trying to help readers to appreciate that the tradition of distant objectivity does not fully capture" the experiences of most of my interviewees as part of the critical minority in Hong Kong's legal profession (2024, 11).

This book generates knowledge and contributes to three strands of literature. First, it contributes to the literature that studies the Rule of Law and legal transplantation from a perspective of intergovernmental relations. This book studies the discourse and practice of the Rule of Law under subnational governance. Hong Kong is a typical semi-autonomous subnational jurisdiction under an authoritarian sovereign state (Yuen and Cheng 2020, 131). Understanding how the Rule of Law and legal transplants can operate under Hong Kong's "One Country, Two Systems" arrangement offers insights into the tensions between the subnational autonomy prescribed by law on the one hand and sovereign control by its constitution on the other. It also serves as a case study to compare other subnational polities, such as Catalonia in Spain, Northern Ireland in the United Kingdom, Québec in Canada, Äland Islands in Finland, West Papua in Indonesia and Kashmir in India (Ghai, ed 2013; Pang 2020, 9).

Second, this book contributes to the literature of the legal profession by associating it with the study of political regimes and contentious politics. Despite the development of various research methods in the study of law, socio-legal studies and the interdisciplinary study of law are not popular in Hong Kong's law schools. Instead, most legal scholars in Hong Kong concentrate more on legal analysis, evaluating controversies in doctrinal interpretation of law, such as China's interpretations of the Hong Kong Basic Law (Chan, Fu and Ghai 2000; Marsden 2006, 117; Yap 2007, 449). While quantitative research that describes the relationship between law and society, such as attitudes towards and beliefs in the Rule of Law by the public in Hong Kong, exists in local scholarship, a qualitative explanation of the relationship between socio-political development and law can be further developed (Kuan 1997; Tai 2015; Lam 2020; Lee and Lo 2020a; 2020b). A social-scientific study of law and politics became more desirable when criminal justice and civil procedure began to be a commonplace strategy of the state to repress the opposition and diminish the civic space from 2014 onwards (Cheng and Yuen 2017; Fu 2018a).

There are two exceptions. One is Tam's study of legal mobilisation and judicial review in the early period of post-colonial Hong Kong (2012). Another one is Jones's comprehensive documentation of the struggles between the state, lawyers and society on the Rule of Law from the post-colonial era until the advent of the Umbrella Movement in Hong Kong (2015). Tam adopted social scientific methods to indicate the capacities of the courts and cause lawyers to promote human rights jurisprudence and protections in the early days. Yet, the change of circumstances in the second decade of Hong Kong's new regime, as found in this book, illustrates a backlash to the Rule of Law and judicial autonomy in this city. A further study of law and politics in Hong Kong in recent years is thus essential.

Contrary to Tam's optimism on legal mobilisation in Hong Kong, Jones provided a less promising picture of the Rule of Law in Hong Kong under the authoritarian rule of the sovereign state. She analyses the significance of the ideology in Hong Kong's political and cultural struggles, highlighting the danger of repression through legalised means by the Chinese state, including the rejection of universal suffrage in 2014. This book continues Jones's discussion on the struggle between the state, legal profession and civil society over the Rule of Law in Hong Kong.

This book's adoption of qualitative methods, such as in-depth interviews, archival research, and participant observation, deepens the understanding of the dynamics of law, politics, and social movements. Legal scholarship in Hong Kong appears to pay less attention to this perspective, and is still overwhelmingly concentrated on the doctrinal study of law. I am confident that this book serves to continue the sociological study of the Rule of Law in Hong Kong, following the steps of Jones and Tam.

Finally, this book contributes to the literature of global China studies, which reflects on China as a global superpower today. The rise of China's economic power in world politics has drawn wide attention from both scholars and political analysts. Recently, think tanks as well as national governments have called China a 'sharp power" instead of the conventional notion of 'soft power" as China commences to leverage its economic capital to expand its influences in politics and culture beyond its territory, including the realms of international laws, standards of international human rights, public health and economic development (Diamond, Plattner and Walker 2016; National Endowment for Democracy 2017; Chan 2018; Hoover Institute 2018; Diamond 2019). As highlighted earlier, China's growing global influence aligns with Hung's argument that it represents an empire-building project disguised as a nation-state. Resistance to such influence is emerging in different continents, including the partner countries of China's Belt and Road Initiative (BRI) (Lee 2017). This book can supplement the debate on the significance of global China, providing evidence on how the domestic legal profession and the Rule of Law respond to the expansion of China's economic influences beyond its territorial jurisdiction.

The remaining eight chapters are organised as follows. Chapters 2 and 3 draws on one of my published works: "Lady Justice or the Golden Calf? The 'China factor' in Hong Kong's legal system" (Lai 2019), analysing the nature of China's authoritarian legal transplantation, its motivations, direct mechanisms and the direct and indirect transplantations of authoritarian legal ideology and institutions through legal imposition and the "United Front Work," a popular strategy of the CCP to co-opt and encroach local legal elites to strengthen the regime's governing capacity and a rule-by-law culture in society.

Chapter 4 begins the analysis of state-bar relations in Hong Kong. It studies how barristers and solicitors interact with the state and respond to perceived threats from authoritarian legal transplantation through two professional bodies of law in Hong Kong: the Bar and the Law Society. It offers a comparative overview of the Bar and the Law Society's public discourse regarding different forms of authoritarian legal transplantation, describing the similarities and differences in language and stances between the two professional bodies.

Chapters 5–8 explain the three strategies activist lawyers adopted in resisting authoritarian legal transplantations in Hong Kong. Chapter 5 focuses on the strategy of civil society empowerment by examining two activist lawyer organisations, Progressive Lawyers' Group and Law Lay Dream, which serve as two instances of lawyers exercising democratic professionalism in civil society. Their organisational, operational, and cultural practices and their impact on resisting authoritarian legal transplantation are explained in a comparative manner. Chapter 6 studies another group of lawyers defending access to justice by providing pro bono legal services for protestors. These activist lawyers or cause lawyers were regarded as resisting authoritarian rule by assisting anti-authoritarian protestors in

Hong Kong's criminal justice system. Their interactions with civil society, protestors and public authorities are explained and evaluated.

Chapters 7 and 8 explain the final strategy of legal resistance: leadership contestation. Chapter 7 focuses on the Bar Council elections since 2017, whereas chapter 8 considers the elections of the leadership of the Law Society of Hong Kong. These two chapters examine why and how, amid a changing political opportunity structure, some liberal lawyers challenged the incumbency of the Bar and the Law Society that performed comprador professionalism for the state's interests, respectively. They then discuss whether and how leadership contestation following critical events inspired the Bar and the Law Society to adopt a robust approach towards emerging threats from the state, and how state-bar relations changed both organisationally and culturally.

Chapter 9 concludes by assessing the contributions and limitations of authoritarian legal transplantation and legal resistance. It includes suggestions for future theoretical and empirical research on the inter-relationship between the Rule of Law, state-lawyer relations, and activist lawyering in anti-authoritarian and decolonising settings. At the end of this chapter, I also discuss how the 2020 National Security Law, imposed by China, has drastically changed Hong Kong's legal and judicial environments, alongside the dynamics between the state, the legal professional community, and civil society, and then possible directions for future research on law and society in Hong Kong under Chinese rule.

References

Adébísí, Folúkẹ́. 2023. *Decolonisation and Legal Knowledge: Reflections on Power and Possibility*. Bristol University Press.

Ahmed, Zahid Shahab, and Maria J. Stephan. 2010. "Fighting for the Rule of Law: Civil Resistance and the Lawyers' Movement in Pakistan." *Democratization* 17 (3): 492–513.

Allan, James. 1998. "Liberalism, Democracy and Hong Kong." *Hong Kong Law Journal* 28 (2): 156–168.

The American Chamber of Commerce in Hong Kong. 2019. "Press Release: Proposed Fugitive Offenders Ordinance." *The American Chamber of Commerce in Hong Kong*, May 30. Accessed August 13, 2020. https://www.amcham.org.hk/news/press-release-proposed-fugitive-offenders-ordinance.

Armstrong, James D. 1977. *Revolutionary Diplomacy: Chinese Foreign Policy and the United Front Doctrine*. University of California Press.

Barclay, Scott, and Anna-Maria Marshall. 2005. "Supporting a Cause, Developing a Movement, and Consolidating a Practice: Cause Lawyers and Sexual Orientation Litigation in Vermont." In *The Worlds Cause Lawyers Make: Structure and Agency in Legal Practice*, edited by Austin Sarat and Stuart A. Scheingold. Stanford University Press.

Barclay, Scott, and Susan S. Silbey. 2008. "Understanding Regime Change: Public Opinion, Legitimacy, and Legal Consciousness." In *The Oxford Handbook of Law and Politics*, edited by Gregory A. Caldeira, R. Daniel Kelemen, and Keith E. Whittington. Oxford University Press.

Benton, Lauren. 2002. *Law and Colonial Cultures: Legal Regimes in World History, 1400–1900*. Cambridge University Press.

Bisharat, George. 1998. "Attorneys for the People, Attorneys for the Land: The Emergence of Cause Lawyering in the Israeli-Occupied Territories." In *Cause Lawyering: Political Commitments and Professional Responsibilities*, edited by Austin Sarat and Stuart A. Scheingold. Oxford University Press.

Blackstone, Amy, Christopher Uggen, and Heather McLaughlin. 2009. "Legal Consciousness and Responses to Sexual Harassment." *Law and Society Review* 43 (3): 631–668.

Bourdieu, Pierre, and Abdelmalek Sayad. 2004. "Colonial Rule and Cultural Sabir." *Ethnography* 5 (4): 445–486.

Brown, Nathan J. 1995. "Law and Imperialism: Egypt in Comparative Perspective." *Law and Society Review* 29 (1): 103–125.

Bush, Richard C. 2016. *Hong Kong in the Shadow of China: Living with the Leviathan*. Brookings Institute Press.

Butler, Daren, and Ece Toksabay. 2020. "Turkish Parliament Passes Disputed Bar Associations Law." *Reuters*, July 11. Accessed August 4, 2020. https://reut.rs/3D5Nqqf.

Cain, Maureen. 1974. "The Main Themes of Marx' and Engels' Sociology of Law." *British Journal of Law and Society* 1 (2): 136–148.

Cairnes, John E. 1887. *Some Leading Principles of Political Economy Newly Expounded*. Macmillan.

Cairns, John W. 2013. "Watson, Walton, and the History of Legal Transplants." *Georgia Journal of International and Comparative Law* 41: 637–96.

Chan, Cora, and Fiona de Londras. 2020. "Introduction: China's National Security in Hong Kong: A Challenge for Constitutionalism, Autonomy and the Rule of Law." In *China's National Security: Endangering Hong Kong's Rule of Law?*, edited by Cora Chan and Fiona de Londras. Hart Publishing.

Chan, Johannes M. M. 2007. "Basic Law and Constitutional Review: The First Decade." *Hong Kong Law Journal* 37 (2): 407–447.

Chan, Johannes M. M. 2018. "A Storm of Unprecedented Ferocity: The Shrinking Space of the Right to Political Participation, Peaceful Demonstration, and Judicial

Independence in Hong Kong." *International Journal of Constitutional Law* 16 (2): 373–388.

Chan, Johannes M. M. 2019. "A Shrinking Space: A Dynamic Relationship Between the Judiciary in a Liberal Society of Hong Kong and a Socialist-Leninist Sovereign State." *Current Legal Problems* 72 (1): 85–122.

Chan, Johannes M. M., H. L. Fu, and Yash Ghai. 2000. *Hong Kong's Constitutional Debate: Conflict Over Interpretation*. Hong Kong University Press.

Chan, Jun., Eric Y. H. Lai, and Tobias E. Kellogg. 2023. *The Hong Kong 2019 Protest Movement: A Data Analysis of Arrests and Prosecutions*. Center for Asian Law, Georgetown University Law Center, October. Accessed January 23, 2024. https://www.law.georgetown.edu/law-asia/wp-content/uploads/sites/31/2023/10/GCAL-HK-2019-ARREST-DATA-REPORT-FINAL-OCT-2023.pdf.

Chan, Kenneth K.L. 2023. "Open Society Contested: Liberal Universalism versus Autocratic Functionalism in Hong Kong." In *Open Society Unresolved: The Contemporary Relevance of a Contested Idea*, edited by Christof Royer and Liviu Matei. Central European University Press.

Chanock, Martin. 1985. *Law, Custom, and Social Order: The Colonial Experience in Malawi and Zambia*. Cambridge University Press.

Chau, Candice. 2021c. "Organiser of Mass Hong Kong Demos Civil Human Rights Front Disbands Citing 'Unprecedented Challenges.'" *Hong Kong Free Press*, August 15. Accessed September 2, 2021. https://hongkongfp.com/2021/08/15/breaking-organiser-of-mass-hong-kong-demos-civil-human-rights-front-disbands-citing-unprecedented-challenges/.

Chen, Albert H.Y. 2020. "Hong Kong in China: The Project of 'One Country, Two Systems' and the Question of National Security." In *China's National Security: Endangering Hong Kong's Rule of Law?*, edited by Cora Chan and Fiona de Londras. Hart Publishing.

Chen, Jianfu. 2007. "The Transformation of Chinese Law: From Formal to Substantial." *Hong Kong Law Journal* 37 (2): 689–739.

Chen, Xunwu. 2016. "Positive Law and Natural Law: Han Feizi, Hobbes, and Habermas." *Journal of East-West Thought* 6 (1): 11–32.

Cheng, Edmund W. 2020. "United Front Work and Mechanism of Countermobilization in Hong Kong." *The China Journal* 83: 1–33.

Cheng, Edmund W., and Samson Yuen. 2017. "How Hong Kong's Umbrella Movement Was Crushed and Pro-Democracy Activists Gradually Silenced." *The Conversation*, November 15. Accessed August 25, 2020. https://theconversation.com/how-hong-kong-umbrella-movement-was-crushed-and-pro-democracy-activists-gradually-silenced-84339.

Cheng, Joseph Y. S. 2009. "The Story of a New Policy." *Hong Kong Journal*. Accessed November 18, 2020. http://www.hkjournal.org/archive/2009_fall/1.htm.

Cheng, Joseph Y. S., ed. 2005. *The July 1 Protest Rally: Interpreting a Historic Event.* CityUHK Press.

Cheung, Anthony B.L., and M. W. L. Wong. 2006. "Judicial Review and Policy Making in Hong Kong: Changing Interface Between the Legal and the Political." *Asia Pacific Journal of Public Administration* 28 (2): 117–141.

Chiu, Man-Chung. 2010. "Going Beyond Globalization and Localization: Articulating a Theory of Justice in Han-Chinese Culture." *Law and Critique* 21 (1): 93–100.

Choi, S.C., and N. K. Lee. 2017. "Legalization of Politics: The Geopolitical Situations of Hong Kong and the Consolidation of Its Rule of Law in the Cold War." *Thoughts and Words Journal* 55: 187–225.

Chua, Lynette J. 2019. "Legal Mobilization and Authoritarianism." *Annual Review of Law and Social Science* 15: 355–376.

Chua, Lynette J., and Mark F. Massoud. 2024. *Out of Place: Fieldwork and Positionality in Law and Society.* Cambridge University Press.

Chu Yee Wah v. Director of Environmental Protection. 2011.

Comaroff, John L. 2001. "Colonialism, Culture, and the Law: A Foreword." *Law and Social Inquiry* 26 (2): 305–314.

Cody, Stephen. 2020. "Dark Law: Legalistic Autocrats, Judicial Deference, and the Global Transformation of National Security." *University of Pennsylvania Journal of Law and Public Affairs* 6 (4): 643–686.

"Comprador." 2021. *Encyclopaedia Britannica.* Accessed January 14, 2021. https://www.britannica.com/money/comprador.

Cownie, Fiona, and Anthony Bradney. 2013. "Socio-legal Studies: A Challenge to the Doctrinal Approach." In *Research Methods in Law,* edited by Dawn Watkins and Mandy Burton. Routledge.

Cummings, Scott L. 2011. "Introduction: What Good Are Lawyers?" In *The Paradox of Professionalism: Lawyers and the Possibility of Justice,* edited by Scott L. Cummings. Cambridge University Press.

Dai, Jianzhong. 2009. "On Several Problems in Legal Transplantation." *Journal of Politics and Law* 2 (3): 107–109.

Dezalay, Yves, and Bryant G. Garth. 2010. *Asian Legal Revivals: Lawyers in the Shadow of the Empire.* University of Chicago Press.

Diamond, Larry J. 2016. *In Search of Democracy.* Routledge.

Diamond, Larry J. 2019. *Ill Winds: Saving Democracy from Russian Rage, Chinese Ambition and American Complacency.* Penguin Books.

Diamond, Larry J, Marc F. Plattner, and Christopher Walker. 2016. *Authoritarian Goes Global: The Challenge to Democracy.* Johns Hopkins University Press.

Dicey, Albert V. 1915. *Introduction to the Study of the Law of the Constitution.* Liberty Classics.

The Director of Immigration v. Master Chong Fung Yuen. 2001. FACV26/2000.

Donnelly, Tom. 2009. "Popular Constitutionalism, Civic Education, and the Stories We Tell Our Children." *The Yale Law Journal* 118 (5): 948–1001.

Dorfman, Zach. 2018. "The Disappeared." *Foreign Policy*, March 29. Accessed August 13, 2020. https://foreignpolicy.com/2018/03/29/the-disappeared-china-renditions-kidnapping/.

Dzur, Albert W. 2008. *Democratic Professionalism: Citizen Participation and the Reconstruction of Professional Ethics, Identity, and Practice*. Penn State University Press.

Eörsi, Gyula. 1979. *Comparative Civil (Private) Law*. Akadémiai Kiadó.

Fallon, Richard H., Jr. 1997. "'The Rule of Law' as a Concept in Constitutional Discourse." *Columbia Law Review* 97 (1): 1–56.

Fanon, Frantz. 1963. *The Wretched of the Earth*. Grove Press.

Farran, Sue. 2013. "The 'Age of Empire': Again?" *The Law Teacher* 47 (3): 345–367.

Fitzpatrick, Peter. 1992. *The Mythology of Modern Law*. Routledge.

Fong, Brian C. H. 2016. "In-Between Liberal Authoritarianism and Electoral Authoritarianism: Hong Kong's Democratization under Chinese Sovereignty, 1997–2016." *Democratization* 24 (4): 724–750.

Fong, Brian C. H. 2017b. "The Rise of Localism in Hong Kong: Counter-Mobilization under the Hurricane of China Factor." *Mainland China Studies* 60 (1): 1–17.

Foreweaker, Joe. 1987. "Corporatist Strategies and the Transition to Democracy in Spain." *Comparative Politics* 20 (1): 57–72.

Foster, Nicholas H. D. 2007. "Comparative Commercial Law: Rules or Context?" In *Comparative Law: A Handbook*, edited by Esin Örücü and David Nelken. Hart Publishing.

Frankel, Ernst. 2017. *The Dual State: A Contribution to the Theory of Dictatorship*. Oxford University Press.

Frantz, Erica. 2018. *Authoritarianism: What Everyone Needs to Know*. Oxford University Press.

Freedom House. 2020. *Freedom in the World 2020: A Leaderless Struggle for Democracy*. Accessed July 31, 2020. https://freedomhouse.org/report/freedom-world/2020/leaderless-struggle-democracy.

Friedman, Milton. 1962. *Capitalism and Freedom*. University of Chicago Press.

Freidson, Eliot. 1983. "The Theory of Professions: State of the Art." In *The Sociology of the Professions: Lawyers, Doctors and Others*, edited by Robert Dingwall and Philip Lewis. The Macmillan Press.

Fu, Hualing. 2018a. "Political Protest in High-Income Societies: The Case of Occupy Central Movement in Hong Kong." In *Law and Politics of the Taiwan Sunflower and Hong Kong Umbrella Movements*, edited by Brian C. Jones. Routledge.

Fu, Hualing. 2018b. "The July 9th (709) Crackdown on Human Rights Lawyers: Legal Advocacy in an Authoritarian State." *Journal of Contemporary China* 27 (112): 554–568.

Fu, Hualing, Carole J. Petersen, and Simon N. M. Young, eds. 2005. *National Security and Fundamental Freedoms: Hong Kong's Article 23 under Scrutiny*. Hong Kong University Press.

Fukuyama, Francis. 2011. *The Origins of Political Order: From Pre-Human Times to the French Revolution*. Profile Books.

Fukuyama, Francis. 2014. *Political Order and Political Decay: From the Industrial Revolution to the Globalization of Democracy*. Profile Books.

Garoupa, Nuno, and Anthony Ogus. 2006. "A Strategic Interpretation of Legal Transplants." *Journal of Legal Studies* 35: 339–363.

Geddes, Barbara, Joseph Wright, and Erica Frantz. 2014. "Autocratic Breakdown and Regime Transitions: A New Data Set." *Perspectives on Politics* 12 (2): 313–331.

Ghai, Yash, ed. 2013. *Practising Self-Government: A Comparative Study of Autonomous Regions*. Cambridge University Press.

Ghai, Yash, Robin Luckham, and Francis Snyder, eds. 1987. *The Political Economy of Law: A Third World Reader*. Oxford University Press.

Gilb, Corinne L. 1966. *Hidden Hierarchies: The Professions and Government*. Harper and Row.

Ginsburg, Tom, and Tamir Moustafa, eds. 2008. *Rule by Law: The Politics of Courts in Authoritarian Regimes*. Cambridge University Press.

Glick, Brian. 2017. "Two, Three Many Rosas! Rebellious Lawyers and Progressive Activist Organizations." *Clinical Law Review* 23: 611–634.

Gobe, Éric, and Lena Salaymeh. 2016. "Tunisia's 'Revolutionary' Lawyers: From Professional Autonomy to Political Mobilization." *Law and Social Inquiry* 41 (2): 311–345.

Gramsci, Antonio. 1971. *Selections from the Prison Notebooks*. Edited and translated by Quintin Hoare and Geoffrey Nowell Smith. Lawrence and Wishart.

Guinier, Lani, Michelle Fine, Jane Balin, Ann Barow, and Deborah L. Stachel. 1994. "Becoming Gentlemen: Women's Experiences at One Ivy League Law School." *University of Pennsylvania Law Review* 143 (1): 1–110.

Gutteridge, Harold C. 1949. *Comparative Law: An Introduction to the Comparative Method of Legal Study and Research*. Cambridge University Press.

Hajjar, Lisa. 2001. "From the Fight for Legal Rights to the Promotion of Human Rights: Israeli and Palestinian Cause Lawyers in the Trenches of Globalisation." In *Cause Lawyering and the State in a Global Era*, edited by Austin Sarat and Stuart A. Scheingold. Oxford University Press.

Halliday, Terence C. 2005. "Legal Professions and Politics: Neocorporatist Variations on the Pluralist Theme of Liberal Democracies." In *Lawyers in Society: Comparative Theories*, edited by Richard L. Abel and Philip S. C. Lewis. Beard Books.

Halliday, Terence C., Lucien Karpik, and Malcolm M. Feeley. 2007. "The Legal Complex in Struggles for Political Liberalism." In *Fighting for Political Freedom:*

Comparative Studies of the Legal Complex and Political Liberalism, edited by Terence C. Halliday, Lucien Karpik, and Malcolm M. Feeley. Hart Publishing.

Halpérin, Jean-Louis. 2010. "Western Legal Transplants and India." *Jindal Global Law Review* 2 (1): 14–40.

Harris, Paul. 2008. "Is Tibet Entitled to Self-Determination?" *China Digital Times*, April 26. Accessed October 16, 2021. https://chinadigitaltimes.net/2008/04/is-tibet-entitled-to-self-determination/.

Henry, Gary T., and Craig S. Gordon. 2003. "Driving Less for Better Air: Impacts of a Public Information Campaign." *Journal of Policy Analysis and Management* 22 (1): 45–63.

Hilson, Chris. 2002. "New Social Movements: The Role of Legal Opportunity." *Journal of European Public Policy* 9 (2): 238–255.

HKTDC Research. 2019. "Legal Service Industry in Hong Kong." Hong Kong Trade and Development Council, July 12. Accessed July 14, 2020. https://hkmb.hktdc.com/en.

HKTDC Research. 2020b. "Legal Services Industry in Hong Kong." Hong Kong Trade and Development Council, June 18. Accessed August 30, 2020. https://research.hktdc.com/en/article/MzEzODc5NTk5.

Ho, Denny K.L. 2004, "Citizenship as a Form of Governance: A Historical Overview." In *Remaking Citizenship in Hong Kong: Community, Nation and the Global City*, edited by Agnes S. Ku and Ngai Pun. eReader version. Accessed October 11, 2021, from Amazon.com.

Hong Kong Bar Association. 2019. *A Brief Guide to Issues Arising from the Fugitive Offenders and Mutual Legal Assistance in Criminal Matters Legislation (Amendment) Bill 2019 ("The Bill")*. June 6. Accessed August 13, 2020. Archived on file with the author.

Hong Kong Special Administrative Region v. Mok Ka To. 2018.

Hong Kong Watch. 2019. *Outdated and Draconian: Hong Kong's Public Order Ordinance*. Accessed July 9, 2020. https://static1.squarespace.com/static/58ecfa82e3df284d3a13dd41/t/5d25c0676c3cb30001e74f6b/1562755179422/hkw+report_jul19+(3).pdf.

Hoover Institute. 2018. *Chinese Influence and American Interests: Promoting Constructive Vigilance*. Stanford University. Accessed June 24, 2020. https://hvr.co/2YCbSkc.

Hui, Mary. 2019. "Everything You Need to Know About Hong Kong's Extradition Law." *Quartz*, June 11. Accessed August 13, 2020. https://qz.com/1635504/everything-you-need-to-know-about-hong-kongs-extradition-law.

Hung, Ho-fung. 2022. *City on the Edge: Hong Kong Under Chinese Rule*. Cambridge University Press.

Hussain, Nasser. 2003. *The Jurisprudence of Emergency: Colonialism and the Rule of Law*. University of Michigan Press.

Jiang, Shigong. 2015. "'Hé Píng Gé Mìng' Zhōng de Sī Fǎ Guǎn Xiá Quán: Cóng 'Mǎ Wéi Kūn Àn' Hé 'Wú Jiā Líng Àn' Tán Xiāng Gǎng Xiàn Zhèng Zhì Xù Zhuǎn Xíng Zhōng de Sī Fǎ Zhǔ Quán Zhī Zhēng." In *Xiāng Gǎng Jī Běn Fǎ Miàn Miàn Guān*, edited by Albert H. Y. Chen and Zou Pingxue. Joint Publishing.

Jones, Carol. 1999. "Politics Postponed: Law as a Substitute for Politics in Hong Kong and China." In *Law, Capitalism and Power in Asia: The Rule of Law and Legal Institutions*, edited by Kanishka Jayasuriya. Routledge.

Jones, Carol. 2010. "Legal Education in Hong Kong: Producing the Producers." In *Legal Education in Asia: Globalization, Change and Contexts*, edited by Stacey Steele and Kathryn Taylor. Routledge.

Jones, Carol. 2015. *Lost in China: Law, Culture and Identity in Post-1997 Hong Kong*. Cambridge University Press.

Jones, Lynn C. 2001. "Career Activism by Lawyers: Consequences for the Person, the Legal Profession, and Social Movements." In *Legal Professions: Work, Structure and Organization*, edited by Jerry Van Hoy. Emerald Publishing Limited.

Kapai, Puja. 2011. "Principled Approach Towards Judicial Review: Lessons from *W v Registrar of Marriages*." *Hong Kong Law Journal* 41 (1): 49–74.

Karpik, Lucien, and Terence C. Halliday. 2011. "The Legal Complex." *Annual Review of Law and Social Science* 7: 217–236.

Katuna, Barret, and Elizabeth Holzer. 2016. "Unobtrusively Stretching Law: Legal Education, Activism, and Reclaiming Title IX." *Social Movement Studies* 15 (1): 80–96.

Killingray, David. 1986. "The Maintenance of Law and Order in British Colonial Africa." *African Affairs* 85 (340): 411–437.

Klug, Heinz. 2001. "Legal Advocacy, Global Engagement: The Impact of Land Claims Advocacy on the Recognition of Property Rights in the South African Constitution." In *Cause Lawyering and the State in a Global Era*, edited by Austin Sarat and Stuart A. Scheingold. Oxford University Press.

Kong, Karen. 2012. "Adjudicating Social Welfare Rights in Hong Kong." *International Journal of Constitutional Law* 10 (2): 588–599.

Ku, Agnes S. 2004. "Negotiating the Space of Civil Autonomy in Hong Kong: Power, Discourses and Dramaturgical Representations." *The China Quarterly* 179: 647–664.

Kuan, Hsin-chi. 1991. "Power Dependence and Democratic Transition: The Case of Hong Kong." *The China Quarterly* 128: 774–793.

Kuan, Hsin-chi. 1997. "Support for the Rule of Law in Hong Kong." *Hong Kong Law Journal* 27 (2): 187–205.

Kwong, Ying-ho. 2015. "Chì Sè Fēng Bào Xià de Fǎ Lǜ Jiè: Wǒ Chéng Fǎ Lǜ Jīng Yīng de Shí Dài Shǐ Mìng." In *Xiāng Gǎng Gé Xīn Lùn: Gé Xīn Bǎo Gāng, Mín Zhǔ Zì Zhì, Yǒng Xù Zì Zhì, Wèi Xiāng Gǎng Qián Tú Ér Zhàn*, edited by Brian C.H. Fong. Azothbooks.

Lai, Yan-ho. 2019. "Lady Justice or the Golden Calf? The 'China Factor' in Hong Kong's Legal System." *Social Transformations in Chinese Societies* 15 (2): 178–196.

Lai, Yan-ho. 2021c. *Pò Jiě Xiāng Gǎng de Wēi Quán Fǎ Zhì: Sǎn Hòu yǔ Fǎn Sòng Zhōng Yǐ Lái de Mín Zhǔ Yùn Dòng.* Showwe.

Lai, Yan-ho. 2023. "Securitisation or Autocratisation? Hong Kong's Rule of Law Under the Shadow of China." *Journal of Asian and African Studies* 58 (1): 8–25.

Lai, Yan-ho. 2024a. *Resistance Through the Cracks: Understanding Hong Kong's Rule by Law and Resistance in the Courtroom in Comparative Perspective.* SpringHill Publishing.

Lai, Yan-ho. 2024c. "Not Just About the Law: Reflections on *A Report on the National Security Regime in Hong Kong (2024)*." *Taiwan Human Rights Journal* 7 (4): 89–110.

Lam, Wai-man. 2020. "Belief in the Rule of Law and Its Resilience in the Hong Kong Political Identity." In *China's National Security: Endangering Hong Kong's Rule of Law?*, edited by Cora Chan and Fiona de Londras. Hart Publishing.

Lau, Siu-kai. 1987. *Decolonization Without Independence: The Unfinished Political Reforms of the Hong Kong Government.* Institute of Social Studies, Chinese University of Hong Kong.

Lau, Siu-kai, and Hsin-chi Kuan. 2002. "Between Liberal Autocracy and Democracy: Democratic Legitimacy in Hong Kong." *Democratization* 9 (4): 58–76.

Leachman, Gwendolyn. 2013. "Legal Framing." In *Studies in Law, Politics, and Society*, edited by Austin Sarat. Emerald Group Publishing.

Lee, Ching-kwan. 2017. *The Spectre of Global China: Politics, Labour and Foreign Investment in Africa.* University of Chicago Press.

Lee, Ching-kwan. 2025. *Forever Hong Kong: A Global City's Struggle for Decolonization.* Harvard University Press (forthcoming, summer 2025).

Lee, Chun-yi, and Chun-yan Yu. 2020. "Diǎn Míng Zhuī Jī Fǎ Guān, 'Sān Quán Zhòng Zài Pèi Hé,' Jiàn Zhì Lì Liáng Rú Hé Zhòng Sù Xiāng Gǎng Fǎ Zhì Guān?" *Initium Media*, 17 September 17. Accessed February 17, 2022. https://theinitium.com/article/20200917-hongkong-judicial-judges-discourse-turning-point/.

Lee, Francis L. F., and Joseph M. Chan. 2018. *Media and Protest Logics in the Digital Era: The Umbrella Movement in Hong Kong.* Oxford University Press.

Lee, Francis L. F., and Chi-kit Chan. 2023. "Legalization of Press Control Under Democratic Backsliding: The Case of Post-National Security Law Hong Kong." *Media, Culture and Society* 45 (5): 916–31.

Lee, Karen M. Y., and Yan Lam Lo. 2020a. "Are Legal Values Gendered? Gender Differences in Support for Judicial Independence in Hong Kong." *International Journal of Law, Crime and Justice* 62. Accessed September 1, 2021. https://doi.org/10.1016/j.ijlcj.2020.100391.

Lee, Karen M. Y., and Yan Lam Lo. 2020b. "Contesting Visions of Hong Kong's Rule of Law and Young People's Political Discontent." *Social and Legal Studies* 29 (6): 858–80.

Legislative Council of the HKSAR. 2011. *LCQ6: Regarding the Judicial Review of Hong Kong-Zhuhai-Macao Bridge*, June 8. https://www.info.gov.hk/gia/general/201106/08/P201106080155.htm.

Levitsky, Steven, and Lucan A. Way. 2010. *Competitive Authoritarianism: Hybrid Regimes After the Cold War.* Cambridge University Press.

Li, Ling. 2019. "Political-Legal Order and the Curious Double Character of China's Courts." *Asian Journal of Law and Society* 6 (1): 19–39.

Lino, Dylan. 2018. "The Rule of Law and the Rule of Empire: A. V. Dicey in Imperial Context." *The Modern Law Review* 81 (5): 739–764.

Linz, Juan J., and Alfred Stepan. 1996. *Problems of Democratic Transition and Consolidation: Southern Europe, South America, and Post-Communist Europe.* The Johns Hopkins University Press.

Liu, Lawrence J., and Rachel E. Stern. 2020. "State-Adjacent Professionals: How Chinese Lawyers Participate in Political Life." *The China Quarterly* 247: 793–813.

Liu, Sida. 2015. "Law's Social Forms: A Powerless Approach to the Sociology of Law." *Law and Social Inquiry* 40 (1): 1–28.

Liu, Sida, and Terence C. Halliday. 2011. "Political Liberalism and Political Embeddedness: Understanding Politics in the Work of Chinese Criminal Defense Lawyers." *Law and Society Review* 45 (4): 831–865.

Lui, Tai-lok, and Brian C. H. Fong. 2014. "Editorial." *China Perspectives*, Special Feature 2014 (1): 3–4.

Ma, Ngok. 2005. "Civil Society in Self-Defense: The Struggle Against National Security Legislation in Hong Kong." *Journal of Contemporary China* 14 (44): 465–482.

Ma, Ngok. 2007. *Political Development of Hong Kong: State, Political Society and Civil Society.* Hong Kong University Press.

Ma, Ngok. 2017. "The China Factor in Hong Kong Elections: 1991 to 2016." *China Perspectives* (3): 17–26.

Magnusson, Eva, and Jeanne Marecek. 2015. *Doing Interview-Based Qualitative Research: A Learner's Guide.* Cambridge University Press.

Maldonado-Torres, Nelson. 2007. "On the Coloniality of Being: Contributions to the Development of a Concept." *Cultural Studies* 21 (2–3): 240–270.

Markesinis, Basil S. 2000. "Our Debt to Europe: Past, Present and Future." In *The Coming Together of the Common Law in the Courtroom and Classroom: The Story of the Last Thirty-Five Years*, edited by Basil S. Markesinis. Hart Publishing.

Marsden, Simon. 2006. "Regional Autonomy, Judicial Criticism, and the 2005 Interpretation: Judicial Independence in Hong Kong Compromised Again." *Hong Kong Law Journal* 36 (1): 117–142.

Marshall, Anna-Maria. 2001. "A Spectrum in Oppositional Consciousness: Sexual Harassment Plaintiffs and Their Lawyers." In *Oppositional Consciousness*, edited by Jane J. Mansbridge and Aldon Morris. University of Chicago Press.

Marshall, Anna-Maria, and Daniel C. Hale. 2014. "Cause Lawyering." *Annual Review of Law and Social Science* 10: 301–320.

Marx, Karl, and Friedrich Engels. 1848. *Manifesto of the Communist Party (The Communist Manifesto)*. Accessed November 6, 2020. https://www.marxists.org/archive/marx/works/1848/communist-manifesto/.

Mattei, Ugo, and Laura Nader. 2008. *Plunder: When the Rule of Law Is Illegal.* Wiley-Blackwell.

Mattei, Ugo, Teemu Ruskola, and Antonio Gidi. 2009. *Schlesinger's Comparative Law*, 7th ed. Foundation Press.

McBarnet, Doreen. 2002. "Transnational Transactions: Legal Work, Cross-Border Commerce and Global Regulation." In *Transnational Legal Processes: Globalisation and Power Disparities*, edited by Michael Likosky. Butterworths.

McCann, Michael. 2004. "Law and Social Movements." In *The Blackwell Companion to Law and Society*, edited by Austin Sarat. Blackwell Publishing.

McCann, Michael, and Helena Silverstein. 1998. "Rethinking Law's 'Allurements': A Relational Analysis of Social Movement Lawyers in the United States." In *Cause Lawyering: Political Commitments and Professional Responsibilities*, edited by Austin Sarat and Stuart A. Scheingold. Oxford University Press.

Meick, Ethan. 2019. "Hong Kong's Proposed Extradition Bill Could Extend Beijing's Coercive Reach: Risks for the United States." *U.S.-China Economic and Security Review Commission*, May 7. Accessed August 13, 2020. https://www.uscc.gov/research/hong-kongs-proposed-extradition-bill-could-extend-beijings-coercive-reach-risks-united.

Meili, Stephen. 1998. "Cause Lawyers and Social Movements: A Comparative Perspective on Democratic Change in Argentina and Brazil." In *Cause Lawyering: Political Commitments and Professional Responsibilities*, edited by Austin Sarat and Stuart A. Scheingold. Oxford University Press.

Meili, Stephen. 2001. "Latin American Cause Lawyering Networks." In *Cause Lawyering and the State in a Global Era*, edited by Austin Sarat and Stuart A. Scheingold. Oxford University Press.

Menski, Werner F. 2006. *Comparative Law in a Global Context*, 2nd ed. Cambridge University Press.

Merry, Sally E. 1995. "Resistance and the Cultural Power of Law." *Law and Society Review* 29 (1): 11–26.

Merry, Sally E. 2000. *Colonizing Hawaii: The Cultural Power of Law. Princeton University Press.*

Merry, Sally E. 2010. "What Is Legal Culture? An Anthropological Perspective." *Journal of Comparative Law* 5 (44): 48–52.

Merton, Robert K. 1972. "Insiders and Outsiders: A Chapter in the Sociology of Knowledge." *American Journal of Sociology* 78 (1): 9–47.

Mertus, Julie. 2011. "From Legal Transplants to Transformative Justice: Human Rights and the Promise of Transnational Civil Society." *American University International Law Review* 14 (5): 1335–1389.

Mertz, Elizabeth. 2007. *The Language of Law School: Learning to 'Think Like a Lawyer'*. Oxford University Press.

Mignolo, Walter D., and Catherine E. Walsh. 2018. *On Decoloniality: Concepts, Analytics and Praxis*. Duke University Press.

Milhaupt, Curtis J., and Katharina Pistor. 2008. *Law and Capitalism: What Corporate Crises Reveal About Legal Systems and Economic Development Around the World*. Chicago University Press.

Miller, Jonathan M. 2003. "A Typology of Legal Transplants: Using Sociology, Legal History, and Argentine Examples to Explain the Transplant Process." *American Journal of Comparative Law* 51 (4): 839–885.

Minutes of Hong Kong Legislative Council. 1967. *Official Report of Proceedings*, November 1.

Mommsen, Wolfgang J. 1992. "Introduction." In *European Expansion and Law: The Encounter of European and Indigenous Law in 19th- and 20th-Century Africa and Asia*, edited by Wolfgang J. Mommsen and Jaap A. de Moor. Berg Publishers.

Munn, Christopher. 2009. *Anglo-China: Chinese People and British Rule in Hong Kong, 1841–1880*. Hong Kong University Press.

Munn, Christopher. 2017. "'Our Best Trump Card': A Brief History of Deportation in Hong Kong 1857–1955." In *Civil Unrest and Governance in Hong Kong: Law and Order from Historical and Cultural Perspectives*, edited by John D. Wong and Michael H.K. Ng. Routledge.

Müller-Chen, Markus, Christoph Müller, and Corinne W. Lüchinger. 2015. *Comparative Private Law*. Dike.

National Endowment for Democracy. 2017. *Sharp Power: Rising Authoritarian Influence*. Accessed June 24, 2020. https://www.ned.org/wp-content/uploads/2017/12/Sharp-Power-Rising-Authoritarian-Influence-Full-Report.pdf.

Nelkin, David. 2001. "Towards a Sociology of Legal Adaptation." In *Adapting Legal Culture*, edited by David Nelkin and Johannes Feest. Hart Publishing.

Ng, Michael H.K. 2016. "Rule of Law in Hong Kong History Demythologised: Student Umbrella Movement of 1919." *Hong Kong Law Journal* 46 (3): 829–848.

Ng, Michael H.K. 2017. "When Silence Speaks: Press Censorship and Rule of Law in British Hong Kong (1850s–1940s)." *Law and Literature* 29 (3): 425–56.

Norton-Kyshe, James William. 1971. *The History of the Laws and Courts of Hong Kong from the Earliest Period to 1898*, 2 vols. Vetch and Lee.

O'Donnell, Guillermo A. 2004. "Why the Rule of Law Matters." *Journal of Democracy* 15 (4): 32–46.

Ogbonnaya, John O., and Chioma V. Iteshi. 2016. "The Jurisprudential Issues Arising from Legal Transplant: An Appraisal." *Journal of Law, Policy and Globalization* 50: 1–12.

Pang, Laikwan. 2020. *The Appearing Demos: Hong Kong During and After the Umbrella Movement*. University of Michigan Press.

Pedriana, Nicholas. 2006. "From Protective to Equal Treatment: Legal Framing Processes and Transformation of the Women's Movement in the 1960s." American Journal of Sociology 111 (6): 1718–1761.

Pedriana, Nicholas, and Robin Stryker. 1997. "Political Culture Wars 1960s Style: Equal Opportunity Employment-Affirmative Action and the Philadelphia Plan." *American Journal of Sociology* 103 (3): 633–691.

Pils, Eva. 2014. *China's Human Rights Lawyers: Advocacy and Resistance*. Routledge.

Pirie, Fernanda. 2013. *The Anthropology of Law*. Oxford University Press.

Pomfret, James. 2019. "EU Lodges Formal Diplomatic Note Against Contentious Hong Kong Extradition Bill." *Reuters*, May 24. Accessed August 13, 2020. https://reut.rs/3c6xxEo.

Rajah, Jothie. 2012. *Authoritarian Rule of Law: Legislation, Discourse and Legitimacy in Singapore*. Cambridge University Press.

Rajah, Jothie. 2024. "Normalising Authoritarianism: Authoritarian Rule of Law in Singapore and Hong Kong." In *The Palgrave Handbook of Political Norms in Southeast Asia*, edited by Gaëlle Facal, Elise L. Micheaux, and Astrid Norén-Nilsson. Springer Nature Singapore.

Raz, Joseph. 1994. *Ethics in the Public Domain*. Oxford University Press.

Rifkind, Malcolm. 2019. "There Is No 'Loophole' in Hong Kong's Current Extradition Law. Rather, It Provides a Necessary Firewall to Protect the Legal System." *South China Morning Post*, June 4. Accessed August 13, 2020. https://www.scmp.com/comment/opinion/article/3012853/there-no-loophole-hong-kongs-current-extradition-law-rather-it.

Rostain, Tanina. 2008. "Professional Power: Lawyers and the Constitution of Professional Authority." In *The Blackwell Companion to Law and Society*, edited by Austin Sarat. Blackwell.

Sarat, Austin, and Stuart A. Scheingold. 1998. "Cause Lawyering and the Reproduction of Professional Authority: An Introduction." In *Cause Lawyering: Political Commitments and Professional Responsibilities*, edited by Austin Sarat and Stuart A. Scheingold. Oxford University Press.

Sarat, Austin, and Stuart A. Scheingold. 2001. "State Transformation, Globalisation, and the Possibilities of Cause Lawyering." In *Cause Lawyering and the State in a Global Era*, edited by Austin Sarat and Stuart A. Scheingold. Oxford University Press.

Sarat, Austin, and Stuart A. Scheingold. 2006. "What Cause Lawyers Do For, and To, Social Movements: An Introduction." In *Cause Lawyers and Social Movements*, edited by Austin Sarat and Stuart A. Scheingold. Stanford University Press.

Schauer, Frederick. 2000. "The Politics and Incentives of Legal Transplantation." *CID Working Paper Series* 2000.44, Harvard University.

Scheingold, Stuart A., and Austin Sarat, eds. 2004. *Something to Believe In: Politics, Professionalism and Cause Lawyering*. Stanford University Press.

Schmidhauser, John R. 1989. "Power, Legal Imperialism, and Dependency." *Law and Society Review* 23 (5): 857–878.

Schmitter, Philippe C., and Terry Lynn Karl. 1991. "What Democracy Is....and Is Not." *Journal of Democracy* 2 (3): 3–16.

Scott, James C. 1985. *Weapons of the Weak: Everyday Forms of Peasant Resistance*. Yale University Press.

Shafqat, Sahar. 2018. "Civil Society and the Lawyers' Movement of Pakistan." *Law and Social Inquiry* 43 (3): 889–914.

Sherr, Avrom, and Julian Webb. 1989. "Law Students, the External Market, and Socialization: Do We Make Them Turn to the City?" *Journal of Law and Society* 16 (2): 225–249.

Siems, Mathias M. 2018. *Comparative Law*. 2nd ed. Cambridge University Press.

Solomon, Peter H., Jr. 2010. "Authoritarian Legality and Informal Practices: Judges, Lawyers, and the State in Russia and China." *Communist and Post-Communist Studies* 43 (4): 351–362.

Spalding, Rose J. 2003. "State Power and Its Limits: Corporatism in Mexico." *Comparative Political Studies* 14 (2): 139–161.

Spamann, Holger S. 2009. "Contemporary Legal Transplants: Legal Families and the Diffusion of (Corporate) Law." *BYU Law Review* 2009 (6): 1813–1878.

Stern, Rachel E. 2017. "Activist Lawyers in Post-Tiananmen China." *Law and Social Inquiry* 42 (1): 234–251.

Stern, Rachel E., and Lawrence J. Liu. 2020. "The Good Lawyer: State-Led Professional Socialization in Contemporary China." *Law and Social Inquiry* 45 (1): 26–48.

Stoler, Ann L., and Frederick Cooper. 1997. "Between Metropole and Colony: Rethinking a Research Agenda." In *Tensions of Empire: Colonial Cultures in a Bourgeois World*, edited by Frederick Cooper and Ann L. Stoler. University of California Press.

Stone, Alan. 1985. "The Place of Law in the Marxian Structure-Superstructure Archetype." *Law and Society Review* 19 (1): 39–68.

Stott, Clifford, Lawrence Ho, Matt Radburn, Ying Tung Chan, Arabella Kyprianides, and Patricio S. Morales. 2020. "Patterns of 'Disorder' During the 2019 Protests in Hong Kong: Policing, Social Identity, Intergroup Dynamics, and Radicalization." *Policing* 14 (4): 814–835.

Stromseth, Jane E., David Wippman, and Rosa Brooks. 2006. *Can Might Make Rights? Building the Rule of Law After Military Interventions*. Cambridge University Press.

Tai, Benny Y.T. 2007. "Developing an Index of the Rule of Law: Sharing the Experience of Hong Kong." *Asian Journal of Comparative Law* 2 (1): 1–19.

Tai, Benny Y.T. 2012. "The judiciary" In *Contemporary Hong Kong Government and Politics: Expanded Second Edition*, edited by Wai-man Lam, Percy L.T. Lui, and Wilson Wong. Hong Kong University Press.

Tai, Benny Y.T. 2015. *Report on rule of law and Legal Culture in Hong Kong*.

Tai, Benny Y.T. 2021. "Authoritarian Rule of Law in Hong Kong." In *Democracy and Rule of Law in China's Shadow*, edited by Brian C. Jones. Hart Publishing.

Tam, Waikeung. 2010. "Political Transition and the Rise of Cause Lawyering: The Case of Hong Kong." *Law and Social Inquiry* 35 (3): 663–687.

Tam, Waikeung. 2012. *Legal Mobilization under Authoritarianism: The Case of Post-Colonial Hong Kong*. Cambridge University Press.

Tamanaha, Brian Z. 2004. *On the Rule of Law: History, Politics, Theory*. Cambridge University Press.

Tamanaha, Brian Z. 2007. "A Concise Guide to the Rule of Law." *Legal Studies Research Paper Series*, Paper 07–2282.

Tamanaha, Brian Z. 2012. "The History and Elements of the Rule of Law." *Singapore Journal of Legal Studies*: 232–247.

Tamanaha, Brian Z. 2017. *A Realistic Theory of Law*. Cambridge University Press.

Terwindt, Carolijn. 2019. *When Protest Becomes Crime: Politics and Law in Liberal Democracies*. Pluto Press.

Teubner, Gunther. 1998. "Legal Irritants: Good Faith in British Law or How Unifying Law Ends up in New Divergences." *Modern Law Review* 61 (1): 11–32.

Tilly, Charles. 1984. "Social Movements and National Politics." In *Statemaking and Social Movements: Essays in History and Theory*, edited by Charles Bright and Susan Harding. University of Michigan Press.

Trevaskes, Susan. 2019. "Socialist Law." In *Afterlives of Chinese Communism: Political Concepts from Mao to Xi*, edited by Christian Sorace, Ivan Franceschini, and Nicholas Loubere. ANU Press and Verso Books.

Tsang, Steve. 2004. *A Modern History of Hong Kong*. Hong Kong University Press.

Turk, Austin T. 1976. "Law as a Weapon in Social Conflict." *Social Problems* 23 (3): 276–291.

Turner, Bertram. 2006. "Competing Global Players in Rural Morocco: Upgrading Legal Arenas." *The Journal of Legal Pluralism and Unofficial Law* 48 (3): 101–139.

Unger, Jonathan, and Anita Chan. 1995. "China, Corporatism, and the East Asian Model." *The Australian Journal of Chinese Affairs* 33: 29–53.

Unger, Roberto M. 2015. *The Critical Legal Studies Movement: Another Time, A Greater Task*. Verso.

United Nations. 1994. "No. 23392. China and United Kingdom of Great Britain and Northern Ireland: Joint Declaration on the Question of Hong Kong (with Annexes). Signed at Beijing on 19th December 1984." *Treaties and International Agreements Registered or Filed and Recorded with the Secretariat of the United Nations* 1399.

Vago, Steven, Adie Nelson, Veronica Nelson and Steven E. Barkan. 2017. *Law and Society*. 11th ed. Routledge.

Vallejos Evangeline Banao, also known as Vallejos, Evangeline B. and Daniel Domingo L. v. Commissioner of Registration and Registration of Persons Tribunal. 2013. FACV19/2012.

Wacks, Raymond. 1989. *The Future of the Law in Hong Kong*. Oxford University Press.

Wang, Chenguang. 2013. "Legal Transplantation and Legal Development in Transitional China." *World Bank Legal Review* 4: 161–178.

Watson, Alan. 1993. *Legal Transplant: An Approach to Comparative Law*. 2nd ed. The University of Georgia Press.

Watson, Alan. 1996. "Aspects of Reception of Law." *The American Journal of Comparative Law* 44 (2): 335–351.

Weber, Max. 1946. *Politics as a Vocation*. Oxford University Press. Accessed July 29, 2020. https://archive.org/details/weber_max_1864_1920_politics_as_a_vocation/page/n1/mode/2up.

Weber, Max. 1978. *Economy and Society*. Edited by Guenther Roth and Claus Wittich. University of California Press.

Whiting, Susan H. 2017. "Authoritarian 'Rule of Law' and Regime Legitimacy." *Comparative Political Studies* 50 (14): 1907–1940.

Wiarda, Howard J. 1997. *Corporatism and Comparative Politics: The Other Great 'Ism'*. M.E. Sharpe.

Wiener, Martin J. 2012. "Some Difficulties of Colonial Judging: The Bahamas 1886–93." In *Judges and Judging in the History of the Common Law and Civil Law: From Antiquity to Modern Times*, edited by Paul Brand and Joshua Getzler. Cambridge University Press.

Wilson, Joshua C. 2011. "Sustaining the State: Legal Consciousness and the Construction of Legality in Competing Abortion Activists' Narratives." *Law and Social Inquiry* 36 (2): 455–483.

Wilson, Sophia. 2017. "Cause Lawyering in Revolutionary Ukraine." *Journal of Law and Courts* 5 (2): 267–288.

Winn, Jane K. and Tang-chi Yeh. 1995. "Advocating Democracy: The Role of Lawyers in Taiwan's Political Transformation." *Law and Social Inquiry* 20 (2): 561–599.

Wong, John D. 2020. "Protests, Politics and Challenges to Hong Kong's Rule of Law." *Harvard Political Review*, March 2. Accessed August 30, 2020. https://harvardpolitics.com/world/protests-politics-and-challenges-to-hong-kongs-rule-of-law.

Wong, John D. 2022. "Constructing the Legitimacy of Governance in Hong Kong: 'Prosperity and Stability' and 'Democracy and Freedom.'" *The Journal of Asian Studies*, First View. Accessed February 17, 2022. https://doi.org/10.1017/S0021911821002230.

Wong, Max W. L. 2011. "Social Control and Political Order: Decolonisation and the Use of Emergency Regulations in Hong Kong." *Hong Kong Law Journal* 41 (2): 449–480.

Wong, Max W. L. 2017. *Re-Ordering Hong Kong: Decolonisation and the Hong Kong Bill of Rights Ordinance.* Wildy, Simmonds and Hill Publishing.

Wong, Stan H.W., Ngok. Ma, and Wai-man Lam. 2018. "Immigrants as Voters in Electoral Autocracies: The Case of Mainland Chinese Immigrants in Hong Kong." *Journal of East Asian Studies* 18 (1): 67–95.

The World Bank. 2019. *Worldwide Governance Indicators.* Accessed July 31, 2020. https://databank.worldbank.org/databases/rule-of-law.

World Economic Forum. 2019. *The Global Competitiveness Report.* Accessed 31 July 2020. https://www3.weforum.org/docs/WEF_TheGlobalCompetitivenessReport2019.pdf.

World Justice Project. 2019. *The WJP Rule of Law Index 2019.* Accessed July 9, 2020. https://worldjusticeproject.org/rule-of-law-index/.

Wu, Jieh-min. 2016. "The China Factor in Taiwan: Impact and Response." In *Handbook of Modern Taiwan Politics and Society*, edited by Gunter Schubert. Routledge.

Yam, Julius, and Po Jen Yap. 2023. "Legalism and Strategic Judicial Decision-Making in Hong Kong." *Hong Kong Law Journal* 53 (1): 207–224.

Yap, Po Jen. 2007. "Constitutional Review under the Basic Law: The Rise, Retreat and Resurgence of Judicial Power in Hong Kong." *Hong Kong Law Journal* 37 (2): 449–474.

Yazdiha, Haj. 2014. "Law as Movement Strategy: How the Islamophobia Movement Institutionalizes Fear through Legislation." *Social Movement Studies* 13 (2): 267–274.

Yuen, Samson, and Edmund W. Cheng. 2020. "Between High Autonomy and Sovereign Control in a Subnational Island Jurisdiction: The Paradox of Hong Kong under 'One Country, Two Systems.'" *Island Studies Journal* 15 (1): 131–150.

Zēng, Zhāo Míng. 2014. "Qí Lù Pái Huái de Zhōng Guó Mèng: Mín Zú Guó Jiā Huò Tiān Xià Dì Guó?" *Reflexion* 25: 25–47.

Zhou, Ling. 2011. "The Independent Director System and Its Legal Transplant into China." *Journal of Comparative Law* 6 (2): 262–291.

Zhu, Han. 2019. "Beijing's 'Rule of Law' Strategy for Governing Hong Kong: Legalisation without Democratisation." *The China Perspective* 2019 (1): 23–33.

Zhuang, Shaohong. 2005. "Legal Transplantation in the People's Republic of China: A Reply to Alan Watson." *European Journal of Law Reform* 7 (1&2): 215–236.

2. China's Authoritarian Legal Transplantation

Abstract: This chapter examines China's implementation of authoritarian legal transplantation in Hong Kong, highlighting the mechanisms and motivations behind this process. Through institutional interventions and elite co-optation, China has reshaped Hong Kong's legal system to align with its political and ideological objectives. The chapter identifies direct transplantation methods, including reinterpretation of the Basic Law, imposition of national laws, and the creation of authoritarian legal discourses. These measures aim to undermine judicial independence, enforce China's sovereignty, and promote nationalism while leveraging economic dependence to exert control. By situating Hong Kong within broader trends of China's global influence, this chapter reveals how legal transplantation consolidates authoritarian governance, transforming Hong Kong's legal traditions into instruments of state control and repression.

Keywords: Authoritarianism, Socialist Law, Judicial Independence, National Security, Sovereignty, Rule by Law

The following chapters will explain how China's process of authoritarian legal transplantation has worked in post-colonial Hong Kong. It will fill an intellectual gap by making sense of how the China factor influences Hong Kong's legal system, which has been serving as a "gateway" between China and the world (Liu and Au 2020, 309). Findings show that China exerts its political and economic influences on the legal system of Hong Kong in four domains: legal institutions, political elections, counter-mobilisation of pro-Beijing lawyers and cross-border political economy. China attempts to increase its legitimacy and supremacy in the normative foundation and practices of law in Hong Kong by transplanting the sovereign's legal rules, legal ideology and discourse on the Rule of Law. The transplantation process is backed by the co-optation of the legal profession under the United Front

Lai, Y. *Legal Resistance under Authoritarianism: The Struggle for the Rule of Law in Hong Kong.*

DOI: 10.5117/9789048558438_CH02

work, which will be further explained in the next chapter. The process of legal transplantation localises ideology, discourses and practices of law that prioritise sovereignty, economic benefits and legal technicality over democratic and liberal values of the Rule of Law. In short, China's authoritarian legal transplantation processes follow a conventional "carrot-and-stick" strategy. It consists of two elements: repression and co-optation. While transplanting its socialist authoritarian legal rules, ideology and practices to pressure Hong Kong's courts and broadly the society to obey, China also uses political and economic benefits to absorb and collaborate with local legal elites through the United Front work.

I follow scholars in China studies to synthesise the acts of China in relation to influencing Hong Kong's legal system as "the China factor." As explained in chapter 1, the China factor refers to which the design and driver of this transplantation project lies in China under the one-party rule of the Chinese Communist Party (CCP). Jieh-Min Wu has conceptualised the China factor as "the process by which the PRC government utilises capital and related resources to absorb other countries and 'offshore districts' into its sphere of economic influence, thereby making them economically dependent on China to further facilitate its political influence" (Wu 2016, 430). He observes the influences of the Chinese government, the presence of Chinese capital, and the cross-strait capital between China and Taiwan as expressions of the China factor in Taiwan's political, economic, social and cultural facets, and how the China factor impacts business behaviours, incumbent's policymaking, mass media, public opinion and political stability in Taiwan (Wu and Liao 2015, 93). These phenomena have been far more intense in Hong Kong, facilitated by the absence of universal suffrage and Hong Kong's return of sovereignty to China in 1997.

The role of external powers in influencing the transition or transplantation of political regimes in foreign countries has been exhaustively discussed in studies of US and Russian politics (Bader, Gravingholt and Kastner 2010, 81; Jackson 2010, 101; Khamzayeva 2012, Wu and Liao 2015). However, in the past decade, scholars have begun to pay more attention to the case of China. Leveraging economic power for political gain is a feature of China's strategy to expand its political influence in the world order. Examples include donations to international organisations such as the World Health Organisation (WHO) and investing in developing countries through the Asian Infrastructure Investment Bank and the Belt and Road Initiative (BRI). The rise of China in the global order is also reflected in its engagement in the international human rights system. China is a United Nations Human Rights Council member and has gained a seat in a consultative group within the Council despite its unsatisfactory record of human rights violations (Albert 2020; Richardson 2020). It's economic and political expansions in both developed and developing countries have attracted scholars to portray China as a new colonial power in the world order today (Diamond, Plattner and Walker 2016). China's rising economic power has facilitated its growing international influence in both the political and economic spheres; this influence, however, is not as straightforward as sometimes presented. Although accounts of China's economic impact are often presented as hegemonic, reality is more nuanced. As Lee argues in her study of Chinese investment in the Zambian copper and construction industries, unlike the Western counterparts, the Chinese capital invested in foreign countries will compromise the recipient government, which faces labour strikes and mobilisation of the opposition (Lee 2017). Her works shed light on the mechanisms and impacts of global China in world politics.

This chapter begins by explaining why China is eager to implement authoritarian legal transplantation through institutional interventions and elite co-optations in Hong Kong, and then examines the direct mechanisms of the legal transplantation and the imposition on Hong Kong's legal system since the transfer of sovereignty in 1997, namely interpretations of the Basic Law, impositions of binding decisions related to the Basic Law, direct as well as indirect transplantations of national legal rules, and the production of authoritarian legal discourse.

China's Motivations

As Linz and Stepan emphasise, the Rule of Law is one of the critical constituents of democratic consolidation (1996). Building solid legal institutions and deepening beliefs in society are intertwined components of engineering for democratic regimes. Nevertheless, the process of state-building is not necessarily moving towards democratisation. If the political authority does not support democratisation, then a liberal notion of the Rule of Law would hardly survive. In contrast, an illiberal idea of the Rule of Law that prioritises the political interests of the incumbency would flourish under authoritarian governance (Bugarič 2014; Drinoczi and Bień-Kacała 2019, 1140).

In 1997, Hong Kong did not undergo a process of decolonisation with independence. Instead, it maintained the status quo at best, as the primary purpose of "One Country, Two Systems" is to preserve the pre-existing institutions inherited from the British colonial administration, including the common law (Lui 2020, 70). However, rather than consolidating the common law tradition and liberal notions of the Rule of Law, China has enhanced its political control over Hong Kong by transplanting its legal ideology and practices into Hong Kong's legal system, including the legal profession itself.

China's motivations of enhancing control over Hong Kong's legal system occurs in threefold. The first one is nationalistic: China, or specifically the CCP, wants Hong Kong to be "decolonised" from the British legacy, so it rebuilds Hong Kong through Chinese nationalism. As defined by Hechter, statecraft of nationalism refers to a process of incorporating "culturally distinctive peripheries" for reducing "the boundaries of the nation and governance unit" and absorbing "culturally distinctive individuals to the dominant culture" (Hechter 2001, 62–63; Fong 2017a, 528). A successful nationalistic project by China thus requires Hong Kong's legal system, legal culture and legal community to be transformed from having characteristics of British colonialism to Chinese ones.

Although China implemented "One Country, Two Systems" in Hong Kong after its handover in 1997, it does not mean that China allowed Hong Kong to develop as a liberal democratic polity mirroring its Western counterparts. This risks Hong Kong seeking independence from Chinese sovereignty. However, a Westernised liberal conception of the Rule of Law had been institutionalised in Hong Kong before its handover. When democratic reform was absent in the colonial era, the British colonisers used law as an alternative way to accommodate redress. Emphasis on legality and judicial independence served as a new technique of governance to substitute politics and to instil individualism instead of a Chinese collective identity among Hong Kong residents (Jones 1999, 46). On one hand, in the 1970s, the colonial administration in Hong Kong introduced new legislations to abolish Chinese customary practices, such as concubinage, in order to eliminate Chinese customary laws and weaken Chinese culture in society (Jones 1999, 54). On the other hand, in 1991, the colonial government adopted the Bill of Rights Ordinance (BORO), leading to a formation of rights-based legal consciousness and expectations of the Rule of Law in the post-colonial era after 1997 (Jones 1999, 62). The BORO highlighted the instrumental value of law in protecting individuals' human rights and limiting government power. Dicey's style of the Rule of Law, requires that both the government and individual be subject to law, is realised in law instead of politics.

The substitution of politics by law consolidated the legitimacy of the British colonial administration in Hong Kong. Eventually, it replaced the national identity that embodied a sense of national belonging and sovereignty with limited citizenship, excluding democratic rights. Chris

Patten, the last governor of colonial Hong Kong, highlighted the Rule of Law as a significant British contribution to Hong Kong's success (Patten, 1996). Its common law legal system was even praised by the last solicitor general of the colonial government of Hong Kong as the "greatest and most treasured legacy to Hong Kong" (McDermott 1997, 263). Yet, from the CCP's perspective, the British Rule of Law project promoted human rights norms, partly free elections, as well as the appreciation of the common law legal system. These were significant obstacles to achieving what the CCP called the "return of the hearts of Hong Kong people" (rén xīn huí guī) and thus national unity between Hong Kong and the mainland (Hung 2020, 374). Beijing's anxiety about achieving its nationalistic state-building project by expanding its encroachments on Hong Kong, ironically, led to further sentimental resistance and distrust towards the new system by the local people, as reflected by the widening differences in the identification between Chinese and 'Hongkongers' after the handover. The identity of Hong Kong as 'Hongkongers' and 'Hongkongers in China' had soared to more than 75 per cent by 2020, while the identity of Chinese and "Chinese in Hong Kong" had dropped to less than 25 per cent (Hong Kong Public Opinion Research Institute 2020c). A similar phenomenon can be found in Taiwan when the public's perceived threat from China was translated to a more robust identification as Taiwanese but not Chinese (Gold and Veg 2020,8).

In China, the constitution, the courts and laws are subject to the ruling party, reflecting the implementation of an "authoritarian Rule of Law" (Whiting 2017, 1935–1936). For the socialist Chinese legal system, serving the state's political goals is the prima facie role of law (Chan 2018, p.374). The courts do not enforce the rights and freedoms warranted in the Constitution of the People's Republic of China, and its interpretation is vested in the political organ rather than an independent judiciary (Chan 2015, 32). The assertiveness of the CCP's authoritarian legality that treats laws as the governing technique of the party-state, like British colonialism, was further reinforced when Xi Jinping came to power in 2012. In the following year, an internal government record was exposed to the public, stating that Western ideas such as "universal values," "civil society," "press freedom" and "judicial independence" should be banned in higher education institutions, labelled by the media as "Seven Ideas that You Should Not Talk About" (qī bù jiǎng). This document evidences the party's resistance to the liberal tradition of legal ideology from the West (*ChinaFile* 8 November 2013; Li 2013).

Mainland Chinese legal norms and practices today are characterised by authoritarian legality, contrary to the common law system in Hong Kong, where norms of human rights, limiting government and judicial independence are well-established. Such norms are well reflected in public opinion. A university survey in 2015 found that more than 90 per cent of respondents strongly agreed or agreed that the Rule of Law and a "just and corruption-free" society are the core values of Hong Kong, whereas "freedom" ranked third (Hong Kong Institute of Asia-Pacific Studies 2015). The tensions between Hong Kong's liberal values of the Rule of Law and China's legal ideology characterised by authoritarianism alongside nationalism persist and draw China to pay greater effort to infringe on Hong Kong's legal system by legal imposition and transplantation.

The second motivation concerns China's anxiety of securing political control over Hong Kong. Such desire has been developed in the beginning of Hong Kong's post-colonial era. To do so, China needs to weaken the checking power of Hong Kong's independent judiciary, which has a strong common law tradition and is committed to the principle of a "separation of powers," as well as to weaponise laws and statutes against the political opposition in the city. Compared with the establishment of the Macau Special Administrative Region in 1999, a neighbouring subnational jurisdiction under Chinese sovereignty, China had less motivation to exert direct interference in Macau's new constitutional order and legal system. From the perspective of the Chinese authorities, the codified civil law tradition in Macau, its inexperienced post-handover legal system, conservative colonial legacies as well as the less contentious political and judicial environment have made Macau's legal system a less threatening institution than Hong Kong (Krebs 2000; Castellucci 2012; Tso 2012; Ip 2019).

Such a comparative perspective further indicates China's motivation to build a new political culture and societal order, as well as to control Hong Kong's common law system. In the first five years after the handover, China interfered in Hong Kong's judicial practice on constitutional review, such as cases concerning the right of abode in Hong Kong. Still, to a large extent, China also exercised "self-imposed restraint" in socio-political-economic spheres – not intervening in the internal affairs of Hong Kong and keeping to its promise to allow self-government (Horlemann 2003, 102). However, this non-interventionist approach ended in 2003 after more than half a million residents in Hong Kong protested against the national security legislation, which was finally withdrawn under pressure (Fong 2017a, 527).

A mainland legal scholar suggested that after that time, Beijing eventually implemented a "new Hong Kong policy" through a "direct involvement" in Hong Kong's constitutional affairs (Cheng 2009). Evidence of the new policy can be found in the National People's Congress Standing Committee (NPCSC)'s interpretation of Hong Kong's Basic Law in 2004, declaring that the central government can decide the pace of Hong Kong's democratisation by giving formal approval before the local government activates any political reform. Such a move by Beijing asserted that "there is no separation of powers, no inherent or residual power of the locality, and Beijing has final control" (ibid.). The support and collaboration of Hong Kong's legal community are essential to consolidate the sovereign state's control in constitutional affairs. Therefore, in the two instances of NPCSC's interpretations of the Basic Law in 2004 and 2005, Beijing's high-ranking officials met members of the legal community from Hong Kong before and after the passage of the interpretations to consolidate their political ties. Since the 20th anniversary of the sovereignty transfer, Chinese officials urged the Hong Kong government to instrumentalise Hong Kong laws as "weapons" to combat the opposition, turning local laws and courts from guardians of political freedoms to government repressive tools against dissent (Zhang 2017; Luo 2020). These events reveal that, the encroachment of Hong Kong's legal system serves the ultimate goal of bringing the city under China's complete political domination.

The third motivation concerns China's economic interests in Hong Kong's legal services market. Hong Kong has been pivotal in China's economic reform since the 1980s by connecting China to overseas markets and capital and serving as an offshore market for China after the sovereignty transfer (Hung 2018, 434-435). China exports capital to Hong Kong and re-exports the capital to other parts of the world as Hong Kong's capital. As of 2018, Hong Kong enjoyed more than 55.5 per cent of China's outward investment stock and more than 60.7 per cent of China's outward capital flow, being the top destination of China's foreign direct investment (HKTDC Research 2020a). The flow of Chinese capital in Hong Kong also boosted the demand for legal services assisting mainland-related investments in terms of the listing of mainland enterprises and setting up offices in Hong Kong (Poon 2020).

The interdependence between Chinese capital and Hong Kong's legal services industries can be found in the increasing shares of mainland enterprises, market capitalisation and fundraising activity of initial public offering (IPO) in Hong Kong's equity market. They have occurred since the introduction of the Mainland and Hong Kong Closer Economic Partnership Agreement (CEPA) between China and Hong Kong. Companies from mainland China consist of red chip companies, state enterprises, and H-share companies, which are incorporated into the mainland and then listed on the Hong Kong Stock Exchange. Between 2004 and 2019, red chip and H-share companies tripled from 304 to 1,241, sharing 51 per cent of the total equity market (figure 2). Moreover, the total capital accumulation by China listed

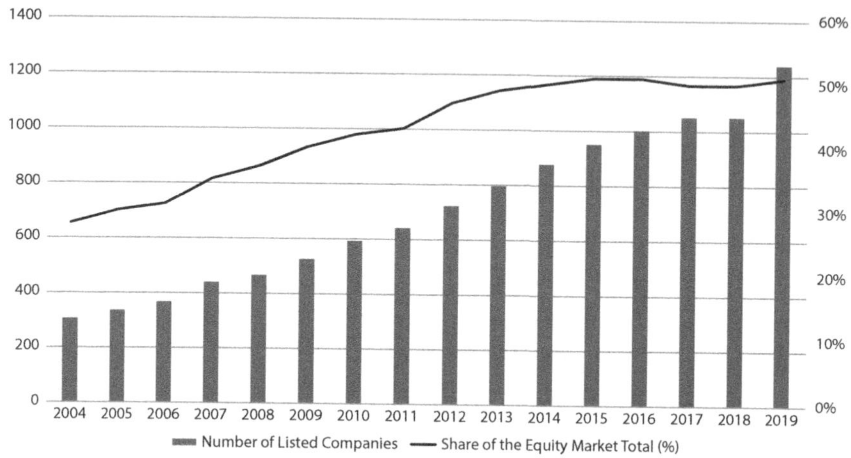

Figure 2. Number of Listed Companies from Mainland China in the Equity Market (2004–2019)
Source: Hong Kong Exchanges and Clearing Limited

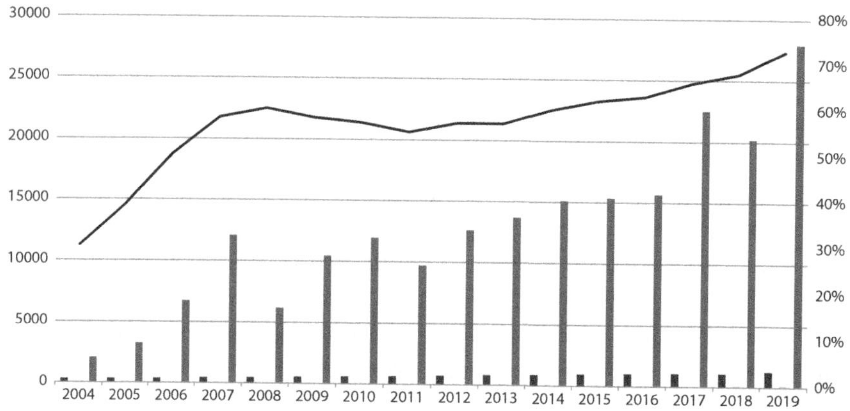

Figure 3. Market Capitalisation of Mainland Enterprises in the Equity Market (2004–2019, HK$ billion)
Source: Hong Kong Exchanges and Clearing Limited

companies in the stock market contributed to 73 per cent of the total equity market share (Figure 3). Chinese IPOs had by 2019 also raised nearly 80 per cent of funds in Hong Kong's local stock market (Figure 4). The huge demand for Chinese corporation listings in Hong Kong's stock market comes with the demand for professional legal services from Hong Kong. At the same time, law firms in Hong Kong would also be attracted by the enormous profits from the merger and acquisition of Chinese capital in Hong Kong.

The Chinese companies, many of which are owned by the Chinese state, represent the significant influence of mainland Chinese capital in Hong

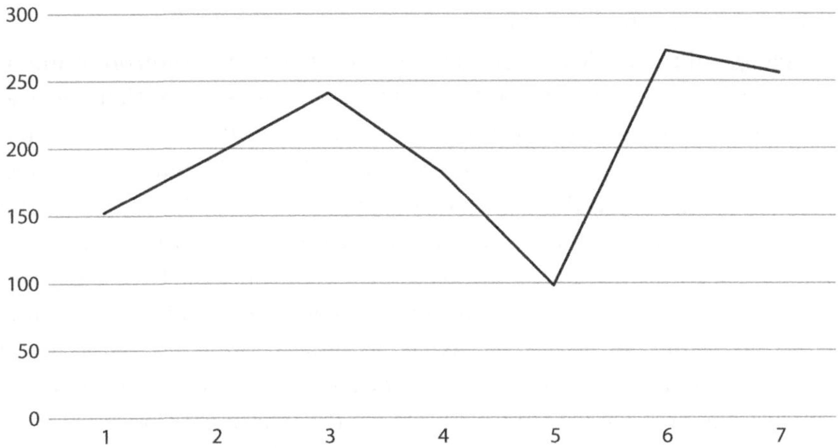

Figure 4. Mainland Chinese IPO Funds Raised (2013–2019, HK$ billion)
Source: Hong Kong Exchanges and Clearing Limited

Kong's financial sector. Chinese economic influence by re-exporting capital from Hong Kong can be expanded with the assistance of the residing legal profession and law firms. As illustrated in the next chapter, the gigantic market opportunities for Hong Kong law firms and chambers are levered by the CCP, which decides and controls capital flow from the mainland to Hong Kong, luring Hong Kong lawyers to co-opt with the CCP. The economic and political ties between local law firms, professional legal bodies and the Chinese state are further entangled.

Direct Transplantation Mechanisms

Direct transplantation mechanisms demonstrate how the CCP transplants national laws, its legal ideology, and practices to Hong Kong's legal system through its powers embedded in the political institutions. It can be read as a form of "institutional transplantation." It is also part of the CCP's state-building project, avoiding abolishing the whole framework of "One Country, Two Systems." The CCP implemented the institutional transplantation through four strategies, namely (1) interpretation of the Basic Law, (2) releasing binding decisions related to the provisions of the Basic Law (3) indirect and direct transplantation of laws promulgated in China, namely national laws (quán guó xìng fǎ lu), and (4) producing official legal discourse in support of the institutional intervention.

Interpretations of the Basic Law

Article 158 of the Basic Law gives the ultimate power of interpretation of the Basic Law to the NPCSC. Yet the same provision requires that only the Court of Final Appeal in Hong Kong can initiate the NPCSC's interpretation of the Basic Law. This is a way to empower the Court of Final Appeal (CFA) and respect judicial independence. Nevertheless, since the handover, the NPCSC has exercised its power to interpret the Basic Law five times, but only one of these interpretations was at the request of the CFA. That case refers to the issue of diplomatic immunity. The other four interpretations were sought by the Chief Executive or introduced independently by the NPCSC per se. These interpretations of the Basic Law changed immigration policies, the procedure of political reform, the length of term of succeeding Chief Executives and disqualifications of electoral candidates and lawmakers due to disapproval of various forms of oath-taking for public office (see table 1).

Under Hong Kong's common law tradition, only the court can interpret the law and make the final judgement of a litigation. Yet, in China, the legislative body, i.e., the NPC and its NPCSC, enjoys the power to interpret the law. The consequence of the NPCSC's re-interpretation of the Basic Law is that judicial autonomy in Hong Kong is weakened. The sovereign state's interpretations of the Basic Law have a binding power in Hong Kong's courts. Hong Kong's judicial authority was also weakened by the NPCSC's action effectively interfering court decisions. This was prevalent in the case of Right of Abode in 1999, when the Chief Executive of Hong Kong sought reinterpretation of the Basic Law, contravening the conditions prescribed in Article 158 of the Basic Law. The message of such top-down and executive-led practices was clear: the executive government and the NPCSC should enjoy greater authority to initiate any interpretation of the Basic Law, and the courts are not superior to the local executive authorities and the sovereign state in matters of constitutional controversy. Even when the executive government appeared to act ultra vires by seeking a Basic Law interpretation from the NPCSC, the court could not stop it. In short, judicial independence and autonomy in Hong Kong are conditioned by the undemocratic executive government of Hong Kong and by the legislature of the unitary Chinese sovereign state.

Binding Decisions by the NPCSC

After the first interpretation of the Basic Law by the NPCSC, Albert Chen, a legal scholar at the University of Hong Kong (HKU), argued that if any legislative acts are not done in pursuance of any provision in the Basic Law,

Table 1. The NPCSC's Interpretations of the Basic Law (1997–2016)

Date	Article(s) of Basic Law	Initiated by	Issue Concerned	Case Concerned	Summary of the content of interpretations	Political Impact(s)
26 June 1999	22(4), 24(2)(3)	The Chief Executive of Hong Kong	The right of abode among children of Hong Kong permanent residents born in mainland China	1/ Ng Ka Ling and another v. the Director of Immigration [1999] HKCFA 72; [1999] 1 HKLRD 315; (1999) 2 HKCFAR 4; [1999] 1 HKC 291; FACV 14/1998 (29 January 1999) 2/ Chan Kam Nga v. Director of Immigration [1999] HKCFA 16; [1999] 1 HKLRD 304; (1999) 2 HKCFAR 82; [1999] 1 HKC 347; FACV 13/1998 (29 January 1999)	A temporal condition was added that children born outside Hong Kong are eligible for the right of abode *only if at least one of their parents had earned permanent residency at the time of their birth.*	Judgement of the Court of Final Appeal was overturned, and the power of the Hong Kong government giving permission to right of abode applicants was taken away by mainland authorities.
6 April 2004	Annex I (7) and Annex II (III)	The NPCSC of China	Selection method of Chief Executive and formation of the Legislative Council	Not Applicable	Two new rules were added to the process of political reform. *Firstly, the Chief Executive must primarily report to the NPCSC on amendment to the method of election. Secondly, the NPCSC has the power to decide whether political reform should commence.*	Future political reform for selecting the Chief Executive and Legislative Council must seek approval from the NPCSC, and the pro-democracy camp's proposal of universal suffrage in 2004 was banned.

Date	Article(s) of Basic Law	Initiated by	Issue Concerned	Case Concerned	Summary of the content of interpretations	Political Impact(s)
27 April 2005	53(2)	The Chief Executive of Hong Kong	Length of term of succeeding Chief Executive	Not Applicable	The succeeding Chief Executive *only needs to fulfil the remaining term of the previous one.*	Donald Tsang, the candidate for the 2005 Chief Executive election, only needed to fulfil the remainder of the first Chief Executive Tung Chee-Hwa's term for 2 years.
26 August 2011	13(1) and 19	The Court of Final Appeal	Diplomatic immunity	Democratic Republic of the Congo and others v. FG Hemisphere Associates LLC [2011] HKCFA 67; (2011) 14 HKCFAR 395; [2011] 5 HKC 395; FACV 6/2010 (8 September 2011)		
7 November 2016	104	The NPCSC of China	Oath-taking of public officials including legislators	1/ Sixtus Leung Chung Hang v. Chief Executive of the Hong Kong Special Administrative Region, Secretary for Justice [2017] HKCFA 55; (2017) 20 HKCFAR 390; FAMV 9/2017 (1 September 2017) 2/ Yau Wai Ching v. Chief Executive of the Hong Kong Special Administrative Region, Secretary for Justice [2017] HKCFA 57; (2017) 20 HKCFAR 390; FAMV 8/2017 (1 September 2017)	*Elected legislators rejecting the oath in a given form or taking the oath "not genuinely or solemnly" will be deprived of their right to assume office without a second chance of oath-taking.*	In total six elected legislators of the opposition camp were disqualified from assuming their offices by the courts.

Sources: Hong Kong Legal Information Institute; Huang and Huang 2016

The Hong Kong courts can legitimately claim that these acts and existing statutes do not have legal force in Hong Kong (Chen 2000, 89).

Chen's hopeful opinion has been buried. As of 2019, the NPCSC had made twenty "decisions" in relation to the HKSAR, including issues of constitutional development and the establishment of port areas at Mainland–Hong Kong transportation hubs (Chan 2020). Among them, four NPCSC's decisions are fundamental to Hong Kong's democratisation and territorial autonomy. These weakened the court's power of constitutional review, as the making of those decisions, which were not prescribed in the Basic Law, are not subject to challenge by local courts (see table 2). In the Basic Law, there is no provision explaining whether and how the NPCSC can announce any "decision" on constitutional matters related to the Basic Law implemented in Hong Kong. If the NPCSC wants to implement something that deviates from the Basic Law provisions, it can either re-interpret the provisions, amend them, or add them to the Annexe of the Basic Law. It has changed the rules of the game in the constitutional affairs between Hong Kong and the mainland by creating a new way to exercise its power over Hong Kong.

Firstly, how the decisions were made bypassed domestic legislative procedures, court proceedings and even public consultations by the executive branch. Secondly, the decisions consolidated the supremacy of the NPCSC's political authority over Hong Kong. In his speech about the NPCSC's decision on the co-location arrangement in 2017, Deputy Secretary General of NPCSC, Li Fei, announced that the decision was final and could not be questioned. He used a Chinese proverb, "one word is as heavy as nine tripods," which implied the boldness of the NPCSC's decision and its absolute authority (E. Ng 2017a). Thirdly, the NPCSC's practice of issuing decisions for Hong Kong has notably diminished the judiciary's role, as a 2020 decision authorises the executive branch to bypass judicial procedures to remove any lawmakers with retrospective power. Finally, there has been a long debate about whether China's constitution can be fully applied to Hong Kong, since Article 5 of the Basic Law clarifies that the socialist system and policies are not applicable. However, the NPCSC decision in 2017 allowed mainland laws to be applied in the territory of Hong Kong, while Articles 52 and 54 of China's constitution were unprecedentedly introduced as a source of the NPCSC decision in 2020, quoting two articles that address the obligations of Chinese citizens in safeguarding national security. The introduction of the Chinese constitution marked China's legal transplantation of constitutional provisions into Hong Kong's local constitutional order (Lam 2020).

The NPCSC used its decision-making powers to facilitate the statecraft of patriotism to consciously rebuild the national identity of the "administrators"

Table 2. Decisions Made by the NPCSC over Constitutional Controversies in Hong Kong

Date	Issue Concerned	Summary of the content of decisions	Political Impact(s)	The Role of the Court
31 August 2014	Method of selection of the Chief Executive by universal suffrage and on the method for forming the Legislative Council	A 1,200-member Election Committee that currently chooses the Chief Executive would perform as a nomination committee, and only the committee can choose 2—3 candidates for Chief Executive elections by simple majority.	The rights of nomination and of candidacy in Chief Executive elections are limited to the nomination committee but not the electorate, and the decision triggered a 79—day Umbrella Movement, and the proposal of a Chief Executive election was vetoed in 2015.	The High Court rejected an application for a judicial review that challenged the validity of the NPCSC decision (Leung Lai Kwok Yvonne v. The Chief Secretary for Administration and others [2015] HKCFI 929; HCAL 31/2015 (5 June 2015)).
27 December 2017	Approval of the co-location arrangement between the mainland and Hong Kong	The co-operation arrangement in the West Kowloon Station of the Guangzhou-Shenzhen-Hong Kong Express Rail Link was approved and was confirmed as consistent with China's Constitution and the Basic Law of Hong Kong, alongside the mainland authorities will exercise jurisdiction over the West Kowloon Station mainland port area in accordance with the laws of the mainland.	Part of the West Kowloon Station territorially located in Hong Kong is regarded as mainland territory governed by mainland laws and its law enforcement, which is outside the framework of the text in the Basic Law	The High Court confirmed in a ruling of judicial review that the NPCSC can exercise supervisory power on any arrangement in compliance with the Basic Law and issue "decisions," thus the basis of the NPCSC decision was constituent with the Basic Law (Ku Chun Hin Zlato v. Secretary for Justice [2018] HKCFI 2657; HCAL 1171/2018 (13 December 2018)).

Date	Issue Concerned	Summary of the content of decisions	Political Impact(s)	The Role of the Court
11 August 2020	Extension of the length of term of the Legislative Council	The 6th Legislative Council (2016–2020) continues performing its duties after the end of 30th September 2020 which was the original date of the end of term. The 6th Legislative Council will extend for no less than one year, and until the term of the next Legislative Council begins.	All members of the 6th Legislative Council extended their length of term. Three pro-democracy legislative council members declined to continue their term of office after 30th September, criticising the decision as unconstitutional and unlawful.	The High Court rejected an application for a judicial review and an injunction that forbids the Chief Executive to amend the length of term of the Legislative Council from four years to five years, as the Court saw the application as ungrounded. (Kwok Cheuk Kin and Chan Kit Bing v. Chief Executive [2020] CFI 1954; HCAL 1595/2020 (14 August 2020))
11 November 2020	Qualification of the members of the Legislative Council	The Hong Kong SAR government can disqualify members of the Legislative Council who allegedly promote Hong Kong independence, refuse China's sovereignty of Hong Kong, collude with foreign countries in intervening in the affairs of Hong Kong, and/or commit any acts that pose a threat to national security.	Four pro-democracy members of the Legislative Council, whose nominations for the Legislative Council election originally scheduled in 2020 were invalidated by the returning officers, were disqualified by the Hong Kong government immediately after the release of the NPCSC decision. Pro-democracy lawmakers responded by resignation *en masse*.	Disqualified members did not give any hint or suggestion that they would seek judicial review

Sources: Websites of the Basic Law of HKSAR; Transport and Housing Bureau of HKSAR Constitutional and Mainland Affairs Bureau of HKSAR; Wisenews; Xinhua News Agency

of Hong Kong. In June 2014, the White Paper on Hong Kong's "One Country, Two Systems" restated those administrators of Hong Kong, including the Chief Executive, judges, government bureaucrats and lawmakers, should be patriotic. The requirement of patriotism was realised in the NPCSC decisions in 2014 and 2020. In the 2014 decision on future methods of electing the Chief Executive, a filtering mechanism was required of the nomination committee that it mainly be made up of pro-China figures, implying that any candidates from the opposition would be excluded from running for election. Six years after, the release of the NPCSC decision in 2020 led to the disqualifications of pro-democracy lawmakers. Zhang Xiaoming, a senior official at China's Hong Kong and Macau Affairs Office (HKMAO), claimed publicly that the consequence of the decision was that "only patriots should be allowed to rule Hong Kong and dissidents must be expelled from the system" (S. Cheng 2020).

Indirect Transplantation of National Laws

China's indirect transplantation of national laws can be found in the Hong Kong government's introduction of the Fugitive Offenders and Mutual Legal Assistance in Criminal Matters Legislation (Amendment) Bill (known as the Extradition Law Amendment Bill or ELAB) in late February 2019. The government claimed that the amendment was a remedy to a legal injustice that was brought to light when a Hong Kong resident was suspected of murdering his girlfriend in Taiwan returned to Hong Kong, which has no extradition agreement with Taiwan (Siu 2019). Nevertheless, the proposed ELAB suggested a mechanism of transferring fugitives that may extend to mainland China, plugging the gap in the extradition of suspects from Hong Kong to China. This matter has not been settled since 1997 (The Legislative Council of HKSAR 2019).

The ELAB was regarded as a removal of a firewall between the judicial system in Hong Kong and the criminal justice system of China, the latter of which is little trusted by the people of Hong Kong, who doubt whether a fair trial would be given to the defendants on the mainland (Chen 2019, 425; Pomfret and Pang 2019). The jurisdictional relationship between Hong Kong and China is not on a level playing field since the Chinese government appoints the Chief Executive of Hong Kong. Thus, the Chief Executive has little room to reject a request for a fugitive to be handed over to the Chinese authorities. The ELAB bill also removes the power of the legislature to review requests for fugitive transfers, and the courts of Hong Kong can only scrutinise the prima facie case provided by the Chinese authorities. The ELAB was reported as providing a legal ground for the Central Commission for Discipline Inspection of the CCP to arrest mainland political elites formally hiding in Hong Kong instead of deploying kidnapping (Lague, Pomfret and Torode 2019).

In referring to extradition agreements, and as already alluded to above about the position of the Chief Executive of Hong Kong vis-à-vis the government of China, the subnational status of Hong Kong is essential. The relationship between China and Hong Kong is not one between two equal (in formal terms) states. It was the realisation that the ELAB was not an equal agreement between two independent jurisdictions, since Hong Kong is a Special Administrative Region subject to the sovereign power of China. The controversy finally led to a six-month long citywide protests in Hong Kong. Although the ELAB was eventually withdrawn in 2019, this episode illustrated the attempt by the CCP to extend its criminal justice system beyond the border of its legal jurisdiction.

Direct Transplantation of National Laws

The NPCSC can add national laws applicable to Hong Kong by listing them in Annex III of the Basic Law. Under Article 18 of the Basic Law, these laws, which do not need to be passed by Hong Kong's legislature, "shall be confined to those relating to defence and foreign affairs as well as other matters outside the limits of the autonomy of the Region." At first glance, the provision is limited. However, the idea of "other matters outside the limits of the autonomy of the Region," and the ambiguity of that provision have allowed interference in Hong Kong's internal affairs. Specifically, China categorised national sovereignty and national security as matters outside Hong Kong's autonomy. Between 1997 and 2020, the national laws listed in Annex III of the Basic Law included laws on diplomatic concerns and matters related to national sovereignty and national security (see table 3).

The transplantation of Chinese national laws in Hong Kong serves two functions: to fulfil the obligations of China in national defence and foreign affairs in Hong Kong, and to promote nationalism and patriotism. Among the 14 national laws listed in Annex III, six facilitate building a national identity in Hong Kong. The national security law (also known as the Hong Kong National Security Law or the NSL) in 2020 relates to national sovereignty and territorial unity. The purpose of promoting patriotism is written in the preamble of the National Anthem Ordinance, and as such legalisation of patriotism is legally enforceable through criminal prosecution. The National Flag and National Emblem Ordinance criminalise speech or non-violent expression that misuses or insults the national flag, emblem, or anthem (Article 6 (3)), as in the National Anthem Ordinance (Article 7). The National Anthem Ordinance further makes the promotion of the national anthem compulsory at schools (Article 9). The government's use of those speech-related criminal laws eventually led to the imprisonment of ordinary

Table 3. List of National Laws Applied in Hong Kong under Annex III of the Basic Law

Date	National Laws	Way of Application	Issues Concerned
1 July 1997	Resolution on the Capital, Calendar, National Anthem and National Flag of the People's Republic of China		National identity
	Resolution on the National Day of the People's Republic of China	Promulgation	National identity
	Declaration of the Government of the People's Republic of China on the Territorial Sea	Promulgation	Diplomacy
	Nationality Law of the People's Republic of China	Promulgation	National identity
	Regulations of the People's Republic of China Concerning Diplomatic Privileges and Immunities	Promulgation	Diplomacy
	Law of the People's Republic of China on the National Flag	Local legislation (1 July 1997)	National identity
	Regulations of the People's Republic of China Concerning Consular Privileges and Immunities	Promulgation	Diplomacy
	Law of the People's Republic of China on the National Emblem	Local legislation (1 July 1997)	National identity
	Law of the People's Republic of China on the Territorial Sea and the Contiguous Zone	Promulgation	Diplomacy
	Law of the People's Republic of China on the Garrisoning of the Hong Kong Special Administrative Region	Promulgation	National defence
4 November 1998	Law of the People's Republic of China on the Exclusive Economic Zone and the Continental Shelf	Promulgation	Diplomacy
27 October 2005	Law of the People's Republic of China on Judicial Immunity from Compulsory Measures Concerning the Property of Foreign Central Banks	Promulgation	Diplomacy
4 November 2017	Law of the People's Republic of China on the National Anthem	Local legislation (4 June 2020)	National identity
30 June 2020	Law of the People's Republic of China on Safeguarding National Security in the Hong Kong Special Administrative Region	Promulgation by NPCSC	National security

Source: The Basic Law of HKSAR

residents (Secretary for Justice v Law Man Chung [2020] CAAR4/2019). Despite the implementation of the BORO which applies the International Covenant on Civil and Political Rights , the NSL can override any domestic legislation in Hong Kong. In other words, national security trumps human rights and civil liberties protection in Hong Kong's legal system.

Production of Official Legal Discourse

To legitimise the sovereign state's direct influence in Hong Kong's legal system, the CCP have been building a favourable legal discourse to rationalise the process of authoritarian legal transplantation, partly by disapproving of Western liberal values embedded in the conventional legal discourse in Hong Kong. Since the handover, the top Chinese government officials responsible for Hong Kong affairs have been fighting to have a more significant say over the constitutional relations between China and Hong Kong, alongside the constitutional arrangements for the Hong Kong government. Such "alternative" discourse consists of three traits: the creation of the concept of "overall jurisdiction", the rejection of the notion of separation of powers, and the emphasis on the political obligation of the judiciary.

Although the idea of "overall jurisdiction" was first introduced in 2014, the CCP had already aggressively addressed the supremacy of China's sovereign power over Hong Kong long before. During a seminar celebrating the tenth anniversary of Hong Kong's transfer of sovereignty in 2007, the chairman of the NPCSC, Wu Bangguo, claimed that Hong Kong does not have "residual power" because "the extent of the power of the Hong Kong SAR Government depends on the extent of power given by the central government" (Chong and Hui 2007). One year later, Cao Erbao, the research director of China's Central Liaison Office in Hong Kong, published an article stating that there are two governing teams in Hong Kong. One refers to the Hong Kong government, while the other comprises "central government authorities responsible for Hong Kong affairs in both mainland China and Hong Kong" (Cheng 2009). The publicised viewpoint of Cao, though not promulgated as laws or regulations, reflected the greater emphasis of the Chinese government in overseeing and engaging in the local governance of Hong Kong, alongside the importance of "One Country" over "Two Systems" (ibid.).

In 2014, a White Paper titled "The Practice of the "One Country, Two Systems" Policy in the Hong Kong Special Administrative Region" was released by China's State Council. The White Paper introduces the concept of overall jurisdiction, claiming that the NPC, NPCSC, the President of China, the Central People's Government and the Central Military Commission can directly exercise jurisdiction over Hong Kong by the constitution of China and the Basic Law of Hong Kong. Moreover, this overall jurisdiction is grounded by the nature of China as a unitary state. This notion interprets the degree of Hong Kong's autonomy as subject to the central leadership's authorisation. Again, the White Paper rejects claims that Hong Kong has "residual power" (the State Council of the PRC 2014).

The phrase "overall jurisdiction" has frequently been quoted in three pro-China newspapers in Hong Kong between 2014 and 2020, justifying the critical events that related to China's exercise of jurisdiction over the local affairs of Hong Kong (see figure 5 and table 4), revealing the government attempt to promote the term and its rationale with the public, and counterbalance the popular belief of separation of powers and judicial independence.

Furthermore, to consolidate the idea of overall jurisdiction, in 2019, Zhang Xiaoming, the Deputy Director of the HKMAO, articulated ten ways the central leadership could exercise its jurisdiction, as regulated by China's Constitution and the Basic Law over Hong Kong. The article was published after a communique of the 4th Plenum of the 19th Central Committee of the CCP was released, assertively stating the Party's commitment to "strictly govern Hong Kong and Macau Special Administrative Regions by the constitution and the Basic Law" (Mai and Zheng 2019). Unlike before, the notion of a "high degree of autonomy" and "Hong Kong people ruling

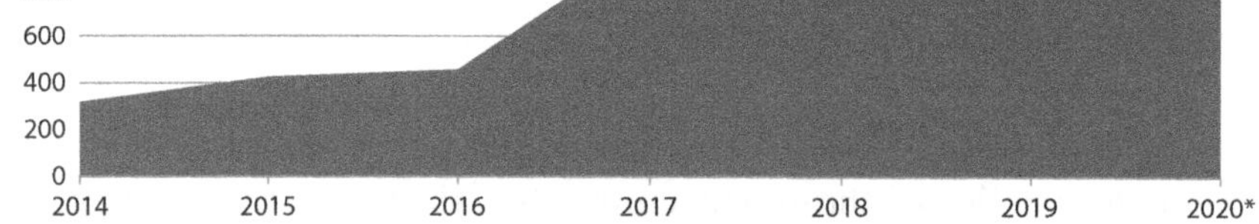

Figure 5. Culminative Frequency of Reports Published by Pro-China Newspapers on "Overall Jurisdiction" (quán miàn guǎn zhì quán)[1]
Source: *Wise news*

1 The source of the figure is based on *Wisenews* (news-searching engine). <https://wisenews.wisers.net/> accessed on 18th November 2020. I counted the number of newspaper reports in three pro-China newspapers that mentioned the Chinese keywords 'overall jurisdiction' (*Quanmian guanzhiquan*) between 1st January 2014 and 18th November 2020. The three newspapers are *Hong Kong Commercial Daily, Ta Kung Pao* and *Wen Wei Po*.

Table 4. Critical Events of China's Intervention in Hong Kong's Constitutional, Legal and Political Affairs

Year	Critical Events
2014	Publication of the White Paper; NPCSC decision on the method of elections of Chief Executive
2015	The proposal of constitutional reform was vetted by Hong Kong Legislature
2016	NPCSC interpretation of Article 104 of the Basic Law
2017	20th anniversary of the handover
2018	NPCSC decision on the co-location arrangement at West Kowloon Station in Hong Kong
2019	The outbreak of the Anti-ELAB Movement
2020*	Promulgation of the National Security Law; NPCSC's decisions on extension of the length of term of the Sixth Legislative Council and on criteria of the disqualification of lawmakers

Source: *Wise news*

Hong Kong" was not addressed. Such change marked a definite shift in the central leadership's rhetoric regarding its policy on Hong Kong: they further gave greater emphasis on "One Country" over "Two Systems."

The Chinese leadership also disapproves of the assertion that Hong Kong follows the principle of separation of powers. The Basic Law of Hong Kong has not declared separation of powers as a constitutional principle. Yet, checks and balances between the executive, legislative and judicial branches are required by the Basic Law (Articles 48-51, 52(2), 52(3), 73, 76, 85, 90). Two former Chief Justices had earlier also confirmed that the principle of separation of powers applies in Hong Kong (Court of Final Appeal of the HKSAR 2001; Ma 2014). However, since 2008, top Beijing officials have begun to change their political rhetoric when describing the three branches of the Hong Kong government. In 2008, Xi Jinping, then vice president of China, asked the executive, legislative and judicial branches of the Hong Kong government to understand and support each other (BBC News Chinese 2 September 2020). His speech was regarded as the beginning of an effort to promote the concept of "cooperation of the three powers." After the 79-day Umbrella Movement of 2014, top officials from Beijing continued to popularise the discourse that undermines separation of powers. In 2015, the director of the Liaison Office for Hong Kong argued that separation of powers could only be applied in sovereign states; it is thus not applicable to Hong Kong. He added that the Chief Executive of Hong Kong stands above the three branches, serving as a hub between the Central People's Government of China and the government of Hong Kong (BBC News Chinese 12 September 2015). In May 2017, the NPCSC Chairman Zhang Dejiang further suggested that Hong Kong does not implement separation of powers but instead is governed by an executive-led government, and the Chief Executive serves as the core. Zhang also restated that the power of the Hong Kong government depends upon the delegation of power from the central government, which enjoys an overall jurisdiction in Hong Kong (Ming Pao Instant News, 27 May 2017). Finally, in 2020, Carrie Lam, the fourth Chief Executive of Hong Kong, officially declared in a press conference that Hong Kong "has no separation of powers". She stated that the executive, legislative and judicial branches are all accountable to the Chief Executive, who is responsible to the central government of China. The Education Bureau also commanded the removal of the notion of separation of powers from textbooks (Cheung and Lau 2020). After Lam's speech, presentation slides of a retired CFA judge, who stated that the doctrine of the separation of powers applied in Hong Kong, were removed from the education bureau's website (Ho 2020).

Removing the notion of separation of powers from Hong Kong's constitutional order serves three functions. First, by emphasising the supreme position of the Chief Executive, the judicial and legislative branches, which are supposed to check and balance executive power, are degraded. The CCP's call for "cooperation" of the three branches – judiciary, legislature, and executive government – is subordinate to the executive authority. In turn, the Chief Executive, appointed rather than elected by the Hong Kong electorate, is accountable only to Beijing. Second, the diminishing authority of the legislative and judicial branches in Hong Kong also assists the increasing influence of China's "overall jurisdiction" over Hong Kong. Such a discursive battle was a prerequisite for the NPCSC to justify its interpretations of the Basic Law, its decisions on Hong Kong's local affairs, and the imposition of a national security law on Hong Kong. The Hong Kong government could not question the legitimacy of these acts. Limiting the jurisdiction of the Hong Kong government is a way to amplify the importance of the Chinese constitution alongside the supremacy of the NPC. Thirdly, dismissing the claim of separation of powers, which the judges in Hong Kong had promoted, is also a rhetorical tactic to undermine judicial authority.

Regarding the political obligation of judges, the State Council's White Paper in 2014 makes clear the political duty of the judiciary. It states that

Hong Kong's administrators, including judges of the courts at different levels and other judicial personnel, should be "patriotic." Furthermore, judges deemed as administrators are asked to love the country as "the basic political requirement". They were also requested for "safeguarding the country's sovereignty, security, and development interests, and ensuring the long-term prosperity and stability of Hong Kong" (the State Council of the PRC 2014). These obligations reveal that the national identification of judges should be tied to their political duties in defending the state's interests. After the launch of the White Paper, 1,800 lawyers joined a silent protest against the narratives of the White Paper, and the former Chief Justice openly disagreed with the notion of "judges as administrators." That said, Beijing did not change its position (So 2014).

Two cases revealed how the discourse on judges' patriotism and political loyalty to China has been developed. The first example was the verdict in the case of seven police officers. They were all sentenced to imprisonment for publicly assaulting a protestor during the Umbrella Movement (HKSAR v Wong Cho Shing and others [2017] DCCC980/2015). Nearly three months after the police officers had been sentenced, major pro-Beijing newspapers in Hong Kong published 126 reports and op-eds criticising the sentences imposed by the Judge, David Dufton, for being too "heavy."[1] State-controlled media platforms in mainland China had heavily criticised the Judge as well. Four days after the sentencing of police officers, the overseas edition of the *People's Daily* published an interview with a law professor in CUHK who commented that there were, at the time, too many British-trained expatriate judges in the Hong Kong legal system, hence the stance of these judges would affect their decisions (Wang 2017). *Southern Weekly* (*Nanfang Zhoumo*), another mainland newspaper, also criticised the judgement as a "bad example" of the Rule of Law in Hong Kong. The report further argued that Judge Dufton's British nationality was problematic and suggested that the national affiliations of public officials in Hong Kong would be an essential issue to be dealt with in the longer term (Liu 2017). This criticism of expatriate judges in Hong Kong was grounded on a nationalistic clash of understanding of the role of judges, following the political requirement of "loving the country" in the White Paper.

1 The figure is based on research in Wisenews (a news-searching engine). https://wisenews.wisers.net/ accessed on 20th November 2020. I counted the number of newspaper reports in three pro-China newspapers that mentioned the Chinese keyword 'seven Police Case" between 18 February 2017 and 18 May 2017. The three newspapers are *Hong Kong Commercial Daily, Ta Kung Pao* and *Wen Wei Po.*

Another example refers to the High Court judgements in cases brought to review the constitutionality of the Emergency Regulations Ordinance (ERO) and the Prohibition of Face Covering Regulation (known as the anti-mask law), which were implemented through the Chief Executive's emergency powers in October 2019 (Kwok Wing Hang and others v Chief Executive in Council and Secretary for Justice [2019] HCAL2945/2019).

Amid the Anti-ELAB Movement, the executive government, including law enforcement, continued to arrest and charge protestors with the public order laws inherited from the colonial administration. Also, the courts appear to have been tasked with finding the political means to handle the protests. The central authorities repeatedly urged the three governmental branches of Hong Kong to cooperate to "end violence and resume public order" (zhǐ bào zhì luàn). They stressed that it was a "common responsibility for Hong Kong's executive, legislative and judicial bodies" (Ting 2019). In response, an anti-mask law was passed by the executive council instead of the legislature to facilitate law enforcement in policing protests. Hence the judicial review against the constitutionality of the anti-mask law and broadly the ERO was initiated by pro-democracy lawmakers. The ruling by two High Court judges favoured the pro-democracy applicants. Not surprisingly, a backlash from the Chinese authorities ensued. The Legislative Affairs Committee of the NPCSC released a statement to "express serious concern" and "strong dissatisfaction" with the decisions. The statement claimed that the NPC was the sole body with authority to determine the constitutionality of laws applicable in Hong Kong and that the High Court's ruling "seriously damages the jurisdiction of the Chief Executive and Hong Kong government" (Xinhua News Agency 19 November 2019).

On the same day, the spokesperson of the HKMAO also criticised the High Court's ruling, arguing that the NPCSC confirmed the constitutionality of the Emergency Regulations Ordinance. He went further to criticise the ruling as an open challenge to the NPCSC's authority and the Chief Executive's governing power. Finally, he urged the Hong Kong government and the judiciary to shoulder their duty to curb violence and restore order together (Lau 2019a). Such criticisms from the top Chinese legislative body denounced the Hong Kong courts' role in constitutional review. The Chinese authorities' request for judges to work with the executive government against the protesters inevitably put political pressure on the judiciary when the appeal process of that High Court's ruling had yet to be exhausted.

Five months later, the Hong Kong government appealed the decision to the Court of Appeal. Its appeal was upheld; the Emergency Regulations Ordinance was found to be following the Basic Law, while a part of the anti-mask law was held unconstitutional. HKMAO backed the ruling of the appellant court, saying that the erroneous ruling of the Court of First Instance had been corrected and that the new ruling would be favourable to the law-based governance of Hong Kong (Z. Chen 2020). The two responses of HKMAO after the two court rulings of the anti-mask law were contrasting examples of how the Chinese sovereignty requests the Hong Kong courts to cooperate with the local executive government, follow the unquestioned authority of the NPC, and ultimately support the Chief Executive who can use the ERO to do what they want with full authority. These instances revealed how the CCP produces favourable legal discourses by mobilising state-owned media and official statements to propagandise such discourses in Hong Kong.

In summary, the institutional dimension of the China factor under authoritarian legal transplantation to Hong Kong is reflected in the NPCSC's interpretations and decisions over the constitutional issues of the Basic Law, its direct transplantation of national laws in Hong Kong, and the production of its authoritarian legal ideology in official records and propaganda favourable to China. Such tactics also adopted the colonial heritage of legal rules that empower the executive government and law enforcement to police protests, incorporating colonial and Chinese authoritarian legality together. These tactics consolidate the notions of supremacy of the NPC and the NPCSC in constitutional issues in the Basic Law, diminish the authority of the local judiciary, and mainstreaming the CCP's discourse on the roles and functions of laws and courts in Hong Kong.

In the next chapter, I explain one major factor that enables China's authoritarian legal transplantation to Hong Kong: China's United Front Work in Hong Kong's legal profession. The United Front Work can be considered as an indirect mechanism of authoritarian legal transplantation, and can be found in Hong Kong's electoral politics, economic governance and state-sponsored counter-mobilisation.

References

Albert, Eleanor. 2020. "China Appointed to Influential UN Human Rights Council Panel." *The Diplomat*, April 8. Accessed November 10, 2020. https://thediplomat.com/2020/04/china-appointed-to-influential-un-human-rights-council-panel/.

Bader, Julia, Jörn Grävingholt, and Antje Kästner. 2010. "Would Autocracies Promote Autocracy? A Political Economy Perspective on Regime-Type Export in Regional Neighbourhoods." *Contemporary Politics* 16 (1): 81–100.

BBC News Chinese. 2015a. "Xiāng Gǎng Zhōng Lián Bàn Zhāng Xiǎo Míng: Tè Shǒu Dì Wèi Chāo Rán Yú Sān Quán." September 12. Accessed November 19, 2020. https://bbc.in/3c1JbQJ.

BBC News Chinese. 2020. "Dèng Xiǎo Píng Dào Lín Zhèng Yuè É: Xiāng Gǎng Sān Quán Fēn Lì Lùn Zhēng de Lái Lóng Qù Mài." September 2. Accessed November 19. https://bbc.in/3koLfqE.

Bugarič, Bojan. 2014. "Protecting Democracy and the Rule of Law in the European Union: The Hungarian Challenge." *LSE 'Europe in Question' Discussion Paper Series*, no. 79.

Castellucci, Ignazio. 2012. "Legal Hybridity in Hong Kong and Macau." *McGill Law Journal* 57 (4): 665–720.

Chan, Johannes M. M. 2015. "Human Rights, the Rule of Law and Democracy: Recent Experience of Hong Kong and China." *University of Hong Kong Faculty of Law Research Paper*, no. 2015/039. Accessed October 16, 2021. https://papers.ssrn.com/sol3/papers.cfm?abstract_id=2641332.

Chan, Johannes M. M. 2018. "A Storm of Unprecedented Ferocity: The Shrinking Space of the Right to Political Participation, Peaceful Demonstration, and Judicial Independence in Hong Kong." *International Journal of Constitutional Law* 16 (2): 373–388.

Chan, Johannes M. M. 2020. "Reconciliation of the NPCSC's Power of Interpretation of the Basic Law with the Common Law in the HKSAR." *Hong Kong Law Journal* 50 (2): 657–684.

Chen, Albert H.Y. 2000. "The Court of Final Appeal's Ruling on the 'Illegal Migrant' Children Case: Congressional Supremacy and Judicial Review." In *Hong Kong's Constitutional Debate: Conflict Over Interpretation*, edited by J. M. M. Chan, H. L. Fu, and Y. Ghai. Hong Kong University Press.

Chen, Albert H.Y. 2019. "A Perfect Storm: Hong Kong-China Rendition of Fugitive Offenders, 2019." *Hong Kong Law Journal* 49 (2): 419–429.

Chen, Zimo. 2020. "HKMAO Backs HK Court Ruling That Anti-Mask Law Constitutional." *China Daily*, April 14. Accessed November 20, 2020. https://www.chinadaily.com.cn/a/202004/14/WS5e952291a3105d50a3d160b4.html.

Cheng, J. 2009. "The Story of a New Policy." *Hong Kong Journal*. Accessed November 18, 2020. Archived on file with the author.

Cheng, Selina. 2020. "Senior Beijing official says only patriots should rule Hong Kong, "dissidents" must be ousted." *Hong Kong Free Press*, 17 November. Accessed 17 November 2020. https://hongkongfp.com/2020/11/17/senior-beijing-official-says-only-patriots-should-rule-hong-kong-dissidents-must-be-ousted/.

Cheung, Tony, and Chris Lau. 2020. "Hong Kong leader Carrie Lam sides with education chief on no "separation of powers" in city, defends move to delete phrase from textbooks." *South China Morning Post*, September 1. Accessed November 19,

2020. https://www.scmp.com/news/hong-kong/education/article/3099729/hong-kong-leader-carrie-lam-insists-there-no-separation.

ChinaFile Editors. 2013. "Document 9: A ChinaFile Translation: How Much Is a Hardline Party Directive Shaping China's Current Political Climate?" *ChinaFile*, November 8. Accessed November 14, 2020. https://www.chinafile.com/document-9-chinafile-translation.

Chong, H.Y., and W.Y. Hui. 2007. "Zhōng yāng shòu yú xiāng gǎng tè qū duō shǎo quán, tè qū jiù yǒu duō shǎo quán! Wú bāng guó yān liǎo xiāng gǎng." *Apple Daily*, June 7. A01.

Court of Final Appeal of the HKSAR. 2001. "Zhōng shěn fǎ yuàn shǒu xí fǎ guān chū xí wǔ cān huì de yǎn cí quán wén." 26 October. Accessed 20 November 2024. https://www.hkcfa.hk/filemanager/speech/en/upload/17/CJ's%20Speech%20at%20a%20luncheon%20(26-10-2001)(Chinese%20only)tc.pdf.

Diamond, Larry, Marc F. Plattner, and Christopher Walker. 2016. *Authoritarian Goes Global: The Challenge to Democracy*. John Hopkins University Press.

Drinoczi, Tamas, and Agnieszka Bień-Kacała. 2019. "Illiberal constitutionalism: The case of Hungary and Poland." *German Law Journal* 20 (8): 1140–1166.

Fong, Brian C. H. 2017a. "One country, two nationalisms: Center-periphery relations between Mainland China and Hong Kong, 1997-2016." *Modern China* 43 (5): 523–556.

Fugitive Offenders and Mutual Legal Assistance in Criminal Matters Legislation (Amendment) Bill 2019. 2019. Legislative Council of the Hong Kong Special Administrative Region of the People's Republic of China. Accessed November 22, 2020. https://www.legco.gov.hk/yr18-19/english/bills/b201903291.pdf.

Gold, Thomas, and Sebastian Veg, eds. 2020. "Introduction." In *Sunflowers and Umbrellas: Social Movements, Expressive Practices, and Political Culture in Taiwan and Hong Kong*. Institute of East Asian Studies, Berkeley.

Hechter, Michael. 2001. *Containing Nationalism*. Oxford University Press.

HKTDC Research. 2020a. "Economic and trade information on China." *The Hong Kong Trade Development Council*, March 16. Accessed November 24, 2020. https://hkmb.hktdc.com/en.

HKSAR v. Wong Cho Shing and others. 2017. DCCC980/2015.

Ho, Kelly. 2020. "Hong Kong Education Bureau removes website slide on separation of powers as part of 'update.'" *Hong Kong Free Press*, September 2. Accessed November 19, 2020. https://hongkongfp.com/2020/09/02/hong-kong-education-bureau-justifies-removal-of-top-judges-slide-on-the-separation-of-powers-as-an-update/.

Hong Kong Institute of Asia-Pacific Studies of the Chinese University of Hong Kong. 2015. "Press Release on 'CUHK Releases Survey Findings on Views on Hong Kong's Core Values.'" October 29. Accessed May 7, 2018. https://www.cpr.cuhk.edu.hk/en/press/cuhk-releases-survey-findings-on-views-on-hong-kongs-core-values/.

Hong Kong Public Opinion Research Institute. 2020a. "PORI Releases the Latest Social and Freedom Indicators." May 8. Accessed July 9, 2020. https://a2022.pori.hk/press-release-en/2020-07-21-pm.html?lang=en.

Hong Kong Public Opinion Research Institute. 2020b. "The Rule of Law, Fairness of the Judicial System, Impartiality of the Courts – Combined Charts." Accessed 13 August 2020. https://a2023.pori.hk/pop-poll/rule-law-indicators-en/g-combined.html?lang=en.

Hong Kong Public Opinion Research Institute. 2020c. "People's Ethnic Identity." Accessed 14 November 2020. https://www.pori.hk/pop-poll/ethnic-identity.

Horlemann, Ralf. 2003. *Hong Kong's Transition to Chinese Rule: The Limits of Autonomy*. Routledge Curzon.

Huang, Zheping, and Huang Echo. 2016. "A brief history: Beijing's interpretations of Hong Kong's Basic Law, from 1999 to the present day". *Quartz*, November 6. Accessed November 15, 2020. https://qz.com/828713/a-brief-history-beijings-interpretations-of-hong-kongs-basic-law-from-1999-to-the-present-day.

Hung, Ching Tung. 2020. "Are Experiences Gained by Hong Kong in East-West Turbulences Being Squandered by China and the World?" In *Evaluation of the C. Y. Leung Administration*, edited by Joseph Y. S. Cheng, City University of Hong Kong Press.

Hung, Ho-fung. 2018. "Chinese State Capitalism in Hong Kong." In *Routledge Handbook of Contemporary Hong Kong*, edited by Tai-lok Lui, Stephen W. K. Chiu, and Ray Yep, Routledge.

Ip, Eric C. 2019. *Hybrid Constitutionalism: The Politics of Constitutional Review in the Chinese Special Administrative Regions*. Cambridge University Press.

Jackson, Nicole J. 2010. "The Role of External Factors in Advancing Non-Liberal Democratic Forms of Political Rule: A Case Study of Russia's Influence on Central Asian Regimes." *Contemporary Politics* 16 (1): 101–118.

Jones, Carol. 1999. "Politics Postponed: Law as a Substitute for Politics in Hong Kong and China." In *Law, Capitalism and Power in Asia: The Rule of Law and Legal Institutions*, edited by Kanishka Jayasuriya, Routledge.

Khamzayeva, Anar A. 2012. *Resilience of Authoritarianism and Its Projection onto International Politics: The Case of Russia*. Doctoral dissertation, Department of Political Science, LUISS Guido Carli, Italy.

Krebs, Judith R. 2000. "One Country, Three Systems? Judicial Review in Macau after Ng Ka Ling." *Pacific Rim Law and Policy Journal* 10 (1): 111–146.

Kwok Wing Hang and others v. Chief Executive in Council and Secretary for Justice. 2019. HCAL2945/2019.

Lague, David, James Pomfret, and Greg Torode. 2019. "How Murder, Kidnappings and Miscalculation Set Off Hong Kong's Revolt." *Reuters*, December 20. Accessed November 22, 2020. https://reut.rs/3qvORep.

Lam, Kay C. Y. 2020. "Besides DQ, What Was Overlooked in NPCSC Decision." *HK Columns* (trans.). *CitizenNews*, November 16. Accessed November 17, 2020. Archived on file with the author.

Lau, Chris. 2019a. "Criminal Lawyer Edwin Choy Opens Up on Resignation from Hong Kong Bar Association, Saying His Outlook on Protest Violence Diverged Too Much from Others." *South China Morning Post*, October 15. Accessed January 29, 2021. https://www.scmp.com/news/hong-kong/law-and-crime/article/3032862/criminal-lawyer-edwin-choy-opens-resignation-hong-kong.

Lee, Ching-kwan. 2017. *The Spectre of Global China: Politics, Labour and Foreign Investment in Africa*. University of Chicago Press.

Li, Raymond. 2013. "Seven Subjects Off Limits for Teaching, Chinese Universities Told." *South China Morning Post*, May 10. Accessed November 14, 2020. https://www.scmp.com/news/china/article/1234453/seven-subjects-limits-teaching-chinese-universities-told.

Linz, Juan J., and Alfred Stepan. 1996. *Problems of Democratic Transition and Consolidation—Southern Europe, South America, and Post-Communist Europe*. The Johns Hopkins University Press.

Liu, Sida, and Anson Au. 2020. "The Gateway to Global China: Hong Kong and the Future of Chinese Law Firms." *Wisconsin International Law Journal* 37 (2): 308–349.

Lui, Tai-lok. 2020. "The Unfinished Chapter of Hong Kong's Long Political Transition." *Critique of Anthropology* 40 (2): 270–276.

Liu, Zunfa. 2017. "Zhè Shì Fǎ Zhì de È Lì." *Nán Fāng Zhōu Mò*, February 23. Accessed November 20, 2020. http://www.infzm.com/content/123087.

Luo, Huining. 2020. "Xiāng Gǎng Wéi Hù Guó Jiā Ān Quán Zhì Dù Bù Gòu Wán Shàn, Xū Jìn Kuài Zhì Dìng Fǎ Lǜ (Quán Wén)." *HK01*, April 15. Accessed September 27, 2021. https://www.hk01.com/%E6%94%BF%E6%83%85/461078.

Ma, Geoffrey. 2014. "Chief Justice's Speech at Ceremonial Opening of the Legal Year 2014." January 13. Accessed 19 November 2020. https://www.info.gov.hk/gia/general/201401/13/P201401130352.htm.

Mai, Jun, and William Zheng. 2019. "China's Communist Party Elite Wrap Up Meeting with Pledge to Safeguard National Security in Hong Kong." *South China Morning Post*, November 1. Accessed November 18, 2020. https://www.scmp.com/news/china/politics/article/3035818/chinas-communist-party-elite-wrap-meeting-pledge-safeguard.

McDermott, John. 1997. "The 'Rule of Law' in Hong Kong after 1997." *Loyola of Los Angeles International and Comparative Law Review* 19 (2): 263–292.

Patten, Chris. 1996. *Hong Kong, Transition: The 1996 Policy Address*. Government Printer.

Pomfret, James, and Jessie Pang. 2019. "Hong Kong Extradition Bill a 'Terrible Blow' to Rule of Law: Patten." *Reuters*, June 6. Accessed November 21, 2020. https://reut.rs/3bYSTTW.

Poon, C. H. 2020. "Legal Service Industry in Hong Kong." *Hong Kong Trade Development Council*, June 18. Accessed December 10, 2020. https://research.hktdc.com/en/article/MzEzODc5NTk5.

Richardson, Sophie. 2020. "China's Influence on the Global Human Rights System: Assessing China's Growing Role in the World." *Human Rights Watch*, September 14. Accessed November 10, 2020. https://www.hrw.org/news/2020/09/14/chinas-influence-global-human-rights-system.

Secretary for Justice v. Law Man Chung. 2020. CAAR4/2019.

Siu, Jasmine. 2019. "Body Folded in Suitcase: Gruesome Details Emerge of Hong Kong Man's Killing of Pregnant Girlfriend in Taiwan." *South China Morning Post*, April 13. Accessed November 21, 2020. https://www.scmp.com/news/hong-kong/law-and-crime/article/3005990/body-folded-suitcase-gruesome-details-emerge-hong-kong.

So, Peter. 2014. "Judges Don't Need to Be Patriots, Says Former Top Judge Andrew Li." *South China Morning Post*, August 15. Accessed November 20, 2020. https://www.scmp.com/news/hong-kong/article/1573867/judges-dont-need-be-patriots-andrew-li.

The State Council of the People's Republic of China. 2014. *White Paper on the Practice of the "One Country, Two Systems" Policy in the Hong Kong Special Administrative Region*. June 10. Accessed November 18, 2020. https://english.www.gov.cn/archive/white_paper/2014/08/23/content_281474982986578.htm.

Ting, Victor. 2019. "As Hong Kong Protests Rage On, Barristers Hit Back at Beijing's Comments on the City's Judiciary and Its Responsibilities." *South China Morning Post*, November 9. Accessed November 20, 2020. https://www.scmp.com/news/hong-kong/politics/article/3037054/hong-kong-protests-rage-barristers-hit-back-beijings.

Tso, Kelvin K. S. 2012. "Fundamental Political and Constitutional Norms: Hong Kong and Macau Compared." *Australian Journal of Asian Law* 13 (1): 25–47.

Wang, Ping. 2017. "Rénmín rìbào hǎiwài bǎn fǎng xiānggǎng fǎlǜ zhuānjiā: Jǐngchá bèi zhòngpàn chōngjī xiānggǎng fǎzhì." *Rénmín Rìbào Hǎiwài Bǎn*, February 21. Accessed November 20, 2020. https://www.thepaper.cn/newsDetail_forward_1623166.

Whiting, Susan H. 2017. "Authoritarian 'Rule of Law' and Regime Legitimacy." *Comparative Political Studies* 50 (14): 1907–1940.

Wu, Jieh-min. 2016. "The China Factor in Taiwan: Impact and Response." In *Handbook of Modern Taiwan Politics and Society*, edited by Gunter Schubert. Routledge.

Wu, Jieh-min, and Mei Liao. 2015. "From Unification-Independence Divide to the China Factor: How Changing Political Identity Influences Voting Behavior." *Taiwan She Hui Xue* 29: 89–132.

Xinhua News Agency. 2019. "Quánguó réndà chángwěihuì fǎgōngwěi fāyánrén jiù xiānggǎng fǎyuàn yǒuguān sīfǎ fùhé ànpànjué fābiǎo tánhuà." November 19. Accessed November 20, 2019. https://www.gov.cn/xinwen/2019-11/19/content_5453345.htm.

Zhang, Dejiang. 2017. "Shùlì guójiā guānniàn shì jīběnfǎ shíshī hé xīn yàoqiú (quánwén)." *Ta Kung Pao*, May 27. Accessed September 27, 2021. http://www.takungpao.com.hk/hongkong/text/2017/0527/84870.html.

Zhang, Dejiang. 2017. "Zhōngyāng hé xiānggǎng shì shòuquán hé bèishòuquán guānxì, qiángdiào bù róng yǐ gāodù zìzhì wéi míng duìkàng zhōngyāng quánlì." *Ming Pao Instant News*, May 27. Accessed November 19, 2020. Archived on file with the author.

3. The United Front Work in Hong Kong's Legal Community

Abstract: This chapter explores China's indirect mechanisms of authoritarian legal transplantation in Hong Kong, focusing on the co-optation of the legal profession through United Front strategies. It examines how the CCP leverages electoral participation, counter-mobilisation, and economic integration to reshape the legal sector. By supporting pro-government lawyers, creating parallel legal organisations, and opening mainland markets to Hong Kong law firms, the CCP fosters political allegiance and propagates authoritarian legal ideology. These efforts undermine the liberal Rule of Law and judicial independence, aligning the legal community with China's state-building goals and its engineering of 'authoritarian rule of law' in Hong Kong.

Keywords: Legal Profession, Co-optation, Countermobilisation, Political Economy, Authoritarianism, China

This chapter continues the discussion of how the China factor has facilitated the authoritarian legal transplantation in electoral, counter-mobilisational and economic domains. Apart from the direct mechanism of authoritarian legal transplantation, the Chinese Communist Party (CCP) also indirectly leverages legal capital in Hong Kong's legal profession to counterbalance the liberal voices on the rule of law, as well as to tame lawyers, who are one of the sources of resistance to socialist legal ideology and authoritarian legality. A well-known strategy of the CCP's encroachment on civil society and the professional sectors is the United Front Work.

British colonisers in Hong Kong had deployed the co-optation strategy by elite absorption from the very beginning. Adapted from the Indian colonial administration, the Hong Kong colonial government selected individuals from the business sectors, professional groups and leaders of local communities to 'represent' the people of Hong Kong, either appointing them as

Lai, Y. *Legal Resistance under Authoritarianism: The Struggle for the Rule of Law in Hong Kong.* Taylor & Francis Group, 2025
DOI: 10.5117/9789048558438_CH03

members of official consultative committees or building partnerships with them (Goodstadt 2005, 10–12; King 1975, 422). For the CCP, its co-optation strategy in Hong Kong commenced in the 1980s with the appointment of individuals to mainland Chinese institutions, including the Chinese People's Political Consultative Conference (CPPCC), the National People's Congress (NPC) and the Basic Law Drafting Committee (Lam and Lam 2013, 306–307). Such appointments were purposive of building connections with local elites, stepping into various professional sectors and consolidating control in society as preparation for the transfer of sovereignty in 1997.

The CCP operates the United Front Work through the United Front Department of the Central Committee of the CCP (Lam and Lam 2013, 304). The Liaison Office of China in Hong Kong, formerly known as the Xinhua News Agency, is directly responsible for coordinating the CCP's United Front activities in the city. Examples of its activities are electioneering, propaganda for the government with their newspapers and counter-mobilisation of pro-Beijing local communities (Yep 2007, 245–264). The United Front Work in Hong Kong can be understood as a policy that "targets people of influence to bring them onside so that they could accept the party line or at least not object to it," to win "the hearts and minds of the Hong Kong community" (Loh 2010, 27). One example is the media industry in Hong Kong: when media tycoons established business ties with mainland Chinese authorities and its market, self-censorship in journalism became a common practice (FLF Lee 2018, 9).

A major tactic of China's United Front Work in Hong Kong is co-opting individuals and organisations ranging from economic elites and professionals to the masses in the grassroots (Lam and Lam 2013, 306; Kwong 2010; Lo 2008). This chapter demonstrates how, as for the legal profession in Hong Kong, the CCP recruits individual lawyers as political candidates to run for elections as a way of popularising a discourse of authoritarian legality, and of building illiberal legal authority in both the legislature and the public. The CCP also introduces economic opening policies in the mainland to build connections and collaborations with Hong Kong law firms and legal professional bodies. Moreover, the CCP sponsors pro-government organisations within the legal community to consolidate ties with pro-government elites in order to promote China's authoritarian legal transplantation.

This chapter is divided into five sections. The first section explains how the CCP co-opts the legal profession in the realm of electoral politics. The second section traces how the United Front Work mobilises lawyers to generate support for the statecraft in the legal sphere. The third section explains how the United Front Work is realised in the economic policies for

Hong Kong lawyers and law firms. The fourth section evaluates the overall performance and impact of authoritarian legal transplantation under the China factor, followed by a conclusion.

Electoral Dimension

The electoral dimension of the China factor over the legal sector refers to the Hong Kong Liaison Office's attempt to build an alliance of governing elites by co-opting pro-government (or pro-Beijing) lawyers to run for the geographical constituencies of the Legislative Council (LegCo) elections. The winning of pro-government lawyers in elections could counterbalance the influence of pro-democracy lawyers in parliamentary politics. Barristers and solicitors such as Martin Lee, Albert Ho and Margaret Ng had become the leading figures in the local democratic movement since the 1980s (Tam 2012, 117). They have eventually became lawmakers in Hong Kong as well. After the enactment of the Bill of Rights Ordinance in 1991, the ideas of human rights and civil liberties attracted more attention from lawyers as well as the public. The presence of lawyers in Hong Kong's political liberalisation became more influential in 2003, when the government proposed a national security bill, which was widely regarded as infringing citizens' civil liberties. Some solicitors, barristers and legal academics, mostly former chairpersons of the Bar including Audrey Eu and Alan Leong, founded the Article 23 Concern Group to express their disapproval of the national security legislation. The Group actively engaged in public by printing and distributing the pamphlets in person on the streets, by speaking to media reporters and by educating high school students (Ma 2005, 477). They became one of the major voices that backed the mobilisation of more than half a million citizens rallying against the bill (ibid.). The government finally postponed the second reading of the bill seven days after the rally because of the loss of majority support in LegCo, occasioned by a twist of position of a pro-Business political party in the Legislative Council (LegCo) (Ma 2005, 481). A year later, four of the Concern Group members were popularly elected as members in the LegCo. In 2006, they grouped together a number of intellectuals and legal professionals to form the Civic Party, which was later dubbed "the Barrister Party" (dà zhuàng dǎng) due to the overwhelming presence of legal counsel in the party leadership (K. Lee 2017a, 95–96). In sum, the vocal position of liberal legal professionals in the democratic movement portrayed lawyers as strong defenders of the Rule of Law, civil liberties and advocates for democratisation.

After 2003, the Chinese state took several actions in attempt of weakening voices of those liberal lawyers and diminish their political weight in Hong Kong. To do so, the state commenced to nurture pro-government lawmakers with a legal professional background. The Hong Kong Liaison Office departed from its passive role to be an active player in domestic politics, particularly in the elections for LegCo.

The LegCo consists of directly elected seats, which are known as the geographical constituency, and indirectly elected seats from the "functional constituency" and "election committee". Seats in the functional constituency were mainly returned by representatives from specific industry or professional sectors following the spirit of corportism. Eventually, seats under the "election committee" were fully abolished until 2021. Of the two paths (geographical and functional constituencies) open to anyone interested in becoming a lawmaker in Hong Kong, the Liaison Office would have known that the seat of legal sector under the LegCo's functional constituency, which is open for competition among practising lawyers in Hong Kong, was the more difficult one because no pro-Beijing candidates had ever won a legal functional seat since 1998. Therefore, the attention was focussed on aiding pro-Beijing lawyers to get elected in the geographical constituency (Figure 6).

In 2008, Priscilla Leung Mei-fun, a new pro-government candidate, won a seat in the Kowloon West Constituency of the LegCo election. She is a barrister and a legal academic at the City University of Hong Kong. Her election campaign was also supported by the Hong Kong Federation of Trade Unions (HKFTU), a labour federation with a long-standing leaning towards Beijing (*Apple Daily News* 27 August 2008). Four years after, Paul Tse, a solicitor, succeeded in winning a seat in the direct election of the Kowloon East constituency in 2012. He later told the press that the Liaison

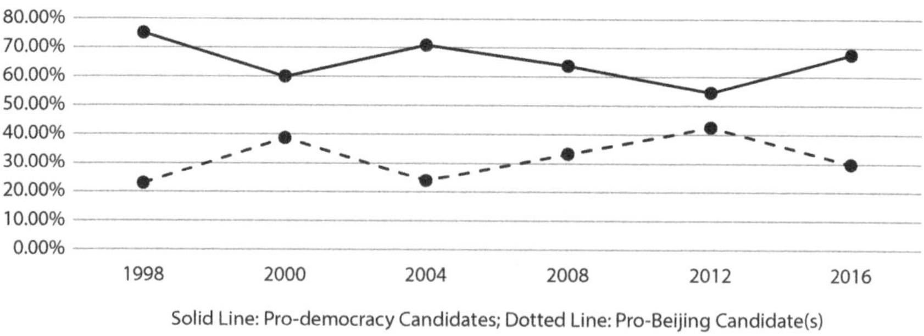

Figure 6. Vote Share (%) of Candidates in the Legal Sector of Functional Constituency Elections of the Legislative Council (1998–2016)
Solid Line: Pro-democracy Candidates; Dotted Line: Pro-Beijing Candidate(s)
Sources: Research based on the reports of Electoral Affairs Commission of HKSAR

Office had supported his candidacy by connecting him to pro-Beijing grassroots associations and significant local figures of the community (*Apple Daily News*, 31 December 2012). In 2016, the pool of pro-government lawyer candidates in direct elections expanded to six, and three of them had pro-Beijing party affiliation. They won seats in each geographical constituency, and a functional constituency in which only electors who had no vote in any other profession-based functional constituencies could elect them (see table 5).

The Liaison Office was behind the expansion of pro-Beijing lawyers in the ranks of lawmakers. The candidates they backed were voluble in thanking their backers. Immediately after the 2016 election, newly-elected lawmaker Junius Ho, a pro-government solicitor, expressed gratitude to the Liaison Office in his public speech (Yuen 2016a). Except for Holden Chow and Horace Cheung who belonged to a major pro-government party, Priscilla Leung, Paul Tse, Junius Ho and Eunice Yung were labelled as "godchildren of the West District" by the opposition and newspaper reports. "West District" is a term understood to symbolise the Liaison Office, in which its official premises is located in the Western area of Hong Kong Island (*Apple Daily Instant News*, 5 September 2016). Aside from these lawmakers, two pro-government candidates with professional qualifications in law also won seats in two functional constituencies other than the legal one.

Table 5. List of Pro-Beijing Lawyers Winning in the Direct Elections of the Legislative Council (2008–2016)

	4th LegCo Election (2008–2012)	5th LegCo Election (2012–2016)	6th LegCo Election (2016–2020)
Kowloon West Constituency	Priscilla Leung Mei-fun	Priscilla Leung Mei-fun	Priscilla Leung Mei-fun
Kowloon East Constituency		Paul Tse Wai-Chun	Paul Tse Wai-Chun
New Territories West Constituency			Junius Ho Kwan-Yiu
New Territories East Constituency			Eunice Yung Hoi-yan*
Hong Kong Island			Horace Cheung Kwok-Kwan**
District Council (2)			Holden Chow Ho-ding**

* Member of New People's Party
** Members of Democratic Alliance for Betterment and Progress of Hong Kong
Source: Research based on the website of the Electoral Affairs Commission of HKSAR.

Such a new force of pro-government or pro-Beijing lawyers inside the LegCo demonstrated the Liaison Office's strategy of rebranding pro-government lawmakers as professional figures equipped with legal expertise. Since Hong Kong's handover to China, the pro-Beijing ruling coalition has consisted of patriotic political parties, blue-collar trade unions and representatives from the business sector. The rise of pro-government legal professionals in LegCo reflects the state's aim to supplement the old patriots in parliamentary politics. Traditional pro-Beijing organisations such as the Hong Kong Federation of Trade Unions (HKFTU) and the Democratic Alliance for the Betterment and Progress of Hong Kong (DAB) are regarded as old-fashioned, grassroots-based communities that provide blind support to the Chinese authorities, discouraging a backing from middle-class citizens and professionals in Hong Kong. Instead, the new pro-Beijing lawmakers from the legal profession were propagandised as an "independent," "professional," and "impartial" new cohort of lawmakers, lending the pro-government camp their professional status, legal expertise and social status. This "brand-building" project can be found in a feature story of the *Hong Kong Lawyer*, an official publication of the Law Society of Hong Kong. Published in November 2016, it interviewed five newly elected lawyer-members of LegCo, all belonging to the pro-government camp. This feature was unprecedented in comparison with the previous elections. Photos of the interviewees were published on the cover of the journal, displaying a positive image of lawyers serving the legislature. Lawyer-members from the pro-democracy camp were not interviewed. A former member of the Law Society publicly criticised the cover story as how Law Society resources being used for political purposes (*Stand News* 18 November 2016).

The 2016 Legislative election was also a turning point for the number of lawmakers with a professional legal background between the pro-government camp and the pro-democracy one. Lawyers from the pro-democracy camp were outnumbered by their pro-government lawyer colleagues (see table 6). In addition, since 2012, pro-government lawyer lawmakers have also been holding the chairmanship of the panel on Administration of Justice and Legal Affairs, enjoying a greater say in agenda-setting over legal affairs in the legislature.

The pro-Beijing lawyer lawmakers act as outspoken advocates of the Chinese authoritarian legality when they defend the application of China's constitution to Hong Kong and the National People's Congress Standing Committee (NPCSC)'s legal interventions. For example, on 7 November 2016, the NPCSC released an interpretation of the Basic Law on issues of oath-taking by opposition lawmakers (see details in chapter 2). Priscilla Leung

Table 6. Number of Lawmakers with Professional Qualifications in Law from Different Political Camps (2004–2020)

	Number of pro-democracy lawmakers with professional qualifications in law	Number of pro-government lawmakers with professional qualifications in law	Total number of lawmakers with professional qualifications in law	Types of legal profession: Solicitor (S) / Barrister (B) / Senior Counsel (SC)
2004–2008	8	1	9	S: 4 B: 1 SC: 4
2008–2012	8	3	11	S: 5 B: 3 SC: 3
2012–2016	6	3	9	S: 4 B: 3(4)* SC: 2(1)*
2016–2020**	5	8	13	S: 7 B: 6 SC: 0

* In the New Territories East by-election of 2016, barrister Alvin Yeung of the Civic Party won the election to take the vacancy due to the resignation of Ronny Ka-wah Tong SC, who became a member of the Executive Council later.
** The length of term of the 6th LegCo was extended at least one year by the NPCSC dated on 11 August 2020. The number of legislators here is recorded between 1 October 2016 and 30 September 2020.
Source: Research based on the website of LegCo; also adapted from the table in Lai 2019, 187

and the other lawyer lawmakers immediately held a press conference on the same day, commenting on the constitutionality of such interpretation. Utilising their legal professional qualifications, those lawyer lawmakers spoke to rationalise the motivations of the NPCSC's interpretation as a "self-restrained response to the lawmakers promoting Hong Kong independence" (*Ming Pao Instant News* 7 November 2016). Another instance refers to which some pro-Beijing lawyer lawmakers formed a "Concern Group" in support for the government proposal of "co-location arrangement" which allowed Chinese law to be directly enforced in a Hong Kong's express railway station in West Kowloon. This will be further discussed in chapter 7. The Concern Group was packaged as a coalition among members from the legal community, including five lawyer-members in the legislature and pro-Beijing law professor Gu Minkang (Cheung 2017a). By speaking at press conferences, as well as challenging pro-democracy lawmakers in debates on legal controversies, pro-Beijing lawyer lawmakers produced alternative, authoritarian and illiberal interpretations of legal and constitutional matters, challenging the liberal legal discourse. Journalists are incentivised to report those pro-government legal arguments and discourses from those lawyer lawmakers for the sake of "balancing reporting", also to avoid being labelled as "prejudicial", "biased" or "unpatriotic."

Overall, pro-Beijing lawyer-members in the legislature have played the role of diluting the established reputation of the pro-democracy camp in legal debates. Pro-Beijing lawyer-lawmakers facilitate the reshaping of the popular understanding of the supremacy of Chinese sovereignty based on the Rule of Law in Hong Kong, attempting to gain greater support from the city's middle class and professionals who do not have a strong political orientation. In addition, their presence in the legislature, and active engagement in legal debates, dilutes the prominence of the public perception of legal principles and discourse that endorsed a liberal notion of the Rule of Law and judicial independence. They have become "defenders" of China's authoritarian legal transplantation in the ruling elite coalition.

Counter-mobilisational Dimension

The CCP's United Front strategy operates beyond the level of the individual. After the transfer of sovereignty, the CCP sponsored several pro-government organisations created by lawyers in Hong Kong, such as the Small and Medium Law Firms Association of Hong Kong (SAMLAW) and the Hong Kong Legal Exchange Foundation (HKLEF). The establishment of "parallel organisations" is a way for authoritarian regimes to establish a "dual structure" that absorbs and marginalises opposition groups in civil society (Ma 2007, 186–188). Dual structure refers to a strategy by which social organisations that are close to or formed by the state would be given positions in official bodies, while those that are unfriendly to the state would be excluded. Examples in Hong Kong include the CCP-sponsored labour organisation the Hong Kong Federation of Education Workers, which acts as a rival to the pro-democracy Hong Kong Professional Teacher's Union; and the Hong Kong Youth and Territory Student Association as a counterpart of the Hong Kong Federation of Students, which was an active social movement group consisting of university student unions (ibid.). The formation of the DAB in 1992 was also another instance of the CCP's support for establishing a counterpart against the pro-democracy parties (Lam and Lam, 307). Parallel organisations within such a dual structure ensure the existence of pro-establishment forces antagonistic to autonomous groups in both civil society as well as professional sectors. Parallel organisations are important platforms for the state to infiltrate and recruit agents in the respective professional and elite communities. A dual structure can also "create divisions within civil society and weaken social movement against the state" (Ma 2007, 187). This strategy is found in the sector of legal profession as well. Two examples are discussed below.

Case 1: The Small and Medium Law Firms Association of Hong Kong

The Small and Medium Law Firms Association of Hong Kong (SAMLAW) was formed in 2012. Claiming itself a "professional association," the objectives of SAMLAW include the promotion of the common interests and enhancement of competitiveness among small and medium law firms in Hong Kong, alongside the cultivation of exchange and collaboration between legal professionals in Hong Kong and the mainland (The Small and Medium Law Firms Association of Hong Kong 2025).

SAMLAW has a strong tie with the governments of Hong Kong and China. At the level of individual ties, the founding President Maggie Chan is a solicitor and in 2018 became a member of both the NPC and the CPPCC. Previously, she was a member of the DAB. In addition, as table 7 shows, the "honorary advisors" of SAMLAW are either selected as members of the NPC, CPPCC or China's Basic Law Committee. Some of the advisors also serve in CCP-sponsored bodies, such as the Qianhai Belt and Road Legal Services Federation, which is a state-regulated organisation in Shenzhen; and the Hong Kong Association for Promotion of Peaceful Reunification of China, which is a branch of the Beijing-based association presided by a member of the CCP's politburo. Finally, one of the advisors of SAMLAW was a former official in the Liaison Office. Their affiliations with the CCP had favoured SAMLAW when it came to connections with lawyer associations in mainland Chinese cities, and to gaining political recognition from state-level officials. Events that cemented these connections included SAMLAW's official visit to the State Council, the NPCSC and the Supreme People's Court in 2017 (see table 7).

SAMLAW began attracting media attention in 2014, when it initiated a counter-mobilising initiative against the pro-democracy campaign Occupy Central with Love and Peace (OCLP). This was the movement that paved the way for the outbreak of the Umbrella Movement in 2014. Launched by a law professor, a sociologist and a veteran protestant pastor, OCLP promoted deliberative democracy and peaceful civil disobedience to bargain for universal suffrage in Hong Kong. SAMLAW followed the government's strong opposition to the campaign and engaged in various counter-mobilisation

Table 7. Profile of People in Small and Medium Law Firms Association of Hong Kong (SAMLAW)

	People	Affiliation (by 2020)
Founding President	Maggie Chan	Member of the NPC and CPPCC; former member of the DAB
Honorary Advisors	Maria Tam	Deputy director of HKSAR Basic Law Committee of the NPC
	Liu Xinkui	Former director of the Legal Division of the Liaison Office
	[Peter Nguyen]	Former judge in Hong Kong
	Carson Wwn	Former member of the NPC
	Zhuang Zhongxi	Former judge in mainland China
	H.F. Ma	Member of the NPC
	Tony Kan	Member of the CPPCC
	Felix Fong	Member of the CPPCC; founding member of the DAB
	Ambrose Lam	Former President of the Law Society of Hong Kong; Partner of a founding law firm of Qianhai Belt and Road Legal Services Federation
	H.M. Leung	Director of Hong Kong Association for Promotion of Peaceful Reunification of China

Source: Extensive research on bibliographies, media reports and the website of SAMLAW

activities. In late April 2014, SAMLAW published a survey of its members' view of the government consultation on political reform and of OCLP. SAMLAW emphasised that more than 76 per cent of the respondents did not support OCLP, and 77 per cent of the respondents agreed that OCLP might damage the Rule of Law in Hong Kong (SAMLAW 25 April 2014). SAMLAW took the survey result as the basis for their antagonistic position towards OCLP. Even though the response rate of the survey was only 26 per cent (157 respondents out of 610 distributed questionnaire), SAMLAW made use of the opinion survey to gain media attention, creating an alternative as well as opposite voice in the public debate on constitutional reform and the civil disobedience campaign.

In June 2014, on behalf of SAMLAW, Maggie Chan published a position paper in support of the White Paper on "One Country, Two Systems." With regards to the controversial notions of "judges as administrators" and "the requirement of loving the country for judges," the position paper proposed an idea of "harmonious co-existence of loving the country and judicial independence," (ài guó yǔ sī fǎ dú lì xū hé xié bìng cún) and emphasised that "loving the country is a legal and political responsibility" (Chan 2014). Two months later, on the day when the NPCSC's decision on the formulation of a candidate-screening mechanism in the proposed suffrage for Chief

Executive was announced, SAMLAW launched an "Anti-occupy Central Helpline," with a group of barristers and solicitors providing assistance to anyone seeking "legal advice [...] to make [a] claim for compensation or relief caused by 'Occupy Central'" (SAMLAW 31 August 2014).

On 28 September 2014, when thousands of protestors gathered outside government headquarters, the law enforcement fired 87 teargas canisters to disperse the crowd; more citizens responded by occupying two more major districts in Hong Kong to express their disapproval of the police action. That was the moment when the Umbrella Movement began, calling for the withdrawal of Beijing's decision barring a genuine universal suffrage. The occupation of three major sites lasted for 79 days. While SAMLAW's helpline continued to operate, Maggie Chan and her colleagues represented a minibus company to seek a court injunction against the protestors in one of the occupied districts (*Chiu Luen Public Light Bus Company Limited v Persons unlawfully occupying or remaining on the public highway namely, the westbound carriageway of Argyle Street between the junction of Tung Choi Street and Portland Street and/or other persons hindering or preventing the passing or repassing of Argyle Street* [2014], HCA2086/2014). At that time, the government failed to clear the occupied zones. Chan's legal intervention was effective: by filing a civil injunction, the Umbrella Movement was reframed from a state-society contention to a court dispute between private actors; as a court dispute, the movement's breach of the rights of other civilians was highlighted (Cheng and Yuen 2017). Eventually, in addition to this plaintiff, Chan's other clients also won cases of civil injunction in all occupied zones, which were later evacuated under the court order (Yang 2019, 468).

After the Umbrella Movement, SAMLAW continued to engage in public debate on legal and political affairs. Maggie Chan was often interviewed by the pro-China media, and SAMLAW issued several statements in alignment with the government position. In 2016, SAMLAW publicly condemned the improper oath-taking of two newly elected lawmakers from the opposition parties. The new lawmakers had intentionally adorned a flag with the words "Hong Kong is not China" and pronounced "China" as "shina (Cheena)," a derogatory term used by Japanese people to refer to Chinese people during the Second World War (Yuen 2016b). The statement of SAMLAW put much weight on "defending the dignity of the nation" and "preventing insults to the country" (M. Chan 2016). Later on, SAMLAW vocally supported the NPCSC's interpretation of the Basic Law on the requirement of oath-taking. The stance and action taken by SAMLAW was part of the state-led effort to justify disqualifying some pro-democracy lawmakers. SAMLAW's active engagement in counter-mobilisation was "awarded" by the CCP as they appointed Maggie Chan as a member of the National People's Congress (NPC) in late 2017 (K. Cheung 2017).

Case 2: Hong Kong Legal Exchange Foundation

Formerly known as the China-Australia-Hong Kong Legal Exchange Foundation, the Hong Kong Legal Exchange Foundation (HKLEF) is another organisation that was founded by pro-government lawyers in 2014. HKLEF focussed on influencing public opinion and popular rhetoric on the Rule of Law. The founding chairman, Lawrence Ma, is a barrister in Hong Kong and Australia, and a member of the DAB as well as the CPPCC. Of the 26 consultants on its Advisory Board, around 30 per cent are either current or former members of the CPPCC. There are also two NPCSC Basic Law Committee members and a former Chinese official in the Ministry of Justice in the Advisory Board (see table 8).

Beside the political background of the members, the intention behind the formation of the HKLEF was also political in nature:

> [We] wanted to balance the voice of the Civic Party. In the political sphere of Hong Kong, the Civic Party should not be the only voice from the legal profession. The Civic Party is not your voice even if you were a barrister (Interviewee (ITV)1804, 22 November 2018).

In short, HKLEF attempted to act as a counterpart to the Civic Party, then popularly known as a "barrister party" and as pro-democratic. Contrary to the Civic Party's advocacy for a Rule of Law that emphasises protection of civil liberties and judicial autonomy, HKLEF supports the state's discourse on the rule of law, which is merely authoritarian legality characterised by Chinese nationalism. HKLEF holds the same position with the Chinese government that the Basic Law is not a mini constitution but just one of the national laws in China. Moreover, it recognised interpretations of the Basic Law by the National People's Congress Standing Committee (NPCSC) as an instrument to stabilise Hong Kong under the framework of "One Country, Two Systems," designed for people in Hong Kong to accept their heritage in China. Adopting Deng Xiaoping's definition of patriots, one of the founding members of HKLEF regarded those who do not accept "One Country, Two Systems" as being reluctant to accept Hong Kong's handover to China, and this in turn, was equivalent to being unpatriotic to the mother country (ITV1804, 22 November 2018).

HKLEF advocates and comments on constitutional disputes. It was actively present in internet media outlets such as the "Silent Majority" and

Table 8. Profile of Consultants in the Hong Kong Legal Exchange Foundation (HKLEF)

	Honorary Consultant (N=1) (%)	Senior Consultants (N=14) (%)	Consultants (N=11) (%)	Total (N=26) (%)
No. of current/former NPC member(s)	1 (100%)	1 (7.14%)	0	2 (7.69%)
No. of current/former CPPCC member(s)	1(100%)	3 (21.43%)	4 (36.36%)	8 (30.77%)
No. of current/former Lawmaker(s)	1(100%)	3 (21.43%)	0	4 (16.67%)
No. of current/former NPCSC Basic Law Committee member(s)	0	2 (14.29%)	0	2 (7.69%)
No. of current/former Chinese Government Official(s)	0	1 (former officer in the Ministry of Justice in China) (7.14%)	0	1 (4.17%)

Source: Extensive research of bibliographies, media reports and the website of HKLEF

the "Speak Out," which were sponsored by an NPC member and a foundation supported by Chinese capitalists (Cheng 2020, 14; Lam et al 2016). HKLEF also took the initiative to counteract the advocacy of pro-democracy parties and organisations on international platforms, such as the United Nations. During the Anti-extradition Bill Movement (Anti-ELAB Movement) in 2019, HKLEF held a press conference to announce its submission to the Secretary General of the United Nations about Hong Kong protests. In the submission, HKLEF asked the United Nations Security Council to investigate whether the United States had sponsored or invested in anyone in the protest, or offered training, as well as planned "unlawful assemblies" and "riots" in the Anti-ELAB Movement (YouTube 17 August 2019). One of the consultants in HKLEF further accused the United States of commending protestors for striving for universal suffrage, in order to make popularly elected lawmakers and the Chief Executive in Hong Kong American proxies (Chow 2019). HKLEF's anti-US statements and interpretations of the Anti-ELAB Movement followed the official rhetoric i.e., that the Movement had "clear colour revolution characteristics" (K. Cheng 2019a). Although no follow-up action was taken, HKLEF demonstrated its counter-balancing strategy against the pro-democracy movement in Hong Kong.

SAMLAW and HKLEF illustrate how lawyer-based parallel organisations tried to make use of their legal capital to operate counter-mobilisation. More than just debating legal and constitutional matters on media platforms as a way of popularising nationalistic and authoritarian legal discourses, they also strategised litigation, election in professional bodies and international advocacy to engage in counter-mobilisation. Their function is similar to that of pro-government lawyer members of LegCo: in their case, supporting the statecraft of the authoritarian legal transplantation and acting as a counterweight to the liberal identity of the legal profession and the liberal Rule of Law discourse in Hong Kong.

Economic Dimensions

Opening economic opportunities for lawyers and law firms in Hong Kong is another strategy of the CCP's co-optation. It is an effective way to achieve a subtle, indirect professional control of a self-regulated legal profession. Since 2003, China has promoted cross-border economic integration by strategic planning, policy instruments and bilateral agreements. The first instance was the CEPA which was signed by the Chinese and Hong Kong governments in 2003 (Trade and Industry Department of HKSAR 14 October 2020). The purpose of the agreement was to consolidate trade and investment cooperation between the mainland and Hong Kong by the provision of investment facilitation, as well as trade liberalisation (Mainland and Hong Kong Close Economic Partnership Arrangement 2003, Article 1). Since then, the CEPA has opened the gate of the mainland legal service market to Hong Kong in a few ways. Firstly, Hong Kong law firms are allowed to open representative offices in the mainland and operate in association with mainland law firms. Secondly, mainland law firms can employ Hong Kong practising lawyers as consultants on the laws of Hong Kong. Thirdly, Hong Kong lawyers who have acquired mainland lawyer qualifications are permitted to take internships in mainland law firms to practise on non-litigation legal work in the mainland under the "Law of the People's Republic of China on Lawyers." Fourthly, permanent residents of Hong Kong who also have Chinese citizenship can sit the legal qualifying examination in the mainland as well as acquire mainland legal professional qualifications under the State Judicial Examination Implementation Measures. Finally, Hong Kong representatives stationed in the mainland representative offices of Hong Kong law firms located in Shenzhen and Guangzhou need not fulfil the residency requirement; for the representatives stationed in the other parts of the mainland, only a minimum residency requirement of two months per year is needed (ibid., Annex 4). These arrangements were designed for Hong Kong lawyers.

Regulatory liberalisation of lawyers in Hong Kong and mainland China continued after the CEPA came into effect. In 2011, practice localisation commenced by loosening cross-border partnerships and qualification requirements between law firms on both sides, permitting them to collaborate as a single partnership. A new qualifying examination that allows Hong Kong solicitors to gain qualifications for legal practice in the mainland was also introduced (Liu and Au 2020, 326). Two years later, the Ministry of Justice in China decided to implement a new measure for lawyers from Hong Kong and Macau who held mainland legal qualifications. This new measure allowed them to expand their scope of practice in the mainland, meaning that they can act as lawyers in the mainland for Hong Kong or Macau-related civil cases including commercial and civil disputes (*China Briefing* 20 August 2013).

The market-opening policies are exclusive, compared with the restrictions against lawyers and law firms from other jurisdictions. This economic privilege bestowed on the Hong Kong legal profession was further expanded to barristers under China's economic initiatives within and beyond its border. In 2017, just prior to the 20th anniversary of Hong Kong's transfer of sovereignty, governments of Hong Kong and China signed a supplementary agreement entitled the Economic Technical Cooperation Agreement (Ecotech Agreement). It was a document facilitating Hong Kong's engagement in China's Belt and Road Initiative (BRI), which aims at expanding China's investment in trade and infrastructure projects in Asia, Africa and Europe. The Ecotech Agreement additionally liberalises Hong Kong's legal service industries to strengthen collaboration between the two jurisdictions. Examples are the Chinese government's support for establishing "cooperation and exchange platforms to enhance business exchange and collaboration," as well as "establishing [Hong Kong] as a centre for international legal and dispute resolution services in the Asia-Pacific region" (Ecotech Agreement, Article 7). Later, the National Development and Reform Commission of the Hong Kong government agreed on an arrangement for "Advancing Hong Kong's Full Participation in and Contribution to the Belt and Road Initiative," affirming Hong Kong as an "important international maritime service hub" by strengthening its maritime law and dispute resolution services for the BRI (HKSAR Government Press Release 14 December 2017). Although barristers cannot practice in the mainland as licensed lawyers, they can engage in alternative dispute resolution. The strategic positioning of Hong Kong as a hub for dispute resolution services, including mediation and arbitration, allows barristers to have a greater share in the legal service markets of China and its partners under the BRI.

Another initiative that is relevant to lawyers is the Guangdong-Hong-Kong-Macau Bay Area, known as the Greater Bay Area. The idea was to implement the regional integration of seven cities and two special administrative regions in the southeast part of China under the central government's 13th five-year plan of 2016. Under the scheme of the Hong Kong government, Hong Kong should be positioned in the Greater Bay Area as a provider of international legal and dispute resolution services in commerce and intellectual property, to benefit the BRI development as well (Greater Bay Area 2025) In 2020, the NPCSC adopted a decision to implement a three-year pilot scheme that allows qualified lawyers in Hong Kong and Macau to practise civil and commercial law there (Ng 2020; *Xinhua Net* 12 August 2020). The Greater Bay Area initiative offers new business opportunities to both solicitors and barristers in Hong Kong. The initiative was welcomed by the Hong Kong government, the professional bodies in law, and even a pro-democracy lawmaker from the legal sector (Lee 2018).

China's economic planning and policies that target the legal services sector of Hong Kong have opened a larger space for the greater integration of Hong Kong's legal profession in the market for legal service in the proposed Bay Area, and broadly mainland China, alongside other jurisdictions that have agreements with China under the BRI. Since these economic initiatives are directed under the political authority of China, it is important to investigate the political consequences for the legal professionals engaged in these economic projects. Although it is too soon to conclude the impact of the BRI and the Greater Bay Area on Hong Kong lawyers, the significance of the CEPA for the legal community of Hong Kong can be examined by tracing the restructuring of competition among law firms established in Hong Kong and China, as well as the degree of politicisation of law firm culture.

Structure of Competition

The CEPA has brought significant changes to the composition of the legal service market in the mainland and Hong Kong. One of the changes lies in the rising number of registered foreign law firms. As of May 2020, the number of representative offices of Hong Kong law firms and foreign law firms (including mainland law firms) based in Hong Kong had risen from 31 in 2003 to 71 in 2020 (Poon 2020). Also, as of 2019, 24 Hong Kong law firms had made association arrangements with their mainland counterparts based on the CEPA (HKTDC Research 12 July 2019). On the other hand, more Chinese law firms also took advantage of the CEPA to set up offices and were registered in Hong Kong. As Figure 7 illustrates, before the commencement of the CEPA in 2004, the share of Chinese law firms only contributed to less than 3 per cent of the total number of registered foreign law firms. The proportion of

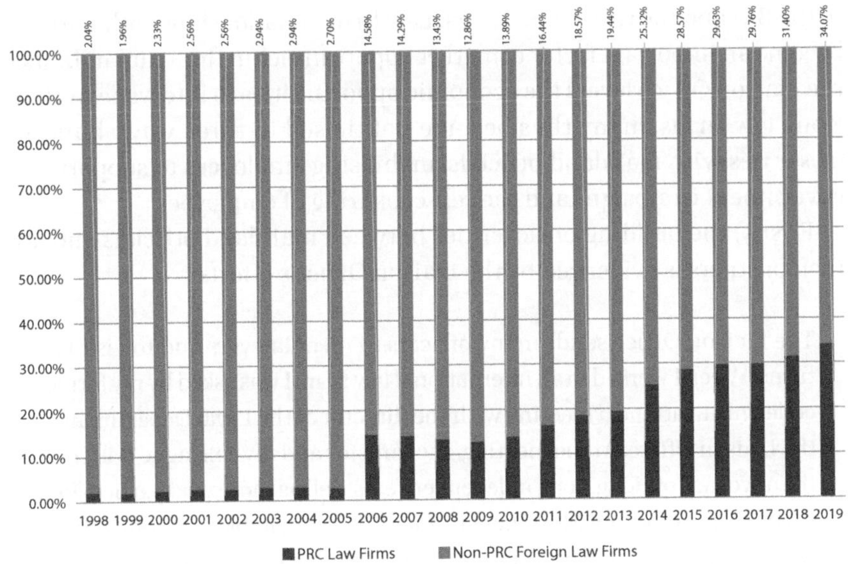

Figure 7. Percentage of Chinese Law Firms Among All Registered Foreign Law Firms in Hong Kong Since the Handover (1998–2020)
Sources: Research based on The Law Society of Hong Kong Annual Reports, 1998–2019 and Liu and Au 2020, 327

Chinese law firms jumped to 14.58 per cent in 2006, and eventually rose to nearly 20 per cent by 2013, reaching almost 30 per cent from 2016 until 2019 (Figure 7). Although Chinese law firms are considered foreign law firms in Hong Kong, as Liu and Au observed, the total number of Chinese law firms is higher than the figure in registered foreign law firms. This is due to many Chinese law firms becoming localised as Hong Kong firms by having Hong Kong solicitors as partners and fulfilling all requirements of local practice (Liu and Au 2020, 326). The rise of Chinese law firms in Hong Kong are signs of greater market competition with local firms, cultural influence in the domestic legal service industry, and the integration of Chinese law and Hong Kong law in the future (Liu and Au 2020, 347–348). For Chinese law firms associated or merged with local law firms, they can now exert influence in the council of the Law Society, the body which regulates solicitor firms and mediates government economic policies for the legal profession.

Politicisation of Law Firms

The legal service market in mainland China is strategised by the economic planning of the Chinese state. For Hong Kong lawyers and law firms that are interested in entering the mainland market, they need to rely on policy changes such as the introduction of the CEPA and state-led projects related to the BRI and the Greater Bay Area. Law firms' relationships with the state become an important factor of market opportunities in the mainland. Since the Liaison Office levers the economic opportunities to intervene in Hong Kong law firms, many thus become politicised in three ways: building closer ties with mainland officials, mobilising employees to support pro-government campaigns and the self-censuring of employees.

Firstly, the building of closer ties between mainland officials and law firm partners is evidenced by the Liaison Office's efforts:

> The Liaison Office sends many officers to meet lawyers and to visit law firms. When I worked in an international law firm, I was asked by my former colleague to attend a meeting with the director of the Legal Department of the Liaison Office. At the meeting, the director and my colleague criticised the advocacy of Hong Kong independence, as well as those who participated in the Occupy Central Movement in 2014 ... It is inevitable that connections will be built with them [the Liaison Office] because if your business is highly dependent on initial public offering in the stock market, which is mostly sourced from the mainland, you will not want to lose business connections with mainland corporations (ITV 1901, 18 January 2019).

The economic motivations for law firm partners to build close ties with the Liaison Office is also reflected in their active engagement in the Course on National Affairs, which is a state-sponsored programme to recruit local elites in Hong Kong to visit the mainland, to better understand the systems and policies of China:

> Many of my friends, who are also lawyers, have voluntarily visited the mainland to join the Course on National Affairs. In a law firm where I previously served, a law firm partner, who was highly "red-dyed" [infiltrated by the CCP], would ask the office manager to circulate those courses via the firm email, inviting the employees to register (ITV 1901, 18 January 2019).

Such practices would generate hierarchal pressure as the circulation of the registration of the Course on National Affairs comes by the official email of the firm, meaning a "suggestion" from the bosses. Similar practice can also be found in the call for a signature campaign against Occupy Central in 2014:

> One of the partners in my law firm is a member of the CPPCC. When a pro-government opinion leader began to collect signatures, I was told

> by some "delivery boys," who were rank-and-file officers in the firm, that they were asked by that partner to sign their names on a statement against Occupy Central (ITV 1935, 29 April 2019).

Besides the top-down efforts, law firms are also politicised by self-censorship among the staff. Unlike top-down censorship, employees of law firms may not be eager to express their opinions on public affairs because of the firms' dependence on mainland Chinese clients and because of peer pressure, particularly colleagues from the mainland:

> My feeling is that many lawyers were unable to exercise free expression. For example, there were times when my colleagues and I were asked to join a black-clad silent march. Yet, most of the clients of the international law firms came from China ... and even though I have my own opinion on some matters [in politics], I don't have the guts to share my views in the firm where all my colleagues are mainland Chinese (ITV 1806, 2 December 2018).

This subtle experience of censorship is not coming from nowhere. The economic dependency on mainland Chinese capital and the rise of Chinese law firms in Hong Kong have opened opportunities for state power to intervene in the law firm culture, in both direct and indirect ways. Such interventions can also be found in professional bodies in law, where news reports unveiled how some law firm partners requested their employees submit proxy forms to the firm in council elections of the Law Society, to secure votes for the conservative candidates (Sing Tao Daily 9 June 2018). This saga will be discussed in chapter 8.

Overall Outcome

The four dimensions of the China factor and its impacts on Hong Kong's legal system are examined in this and the previous chapters. How shall we assess their outcomes? One parameter is to evaluate their contributions to China's authoritarian legal transplantation to Hong Kong. The transplantation process is facilitated in part by the United Front work, which can be seen as a governing technique to consolidate China's political control of the legal profession in Hong Kong to aid the nationalistic engineering, as well as to facilitate China's economic development amid globalisation. The four dimensions of the China factor cover different aspects of authoritarian legal transplantation, yet only some succeeded in achieving the goals.

The institutional dimension of the China factor is a direct expression of the authoritarian legal transplantation of Chinese laws, legal ideology and legislative practices to Hong Kong. It aims at consolidating direct control of the CCP over political and legal institutions of Hong Kong and at deepening the nation-rebuilding project in this former British colony. The NPCSC's interpretations of the Basic Law and its decisions on legal controversies in Hong Kong have engendered significant effects on the constitutional development and the fate of political opposition in Hong Kong. When the executive government of Hong Kong and the NPCSC can take the initiative of re-interpretating the Basic Law without the involvement of Hong Kong's Court of Final Appeal, and when the NPCSC can promulgate any decisions on legal and constitutional matters without any domestic consultation or court proceedings, the intervention of the NPCSC in Hong Kong's legal and political systems has been institutionalised and routinised. These interventions have created new barriers of democratisation in Hong Kong, such as the creation of a candidate-filtering mechanism in favour of the CCP in the proposed reform of the Chief Executive election in 2014 and the interpretation of the oath-taking of public officials in 2016. These sagas laid grounds for disqualifying six lawmakers in 2017. Political opposition in Hong Kong was further side-lined and even dismissed from participating in the legislature after the direct transplantation of the National Security Law (NSL) and enforcing institutions, which were promulgated and enacted by the CCP in 2020. Twelve pro-democracy figures were disqualified from running for LegCo elections in the same year because of their explicit opposition to the national security law. Four pro-democracy lawmakers were dismissed by the Chief Executive when the NPCSC announced a decision to empower the executive government with unseating lawmakers for endangering national security law without scrutiny of the courts (Civil Rights Observers 2020 a and b). These actions repressed political dissent and warranted the implementation of what the 2014 White Paper called the "comprehensive jurisdiction" of China in Hong Kong's governing institutions.

A chilling-effect within the judiciary also generated after the 2014 White Paper, which insisted the obligation for judges to "love the country" and "safeguard national security and development interests." Examples can be found in the controversy of the Hong Kong government's proposal on amending the extradition law in 2019. Hong Kong judges with anonymity told newspapers of their worry that judicial independence would be compromised, since the Chinese government would put political pressure on judges charged with deciding on the extradition of "high-profile suspects" back to the mainland (Torode and Pomfret 2019). The second Chief Justice of Hong Kong was also reported of being pressurised by "Communist Party officials pushing Beijing's view that the Rule of Law ultimately must be a tool to preserve one-party rule" (Torode and Pomfret 2020). China's legal transplantation by institutional intervention has consolidated state control in the political order of Hong Kong, including the judiciary. That said, Hong Kong peoples' national identification and sense of belonging to China have not risen after such legal engineering, as demonstrated in public opinion surveys. Popular trust towards the "One Country, Two Systems," as reflected in a public opinion index, sharply declined since 2019, as found by a research institute just before the implementation of the NSL (*Path of Democracy* August 2020, 12).

China's intervention in Hong Kong's legal system appears to result in a general and demonstrable decline in public trust in the legal system, although the Rule of Law and judicial independence have remained as top core values in this city (Hong Kong Institute of Asia-Pacific Studies 2015; Centre for Communication and Public Opinion Survey 2017). Hong Kong has been placed high in the worldwide ranking of the Rule of Law. Its judicial independence was ranked eighth out of 141 countries in the *Global Competitiveness Report 2019* (Schuwab 2019). Hong Kong was graded sixteenth out of 126 countries and jurisdictions in the *World Justice Project Rule of Law Index* in the same year (2019). However, popular confidence in the Rule of Law in Hong Kong has declined since 2019. One survey report released by the pro-government thinktank "Bauhinia Foundation Research Centre" revealed that more than half of the respondents were displeased with the overall performance of the Rule of Law in 2019, while the average score of "prevention of the abuse of power by the government" had dropped from 5.23 out of 10 to 3.61 (2019). Another survey report also indicated a general decline in public confidence towards the Rule of Law, fairness of the judicial system and impartiality of the courts in Hong Kong, pointing out that the scores of "the Rule of Law indicator" had dropped from 6.20 out of 10 in 2019 to 4.45 in 2020 (Hong Kong Public Opinion Research Institute 2020a & 2020b).

The discrepancies between international recognition and local dissatisfaction over the Rule of Law in Hong Kong, as well as the significant drop in confidence towards the institutions of the rule, can be explained by the ways the sovereign state accommodates the tensions between its socialist authoritarian legality and Hong Kong's common law system. In the eyes of the public, the common law in Hong Kong is perceived as endorsing a liberal notion of the Rule of Law; at the very least, it means limiting the government and asserting the independence of the judiciary. However, as aforementioned, the design of "One Country, Two Systems" involves an inherent conflict of two legal systems backed by different ideologies, principles and practices. The public expects the city's legal system to operate impartially and independently from the influences of the sovereign state, whose judicial system is not perceived as meeting the standards of the Rule of Law and judicial independence. In contrast, the CCP demonstrates its sovereignty over Hong Kong's legal system by exercising powers to interpret provisions of the Basic Law and make decisions that change Hong Kong's constitutional practices. On one hand, the Chinese sovereign wants to uphold its authority over Hong Kong; on the other hand, tightening its rule would cause resistance from Hong Kong society, and the Hong Kong government's legitimacy would also be contested.

Has authoritarian legal transplantation from China succeeded apart from the direct mechanism? It is essential to observe the contributions of other dimensions of the China factor to Hong Kong's legal system. The electoral dimension of the China factor aims at strengthening political control and consolidating the authoritarian legal ideology of the CCP in Hong Kong via nurturing pro-government legal elites as lawmakers in the city. Nevertheless, some pro-government lawyer members in the LegCo created much embarrassment for the establishment in the end. The first instance occurred in 2017, when the former Chief Executive of Hong Kong, CY Leung, was found intervening in a legislative investigation into his past receipt of HKD$50 million payment from an Australian company before he became the Chief Executive of Hong Kong in 2012 (Cheung and Kao 2017). Holden Chow, a pro-government solicitor member of LegCo and a vice-chairman of the select committee of the investigation, was found to have held behind-the-scenes communications with CY Leung about the scope of the investigation into the possible conflict of interests. Chow allegedly accepted Leung's suggestion, documented in a proposal from the Chief Executive office, which crucially amended the document prepared for the investigation panel (Cheung and Kao 2017). Chow's behaviour was widely criticised by both the opposition and pro-government camps, and he finally resigned from the panel (Tsang and Cheung 2017).

The second instance came in 2019, when Junius Ho, a solicitor elected as a lawmaker in 2016, was alleged to have had connections with the "white-clad mob" that indiscriminately attacked civilians inside a Hong Kong MTR station after an Anti-ELAB rally held on 21 July. In video clips, Ho was found shaking hands with men in white t-shirts and thanking them as "heroes" before the attack. Ho did not deny his act in the clips but argued that the attack was a "normal reaction" to protesters bringing violence to a peaceful community (Sum and Su 2019). Ho's response caused criticism not only from civil society, but also from academic institutions overseas. Three months after the attack, Ho was stripped of an honorary law degree awarded by Anglia Ruskin University in the UK, after the university investigated complaints made against him (Lum 2019). However, he was soon awarded an honorary doctoral degree by the China University of Political Science and Law, making the offering of the degree a clear political response by Beijing (K. Cheng 2019d). While the formation of state-sponsored lawyer-lawmakers was supposed to rebrand the pro-government camp with legal professional and elitist images, the performance of Ho caused the opposite effect.

What about the counter-mobilisational dimension? Compared with SAMLAW, HKLEF played a greater role in debating with liberal and progressive lawyers on legal and constitutional matters. It was repeatedly interviewed by and submitted commentaries to newspapers in Hong Kong as well as mainland China. As shown in table 9, the number of media reports and op-eds on HKLEF in newspapers within "Greater China," which covers regions of mainland China, Hong Kong, Macau and Taiwan, had significantly risen from 50 in 2014 to 581 in 2020. Two state-owned newspapers in Hong Kong had shared nearly 70 per cent of the coverage of HKLEF. It is obvious that HKLEF has served as a supplier of legal discourse and commentaries to pro-government media in Hong Kong. In March 2021, ten months after the China's imposition of the NSL on Hong Kong, a new electoral system for Hong Kong was introduced by the NPC. The new system replaces personal votes with corporate votes in many sectors of the Election Committee elections, including the legal ones. SAMLAW and HKLEF become two of the 30 corporate voters under the new electoral reform, enjoying the power to elect 15 members of that sector (C. Chau 2021a). It demonstrates Beijing's support for SAMLAW and HKLEF, and its attempt to enhance pro-Beijing lawyer allies by further integrating counter-mobilisation and political elections in the future.

The significance of the economic dimension of the China factor should also be considered. Authoritarian legal transplantation by China is not confined to the transplantation of laws and legal ideology. The cross-border economic policies for Hong Kong lawyers since 2003 have restructured the market share between local law firms and the Chinese ones in Hong Kong. Such economic opportunities shaped behaviours of law firms as well as legal professional bodies like the Law Society, and their behaviours did influence or counterbalance the liberal notion of the Rule of Law in the legal profession and the Hong Kong society. As Liu and Au predicted, the rise of Chinese law firms in Hong Kong, as well as the increase in the recruitment of Hong Kong lawyers in Chinese law firms, would alone facilitate hybridisation

Table 9. Coverage of HKLEF in Newspapers (2014–2020)[1]

	No. of reports or op-eds in newspapers of the Greater China	No. of reports or op-eds in state-owned newspapers	Percentage of reports or op-eds in state-owned newspapers (%)
2014	50	23	46.00
2015	178	103	57.87
2016	366	138	37.70
2017	166	104	62.65
2018	200	156	78.00
2019	373	234	62.73
2020 (Until 30/11)	581	407	70.05

Source: Research based on *Wisenews*

of Chinese law and Hong Kong law and a resemblance to the ecology of mainland law firms in the future (Liu and Au 2020, 346–347). Moreover, the ecology of the legal service market has paved the way for a greater degree of politicisation of law firm culture, when law firm partners are mobilised to engage in counter-mobilisation and political alignment with the state under the United Front Work. After all, China's cross-border initiative for Hong Kong lawyers, such as the BRI and the Greater Bay Area, are not just economic projects, but a political mission for the CCP to expand the political influence beyond its territory and to strategise the coastal area of Southeast China for development. The ties between the CCP and the legal profession are indeed politically-driven.

Economic opportunities are certainly an important agenda for state-lawyer co-optation, as reflected in the interactions between political authorities and the Law Society as well as the Bar. This is because solicitors and barristers are nowadays both able to provide legal services in mainland China in different ways. However, as demonstrated in the following chapters, the results of the council elections of the two professional bodies did not always homogeneously reflect the significance of the economic side of the China factor.

Conclusion

By using the analytical framework of the China factor, chapters 2 and 3 reveal that China neither adopts the past trajectory of British colonialism that exerted indirect rule, nor implements a direct rule like the French colonisers in Africa. Rather, China's approach is hybridised. More than just top-down encroachment by the exercise of sovereign power through law, China also uses a variety of influencing mechanisms to control the legal profession, and its engagement in civil society and the market. The interrelationships between law, politics, economy and society are thus proven and amplified.

China's institutional intervention in the legal system, recruitment of pro-government lawyers in political elections, formation of lawyer-based organisations and provision for economic opportunities in the mainland are purposive of an advancing authoritarian transplantation of Chinese socialist laws, legal ideology and the building of a political allegiance of the legal profession to the sovereign state. The dissemination of authoritarian legal ideology and the repeated promotion of the absolute sovereign power are facilitated by pro-government lawyers with a law background and counter-mobilisation by state-sponsored legal associations. At the same time, the political and economic influences of China also pose an impact on the political orientation and participation of solicitors in law firms.

Lawyers are one of the significant parties in defending the Rule of Law and upholding judicial autonomy. Whether lawyers' conventional beliefs of and commitments to the Rule of Law would be compromised depend on the scope and scale of authoritarian legal transplantation, as well as the resilience of lawyers themselves. Resilience of lawyers concerns the agency of lawyers, either in an individual or a collective form, to resist the authoritarian rule. Although the China factor enables the Chinese and Hong Kong governments to pressure judges, lawyers and political opposition, not all lawyers accept the offer. While there are lawyers who are willing to be compradors for the political authority, some lawyers choose to confront the process of authoritarian legal transplantation in different ways.

References

Arrangement between the National Development and Reform Commission and the Government of the Hong Kong Special Administrative Region for Advancing Hong Kong's Full Participation in and Contribution to the Belt and Road Initiative. 2017. HKSAR Government Press Release, December 14. Accessed December 10, 2020. https://gia.info.gov.hk/general/201712/14/P2017121400551_274123_1_1513236929437.pdf.

Bauhinia Foundation Research Centre. 2019. "Survey on Public Perceptions towards the Rule of Law in Hong Kong." December 18. Accessed July 9, 2020. http://www.bauhinia.org/index.php/english/research/106.

"Bèi tī bào fā xìn gōng lián huì yuán zhǐ shì tóu piào, èr líng líng bā lì fǎ huì xuǎn jǔ Zhèng Yào Táng chū miàn pèi piào chēng Liáng Měi Fēn." 2008. *Apple Daily,* August 27, A07.

Centre for Communication and Public Opinion Survey of the Chinese University of Hong Kong. 2017. "Press Release: Survey Result of Public Opinion and Political Development in Hong Kong." July 7. Accessed May 7, 2018. Archived on file with the author.

Chan, Maggie. 2014. "Ài guó yǔ sī fǎ dú lì xū hé xié bìng cún." The Small and Medium Law Firms Association of Hong Kong, June 19. Accessed December 17, 2020. https://www.samlaw.hk/images/files/2014/2014-06-19譴責暴力維護法治_記者茶聚/香港中小型律師行協會愛國與司法獨立須和諧並存.pdf.

Chan, Maggie. 2016. "SAMLAW Statement Dated 16th October 2016." The Small and Medium Law Firms Association of Hong Kong, October 16. Accessed December 17, 2020. https://www.samlaw.hk/index.php/lastnews/162-re-samlaw-statement-dated-16th-october-2016.html.

Chau, Candice. 2021a. "Hong Kong Legal Sector Influence 'Diluted' in Election Committee under Election Revamp Plan, Says Lawmaker." *Hong Kong Free Press,* April 15. Accessed June 30, 2021. https://hongkongfp.com/2021/04/15/hong-kong-legal-sector-influence-diluted-in-election-committee-under-election-revamp-plan-says-lawmaker/.

Cheng, Edmund W. 2020. "United Front Work and Mechanism of Countermobilization in Hong Kong." *The China Journal* 83: 1–33.

Cheng, Edmund W., and Samson Yuen. 2017. "How Hong Kong's Umbrella Movement Was Crushed and Pro-Democracy Activists Gradually Silenced." *The Conversation,* November 15. Accessed August 25, 2020. https://theconversation.com/how-hong-kong-umbrella-movement-was-crushed-and-pro-democracy-activists-gradually-silenced-84339.

Cheng, Kris. 2019a. "Beijing Deems Hong Kong Protests 'Colour Revolution,' Will Not Rule Out Intervention." *Hong Kong Free Press,* August 8. Accessed December 17, 2020. https://hongkongfp.com/2019/08/08/beijing-deems-hong-kong-protests-colour-revolution-will-not-rule-intervention/.

Cheng, Kris. 2019d. "Pro-Beijing Lawmaker Junius Ho Receives Honorary Degree from Chinese University after UK Degree Withdrawn." *Hong Kong Free Press,* December 6. Accessed December 23, 2020. https://hongkongfp.com/2019/12/06/pro-beijing-lawmaker-junius-ho-receives-honorary-degree-chinese-university-uk-degree-withdrawn/.

Cheung, Karen. 2017. "Anti-Occupy Figures Elected as Hong Kong Representatives in China's National Legislature." *Hong Kong Free Press,* December 19, updated March 31, 2020. Accessed November 20, 2020. https://hongkongfp.com/2017/12/19/anti-occupy-figures-elected-hong-kong-representatives-chinas-national-legislature/.

Cheung, Tony. 2017a. "Third Concern Group Set Up on Hong Kong's Controversial Border Plan for China Rail Line; Coalition Insists It Is Legal." *South China Morning Post,* August 8. Accessed November 22, 2020. https://www.scmp.com/news/hong-kong/politics/article/2105928/third-concern-group-set-hong-kongs-controversial-border-plan?utm_source=facebook.com&utm_medium=referral.

Cheung, Tony, and Ernest Kao. 2017. "Hong Kong Leader Leung Chun-ying Admits Intervening in Probe into HK$50 Million Payment." *South China Morning Post,* May 16. Accessed December 23, 2020. https://www.scmp.com/news/hong-kong/politics/article/2094482/hong-kong-leader-cy-leung-admits-role-proposal-change-scope.

Chiu Luen Public Light Bus Company Limited v. Persons unlawfully occupying or remaining on the public highway namely, the westbound carriageway of Argyle Street between the junction of Tung Choi Street and Portland Street and/or other persons hindering or preventing the passing or repassing of Argyle Street. 2014. HCA2086/2014.

Chow, Lok Yiu. 2019. "Mǎ Ēn Guó Qù Xìn Lián Hé Guó Mì Shū Cháng Gào Zhuàng, Chì Měi Guó Zhǐ Shǐ Xiāng Gǎng Bào Luàn." *Inmediahk,* August 16. Accessed December 17, 2020. https://www.inmediahk.net/node/1066554.

Civil Rights Observers. 2020a. *Brief Reports on National Security Law (July–August 2020).*

Civil Rights Observers. 2020b. *Brief Reports on National Security Law (September–November 2020).*

"[Duǎn Piàn] [Fǎ Xué Jiāo Liú Jī Jīn Huì Qù Xìn Lián Hé Guó] Cù Chá Měi Guó Cān Yǔ Xiāng Gǎng Bào Luàn Qíng Kuàng, Mǎ Ēn Guó: Hěn Duō Biǎo Miàn Zhèng Jù Xiǎn Shì Měi Guó Bàn Yǎn Zhòng Yào Jiǎo Sè." 2019. YouTube, August 17. Accessed December 17, 2020. https://www.youtube.com/watch?v=H9j7TXtS8zs.

"[Duǎn Piàn: Huí Yīng Shì Fǎ] Chēng Zhōng Yāng Èr Yuè Yǐ Kāi Shǐ Tǎo Lùn Shì Fǎ, Liáng Měi Fēn: Zhōng Yāng Gǎn Jué Wàng, Xiàn Yǐ Hǎo Kè Zhì (14:46)." 2016. *Ming Pao Instant News,* November 7. Accessed November 22, 2020. https://news.mingpao.com/ins/%E6%B8%AF%E8%81%9E/section/20250209/s00001.

Goodstadt, Leo. F. 2005. *Uneasy Partners: The Conflict Between Public Interest and Private Profit in Hong Kong.* Hong Kong University Press.

Greater Bay Area. 2025. "Home Page. Accessed April 5, 2025. https://www.bayarea.gov.hk/en/home/index.html .

"Hé Jūn Yáo Lùn Lu Shī Huì Gǎi Xuǎn, Lǎo Bǎn Yǒu Quán Yào Yuán Gōng Shòu Quán Piào." 2018. *Sing Tao Daily,* June 9. Accessed November 20, 2024. https://hk.news.yahoo.com/%E4%BD%95%E5%90%9B%E5%A0%AF%E8%AB%96%E5%BE%8B%E5%B8%AB%E6%9C%83%E6%94%B9%E9%81%B8-.

HKSAR Government Justice Department. 2020. "Justice Department Welcomes NPC Standing Committee's Decision to Allow HK Law Practitioners to Work in

Greater Bay Area." *Xinhua Net*, August 12. Accessed December 10, 2020. http://en.people.cn/n3/2020/0812/c90000-9720726.html.

HKTDC Research. 2019. "Legal Service Industry in Hong Kong." Hong Kong Trade and Development Council, July 12. Accessed July 14, 2020. https://hkmb.hktdc.com/en.

Hong Kong Institute of Asia-Pacific Studies of the Chinese University of Hong Kong. 2015. "Press Release on 'CUHK Releases Survey Findings on Views on Hong Kong's Core Values.'" October 29. Accessed May 7, 2018. https://www.cpr.cuhk.edu.hk/en/press/cuhk-releases-survey-findings-on-views-on-hong-kongs-core-values/.

"Jiàn zhì pài wǔ yì yuan dēng lu shī huì guān fāng kān wù fēng miàn, bèi zhì yí yòng gōng jiā zī yuán zhèng zhì xuān chuán." 2016. *Stand News*, November 18. Accessed November 22, 2022. Archived on file with the author.

King, Ambrose Y. C. 1975. "Administrative Absorption of Politics in Hong Kong: Emphasis on the Grass Roots Level." *Asian Survey* 15, no. 5: 422–439.

Kwong, Bruce K. K. 2010. *Patron-Client Politics and Elections in Hong Kong*. Routledge.

Lam, L. C., K. L. Chan, H. Y. Fung, and K.H. Cheung. 2016. "[Tè shǒu xuǎn zhàn] Zhōng jí jīn zhǔ pù guāng: qí xīn jī jīn yōng èr qiān wàn xiàn jīn chǔ bèi 2016." *HK01*, May 6. Accessed December 17, 2020. https://www.hk01.com/%E7%A4%BE%E6%9C%83%E6%96%B0%E8%81%9E/19657/%E7%89%B9%E9%A6%96%E9%81%B8%E6%88%B0-%E7%B5%82%E6%A5%B5%E9%87%91%E4%B8%BB%E6%9B%9D%E5%85%89-%E9%BD-%8A%E5%BF%83%E5%9F%BA%E9%87%91-%E6%93%81%E4%BA%8C%E5%8D%83%E8%90%AC%E7%8F%BE%E9%87%91%E5%84%B2%E5%82%99.

Lam, Wai-man, and Kay C. Y Lam. 2013. "China's United Front Work in Civil Society: The Case of Hong Kong." *International Journal of China Studies* 4, no. 3: 301–325.

Lee, Francis L. F. 2018. "Changing Political Economy of the Hong Kong Media." *China Perspectives* 3: 9–18.

Lee, Karen M. Y. 2017a. "Lawyers and Hong Kong's Democracy Movement: From Electoral Politics to Civil Disobedience." *Asian Journal of Political Science* 25, no. 1: 89–108.

Lee, W. Y. 2018. "[Dà wān qū zhuān fǎng] Guō Róng Kēng chàng chéng lì wān qū zhòng cái zhōng xīn, zhù nián qīng lu shī zēng zhí yè jīng yàn." *HK01*, May 16. Accessed December 10, 2020. https://www.hk01.com/%E6%94%BF%E6%83%85/186302/%E5%A4%A7%E7%81%A3%E5%8D%80%E5%B0%88%E8%A8%AA-%E9%83%AD%E6%A6%AE%E9%8F%97%E5%80%A1%E6%88%90%E7%AB%8B%E7%81%A3%E5%8D%80%E4%BB%B2%E8%A3%81%E4%B8%AD%E5%BF%83-%E5%8A%A9%E5%B9%B4%E8%BC%95%E5%BE%8B%E5%B8%AB%E5%A2%9E%E5%9F%B7%E6%A5%AD%E7%B6%93%E9%A9%97.

Liu, Sida, and Anson Au. 2020. "The Gateway to Global China: Hong Kong and the Future of Chinese Law Firms." *Wisconsin International Law Journal* 37, no. 2: 308–349.

Lo, Sunny S.H. 2008. *The Dynamics of Beijing-Hong Kong Relations: A Model for Taiwan?* Hong Kong University Press.

Lum, Alvin. 2019. "British University Strips Pro-Beijing Lawmaker Junius Ho of Honorary Degree over Remarks during Hong Kong Protests." *South China Morning Post*, October 29. Accessed December 23, 2020. https://www.scmp.com/news/hong-kong/politics/article/3035297/british-university-strips-pro-beijing-lawmaker-junius-ho.

Ma, Ngok. 2005. "Civil Society in Self-Defense: The Struggle against National Security Legislation in Hong Kong." *Journal of Contemporary China* 14, no. 44: 465–482.

Ma, Ngok. 2007. *Political Development of Hong Kong: State, Political Society and Civil Society*. Hong Kong University Press.

Mainland and Hong Kong Close Economic Partnership Arrangement 2003. Trade and Industry Department of the Government of Hong Kong Special Administrative Region, June 29. Accessed December 8, 2020. https://www.tid.gov.hk/english/cepa/files/main_e.pdf.

Mainland and Hong Kong Close Economic Partnership Arrangement 2020. Trade and Industry Department of the Government of Hong Kong Special Administrative Region. Accessed 8 December 2020. https://www.tid.gov.hk/english/cepa/index.html.

Mainland and Hong Kong Closer Economic Partnership Arrangement: Agreement on Economic and Technical Cooperation (Ecotech Agreement) 2017. Trade and Industry Department of the Government of Hong Kong Special Administrative Region, June 28. Accessed December 8, 2020. https://www.tid.gov.hk/english/cepa/legaltext/files/cepa15_main.pdf.

Ng, Kang-Chung. 2020. "Hong Kong Lawyers Can Soon Earn Qualification to Practise in Greater Bay Area under New Pilot Scheme." *South China Morning Post*, October 22. Accessed December 10, 2020. https://www.scmp.com/news/hong-kong/politics/article/3106710/hong-kong-lawyers-can-soon-earn-qualification-practise.

One Country, Two Systems Index 2020. Path of Democracy. Hong Kong.

Poon, C. H. 2020. "Legal Service Industry in Hong Kong." *Hong Kong Trade Development Council*, June 18. Accessed December 10, 2020. https://research.hktdc.com/en/article/MzEzODc5NTk5.

"Restrictions Eased for Qualified Hong Kong and Macau Lawyers Practicing in Mainland China." 2013. *China Briefing*, August 20. Accessed December 10, 2020. https://www.china-briefing.com/news/restrictions-eased-for-qualified-hong-kong-macau-lawyers-practicing-in-mainland-china/.

"Róng Hǎi En duó xīn dōng yì xí, xī huán qì zī qì nǚ dà sheng." 2016. *Apple Daily Breaking News*, September 5. Accessed January 13, 2019. Archived on file with the author.

Schwab, Klaus, ed. 2019. *The Global Competitiveness Report 2019*. World Economic Forum. Accessed July 9, 2020. https://www3.weforum.org/docs/WEF_TheGlobalCompetitivenessReport2019.pdf.

The Small and Medium Law Firms Association of Hong Kong. 2014a. "Methods for Selecting the Chief Executive in 2017." April 25. Accessed December 17, 2020. https://www.samlaw.hk/index.php/lastnews/89-2017.html.

The Small and Medium Law Firms Association of Hong Kong. 2014b. "Press release: Free "Anti-Occupy Central" helpline starts talking calls tomorrow." August 31. Accessed December 17, 2020. https://www.samlaw.hk/images/files/2014/2014-08-31Anti-Occupy_Central_Helpline_Press_Releases/SAMLAWAnti-Occupy_Central_Helpline_Press_Releases_with_signature.pdf.

The Small and Medium Law Firms Association of Hong Kong. 2025. "Home Page". Accessed April 5, 2025. https://www.samlaw.hk .

Sum, Lok-kei, and Xinqi Su. 2019. "Pro-Beijing Lawmaker Junius Ho Defends White-Clad Mob That Attacked Civilians in Hong Kong MTR Station, Says They Can Be 'Pardoned for Defending Their Home'." *South China Morning Post*, July 22. Accessed December 23, 2020. https://www.scmp.com/news/hong-kong/politics/article/3019621/pro-beijing-lawmaker-junius-ho-defends-white-clad-mob.

Tam, Waikeung. 2012. *Legal Mobilization Under Authoritarianism: The Case of Post-Colonial Hong Kong*. Cambridge University Press.

Torode, Greg, and James Pomfret. 2019. "Exclusive: Hong Kong Judges See Risks in Proposed Extradition Changes." *Reuters*, May 29. Accessed December 23, 2020. https://www.reuters.com/article/us-hongkong-politics-extradition-judges-idUSKCN1SZ09U/.

Torode, Greg, and James Pomfret. 2020. "Hong Kong Judges Battle Beijing over Rule of Law as Pandemic Chills Protests." *Reuters*, April 14. Accessed December 23, 2020. https://www.reuters.com/investigates/special-report/hongkong-politics-judiciary/.

Tsang, Emily, and Tony Cheung. 2017. "Opposition Ramps Up Bid to Impeach Hong Kong Leader for Intervening in Fee Probe." *South China Morning Post*, May 19. Accessed December 23, 2020. https://www.scmp.com/news/hong-kong/politics/article/2094923/lawmaker-holden-chow-quits-ugl-investigation-panel-wake-cy.

World Justice Project. 2019. *The WJP Rule of Law Index 2019*. Accessed July 9, 2020. https://worldjusticeproject.org/rule-of-law-index/.

"Xiè Wěi Jùn Zhōng Rèn Shì 'Xī Huán Qì Zī'." 2012. *Apple Daily*, December 31, A03.

Yang, Shen. 2019. "In the Name of the Law: Legal Frames and the Ending of the Occupy Movement in Hong Kong." *Law and Social Inquiry* 44, no. 2: 468–490.

Yep, Ray. 2007. "Links with the Mainland." In *Contemporary Hong Kong Politics*, edited by Wai-Man Lam, Percy L. T. Lui, and Wilson Wong. Hong Kong University Press.

Yuen, Chris. 2016a. "Incoming Lawmaker Junius Ho Thanks China Liaison Office and Others for Support." *Hong Kong Free Press*, September 5. Accessed November 22, 2020. https://hongkongfp.com/2016/09/05/incoming-lawmaker-junius-ho-thanks-china-liaison-office-others-support/.

Yuen, Chris. 2016b. "Over 44,000 sign petitions against Youngspiration's Yau Wai-ching amid "Chee-na" oath fallout." *Hong Kong Free Press*, October 14. Accessed December 17, 2020. https://hongkongfp.com/2016/10/14/over-44000-sign-petition-against-youngspirations-yau-wai-ching-amid-chee-na-oath-fallout/.

4. Professional Rule of Law Discourse under State-Bar Relations

Abstract: This chapter examines the evolving relationship between Hong Kong's legal professional bodies—the Bar Association and the Law Society—and the political authorities amid China's authoritarian legal transplantation. It highlights the divergence in their rhetoric: the Bar, emphasising judicial independence and the Rule of Law, often confronts state overreach, while the Law Society, prioritising law and order, mostly maintains a cooperative stance. Drawing on comparative analyses of public statements from 1997 to 2020, the chapter explores how economic incentives and political co-optation shaped a "comprador professionalism" within the Bar and the Law Society. The discussion reveals the professional bodies' contrasting roles in navigating authoritarian pressures and their implications for legal autonomy, civil liberties, and constitutional governance in Hong Kong.

Keywords: Bar Association, Law Society, Judicial Independence, Professionalism, Authoritarian Governance, Rule of Law

> Although many people think this role [of speaking up for the Rule of Law] ought to be fulfilled by the Chief Justice or the judiciary, the judiciary shouldn't be speaking too much. The judiciary and judges speak through their judgements; detailed though they are, it's left to the people interested in the law to speak out. When the judiciary, for example, is attacked, these include the Secretary for Justice, and they include the lawyers, such as the Bar and The Law Society (The Hon Geoffrey Ma, the former Chief Justice of Hong Kong, 10 November 2020).

A significant indicator of the success of legal transplantation lies in the response of stakeholders living in the transplanted jurisdiction. As Jones suggests, the reception of legal transplantation "owes much to national and local histories, as well as whether interested parties within a society regard it as advantageous"

Lai, Y. *Legal Resistance under Authoritarianism: The Struggle for the Rule of Law in Hong Kong.* Taylor & Francis Group, 2025
DOI: 10.5117/9789048558438_CH04

(Jones 2010, 120). Hence, whether reception, adaptation or resistance occurs in the political institutions, the legal community and civil society could impact the process and outcome of the transplantation, subject to the capacities and resilience of those stakeholders. Among the stakeholders in society, independent professional bodies in law are expected to have a significant voice as they are meant to support the operation of the existing legal system and regulate the legal profession. They police the conduct of lawyers and protect their professional interests, which are generally defined by the professional bodies themselves. Legal professional bodies are sensitive to market signals and political authority, as they are significant forces that influence, regulate and even control the well-being and welfare of the legal profession.

The Hong Kong Bar Association (The Bar) and the Law Society of Hong Kong (The Law Society) are the two statutory professional bodies for regulating lawyers in Hong Kong. When Geoffrey Ma, formerly the Chief Justice of Hong Kong, gave a keynote speech to the International Bar Association in 2020, he suggested that the organised legal profession, meaning the Bar and the Law Society, should speak up for the Rule of Law and defend the judiciary from any attacks.. Has Ma's expectation been realised under China's authoritarian legal transplantation in Hong Kong?

This chapter provides an analysis of the state-bar (including both barristers and solicitors) relations in Hong Kong, the similarities and differences between the Bar and the Law Society in terms of their public responses to authoritarian legal transplantation by China. Based on the comparative study of published statements and submissions of the Bar and the Law Society between 1997 and 2020, this chapter argues that the Bar and the Law Society have adopted divergent rhetoric and writing styles in public legal discourses that respond to different strategies of the Chinese authoritarian transplantation. While the Bar stressed the Rule of Law as limiting government and adopted confrontational statements towards the political authorities of Hong Kong and China, the Law Society has put a greater emphasis on law and order. The latter is inclined to be less critical of the statecraft in the legal sector. Before comparing the Bar and the Law Society's public discourse, the next section provides an overview of Hong Kong's state-bar relations from institutional and cultural perspectives.

Statutory Relationship Between the State and Legal Professional Bodies in Hong Kong

The Legal Practitioners Ordinance (CAP 159) regulates the relationship between the Hong Kong government and legal professional bodies, including the Bar and the Law Society. The ordinance states that all solicitors in Hong Kong are court officers. Still, the Law Society plays a vital role as the court can only admit a solicitor once a certificate from the Law Society is received (Articles 3(1)(1B)(2) and 4(1)(1A)). The Law Society prescribes standard requirements for solicitors to be admitted, issues practising certificates to solicitors, holds power of investigation, inspection and sanction against misconduct by solicitors, and intervenes in a solicitor's or foreign lawyer's practice on particular grounds. The grounds include dishonesty and bankruptcy of law firms, and complaints against solicitors or foreign lawyers to the Solicitor Disciplinary Tribunal for disciplinary action. All Solicitor Disciplinary Tribunal Panel members are appointed by the Chief Justice of Hong Kong (Cap.159, Articles 3, 9, 10 and 26A; The Law Society of Hong Kong, 2013).

Barristers, who are self-employed legal professionals in Hong Kong, are admitted by the court after complying with the requirements prescribed by the Bar and are granted practising certificates from the Bar Council (Cap.159, Articles 27, 30 and 31). The Bar Council has the power to admonish barristers found guilty of misconduct, while the Barristers Disciplinary Tribunal takes on the role of punishment (Cap.159, Articles 34–37; *The Hong Kong Bar Association* 2020). In addition, the Chief Justice can consult the Bar Council chairman and the Law Society president on the appointments of senior counsel (silk) and honorary senior counsel (Cap. 159, Article 31A). In short, the legal profession in Hong Kong is self-regulatory as prescribed by law.

The Bar and the Law Society also enjoy privileges to engage in ceremonial events, consultation in professional education and training programmes, official provision of legal aid services, judicial appointments and public policymaking. For example, since the sovereign transfer in 1997, the chairman of the Bar and the president of the Law Society continue to speak on behalf of the profession at the "Opening of the Legal Year," which is transplanted from the English legal tradition, serving as a ceremonial event for judges and lawyers at the start of the legal year. As for professional legal education and training, they are standardised not only by law schools in Hong Kong, which admit students for the postgraduate certificate in law programmes and provide qualifying exams, but also in the Standing Committee on Legal Education and Training, which was established in 2005 under the Legal Practitioners Ordinance (Article 74A). The committee is responsible for reviewing and evaluating education and training programmes for future lawyers in Hong Kong and giving recommendations to law schools and institutions that provide vocational training in law (Article 74A (2)). The Bar and the Law Society can nominate four people to join the 17-member committee, and the rest are nominated by the judiciary and law schools in Hong Kong, subject to the appointment of the Chief Executive (Article 74A(3)).

Regarding legal aid services, the councils of the Bar and the Law Society are consulted by the Chief Executive on the appointment of members of the Legal Aid Services Council, which supervises the Department of Legal Aid and advises the government on legal aid policy. However, under the Legal Aid Service Council Ordinance (Cap. 489), the Chief Executive can appoint anyone other than those recommended by the councils of the Bar and The Law Society (Articles 3, 5(3) and 5(4)). When it comes to judicial appointments in which only legal professionals are eligible for the position of judges, councils of the Bar and the Law Society can recommend any of their lawyer members as members of the Judicial Officers Recommendation Commission, in which all members are appointed by the Chief Executive of Hong Kong (Judicial Officers Recommendation Commission Ordinance (Cap.92), Article 3(1)(1A)). Yet, as with the settings of the Legal Aid Services Council, the Chief Executive is not required to appoint the referred barristers and solicitors by the legal professional bodies (Article 3(1)(1B)).

Concerning policymaking, the Bar and the Law Society can voluntarily submit reports and recommendations in public policy and legislation consultation processes to the Hong Kong government, and they are often invited to join discussions on the Panel on Administration of Justice and Legal Services in the Legislative Council (LegCo). These channels are platforms for the Bar and the Law Society to express their positions on matters of human rights and the Rule of Law. For instance, during the consultation process of the draft Bill of Rights Ordinance (BORO) in 1990, both the Bar and the Law Society submitted opinions. While the Law Society mainly focused on the rejection of a provision on inter-citizen disputes and the need for a one-year freeze period for some specific provisions after the passage of the BORO, the Bar demonstrated a more progressive position by requesting the government to include chapter 3 of the Basic Law, which later became the mini-constitutional document of Hong Kong after its sovereignty transfer to China in 1997, into the draft bill (Wong 2017, 99–101). Chapter 3 of the Basic Law stipulates most of the fundamental human rights prescribed in the International Covenant on Civil and Political Rights (ICCPR). This historical event demonstrates that even before the sovereignty transfer, the Bar was eager to take further steps to commit to defending human rights, which is an essential pillar of constituting a liberal Rule of Law in post-handover Hong Kong.

In summary, the legal and institutional frameworks in Hong Kong have given the Bar and the Law Society official status to regulate lawyers via the quality control of legal education, vocational training, admission and discipline to guarantee the monopolisation of the legal service market by the legal profession. The Bar and the Law Society also enjoy statutory positions in legal aid policy and appointments alongside promotions of judges in Hong Kong. However, these formal arrangements cannot fully picture the dynamics between the state and the organised legal profession. Both formal and informal power relationships between the Chinese authority and the legal professional bodies are significant in developing the legal profession and the Rule of Law in Hong Kong. Such relationships go beyond the legal and institutional settings in Hong Kong. Moreover, the legal framework of the Bar and the Law Society cannot illuminate how they interact with both Hong Kong and Chinese authorities over legal as well as constitutional controversies. The formal state-bar relations do not explain how does state powers penetrate in the two professional bodies in a subtle and inform way, such as the United Front Work that cultivates and reinforces "comprador professionalism".

As described in chapter 1, comprador professionalism captures how legal professional bodies tends to collaborate, legitimise and aid the state by stressing on the economic and technical characters of legal practices, political neutrality and non-partisanship as covers of their collaborative position with the state. Understanding how the Bar and the Law Society fostered their relationships with the Chinese and Hong Kong political authorities unravels the emergence of comprador professionalism in the two professional bodies after the handover.

Comprador Professionalism in the Bar

The Bar Council, as the annually elected leadership of the Bar, had been vocal in constitutional affairs and human rights issues when the Basic Law was officially implemented in Hong Kong. The Bar has also promoted discourse of the Rule of Law and judicial independence beyond Hong Kong's border. For instance, the Bar Council sent its members to East Timor, which became independent from Indonesia in 1999, to train domestic judges and lawyers and promote a jury system (Lum 2021). Moreover, many retired chairpersons of the Bar were outspoken in the public domain. One outstanding example was held in 2003, as some former chairpersons of the Bar formed the Article 23 Concern Group as a collective way to advocate their opposition to the proposed bill of national security law in Hong Kong (see chapter 3). That said, the Bar at that time did not fundamentally oppose the legislation of the national security law in 2003 but instead adopted a reformist approach to persuade the government to make concessions moderately. The Bar, as a professional body, remained friendly and cooperative with the governments of Hong Kong and China, despite its occasional public disagreement with the government.

Even during the British colonial rule, the Chinese Communist Party (CCP) had revealed its intention to consolidate its United Front Work in local elites in Hong Kong, including members of the Bar Council (Loh 2011; Lee 2018). After the sovereignty transfer, the CCP's United Front Work became more apparent. In 2008, Rimsky Yuen, a Bar chairman who sought a second term of office, was appointed as a member of the Guangdong Provincial Committee of the Chinese People's Political Consultative Conference (CPPCC). The appointment was announced before the annual general meeting of the Bar that elects the Bar chairman. Hence this news caused a backlash and criticism from some senior counsel. A mainland Chinese legal scholar Wang You-Jin also commented that since the CPPCC members are obliged to "love the country and the party," Yuen could not uphold political neutrality if he got re-elected (*Radio Free Asia* 6 January 2008).

Later on, ten former chairpersons of the Bar released a joint letter asking Yuen to resign. However, Yuen insisted on running for his second term. In the end, he won the chairmanship without rivals. He then stressed that his acceptance of the CCP's appointment was due to his wish to "raise the Rule of Law in Guangdong Province. " He also dismissed the claim that the appointment was part of China's United Front Work (*The Apple Daily* 18 January 2008). Under Yuen's leadership, the Bar and the Chinese government commenced various exchange activities and collaboration in developing legal service markets and training in the mainland.

A joint academic programme at Peking University was one outstanding example of the collaboration between the Bar and the mainland Chinese authorities. The Bar Council hosted this programme at the Peking University Rule of Law Research Centre. The programme was initially a weekly course titled "The Essentials of the Common Law: Public Law". It consisted of four lectures and mooting (mock court litigation), and the topics of lectures included "the concept of the Rule of Law", "principles of common law", "natural law", "court proceedings in different levels of courts", "judicial review", "human rights protections", "international trade dispute resolutions" and "commercial arbitration". Lectures and mooting were instructed and convened by barristers from Hong Kong and mainland law professors (Peking University Rule of Law Research Centre and Hong Kong Bar Association 2011–13, 2014 and 2015). In 2017, the Bar Council further opened a course on "international arbitration" at Peking University (*Ming Pao Instant News*

30 August 2018). In these two courses, outstanding students were awarded scholarships to visit Hong Kong's judiciary and law enforcement agencies and to join internships in local chambers.

Such joint teaching modules demonstrate a collaborative relationship between the Bar and mainland academic institutions to promote the common law notion of the Rule of Law in mainland China's soil. The Bar's partnerships with mainland institutions also occur in economic and political spheres. Like the Law Society, the Bar has two standing committees responsible for issues related to the members' interests in practising on the mainland. The Bar had signed memorandums of understanding (MoUs) with the CCP-led mainland institutions, such as the Shanghai Bar Association and the China Enterprise Association, to advance opportunities for Hong Kong barristers to be in-house counsel and legal consultants in mainland law firms. This was approved by the Ministry of Justice in China (W. Tam 2017, 1).

Moreover, backed by the Ministry of Justice in China, 37 agreements were signed between a mainland law firm and a Hong Kong barrister, who can thus practice as a legal consultant in the mainland (W. Tam 2017, 2). In addition, the Bar maintained regular official visits to state bodies in Beijing and made public statements to report its visits (W. Tam 11 January 2016). The Chinese government was also willing to connect with the Bar for the sake of achieving the United Front Work. As experienced and observed by a former chairman of the Bar, at least between 2007 and 2017, the vocal position of the Bar on specific constitutional issues had not diminished the mutual respect between the Bar and the Chinese government. He viewed such smooth relationship was attributed to the CCP's "United Front mentality":

> You may say it is a kind of the United Front Work ... yet in the eyes of the mainland authorities, the Bar is a credible organisation in Hong Kong. Hence, they do not have to break our relationship. They would take our public statements [on specific issues] as balanced views, rather than treating us as a political opposition group. [Through building relationship with the Bar] China can also tell the world that it can tolerate diverse opinions... The Bar was able to uphold exchanges with mainland authorities without "kowtowing" (ITV1918, 18 March 2019).

Developing a State-adjacent Law Society

The economic incentive structure of the solicitor community in Hong Kong reinforces a state-adjacent character of the leadership in the Law Society.

Such structure helps the Law Society stabilise its political agenda and cooperations with both the Hong Kong and Chinese authorities to avoid creating tensions, thus safeguard solicitors' professional interests and secure their comprador status.

Professional interests here are defined as any means of maintaining and advancing the monopolisation of a profession's knowledge, skills, training and standards. The means are supposed to be controlled by a regulatory body. Professional interests are both tangible and intangible. Tangible interests refer to the economic opportunities given by the state, which endorses monopolisation in the market so that members of the profession can enjoy better profit-making. Intangible interests include policies and agreements to secure a professional monopoly, such as training, licensing and standardising professional services. The Law Society needs to advance and sustain professional interests by maintaining collaborations with or co-optation by the state. Thus, political confrontation against the authority is unfavourable.

The Law Society had been expanding market opportunities in mainland China to advance tangible professional interests even before the Hong Kong's sovereignty transfer to China, as the Chinese government implemented the "reform and open door" policy and leveraged Hong Kong as a global gateway to the Chinese market since the 1980s. To do so, the Law Society needed to deepen economic and professional ties with relevant parties in the mainland. These parties are not independent of politics in the mainland, as many of them are governed or observed by the CCP . One indicator of the Law Society's close ties with the mainland Chinese institutions is the number of activities that the Law Society organised or attended in the mainland through its subdivison, namely "the Greater China Legal Affairs Committee" (GCLAC), which is a sub-committee under the Law Society's External Affairs Standing Committee. The GCLAC originated from the China Lawyer Committee under the same standing committee in 1993. It changed its name from China Legal Affairs Committee in 1995 to Mainland Legal Affairs Committee in 1997 and finally renamed as GCLAC in 2012. Legal affairs concerning Macau and Taiwan were covered under the revised terms of reference (Annual Reports of the Law Society 1993, 1995, 1997 and 2012). However, the committee's significant attention has always been on the mainland.

Over the years, the GCLAC has initiated many outbound activities and programmes with law schools in the mainland, set up training programmes for Chinese junior lawyers and trainees, engaged in partnerships and "road-show" promotion programmes with the Hong Kong government in mainland cities, hosted business trips and official visits with lawyer associations and local governments, and organised or attended conferences and forums in different provinces to promote legal services of Hong Kong lawyers (Annual Report of the Law Society 1993–2019).

Another indicator of partnership refers to the number of agreements signed between the Law Society and professional bodies in the mainland. By the end of 2019, the Law Society had signed cooperation agreements and MoUs with 34 lawyer associations in the mainland and the All China Lawyers Association (ACLA) (Annual Report of the Law Society 2019, 38–39). These agreements aim to facilitate solicitor firms in Hong Kong to enter the mainland market, or vice versa, under the Mainland and Hong Kong Closer Economic Partnership Arragement (CEPA). However, unlike Hong Kong, lawyer associations in China are government entities (McMorrow, Liu and Rooij 2017, 267). The Law Society's ties with them are thus not just economic or professional partnerships, but a political co-optation. Such political-economic bonding between the Law Society, the legal service market and those state-led mainland institutions constitutes a significant demand factor for both the leadership and many members of the Law Society to perform publicly conservatively in domestic constitutional and legal controversies.

The critical feature of comprador professionalism lies in the intersection of politics and the market. The priority of stretching economic opportunities in the mainland is also consolidated by the Law Society's leadership. Based on the existing records in the annual reports of the Law Society, a statistical dataset of the presidency in the Law Society from 1997 to 2019 is compiled below (see table 10). It illustrates that many presidents of the Law Society have served in the Standing Committee of External Affairs that oversees the GCLAC and the newly formed Belt and Road Committee for years. Since the sovereignty transfer, more than half of the presidents have served on the council as a member for at least 60 per cent between 1997 and 2019. Seven presidents were members of the GCLAC at least 40 per cent of the time between 1997 and 2019; four of them had fully participated in the Belt and Road Committee since it was created. Their experiences of building ties with China for business development of Hong Kong's solicitor firms, alongside their active engagement in Chinese cross-border economic projects like the BRI, would be a strong motivation for the Law Society council to maintain a depoliticised professional body that would be less confrontational and contentious with the Hong Kong government and the Chinese state. In short, the leadership structure in the Law Society council has consolidated the vision of comprador professionalism in the Law Society for decades.

Table 10. Years of Service of Presidents in the Law Society (1997–2019)

Year	President	Years of Service in the Council (1997–2019)	%	Years of Service in the Standing Committee of External Affairs (1997–2019)	%	Years of Service in the GCLAC Members since 1997 (%)	%	Years of Service in the Belt and Road Committee (2016–2019)	%
2019	Melissa K. Pang	15	65%	18	78%	4	17%	4	100%
2018	Melissa K. Pang	15	65%	18	78%	4	17%	4	100%
2017	Thomas S. T. So	15	65%	8	35%	10	43%	4	100%
2016	Thomas S. T. So	15	65%	8	35%	10	43%	4	100%
2015	Stephen W. S. Hung	17	74%	18	78%	10	43%	4	100%
2014	Stephen W.S. Hung	17	74%	18	78%	10	43%	4	100%
2013	Ambrose Lam	12	52%	8	35%	12	52%	0	0%
2012	Dieter Yih	13	57%	1	4%	0	0%	0	0%
2011	Junius K. Y. Ho	21	91%	5	22%	10	43%	0	0%
2010	Huen Wong	19	83%	13	57%	0	0%	4	100%
2009	Huen Wong	19	83%	13	57%	0	0%	4	100%
2008	Lester G. Huang	12	52%	5	22%	0	0%	0	0%
2007	Lester G. Huang	12	52%	5	22%	0	0%	0	0%
2006	Peter C. L. Lo	19	83%	5	22%	0	0%	0	0%
2005	Peter C.L. Lo	19	83%	5	22%	0	0%	0	0%
2004	Michael J. Lintern-Smith	21	91%	4	17%	0	0%	0	0%
2003	IP Shing Hing	15	65%	11	48%	15	65%	0	0%
2002	IP Shing Hing	15	65%	11	48%	15	65%	0	0%

Year	President	Years of Service in the Council (1997–2019)	%	Years of Service in the Standing Committee of External Affairs (1997–2019)	%	Years of Service in the GCLAC Members since 1997 (%)	%	Years of Service in the Belt and Road Committee (2016–2019)	%
2001	Herbert H.K. Tsoi	9	39%	2	9%	10	43%	0	0%
2000	Herbert H.K. Tsoi	9	39%	2	9%	10	43%	0	0%
1999	Anthony W.K. Chow	8	35%	12	52%	19	83%	0	0%
1998	Anthony W.K. Chow	8	35%	12	52%	19	83%	0	0%
1997	Anthony W.K. Chow	8	35%	12	52%	19	83%	0	0%
1996	Christopher C. Chan	1	4%	0	0%	0	0%	0	0%
1995	Roderick B. Woo	3	13%	3	13%	2	9%	0	0%
1994	Roderick B. Woo	3	13%	3	13%	2	9%	0	0%
1993	Roderick B. Woo	3	13%	3	13%	2	9%	0	0%

Source: Annual Reports of the Law Society of Hong Kong and *Wisenews*

In the past, some former presidents of the Law Society have even engaged in political elections and built political affiliation with the state. Huen Wong and Junius Ho, presidents between 2009 and 2011, had run for the LegCo elections with endorsements by pro-establishment figures and members of the CPPCC in 2008, 2012 and 2016 individually (*Apple Daily* 13 August 2012). Moreover, the other two presidents were the CCP's political consultants during their terms of office. Dieter Yih was a member of the Guangdong Provincial Committee of the CPPCC when he was still presiding over the Law Society in 2013, while Thomas So commenced his office as a member of the National Committee of the CPPCC in 2018 (*Ming Pao* 15 January 2013). The CPPCC appointment is one of the obvious instruments of the United Front Work. The appointments of Yih and So are evident of the CCP's attempt to boost political co-optation with the leadership of the Law Society.

The state-embedded leadership of the Law Society have been less interested in criticising the state, even though progressive voices could be found in the Law Society's subordinate committees. For example, it was revealed in a news report that in 2014, while the Constitutional Affairs and Human Rights Committee passed a draft submission questioning the National People's Congress Standing Committee's (NPCSC) decision on the Chief Executive elections on 31 August, the council did not release it after receiving the submission. Moreover, when the council circulated an email to all members on their opinions of the government-proposed constitutional reform in 2015, they did not mention anything about the draft submission of the constitutional reform proposal. As a result, the council was questioned by members of the Law Society and the public for misleading the internal consultation as the council disregarded the efforts of the responsible committee at all (Lum 2017). Such a move revealed how the council could minimise potential contention with the political authority through bypassing its subordinate committees' stances and arguments.

Regarding intangible professional interests, ever since the 1990s, the Bar and the Law Society have had a constant but subtle contest over their jurisdictions over professional monopoly of the legal sector in Hong Kong. In 1993, the Law Society proposed a fusion of the two branches of the legal profession, that are barristers and solicitors. In the end, it was rejected by the Bar. In 2000, a similar debate between the two professional bodies resumed when the Law Society called for solicitors being entitled to have the right of audience in the High Court, where the right of audience have been long occupied by barristers (Sin 2001, 496–497). Sin correlated these events with the usually ambivalent position of the Law Society towards the government, implying that it sided with the government for its members' interests (Sin 2001, 496–498). The latest attempt of the Law Society to exert greater control of the profession was the council's decision to introduce a joint entrance examination in 2016, making itself the sole provider of qualifying examinations for students receiving a professional legal education (Hung 2016). Nevertheless, the statutory Standing Committee on Legal Education and Training dismissed the proposal in 2018, as the concerned the proposal established a "path to monopoly [of the Law Society]" (Standing Committee on Legal Education and Training 2018). Although the Law Society postponed introducing a new examination afterwards, it did not abandon its decision.

Further, the Law Society proposed an examination of its own, as an alternative route for people who seek to become a legal practitioner in Hong Kong (The Law Society of Hong Kong 29 May 2020). The state is one of the stakeholders in professional control and amending the laws of admission to solicitors. The Law Society, therefore, would have less motivation to challenge the authority and legitimacy of the Hong Kong and Chinese governments to avoid losing support for extending solicitors' professional monopoly.

In the next section, I will look closely at the public discourse on the six themes related to authoritarian legal transplantation and constitutional affairs in Hong Kong.

Professional Discourse in Response to Authoritarian Legal Transplantation

In many instances, the Bar and the Law Society addressed their concerns on legal and constitutional controversies via public statements, submissions and the annual speeches of their leaders in the opening of the legal year. Sometimes, the Bar and the Law Society jointly released statements to restate the importance of judicial independence, and to condemn any personal attacks against individual judges by people who disapproved of judicial decisions.

Although both the Bar and the Law Society emphasise their stances as impartial and politically neutral, their responses to many events of China's authoritarian legal transplantation and constitutional developments in Hong Kong illustrated their divergence in interpreting the concept of the Rule of Law, law and order and attitudes towards the Hong Kong and Chinese political authorities. Public statements by the Bar and the Law Society on significant legal and constitutional controversies between 1997 and 2020 are summarised in the following tables. They are categorised into six themes: (1) constitutional order, (2) constitutional development, (3) the NPCSC's interpretations of and decisions on the Basic Law, (4) indirect legal transplantation by China and the related events, (5) direct legal transplantation and (6) national security. This section will analyse each theme one by one.

Constitutional Order

China has repeatedly attempted to reshape the discourse of Hong Kong's constitutional order in aspects of the relationship between the executive, legislative and judicial branches of the Hong Kong government, the creation of China's overall jurisdiction in Hong Kong, and re-asserting the power of the central authorities to intervene in Hong Kong's legal and constitutional affairs (see chapter 2). These discourses constitute a form of ideological legal transplantation to Hong Kong to dismiss the popular notions of separation of powers and judicial autonomy in the city. While the Bar took an active role in rebuking the discourse from the Chinese authorities, the Law Society responded passively or chose to be silent.

The Bar held a bold view against the claim of "no separation of powers in Hong Kong" and the call for "cooperation of the three branches" of the executive government, the legislature and the judiciary of Hong Kong. In contrast, the Law Society did not publish any statements on this matter. The Bar also took a proactive voice against top Chinese officials' comments on the judgement by the Court of First Instance against the emergency powers of the Chief Executive and a new anti-mask law, promulgated by the same emergency power in 2019, which was pending appeal at that time. The Bar firmly criticised the claim of the Legislative Affairs Commission of the NPCSC that "only the NPCSC could review the constitutionality of laws in Hong Kong" as legally incorrect. Five months after, when the appellant court ruled in favour of the government, the two major central government bodies openly "approved" the judgement. This caused a backlash from the Bar, which released a statement arguing that the official approval from the two bodies were perceived as an interference of "One Country, Two Systems." However, the Law Society responded subtly to this controversy, claiming that it was not supposed to comment on a court case and only stating that no acts should be perceived to undermine judicial independence and the Rule of Law.

The only common ground between the Bar and the Law Society on the disputes regarding Hong Kong's constitutional order was their support for judicial independence after the White Paper on "One Country, Two Systems" was released by China's State Council in 2014. Both legal professional bodies upheld the importance of judges not being part of the "administrators" as the White Paper claimed. That said, it is evident that the Law Society intentionally avoided commenting on the central authorities intervening constitutional matters in Hong Kong, whereas the Bar remained firm in publicly expressing their legal opinions opposite to the government's views (see table 11).

Constitutional Development and Democratic Governance

According to Article 45 of the Basic Law,

> The method for selecting the Chief Executive shall be specified in light of the actual situation in the Hong Kong Special Administrative Region and by the gradual and orderly progress principle. The ultimate aim is the selection of the Chief Executive by universal suffrage upon nomination by a broadly representative nominating committee by democratic procedures.

In 2007, the Bar highlighted the importance of compliance with international standards of universal suffrage in any constitutional proposal. Surprisingly, the Law Society took a further step by proposing the formation of a future "nominating committee" with a sector-specific approach, which could be identical to the composition of the existing Election Committee. The nominating committee should be made up by universal suffrage or of directly elected lawmakers and district councillors. This reflected that the Law Society had supported a greater representativeness in constitutional reforms, just like the Bar. However, the Law Society was silent about post–2014 events that undermined the democratic character of the legislature, which posed adverse effects to the democratic development in Hong Kong. While the Bar was unreservedly critical of the executive-driven disqualification of candidates in a by-election of the LegCo in 2018, as well as the government's decision to postpone the 2020 LegCo election by using the executive's emergency powers, the Law Society did not offer any public pronouncements. In addition, the Law Society avoided commenting on the Department of Justice's decision not to prosecute CY Leung, the former Chief Executive, who was accused of receiving HK$50 million from an Australian engineering firm. However, the Bar criticised the Department of Justice's decision, as they departed from previous practice of seeking independent counsel's advice in this case (see table 12).

NPCSC's Interpretations of and Decisions on the Basic Law

A blunt divergence of the attitude and stance towards the NPCSC's interpretations and decisions on provisions of the Basic Law can be found in the

Table 11. Summary of the Responses of the Bar and the Law Society on Hong Kong's Constitutional Order (1997–2020)

Events	The Hong Kong Bar Association	The Law Society of Hong Kong
Xi Jinping's Comments on "Cooperation of the Three Branches" in Hong Kong (2008)	9 July 2008: Although not attributing Xi's speech to "any intention to interfere with the independence of [the] judiciary," the importance of an independent judiciary in the HKSAR should be recognised, reiterated and affirmed to maintain the Rule of Law and long-term stability and prosperity in Hong Kong.	No response
Release of the State Council's White Paper "On the Practice of "One Country, Two Systems" in the HKSAR (2014)	11 June 2014: Respect for the Rule of Law "means far more than merely "doing things according to law" or "governing according to law," and "judges and judicial officers of the HKSAR are not to be regarded as part of "Hong Kong's administrators" or part of the governance team upon whom a political requirement is imposed."	25 June 2014: "The Rule of Law and independence of the judiciary are indispensable and sacrosanct foundations for the Hong Kong legal system." Expected the government to uphold the principle of which judges "are not regarded as part of the executive authorities." Yet, the White Paper "must be read as a whole."
Comments of the Chinese authorities on court judgements on the "Emergency Regulations Ordinance and Prohibition on Face Covering Regulation" that "the NPCSC is the only body that could decide whether Hong Kong laws comply with the Basic Law"(2019)	19 November 2019: The comments of the NPCSC's Legislative Affairs Commission are "legally incorrect." Any NPCSC's interpretation of the Basic Law "before the conclusion of the entire judicial process" would be read as putting pressure on the judiciary.	21 November 2019: "It is not the practice of the Law Society to comment on individual cases, which may be the subject of an appeal," and "nothing should be said or done that will undermine, or will be perceived to undermine, judicial independence and the Rule of Law."
	14 April 2020: The "expressed approval" from the Hong Kong and Macau Affairs Office and the China Liaison Office in Hong Kong "could easily be perceived as interference in contravention of the principle of one-country, two-systems enshrined in the Basic Law."	

Events	The Hong Kong Bar Association	The Law Society of Hong Kong
The Status and Functions of the PRC Liaison Office in Hong Kong (2020)	20 April 2020: The Hong Kong and Macau Affairs Office and the China Liaison Office in Hong Kong are "bound by the Basic Law, including the prohibition of interference in the internal affairs of the HKSAR." There is also no provision in the Basic Law that "confers [the two bodies] the power of supervision over affairs which the HKSAR administers on its own."	No response
	27 April 2020: Sent a letter to the Secretary for Constitutional and Mainland Affairs about the constitutional position of the status of the China Liaison Office in Hong Kong.	
	15 May 2020: Sent a follow-up letter to the Secretary for Constitutional and Mainland Affairs, who has yet to reply to the Bar's letter.	
Comments of the Chinese and Hong Kong authorities on the notion of 'separation of powers" in Hong Kong (2020)	2 September 2020: The judiciary should not be regarded as part of a governance team. The notion of "no separation of powers principle in the HKSAR," made by the Chief Executive and secretary for education, is "unfounded and inconsistent with the unambiguous provisions of the Basic Law prescribing and delineating the functions of the three branches of government."	No response

Sources: The Hong Kong Bar Association, the Law Society of Hong Kong and K. Lee 2017b

Table 12. Summary of the Responses of the Bar and the Law Society on Constitutional Development and Democratic Governance (1997–2020)

Events	The Hong Kong Bar Association	The Law Society of Hong Kong
Constitutional Development in Hong Kong (2004)	15 April 2004: The government failed to implement a wider consultation on the Chief Executive's report on constitutional development to NPCSC before submission.	27 September 2004: Members of the Election Committee should increase from 800 to 1,200; additional members can be elected by 400 district council constituencies.
	18 March 2005: Corporate voting in the Election Committee and functional constituencies in the Legislative Council should be abolished.	
The Green Paper on Constitutional Reform in Hong Kong (2007)	24 August 2007: Elections of the Chief Executive and the Legislative Council should be "fully in line with Article 25 of the ICCPR" and should not "contain any discriminatory distinctions or unreasonable restrictions."	10 October 2007: A 'sector-specific approach to a broadly representative nominating committee" is inconsistent with the Basic Law on universal suffrage of Chief Executive elections. Nominating committee should be formed by universal suffrage or directly elected lawmakers and/or district council members.
Constitutional Reform on Chief Executive Election (2014)	28 April 2014: Disagreed with forms of nomination "other than nomination by a broadly representative nominating committee in accordance with democratic procedures." Corporate voting, as a usual practice in elections of the Election Committee in Hong Kong, should be abolished in methods of selecting the nominating committee.	5 May 2014: Civil nomination or nomination by political parties are inconsistent with the Basic Law, so are any proposals that "waters down the constitutional role of the nominating committee."

Events	The Hong Kong Bar Association	The Law Society of Hong Kong
Disqualification of Candidates in By-election of the Legislative Council of the HKSAR (2018)	14 February 2018: the substantive power of the returning officer, as affirmed in previous court ruling, was "regrettably equivalent to the introduction of a political screening process for any prospective candidate, and there is no fair, open, certain and clear procedure to regulate this process," and "the requirement of "upholding the Basic Law" is a vague and imprecise political concept, which has now to be interpreted and administered by a civil servant under a closed-door inquiry."	No response
Department of Justice's Decision Not to Prosecute Former Chief Executive CY Leung (2018)	21 December 2018: The Department of Justice's "failure to instruct and obtain independent counsel's advice represents a departure from past convention" in cases that involve senior government officials, and which were perceived to be of a politically sensitive nature. Thus, it should "review its decision after obtaining independent counsel's advice."	No response
The Hong Kong Government's Decision to Postpone the Legislative Council Election (2020)	2 August 2020: The legal and evidential basis of the government's decision to postpone elections was in doubt, and the government did not consult experts and civil society about the decision. The government's decision to seek the NPCSC to resolve the question of the term of office of the Legislative Council, arising from postponing the election, was "contrary to the principles of legality and legal certainty" and "degraded" the Rule of Law in Hong Kong.	No response

Sources: The Hong Kong Bar Association, the Law Society of Hong Kong and K. Lee 2017b

public statements between the Bar and the Law Society as early as in 1999. While the Bar openly expressed its legal arguments against the actions of the NPCSC, the Law Society often took a state-adjacent approach in giving comments on the substance of the matters. It even took firm positions to justify the NPCSC's actions occasionally.

In the first interpretation of the Basic Law by the NPCSC in 1999, which dealt with the judgement of the Court of Final Appeal on the right of abode in Hong Kong, the Bar made a firm statement disapproving the Hong Kong government's initiative to seek the NPCSC's re-interpretation of the relevant provisions in the Basic Law, as this attempt contravened the requirement in Article 158 of the Basic Law that only the Court of the Final Appeal should seek the NPCSC's interpretation. However, the Law Society declared that it was lawful for the NPCSC to interpret the Basic Law, and "it was up to the government to make a political decision." Without giving a clear position on the procedures, contents and impact of the interpretation of the Basic Law, the Law Society was indirectly endorsing the acts of the political authorities. In subsequent interpretations of the Basic Law by the NPCSC, such as the interpretation related to the resignation of the first Chief Executive in 2005 and that related to the validity of oath-taking by two newly-elected members of the LegCo, the Law Society only repeated its call for the NPCSC to "exercise restraint" when enforcing its power. On the contrary, the Bar relentlessly opposed these interpretations, expressing its disappointment and deep regrets for the sovereign state's acts.

Contrasts between the Bar and the Law Society were also tangible in their views over the NPCSC's decisions related to the Basic Law after the release of the NPCSC's decision to affirm the constitutionality of the co-location arrangement in an express railway station in Hong Kong in mid–2017. The proposed arrangement allows laws of China to apply inside the port area. The Bar issued a strong statement against the co-location proposal, arguing that the allowance of the direct application of Chinese laws inside the railway station has no convincing legal basis. Nonetheless, the Law Society only suggested the government to "clarify the legal basis" of the decision on one hand but supported the benefits of the co-location arrangement on the other. In 2020, the Law Society repeatedly used similar wordings after the NPCSC decided to empower the executive government of Hong Kong by entitling it to disqualify any lawmakers allegedly breaching national security. However, the Bar boldly disapproved of the NPCSC decision as undermining due process and fairness in the principle of the Rule of Law. In short, the Bar repeatedly opposed the NPCSC's interventions in Hong Kong's constitutional affairs. The Law Society, however, stayed away from substantial debates on those issues or aligned itself with the acts of the political authorities (see table 13).

Indirect Legal Transplantation and Resistance from Civil Society

Chapter 2 explained the government's introduction of the Extradition Law Amendment Bill (ELAB) in 2019, which served as an indirect legal transplantation of China to Hong Kong since the amendment allows extraditing fugitives to the Chinese justice system, and the Hong Kong jurisdiction would have little say in the sovereign's requests. The Bar was very active in commenting and debating the concerns of the legislation, while the Law Society only formally expressed its position once. The Bar repeatedly disapproved of the government proposal, arguing that an extradition agreement with China would undermine the Rule of Law in Hong Kong, in light of the poor track record of the Chinese justice system. The Bar had been calling for more comprehensive public consultation and not rushing the legislation before the proposed second reading of the bill. After the mass demonstration and the following clashes outside the LegCo complex on 12 June 2019, the Bar's stance evolved further when it requested that the government withdraw the bill and promise not to introduce it without full and open consultation.

Unlike the Bar's course of action, the Law Society only called on the government "not to rush the legislative exercise" for the sake of a more extensive consultation. In the same statement, the Law Society attached a document that quoted members' opposing views of the amendments as "equally valuable views" of the Law Society. Since the Law Society did not endorse the opposing views, it could be immune from having any bold standpoint regarding the bill. Furthermore, the Law Society did not call for a withdrawal of the bill, which was a popular demand yet unfavourable to the government's position. Instead, the Law Society released a statement to express regret over the "violent conflict" after the clash between riot police and protestors on 12 June 2019.

As the Anti-ELAB Movement was initially highly characterised as an opposition to China's extradition, it is also worth addressing the difference between the Bar and the Law Society regarding their demands and attitudes towards the Anti-ELAB movement. First, the Bar condemned different actors during the movement in 2019, ranging from protestors who breached court injunctions by blocking the airport and other public transport systems to organised groups of gangsters who attacked civilians and the police force that was allegedly abusing its power against protestors and lawyers in police stations. Second, the Bar highlighted the comprehensive features of the Rule of Law after the protestors' siege of the LegCo complex on 1 July 2019. While

Table 13. Summary of the Responses of the Bar and the Law Society on the NPCSC's Interpretations of and Decisions on the Basic Law (1997–2020)

Events	The Hong Kong Bar Association	The Law Society of Hong Kong
NPCSC's 1st Interpretation of the Basic Law on the Right of Abode (1999)	5 May 1999: The interpretation will 'seriously and irreversibly damage judicial independence."	17 May 1999: The NPCSC's interpretation of Basic Law provision is "lawful," and it was "up to the government to make a political decision."
	18 May 1999: Deeply regretted the government's decision to seek the NPCSC's interpretation of the Basic Law.	
NPCSC's 3rd Interpretation of the Basic Law on the Length of Terms of Office of the Chief Executive (2005)	14 April 2005: Disappointment of the interpretation by the NPCSC and the decision of the acting Chief Executive to request for such interpretation.	28 April 2005: The interpretation "was not necessary" and it is preferable that it "be resolved through the Hong Kong courts." Any interpretation of the Basic Law "must be used with caution and restraint."
NPCSC's 5th Interpretation of the Basic Law on Oath-taking of Public Officials (2016)	2 November 2016: The interpretation would "deal a severe blow" to the independence of the judiciary and the power of final adjudication of the Hong Kong court as legal proceedings of the issue commence.	8 November 2016: Frequent interpretations of the Basic Law by the NPCSC would undermine the independence of the judiciary, and the NPCSC should exercise restraint in invoking its power.
	7 November 2016: "Deep regrets" for the interpretation by the NPCSC as it is unnecessary and "indeed would do more harm than good" to issue the interpretation "in haste at this juncture."	
NPCSC's Decision on Method of Selection of the Chief Executive of the HKSAR (2014)	(The Bar did not respond.)	(The Law Society did not respond.)

Events	The Hong Kong Bar Association	The Law Society of Hong Kong
NPCSC's Decision on Co-location Arrangement of West Kowloon Station of the Guangzhou-Shenzhen-Hong Kong Express Rail Link in Hong Kong (2017–2018)	16 September 2017: The Bar "has not yet made a decision or adopted a position on whether the co-location arrangement is or is not permissible under the Basic Law."	18 January 2018: Recognised the 'social and economic benefits as well as the advantages of the Express Rail Link and the co-location arrangement," but its legal basis should be clarified by the Hong Kong government.
	19 October 2017: "The Bar is monitoring the development closely and will publish its views if and when appropriate."	
	28 December 2017: the Bar is "appalled" by the NPCSC's decision, which is "the most retrograde step to date in the implementation of the Basic Law, and severely undermines public confidence in "One Country, Two Systems" and the Rule of Law in the HKSAR," and is "unconvincing and unsatisfactory" in providing a "firm legal basis."	
NPCSC's Decision on Qualification of Lawmakers in Hong Kong the Power of the Chief Executive in Disqualifying Lawmakers (2020)	12 November 2020: The NPCSC's decision, which was apparently sought by the Hong Kong government, greatly impaired legal certainty in Hong Kong as the government applied the decision in a retrospective manner and based its decision to disqualify four lawmakers "entirely on the decisions of the relevant returning officers." Thus "basic principles of fairness and due process inherent" in the Rule of Law were violated.	13 November 2020: The government should address the concerns of the legal basis of disqualifying lawmakers, due process, transparency and accountability, alongside legality of the empowerment of the HKSAR government to disqualify members of the Legislative Council.

Sources: The Hong Kong Bar Association, the Law Society of Hong Kong and K. Lee 2017b

the government strongly condemned the siege as breaking the Rule of Law in Hong Kong, the Bar emphasised that the Rule of Law is not just about law and order; "respect for human rights and civil liberties, an open and accountable executive, effective checks and balances under the doctrine of separation of powers, and an independent judiciary" also constitute the Rule of Law with equal weight. Third, the Bar had advocated six times for setting up an independent commission of inquiry by the laws of Hong Kong to investigate police administration and the causes of the movement. It emphasised that an independent inquiry could protect witnesses with immunity from lawsuits and would be led by a judge.

The Law Society mainly targeted protestors in its official statements, condemning the unlawful violence thrice. It did not pay any attention to the alleged police brutality in the public statements. Regarding the call for a commission of inquiry, the Law Society suggested that an investigation is not necessarily statutory, although a statutory independent commission of inquiry enjoys the power to summon witnesses and court evidence under the Commission Inquiry Ordinance (Cap. 86, Article 4(1)). Overall, while the Bar had repeatedly emphasised the comprehensive nature of the Rule of Law in its statements related to the protest events and public order policing, the Law Society paid more attention to addressing the importance of law and order, which was in alignment with the government position of "stopping violence and chaos," and to avoid recommending a formation of a statutory independent inquiry, which was in line with the demands of protestors and the major public opinion at that time (see table 14). The Law Society's position was favourable to the government, which repeatedly objected to setting up a commission of inquiry to investigate the policing of the Anti-ELAB Movement (Pang and Wu 2020).

Direct Legal Transplantation and National Security

Two events of China's direct authoritarian legal transplantation to Hong Kong revealed the convergence and divergence of views and responses between the Bar and the Law Society. The first instance refers to the local legislation of the national anthem bill in 2020, which was three years after a national anthem law was enacted in mainland China by the NPCSC. Neither the Bar nor the Law Society made statements questioning the legitimacy and necessity of the NPCSC's demands for implementing those national laws in Hong Kong. They did not fundamentally reject the implementations that can punish citizens merely by booing the national anthem. Instead, they provided technical suggestions for the national anthem bill as a domestic adaptation of the national legislation. Their suggestions and concerns on

Table 14. Summary of the Responses of the Bar and the Law Society on Indirect Legal Transplantation (1997–2020)

Events	The Hong Kong Bar Association	The Law Society of Hong Kong
Introduction of the Fugitive Offenders And Mutual Legal Assistance in Criminal Matters Legislation (Amendment) Bill (known as the Extradition Law Amendment Bill) (2019)	4 March 2019: Since 1997 the HKSAR government has been 'seeking to put in place *ad hoc* rendition arrangements in apparent breach of its commitment for full consultation on this delicate matter." The proposal removed the oversight power of the legislature. Thus, the proposal "potentially undermined the reputation of Hong Kong as a free and safe city governed by the Rule of Law" and could not 'secure comparable minimum rights enjoyed by persons" in Hong Kong's criminal justice and prison systems. 2 April 2019: "Not supportive" of the government proposal. The HKSAR government should not rush into the legislative process that would "undermine the international reputation of Hong Kong." A "full and wide-ranging consultation" for the public was needed. 6 June 2019: Published a Q and A like brief guide on the key issues of the bill for the public. 12 June 2019: Urged the government to withdraw the bill for a full and proper consultation" given the "widespread and deep-seated public unease with the bill" as reflected in the "massive turnout at the protest against the bill on 9th June 2019." 21 June 2019: Agreed that the bill would "fundamentally imperil the operation of the Rule of Law in Hong Kong." Urged the government, which just suspended the bill, "to withdraw the bill and make a commitment that it will not introduce any legislation on the question of surrender of fugitives and cross-border legal assistance without full and open consultation involving the Hong Kong public and others who have an interest in the subject matter."	5 June 2019: The HKSAR government should not "rush the legislative exercise" as there 'should be a comprehensive review of the extradition regime in Hong Kong and an extensive consultation with the stakeholders and the community." The Law Society received different views, and there were also "equally valuable" views in the Law Society that the legislation did not address the concerns of the differences between the criminal justice system of the HKSAR and that of mainland China.

Events	The Hong Kong Bar Association	The Law Society of Hong Kong
On Protest Events and Violent Conflicts in the Anti-extradition Movement and the Related Public Order Policing (2019)	5 July 2019: It is important to maintain law and order, but the Rule of Law encompasses equally important components other than compliance with the law, such as "respect for human rights and civil liberties, an open and accountable executive, effective checks and balances under the doctrine of separation of powers, and an independent judiciary."	13 June 2019: 'sad and regrettable" regarding the "violent conflicts" in Admiralty and Central districts of H^{on}g Kong on 12th June 2019.
	24 July 2019: Condemned "the violent and indiscriminate attacks on ordinary unarmed passers-by, rail passengers and members of the press at the Yuen Long West Rail Station and its vicinity on Sunday night by an organized group of gangsters."	2 July 2019: 'strongly condemns the violent siege of the Legislative Council building on 1 July 2019 by some protesters who attacked the police and vandalised public property."
	2 September 2019: Condemned "the acts of individuals over the past weekend which constituted serious obstruction and interference in the operation of the Hong Kong International Airport and the MTR and damage to airport and MTR property in open defiance of injunctions granted by the court."	3 September 2019: Condemned "all forms of unlawful violence." Reminded anyone disobeying the court injunction by paralysing the airport and other public transport they would be in contempt of court as a 'serious matter." Urged the law enforcement to investigate concerns of the police allegedly exerting unnecessary force against passengers inside MTR stations.
	3 September 2019: Condemned "any abuse of power by the police force." Alleged the police of "using excessive force to disperse protestors and in making arrests" as shown in television and video footage, obstruction of legal assistance to arrested protestors at police stations, and violations of the Police General Orders.	

Events	The Hong Kong Bar Association	The Law Society of Hong Kong
On Popular Demand for an Independent Commission of Inquiry into the Anti-Extradition Movement and the Related Public Order Policing (2019)	21 June 2019: Believed that "an independent commission of inquiry be set up to fully investigate the relevant events" and "guidelines on the use of force by the police against protestors" would be fair and "of great value" to the public and the law enforcement. 5 July 2019: The government should set up a statutory independent inquiry. The Independent Police Complaint Council could not meet "the scope of powers and potential areas of investigation of a statutory independent inquiry," and lacks the power to protect witnesses who do not enjoy immunity from lawsuits. 24 July 2019: Repeated the call for an independent inquiry of the administration of the police force. 2 September: Repeated the call for "the establishment of an independent commission of inquiry to look into the events occurring since June [2019]." 3 September: "An independent inquiry will offer the truth that the public and the police deserve and may restore public confidence in our police force." 14 January 2020: Sent a letter to the Chief Executive and released a 'summary guide" of the Bar's call for "establishing a commission of inquiry into the social unrest in Hong Kong."	1 August 2019: "Inquiries may be conducted in a variety of ways and not necessarily by way of a statutory one." Provided suggestions to the future investigation by the Independent Police Complaint Council.

Sources: The Hong Kong Bar Association and the Law Society of Hong Kong

the ambiguity of terms being used in the bills, such as "disrespectful" of the national anthem, reflected their eagerness to harmonise the national laws with the common law principles (see table 15).

The second instance refers to the NPCSC's imposition of a new national security law (the NSL) for Hong Kong in 2020. In response to the legal imposition, the Bar and the Law Society differed twofold. The Bar released eight public statements and letters to relevant government officials to express their worries about the "problematic features" of the substance and the legislative process of the NSL. The national security law was drafted secretly, meaning no consultations were held for the public, civil society, and legal professional bodies. In contrast, the Law Society only published two statements.

The Bar went further to bluntly question and to challenge the legislation. The Bar's disapproval of the legislation included a lack of transparency in the drafting process, the establishment of a national security agency being directly subject to the central government in Hong Kong, and the power of the Chief Executive in designating judges to try cases related to national security. Furthermore, the Bar published a "Q and A" (Question and Answer) to raise public awareness of the legislation. The Bar also openly demanded the Chinese and Hong Kong authorities to release the draft bill before it was passed in China. After several failed attempts to fulfil its demands, the Bar heavily criticised the legislation. It stated that the new national security law "erodes the high degree of autonomy" in Hong Kong and undermines "independent judicial power, the enjoyment of fundamental rights and liberties, and the vesting of legislative and executive power in local institutions."

For the Law Society, despite its concern over the Chief Executive's power to designate judges in trials of national security, its public pronouncements were expressed in a lenient manner, affirming the power of the NPC to institute laws for safeguarding national security, and "respectfully requesting" that the NPCSC take the Law Society's suggestions into account. The statements of the Law Society did not challenge the legislation per se as undermining judicial independence and the Rule of Law in Hong Kong. They only asked the Chinese authorities to "exercise restraint upon invoking its power under the Chinese constitution" (see table 16).

Conclusion

Overall, the above comparisons illustrate similarities and differences between the Bar and the Law Society when they engaged in public debate and provided legal opinions to the governments of Hong Kong and China on

Table 15. Summary of the Responses of the Bar and the Law Society on Direct Legal Transplantation (1997–2020)

Events	The Hong Kong Bar Association	The Law Society of Hong Kong
National Anthem Bill (2019)	2 April 2019: Accepted that certain disrespectful behaviours against the national anthem should be prohibited by law, but "if and when conduct is to be criminalised, the prohibited conduct should be clearly defined in compliance with the principle of certainty of the law" and should not "unduly restrict citizens" constitutional right to freedom of expression." The usual limitation period of prosecution should be applied to maintain public confidence in the Rule of Law.	21 May 2019: The proposed "two-year period after the alleged crime has been committed" was too long, and the terms in the legislation such as 'solemnly," "disrespectful" and "dignity" need clearer definition to uphold legal certainty and predictability as paramount in criminal law.

Sources: The Hong Kong Bar Association and the Law Society of Hong Kong

Table 16. Summary of the Responses of the Bar and the Law Society on National Security (1997–2020)

Events	The Hong Kong Bar Association	The Law Society of Hong Kong
Proposed Legislation of National Security under Article 23 of the Basic Law (2002–2003)	22 July 2002: Any legislation of Article 23 should comply with the Basic Law and international human rights conventions, and the government should enact the laws itself. Also, existing laws are sufficient to prohibit crimes listed in Article 23. 9 December 2002: Disagreed with the government proposal and regarded it as failing to comply with "the minimum standards contained in the ICCPR and ICESCR" and the Johannesburg Principle, and the drafting in the legislation is ambiguous and loose. 13 February 2003: The first and second readings of the bill should be deferred, allowing room for public discussion. 4 July 2003: (After the 500,000 citizens" rally on 1st July) The bill "represents a real threat to the rights and freedoms of the residents of Hong Kong and regretted the government's refusal to make provision for public interest." The government should "withhold the resumption of the second reading of the bill."	18 December 2002: The HKSAR "has a constitutional obligation to enact laws pursuant to Article 23." 12 June 2003: "There appears to be no need to rush into legislation. LegCo should adopt a more sensible timetable." (The Law Society did not make further statements after the 1 July rally and the further revisions of the bill on 4 July.)

Events	The Hong Kong Bar Association	The Law Society of Hong Kong
Implementation of the Law of the People's Republic of China on Safeguarding National Security in the HKSAR (2020)	25 May 2020: The proposed legislation had some "worrying and problematic features" and "caused deep unease in the local and international community." Urged the HKSAR government to address the "fundamental constitutional and legal concerns" of the legislation. 2 June 2020: A "meaningful public consultation on the proposed legislation with the public in the HKSAR is crucial," and expressed the hope "to be provided with a copy of the draft legislation when it is ready" to provide "constructive comments on its form and content." 12 June 2020: Offered suggestions for the principles, forms and contents of the proposed legislation by the NPCSC. Any national security agency of the Central People's Government in the HKSAR, together with their personnel, should abide by the laws of the HKSAR, and should not have any law enforcement powers, and should not be granted any civil and criminal immunity under the laws of the HKSAR. 19 June 2020: The NPCSC should "disclose the draft legislation for consideration by the public in the HKSAR as soon as possible." Urged the Chief Executive to make public "the contents of the proposed national security law, if that has not already been done, in good time before it is brought into force." Also released a Q and A on the proposed national security law to the public.	11 June 2020: Recognised the NPC under the Chinese constitution "has the power to decide on and to institute a law for maintaining national security," and considered the NPC should "exercise restraint in invoking its power under the constitution to introduce laws to be applied to the HKSAR." Provided some suggestions of NPCSC's preparation of the legislation. 24 June 2020: The Chief Executive should follow the recommendation of the Judicial Officers Recommendation Commission to designate judges to handle cases concerning national security. "Respectfully requested" the NPCSC "to take into consideration the proposals" of the Law Society's preliminary observation.

Events	The Hong Kong Bar Association	The Law Society of Hong Kong
	23 June 2020: The power of the Chief Executive to designate judges to try national security criminal offences is "contrary to the intent and spirit of the Basic Law" and threatens "perceived or actual judicial independence."	
	29 June 2020: The draft national security law has yet to be made public thus the secretary for constitutional and mainland affairs and the secretary of justice should "outline to the legal profession the important features of the national security law" urgently.	
	1 July 2020: Provisions of the national security law operate to "erode the high degree of autonomy guaranteed to the HKSAR under the Basic Law and the Sino-British Joint Declaration" and "to undermine core pillars of the "One Country Two Systems" model including independent judicial power, the enjoyment of fundamental rights and liberties, and the vesting of legislative and executive power in local institutions."	
	3 July 2020: An authentic English version of the new national security law is "an urgent need."	

Sources: The Hong Kong Bar Association, the Law Society of Hong Kong and K. Lee 2017b

policy and legislative matters. The divergence of the two legal professional bodies' understanding of the Rule of Law, and of their positioning towards the government's actions and policies on legislative and constitutional matters are ostensible. The Bar's public discourse consistently addressed the importance of the Rule of Law, which in its view, is more than just upholding law and order. The Bar was outspoken and did not refrain from publicly questioning the government's proposed legislation, public speeches, and actions that challenged conventional practice and understanding of judicial independence and the Rule of Law in Hong Kong. In many instances outlined above, the Bar's public statements have more significant publicity than the Law Society, given the Bar's track record of defending civil liberties in the early 1990s and its reputation of independence.

In contrast, the Law Society is considerably more cautious and tends to exercise restraint in its public discourse on legal and constitutional controversies in Hong Kong. It frequently expressed support of the Chinese sovereignty's intervention in constitutional matters in Hong Kong. It repeatedly refrained from commenting on the substance of legal and constitutional disputes, preferring to call for the political authorities to practice self-restraint. The Law Society sometimes opted not to give any official comments on politically sensitive legal issues and chose to stand with the government, which can be found in the Law Society's public pronouncements against democratic protestors.

The divergence between the Bar and the Law Society can also be discovered in the speeches of the leaders of the two professional bodies at the opening of the legal year. In 2020, the chairman of the Bar, Philip Dykes, paid tribute to barristers and solicitors who provided legal assistance to arrested protestors at police stations during the Anti-ELAB Movement, as well as engaged in criminal defence on behalf of the charged protestors. Dykes called for better measures to safeguard arrestees' constitutional rights of access to lawyers (Dykes 2020). The speech by the president of the Law Society, Melissa Pang, however, stressed the principle of obedience to the law as "non-negotiable and uncompromisable." Pang asserted, "every wilful disobedience of the law is an erosion on our Rule of Law". Although both leaders disapproved of unlawful violence in protest events, the Bar's speech focused on the legal rights of the arrested protestors. On the other hand, the Law Society's position was in alignement with the government's priority of "restoring law and order" (*Channel News Asia* 10 December 2019).

As this chapter explained in the beginning, although professional bodies like the Bar and Law Society could be outspoken in political and legal controversies in Hong Kong, their nature as professional and regulatory bodies of the legal profession would prevent them from going too far to fight against the Hong Kong government, which has the absolute power to exercise professional control against the Bar and the Law Society, such as diminishing lawyers' professional autonomy through legislative amendments.

State-Bar relations in Hong Kong can serve as a backdrop of why and how local liberal and activist lawyers carried out resistance. Under the unfavourable power structure between the state and legal professional bodies, some activist lawyers focused on utilising their legal expertise outside the "establishment": they preferred to invest their legal capital in civil society development and democratisation movement. However, some of them still chose to struggle for an official position within their respective legal professional bodies to challenge the state-adjacent or comprador-like culture within professional bodies, promote their liberal values within the establishment, as well as to resist authoritarian rules intervening in the Bar and the Law Society.

In short, these institutional constraints did not stop individual lawyers from exercising their political agency. Lawyers' public spirit and legal activism have been repeatedly engendered by a widening group of activists or political lawyers in the democratic movement of Hong Kong. In particular, critical events in Hong Kong's legal and constitutional development dissimilated threats and fostered the awakening of lawyers' political agency. In the following chapters, I will analyse how Hong Kong's activist lawyers engaged in civil society empowerment, in providing legal support for protestors as part of anti-authoritarian resistance, and in contesting leadership in the Bar and the Law Society through running for the their council elections.

References

"A Conversion with the Honourable Chief Justice Geoffrey Ma Tao-li." *GBM* 2020. International Bar Association, November 10. Accessed January 3, 2021. https://ibanet-org.zoom.us/rec/play/MF6R_RoimgwNrFX01KCsg85vYXE7CFnd5dhjwycPDq6P7hHWxpJgLgb5sZWcBUz_1BqgzcsfB7GqzZQp.xj_4gEk-DPnS_ZFW?startTime=1604995208000&_x_zm_rtaid=NjgEmUyKTnm3yQKW8Mfm-Q.1605107701848.392f7b76476a21cabcade74076a67a57&_x_zm_rhtaid=848.

"Bèi zhǐ yǔ dà lu shī gōng huì běi dà kè chéng 'nào shuāng bāo' zhì diào zhěng, Tán Yǔn Zhī chì Yú Ruò Wēi zī xùn cuò." 2018. *Ming Pao Instant News*, August 30. Accessed January 30, 2021. Archived on file with the author.

Code of Conduct 2020. The Hong Kong Bar Association. Last updated 4 June. Accessed January 12, 2021. https://www.hkba.org/content/code-conduct.

Comprehensive Review of Legal Education and Training in Hong Kong: Final Report of the Consultants. 2018. Standing Committee on Legal Education and Training of the Hong Kong Special Administrative Region, April. Accessed January 27, 2021. https://www.sclet.gov.hk/eng/pdf/final2018.pdf.

"Dà lu shī gōng huì shí qián zhǔ xí quàn tuì, Yuán Guó Qiáng sǐ lài." 2008. *Apple Daily,* 18 January, A02.

Dykes SC, Philip. 2020a. "Speech Given at the Opening of the Legal Year." Hong Kong Bar Association, January 13. Accessed January 26, 2021. Archived on file with the author.

The Essentials of the Common Law: Public Law Course Reports 2011–13. Peking University Rule of Law Research Centre and the Hong Kong Bar Association.

The Essentials of the Common Law: Public Law Course Reports 2014. Peking University Rule of Law Research Centre and the Hong Kong Bar Association.

The Essentials of the Common Law: Public Law Course Reports 2015. Peking University Rule of Law Research Centre and the Hong Kong Bar Association.

"Fǎ lu jiè: Wáng Guì Xun huò dà duī 'hóng' rén tí míng." 2012. *Apple Daily,* 13 August, A06.

"Hong Kong Leader Carrie Lam Does Not Rule Out Reshuffle, Says Focus Is Restoring Order." 2019. *Channel News Asia,* December 10. Accessed January 26, 2021. Archived on file with the author.

The Hong Kong Solicitors' Guide to Professional Conduct. 2013. The Law Society of Hong Kong. Accessed January 13, 2021. https://www.hklawsoc.org.hk/en/Support-Members/Professional-Support/Professional-Guide/The-hong-kong-solicitors-guide--to-professional-conduct--volume-1.

Hung, Stephen. 2016. "Ceremonial Opening of the Legal Year 2016: Speech by Mr. Stephen Hung, President of the Law Society of Hong Kong." The Law Society of Hong Kong, January 11.

Jones, Carol. 2010. "Legal Education in Hong Kong: Producing the Producers." In *Legal Education in Asia: Globalization, Change and Contexts,* edited by Stacey Steele and Kathryn Taylor. Routledge.

The Law Society of Hong Kong Annual Reports 1998–2019. The Law Society of Hong Kong.

The Law Society of Hong Kong. 2020a. "Statement by the Law Society of Hong Kong on Proposals for the Law Society Examination and the Common Entrance Examination under Rule 7(a) of the Trainee Solicitors Rules Cap. 159J." The Law Society of Hong Kong, May 29. Accessed January 27, 2021. https://www.hklawsoc.org.hk/-/media/HKLS/Press-statement/EN/2020/20200529a_EN.pdf?rev=e7bc550a8050413ea915cc090266b6ac&hash=7D698030615D85637A14D015D1F0BB44.

Lee, Karen M. Y. 2017b. "Lawyers as an Interest Group in Hong Kong's Democracy Movement." In *Interest Groups and the New Democracy Movement in Hong Kong,* edited by Sonny Shiu-Hing Lo. Routledge.

Lee, Martin. 2018. "Wǒ shì fǒu yǐ bèi tǒng zhàn liǎo?" *Apple Daily*, January 10. Accessed January 29, 2021. Archived on file with the author.

Loh, Christine. 2018. *Underground Front: The Chinese Communist Party in Hong Kong, Second Edition*. Hong Kong University Press.

"Lu shī huì huì cháng dāng yuè zhèng xié rě zhì yí." 2013. *Ming Pao Daily News*, 15 January, A02.

Lum, Alvin. 2017. "Zhèng gǎi zī xún zāo fù hé, dà lu shī gōng huì zēng 'zǒu wèi' huí yīng." *CitizenNews*, September 16. Accessed January 29, 2021. Archived on file with the author.

Lum, Alvin. 2021. "Zài zuì huài de shí dài bān huí xiāng gang——Xià Bó Yì (Paul Harris)." *CitizenNews*, January 30. Accessed January 31, 2021. Archived on file with the author.

McMorrow, Judith, Sida Liu, and Benjamin Van Rooij. 2017. "Lawyer Discipline in an Authoritarian Regime: Empirical Insights from Zhejiang Province, China." *Georgetown Journal of Legal Ethics* 30 (Spring): 267–300.

Pang, Jessie, and Sarah Wu. 2020. "Hong Kong Leader Rejects Protesters' Call for Independent Police Probe." *Reuters*, May 15. Accessed January 24, 2021. https://reut.rs/30dodIQ.

Sin, Wai Man. 2001. "Law, Politics and Professional Projects: The Legal Profession in Hong Kong." *Social and Legal Studies* 10 (4): 483–504.

Tam SC, Winnie. 2016. "Speech of the Chairman of the Hong Kong Bar Association Winnie Tam SC, at the Opening of the Legal Year." The Hong Kong Bar Association, January 11. Accessed January 29, 2021. Archived on file with the author.

Tam SC, Winnie. 2017. "Report on Committee on China Practice Development 2017." The Hong Kong Bar Association, December. Accessed January 29, 2021. Archived on file with the author.

Wong, Max W. L. 2017. *Re-ordering Hong Kong: Decolonisation and the Hong Kong Bill of Rights Ordinance*. Wildy, Simmonds and Hill Publishing.

"Xiāng gǎng dà lu shī gōng huì zhǔ xí chū rèn zhèng xié wěi yuán yǐn qǐ zhì yí." 2008. *Radio Free Asia*, January 6. Accessed January 29, 2021. https://www.rfa.org/cantonese/news/hongkong_politics_beijing-20080116.html.

5. Organised Lawyers in Civil Society Empowerment

Abstract: This chapter examines how Hong Kong's activist lawyers resisted authoritarian legal transplantation by empowering civil society through the Progressive Lawyers Group (PLG) and Law Lay Dream (LLD). It explores their origins in the Umbrella Movement, contrasting their approaches: the PLG focused on public legal education, media advocacy, and social mobilisation, while LLD emphasised vernacularised legal commentaries and grassroots engagement. Both groups enhanced civil society's legal literacy, provided legal training, and democratised the profession by nurturing liberal values among young lawyers. Despite challenges in sustaining leadership and balancing activism with professionalism, their efforts fostered resilience within the legal and civil communities, creating a "middle democracy" that bridges professional expertise with grassroots resistance against authoritarian governance.

Keywords: Activist Lawyers, Legal Education, Mobilisation, Middle Democracy, Human Rights, Rule of Law Culture

Social movements often promote or resist changes to the existing order, whereas lawyers, as a state-protected monopoly in the legal service market, tend to favour the status quo (Halliday 2005, 375). In many instances, however, lawyers with public spirit are willing to get involved in political activism, social mobilisation and civil resistance. They are usually considered as activist lawyers. How do they engage in political advocacy and social movement while upholding legal professionalism?

This chapter explains how activist lawyers in Hong Kong are organised outside the legal establishment to resist China's authoritarian legal transplantation. I compare two activist lawyer organisations in Hong Kong, namely the Progressive Lawyers Group (hereafter PLG) and Law Lay Dream (hereafter LLD). The PLG was formed in 2014 and disbanded in 2021, whereas

Lai, Y. *Legal Resistance under Authoritarianism: The Struggle for the Rule of Law in Hong Kong.* Taylor & Francis Group, 2025
DOI: 10.5117/9789048558438_CH05

LLD was established in 2017 and is now virtually defunct. They are considered activist lawyer organisations because, on the one hand, they were founded by local legal professionals and law students; on the other, their primary businesses were highly relevant to civil society empowerment, mobilisation and different forms of political and legal activism. In short, their work was either promoting social change and resisting policy alongside legislative reforms proposed by the political authorities.

This chapter argues that Hong Kong's activist lawyers were able to resist authoritarian legal transplantation through empowering local civil society. This chapter also demonstrates that it is also feasible to reconcile the tensions between engaging in legal activism and upholding legal professionalism. Here, activist lawyers resisted the statecraft by disseminating liberal and progressive discourse on the Rule of Law. This method counterbalanced the authoritarian legal ideology, empowered civil society organisations and activists with legal knowledge as well as practical skills and consolidated democratic culture both within the legal profession and civil society.

The formation of the PLG and LLD was attributed to the legacy of lawyers' political awakening since 2014, which engendered a commitment to advancing democracy and building resilience against the perceived threats from authoritarian legal transplantation. Both PLG and LLD had taken many initiatives to strengthen their ties and collaborations with activist groups and civil society organisations by providing legal knowledge, training and networking to mobilise legal resources in social movements. Eventually, they tried to democratise the legal profession and reconcile the tensions between professionalism and activism through mobilising lawyers to promote democratic norms and practices within the legal community. By doing so, they contributed to internalising the public-spirit of the legal profession.

An Overview of Lawyers in Hong Kong's Democratic/Anti-authoritarian Movement

Throughout the history of Hong Kong, only a minority of lawyers involved in political movements, particularly in late colonial times. Mostly, they attempted to advance democratic reforms through direct political participation. From the mid–1980s onwards, some solicitors and barristers were enthusiastic about promoting democratisation. They included Albert Ho, Margaret Ng and Martin Lee, who later became famous political leaders in pro-democracy parties in Hong Kong. However, they were often considered as as politicians, and they could not represent the political orientation of most of the legal profession while activist lawyering remained uncommon (Dezalay and Garth 2010, 212-215; Jones 2007). After the 1997 sovereignty transfer, more lawyers, mainly barristers, became active in fostering democratisation in the city. This can be appreciated in three ways. First, some barristers were collectivised to be part of the apparatus for social mobilisation. One outstanding example was the movement against national security legislation in 2003. Some former chairmen of the Bar formed the Article 23 Concern Group, vocally raised their reservations to the proposed bill. The Concern Group became a popular engine in mobilising citizens to protest against the law. Four concern group members won seats in the Legislative Council (LegCo) elections in the following year and founded a pro-democracy Civic Party in 2006 (see chapter 3).

Second, lawyers ran for political elections in which some of the seats in LegCo and the Election Committee were assigned to the legal profession. Before 2021, all solicitors and barristers in Hong Kong can cast a ballot to select their representative (the Legal Sector in the Functional Constituency) in the LegCo. In addition, 30 seats in the Election Committee were dedicated to the legal profession (Young and Cullen 2010). Running for election was thus a channel for lawyers to engage in politics with their professional role in society.

Third, many lawyers attended the "black-clad" silent marches to express their dissatisfaction with the state's action that allegedly damaged the Rule of Law and judicial independence in Hong Kong (Barrow, 2023). The six silent marches were called by liberal figures in the profession, including pro-democracy lawmakers and members of the legal sector of the Election Committee (Torode and Roantree 2019; Channel News Asia 7 August 2019). Participants did not chant slogans during the marches when rallying towards the Building of the Court of Final Appeal or the Office of the Secretary for Justice. They protested silently and solemnly. The marches demonstrated the solidarity of the legal profession, expressing their resilience in defending the Rule of Law, and caught the attention of international media outlets (see chapter 1).

However, the three methods above also reflect the limitations of the ways lawyers involved in Hong Kong's democratic movement in the early days of sovereignty transfer. Standing as a candidate for political elections seemed to be the only choice for lawyers to engage in democratisation when famous figures from the profession had become lawmakers to maintain their significance in promoting the liberal values of the Rule of Law in Hong Kong. Lawyers who engaged in the democratic movement in Hong Kong were mainly lawyers with high seniority, whereas junior barristers and solicitors were often out of the picture. Besides, joining demonstrations and marches was not sustainable. They were ad hoc events only. Indeed, lawyers' engagements in Hong Kong's democratic movement were mainly individual choices rather than collective effort. This is partly attributed to the professional legal culture that being less politically outspoken is essential for maintaining job security among junior lawyers .

Against this backdrop, the emergence of the PLG and LLD was exceptional in Hong Kong's legal history. Utilising their legal capital, these two groups chose an alternative way to engage in democratisation movement, empower civil society and resist the sovereign state's authoritarian project.

Formation of the Progressive Lawyers Group and the Law Lay Dream

The White Paper, the Umbrella Movement and the Progressive Lawyers Group (PLG)

Two political events in 2014 paved the way for the formation of the PLG. The first event refers to the release of the White Paper by China's State Council. As discussed in previous chapters, the White Paper introduced the idea of "overall jurisdiction", meaning that the Chinese central leadership enjoyed the power to exercise its jurisdiction over different aspects of Hong Kong's political and legal institutions. What touched the nerve of the legal sector was the State Council's interpretations of the roles and functions of judicial officials in Hong Kong. The White Paper categorised judges as administrators of Hong Kong, having responsibilities for "correctly understanding and implementing the Basic Law, of safeguarding the country's sovereignty, security and development interests, and of ensuring the long-term prosperity and stability of Hong Kong." Moreover, the White Paper asked judicial officials to "love the country" as a prerequisite for taking office.

Despite the Bar's statement that expressed reservations on the descriptions of the role of judges in the White Paper, Ambrose Lam, who served as the president of the Law Society at the time, appeared to be a vocal supporter of the White Paper. He openly endorsed the White Paper, saying that the requirement for judges to "love the country" would not affect judicial independence. He further commented in a radio programme that "the [Chinese] Communist Party is so great that it brings the nation to a new age" and emphasised that he spoke on behalf of the Law Society (Cheung 2014).

Lam's comments attracted criticism from the members of the legal community. Nine solicitors as well as paralegals collected 240 solicitors' signatures as a petition to call on the Law Society to hold an extraordinary general meeting and to arrange a voting of (1) no confidence in Lam as the president, (2) Lam's withdrawal of his speech on the White Paper, and (3) urging the Law Society to release a statement that the Rule of Law and independence of judiciary should be upheld, as a response to the White Paper (Lam and Chu 2014; *Stand News* 13 August 2015). All motions were passed in an emergency general meeting held in August 2014, with 60 per cent of votes showing no confidence in Lam (Ng 2014a). The result was unexpected since, conventionally, the ballot boxes of the Law Society had been dominated by proxy votes collected by heads of law firms, who were usually pro-government in political matters. Five days after the voting, Lam resigned from the presidency, stating that his move was to unite the Law Society (Ng 2014b).

The unexpected victory in removing Lam from office enthused some active solicitors to plan to set up a platform to gather lawyers who shared the belief in defending the Rule of Law and public advocacy. In theire view, establishing a new platform for lawyers could maintain momentum after the emergency general meeting (ITV1924, 28 March 2019). It could also avoid further division within the profession:

> The young lawyers realised that the profession would be further divided if they persisted in firing on the Law Society. Thus, they could enjoy greater freedom if they could gather a group of people with shared beliefs (ITV1902, 29 January 2019).

Forming a new organisation could also preserve and carry on the legacy of the Umbrella Movement . These lawyers envisioned that setting up a new organisation could build solidarity among liberal and junior lawyers who supported the Umbrella Movement, and broadly the democratic movement in Hong Kong. The Umbrella Movement was sparked on 28 September 2014, a month after Beijing decided to set up a strict screening mechanism to vet candidates for future chief executive elections. During the 79-day protests, citizens occupied three major city hubs to pressure the government to accept the demand for a "genuine universal suffrage". Although the occupations failed to win any CCP concessions on democratic reform, the movement had awakened many middle-class professionals in Hong Kong and spawned a variety of pro-democracy groups that represented different industries, such as medical doctors, nurses, social workers, accountants and experts in financial markets (Ng and Lai 2015). The political awakening of professionals after the Umbrella Movement intersected with the aspiration of those lawyers excited by the removal of Ambrose Lam's presidency, motivating some active lawyers to create a pro-democracy professional group within the legal sector:

> Everyone sympathetic to the Umbrella Movement is wondering what to do to take the fight for democracy forward. One of the ideas among some lawyer friends is that we should form a group to keep up the spirit of the movement (ITV1944, 17 May 2019).

On 27 January 2015, the PLG was publicly launched as part of the "post-Umbrella Movement professional political groups," in which founders aimed at "instilling hope amid the post-Umbrella hopelessness" (Ma 2020, 236). The formation of the PLG was an effort to institutionalise the momentum, and offer aspirations and channels for the politically awakened lawyers to closely engage in civil society and the democratic movement.

The Umbrella Movement, the Oath-taking Saga and Law Lay Dream (LLD)

Like the PLG, the creation of LLD can be traced back to the same movement and the subsequent political repression against pro-democracy forces by law. The LLD was formed in February 2017. Its founders had been engaged in legal advocacy since 2014, just before the outbreak of the Umbrella Movement. At the time, some law students, including two of my interviewees, formed Law Students Political Reform Concern Groups in the three university law schools in Hong Kong, namely the University of Hong Kong (HKU), the Chinese University of Hong Kong (CUHK) and the City University of Hong Kong (CityU). During the Umbrella Movement, the concern groups issued joint statements on social media platforms in support of acts of civil disobedience, demonstrating solidarity between law students and the democratic movement at that time (*Inmediahk* 13 October 2014). Yet those concern groups ceased operations after the government proposal of political reform was vetoed by pro-democracy lawmakers following the Umbrella Movement (ITV1912, 4 March 2019; ITV1922, 21 March 2019).

These law students later became founders of LLD mainly because of the "oath-taking saga" at the beginning of the sixth term of LegCo in 2016. At the oath-taking session, before assuming their office in LegCo, two new lawmaker-elects, Sixtus Leung and Wai-ching Yau, displayed a flag written "Hong Kong is not China"; Yau then read People's "Republic of China" with derogatory terms used by Japanese people to refer to Chinese people during the Japanese invasion of China between 1937 to 1945. Some regarded this as offensive to the Chinese people (Steger 2016). Their behaviour was widely criticised by the pro-government camp and beyond as damaging national sentiment. Later, the Chief Executive filed a judicial review against the validity of the oaths of Leung and Yau. The controversy was further ignited when the National People's Congress Standing Committee (NPCSC) reinterpreted Article 104 of the Basic Law, stating that upholding the Basic Law of Hong Kong and bearing allegiance to Hong Kong and China are "legal requirements and preconditions for standing for election" alongside taking up public office. Any oath taker who does not read out the oath 'sincerely and solemnly" will be disqualified from assuming public office (7 November 2016).

The NPCSC's interpretation of the Basic Law, although had already occurred four times since Hong Kong's sovereignty transfer, was seen as unprecedented because the interpretation was announced when a litigation was still pending (Chan 2018). Suspicion of compromising judicial independence stimulated at least 2,000 lawyers to silently marching against the NPCSC's act of interpretation (*The Strait Times*, 8 November 2016).

In the end, the Court of Appeal decided the oaths of Leung and Yau were invalid. They could not assume their office in the legislature (*Chief Executive of the Hong Kong Special Administrative Region and Another v. Yau Wai Ching and Others* [2016] HCMP 2819/2016). Leung and Yau's appeal failed at the appellant court and was rejected at the Final Court of Appeal (*Sixtus Leung Chung Hang v. Chief Executive of the Hong Kong Special Administrative Region, Secretary for Justice* [2017] FAMV 10/2017; *Yau Wai Ching v. Chief Executive of the Hong Kong Special Administrative Region, Secretary for Justice* [2017] FAMV 8/2017).

The oath-taking saga and the lawyers' march inspired some solicitors and law students from the concern groups to discern what they could do further (ITV1926, 30 March 2019). Those students banded together with some junior solicitors and paralegals. At the beginning, they only planned to publish online their legal analysis as a brief guide on the NPCSC's interpretation of the Basic Law (ITV1912, 4 March 2019; ITV1923, 21 March 2019). However, they changed their mind and decided to set up a social media platform to disseminate their legal analysis and commentaries for raising public awareness. This strategy also modelled an effort made by a 'netizen' who published a Facebook page called "Charles Not a Lawyer" to comment on issues of law and lawyering in Hong Kong between 2015 and 2020. Finally, eight law students, legal executives and practitioners founded LLD and launched a Facebook page on 14 February 2017 (ibid.).

Organisational Characteristics and Strategies

Regarding goals, both the PLG and LLD share commonalities. Yet, their membership composition, legal ideologies, organisational structures and collective identities slightly differ. These characteristics have underpinned their convergence alongside divergence of strategies and tactics to produce a liberal and progressive legal discourse and to strengthen ties with and the capacities of partner groups in civil society.

Organisational Characteristics

Unlike the Bar and the Law Society, which generally stress safeguarding the Rule of Law as their core value, the PLG and LLD envisioned core elements of political liberalism as their principal values. In its press release, the PLG stressed its commitment to "the upholding of the Rule of Law, judicial independence, democracy, human rights, freedoms and justice," and they made it clear that as an organisation, they were at "the forefront" of Hong Kong's democracy movement. LLD's vision of the Rule of Law is tied to human rights, fair trial and equality. One of the LLD founders elaborated LLD's approach was to "take a politicised path to deliberate with supporters of democracy and freedom and seek legal reform." (Kristine 2018). Regarding member composition, there were overlapping memberships between LLD and the PLG, but the group size of LLD was much smaller than that of the PLG. By 2019, LLD had 15 members, of which only half were active.

In contrast, when the PLG was formed, it had nearly forty founding members and ten core members (ITV1930, 17 April 2019; *Stand News,* 13 August 2015). By March 2019, members of PLG increased to around 100, which consisted of law students, solicitor trainees, junior solicitors and barristers (ITV1927, 30 March 2019). This was partly because law students and lawyers could join the membership by self-recommendation to existing members for referral, and their application would be considered after a screening procedure with due diligence (ITV1920, 20 March 2019). On the other hand, LLD recruited members by invitation instead of making open calls.

Having registered under the Societies Ordinance of Hong Kong (Cap. 151), the PLG had a well-defined document of articles of association to guide its operation. Regarding leadership, the PLG was led by a core committee with at least one to four convenors as spokespersons. The core committee members could hold office for two to six years maximum. Still, in practice, the terms of convenors were regularly rotated between one to two years to relieve their burden in this voluntary office (ITV1903, 30 January 2019; ITV1927, 30 March 2019). Regarding the division of labour, the PLG had several functional teams for members to engage in the organisation's advocacy campaign, such as a translation team drafting bilingual statements, a writing team responsible for the regular articles in newspaper columns, and a multimedia team managing and promoting social media accounts (ITV1906, 20 February 2019). For ad hoc statements in response to public affairs, the PLG also had a standardised practice. Once the core committee decided to publish a statement, it will be posted in their chatroom on Telegram, a social media platform, to call for volunteers to help with legal research and drafting. Once volunteers, usually law students and barristers completed a first draft, the core committee would decide whether and how to publish it and ask the translation team to work on a bilingual version of the statement (ITV1920, 20 March 2019).

The characteristics of the division of labour, and the hierarchal leadership of the PLG contrasted with LLD, which positioned itself as a loosely organised "civil legal commentary group." They only concentrated on publishing commentary on case law and legal issues. LLD had no spokesperson, and most of the authors of its articles and commentaries were pseudonymised. In addition, as most of the founding members of LLD were law students and paralegals, they had fewer financial resources to diversify strategies and sustain the organisation. Yet, the loose organizational feature of LLD was also advantageous as it could perform their commentary role with greater flexibility and individuality. Members of LLD were allowed individualistic writing style in their commentaries:

> We do not wait until a consensus on a legal standpoint is reached. We decide to write a commentary once we have agreed to tackle a legal issue. It's a bottom-up practice. When one of us drafts a work, the other reviews and edits it (ITV1922, 21 March 2019).

> LLD serves as a medium of civil society empowerment; otherwise, civil society would have no voice in legal matters. Unlike the PLG, which empowers civil society with organisational power, LLD concentrates on writing commentaries (ITV1945, 24 May 2019).

The differences between the PLG and LLD, in terms of organisational characteristics, influenced their choices of tactics. Regarding education, PLG's alignment with local democratic movements drove the group to combine public legal advocacy with social mobilisation. In contrast, LLD stressed popularising the understanding of legal issues and critique of court trials for stimulating public debate.

Public Legal Education

The PLG promoted public legal education by dissimilating a liberal discourse of the Rule of Law through mass media platforms and by producing creative materials online to make basic legal knowledge publicly accessible. For LLD, its public legal education campaign mainly rested in its publication of carefully researched commentaries on social media platforms and digital media outlets. Both groups aimed to consolidate a Rule of Law culture in Hong Kong society.

Rather than just publishing official statements and legislative submissions like the Bar and Law Society, the PLG made more effort on media campaigns against the state's production of authoritarian legal discourse. Having members with experience in press liaison, the PLG built local and overseas media connections, responded to enquiries from journalists on matters of Hong Kong law, and sent members to join radio and television programmes to engage in public debates and to express the organisation's viewpoints. Moreover, in 2019, the PLG published a "Rule of Law Report 2018", documenting and commenting on all legal, legislative, and constitutional issues related to the city's quality of the Rule of Law (Progressive Lawyers Group 2019b). The PLG's diverse materials for public legal education earned an excellent network with and appreciation by reporters. In return, convenors and members of the PLG were consulted by journalists for comments when they were investigating legal issues (ITV1906, 20 February 2019).

One of the PLG's media tactics was running regular columns in newspapers. The PLG established several columns for commentary in local newspapers such as *Ming Pao* or *Hong Kong Free Press*. Conversely, it also published soft-toned articles in a column titled "Fa Zheng Ba Si" in a now-defunct local newspaper, *Apple Daily*. The title translates to "brothers and sisters of the PLG." The choice of the title reflects the PLG's target audience of young people in Hong Kong (ibid.). Run by the Chinese writing team of the PLG, the authors made use of this column to share the everyday routine of the legal profession, as well as opinions on different socio-political-legal issues. These publications often used laypeople's language and phrases that are catchy to young people, portraying a more dynamic image of the activist lawyers to the public. Between 2016 and 2020, the column published 219 articles, accompanied by the PLG multimedia team; these articles were also uploaded online to reach higher hit rates on social media platforms such as Facebook and Twitter (now called "X").

Another achievement of the PLG in public legal education is its production of "lazy packs" (懶人包), which literally means "a package for lazy people" in Chinese. The lazy packs served as brief guides to various legal issues for the public. They consisted of different frequently asked questions and various infographics responding to a widespread need for a greater understanding of specific legal issues. Infographics were then circulated via social media platforms. As part of its mission, the PLG hoped to make legal knowledge more accessible to the public through the wide circulation of the graphical packages (ITV2008, 8 June 2020). Table 17 shows that 21 lazy packs , including written frequently asked questions (FAQs), were published by the PLG, and 17 of them were related to the issues of policing and criminal justice during the Anti-Extradition Bill Movement (the Anti-ELAB Movement) in 2019. The massive publication of the lazy packs in 2019 was attributed to the urgent need for legal information, as discerned by members of the PLG. For instance, the first set of infographics on the Anti-ELAB Movement, titled "Stop and Search Lazy Pack", was a response to the rise in tension between the police and protestors on the eve of the scheduled second reading of the Extradition Law Amendment Bill (ELAB), as police officers began to stop and search civilians around the legislature and underground stations nearby (Griffiths et al. 2019). As recalled by a member of PLG,

> We felt we must do something as it was becoming an urgent matter. We drafted a brief guide overnight, focusing on the scope and limitations of police power to stop and search, and thus, a lazy pack was published. Later, as many of us were pro bono lawyers supporting arrested protestors, many more issues [on police power] arose, so we made more lazy packs (ITV2008, 8 June 2020).

The lazy packs were designed for young protestors and people with little knowledge of Hong Kong's criminal law. Each infographic tackled one puzzle or question on law and provided precise answers. The size and resolution of each infographic fit the design of social media platforms, thus were convenient for the social media circulation and the younger generation of netizens in the city.

LLD mainly provided public legal education through publishing online legal commentaries. Between 2017 and 2020, LLD published a total of 259 online commentaries. They can be classified thematically in table 18 as follows: (1) constitutional order, which expresses their disagreement with different forms of authoritarian legal transplantation from China; (2) court trials; (3) criminal justice; (4) judicial institutions; (5) democratic institutions; (6) professional legal culture; (7) human rights; and finally (8) civil society events. Except for themes (1), (6) and (8), the rest are divided into two sub-themes in the table. In total, there are 13 themes and sub-themes.

Table 17. List of Lazy Packs and FAQs for Public Legal Education by the Progressive Lawyers Group

Date	Title	Related Issues
8 November 2016	The Progressive Lawyers Group and the NPCSC Interpretation: Detailed Legal Analysis and FAQs	The 5th Interpretation of Basic Law (Article 104) by the NPCSC
15 September 2017	FAQs on Hong Kong Government's Co-location Proposal	The proposed co-location arrangement of the Guangzhou-Shenzhen-Hong Kong Express Railway Link by the Hong Kong government
6 June 2019	Why Extradition Law Amendment Should Not Pass	The proposed ELAB to be tabled for the reading at LegCo
12 June 2019	Stop and Search – lazy pack (the English version was released on 14 June 2019)	Controversies of public order policing and the alleged abuses of the rights of citizens in the Anti-ELAB Movement
21 June 2019	Are You a Registered Voter?	Voter registration for the District Council elections in November 2019
19 July 2019	What is Bail? What is the Release of Bail Without Charge? – lazy pack (Chinese only)	Controversies of public order policing, criminal prosecutions and the alleged abuses of the rights of citizens in the Anti-ELAB Movement
19 July 2019	Arrest – lazy pack	
20 July 2019	House Search – lazy pack (Chinese only)	
26 July 2019	Police's Letter of Objection – info pack	
5 August 2019	Riot – info pack	
7 August 2019	Jury – lazy pack (Chinese only)	
10 August 2019	Parents and Children – lazy pack (Chinese only)	
23 August 2019	Medical Workers Making Contacts with Family Members of Patients – lazy pack (co-authored with *Médecins Inspirés*, Chinese only)	
27 August 2019	Evidence Preservation – info pack (Chinese only)	
14 September 2019	Know Your Rights at Hong Kong Protests: FAQ with the Progressive Lawyers Group (English only)	
15 September 2019	Request for Unlocking Phones – lazy pack (the English version was released on 2 November 2019)	
28 September	Special Edition of the 5th Anniversary of the Umbrella Movement: Arrest – lazy pack (Chinese only)	

Date	Title	Related Issues
6 October 2019	Anti-mask Law – info pack	
5 November 2019	Can Police Officers Enter Private Estate to Enforce the Law? – lazy pack (Chinese only)	
12 May 2020	Three Reasons Against the National Anthem Bill – lazy pack (Chinese only)	The proposed National Anthem Bill to be tabled at LegCo
21 January 2021	Money Laundering – info pack	The arrest of an online radio programme host being suspected of money laundering by sponsoring protestors in exile

Source: Research based on archives of the PLG's Facebook page and official website

These commentaries were primarily written in vernacular and accessible languages to familiarise the public with court rulings and judgements. Most of the court's decisions in Hong Kong are written in English, whereas only some of them are accompanied by a Chinese executive summary. The legal jargon and technical language in those judgements discourage readership and discussion by the public. The use of vernacular and sometimes slang by LLD were more attractive to their target audience. LLD's writing style can help to widen the circulation of its published works alongside readership, to empower the audience to understand and thus be reasonably critical of the legal system, the court trials and judicial decisions:

> Not everyone knows how to read a court judgement... they would feel powerless as they do not know how to criticise a court ruling. In the end, they might exercise personal attacks against the judges. We can highlight the problems of the trials and the judgements ... Once you know the arguments, you can speak louder (ITV1945, 24 May 2019).

For instance, in one commentary on a verdict against 16 activists whose sentence of unlawful assembly was reviewed by the Department of Justice in 2017, LLD summarised the arguments of the Court of Appeal in written Chinese and rebuked the court's arguments without using any jargon or technical terms that appeared in the judgement (Law Lay Dream 2017). Another commentary also demonstrated how LLD balanced vernacularity and legal technicality. It used oral Cantonese to comment on a speech by Teresa Cheng, the Secretary for Justice in Hong Kong at that time, criticising her ignorance of the principles of international law on sanctioning officials

Table 18. Online Publication by Law Lay Dream (2017–2020)

	(1) Constitutional Affairs (% of Total Publication)	(2) Court Trials (% of Total Publication)		(3) Criminal Justice (% of Total Publication)		(4) Judicial Institutions (% of Total Publication)		(5) Democratic Institutions (% of Total Publication)		(6) Professional Legal Culture (% of Total Publication)	(7) Human Rights (% of Total Publication)		(8) Civil Society Events (% of Total Publication)	Total (% of Total Publication)
		Case Commentary	Case Diary	Law and Crimes	Law Enforcement	Judiciary	Legal Aid	District Council	Legislative Council		Local Rights Issues	International Affairs		
2017	4	33	4	23	3	7	2	0	5	4	11	1	3	100
2018	0	27	2	8	1	3	0	0	1	3	4	3	1	53
2019	0	7	1	23	22	0	0	0	10	1	6	0	0	70
2020	3	5	0	7	10	2	0	6	0	0	2	1	0	36
Total	7 (2.7)	72 (27.8)	7 (2.7)	61 (23.6)	36 (13.9)	12 (4.63)	2 (0.8)	6 (2.32)	16 (6.18)	8 (3.1)	23 (8.9)	5 (1.9)	4 (1.5)	259 (100)

Source: Research based on archives of the Facebook pages of LLD, *Inmediahk*, and *Stand News*

accused of human rights abuses. Then, the author explained the United Nations report on economic sanctions in formal written Chinese, quoting the relevant paragraphs with citations (Law Lay Dream 2020).

On some occasions, LLD even used heavily politicised language and rhetoric in their online commentaries, significantly when they opined on the actions of the law enforcement after the outbreak of the Anti-ELAB Movement. After the protestors of the Anti-ELAB Movement stormed the LegCo Complex on 1 July 2019, LLD published a statement-like opinion affirming its respect for the protestors' demands, support for dissolving the legislature, which was not formed by universal suffrage, and condemned the police for disproportionate use of force against protestors. In that opinion, LLD did not address the breaking of the law and vandalism of the protestors inside the legislature but highlighted that those protestors did not intend to harm anyone (*Stand News* 2 July 2019). Its sympathy for protestors is contrasted with its disapproval of the police. Between 2019 and 2020, LLD repeatedly used the term "black cop" in the title and main texts of its commentaries. The term was widely adopted by protestors to derogatorily label police officers who were involved in policing the Anti-ELAB protests by allegedly breaking the law and police general orders.

LLD had no reservations in employing swear words in the titles of their commentaries against police officers, who allegedly contravened the standard prescribed in legal provisions while policing protests. This is something the PLG did not do. As one LLD member explained, the small-team nature of LLD allowed greater room for individual authors to express their individuality even by using foul language, with grievance and outrage, to criticise the alleged misconducts of the law enforcement in handling protestors, journalists and civilians (ITV1922, 21 March 2019; Law Lay Dream 2019b, 2019c and 2019d). Using indecent and derogatory language might be considered controversial for a legal commentary. However, it is revealed that LLD mainly targeted the younger generation of pro-democracy netizens and activists. The use of swear words fit in the target audience's appetite. The use of layman's language and provoking rhetoric proved to be leverage for LLD to attract readers and to popularise its legal discourse for public legal education.

Solidarity with Civil Society

The PLG upheld good relationships with civil society organisations and political parties in Hong Kong's democratic movement. As one of the post-Umbrella professional political groups, PLG had repeatedly issued joint statements with its fellow organisations to address domestic political and legal issues and to express their stance (see table 19). Furthermore, the PLG also joined other professional political groups in policy advocacy, such as joint submissions on Hong Kong's human rights development to the UN treaty bodies and the Human Rights Council. The last joint statement by the PLG was an open letter to the chairman of the NPCSC. The letter was signed by 86 domestic and international non-governmental organisations before China's implementation of a national security law (the NSL) in Hong Kong. The groups called for the withdrawal of the legislation, which was alleged of not conforming to international human rights laws and standards (Progressive Lawyers Group 2020).

The PLG stressed the importance of communications with Hong Kong expatriates and the international community since Hong Kong has long been an international financial hub for foreign investment. It saw that the value of the publication of statements is more than just public legal education in the local community. Releasing English translations of statements, evidence-based reports, and policy submissions were instruments to build stronger ties with the global community:

> The English translation of our statements strategically targets the international community and international press, which will thus pay more attention to Hong Kong. Many foreign journalists struggle to pick up what's happening in Hong Kong, so they often quote our English statements and know who we are (ITV1920, 20 March 2019).

Apart from publishing statements and reports, the PLG also worked with pro-democracy parties and civil society organisations to draft legislative proposals and amendments of bills (ITV1930, 17 April 2019). In 2014, the Hong Kong government introduced an amendment bill on copyright, but the proposals were controversial as they put free speech, free press and the rights to secondary creations at stake (Mo 2017, 211; Progressive Lawyers Group 2015). After the creation of the PLG in 2015, its members began to advocate for revising the proposed bills by drafting amendment proposals, lobbying civil society partners and political parties, as well as deliberation tactics in legislative debates:

> We mainly provided a legal perspective and details on how our amendments would work. When political parties and civil society organisations decided to filibuster during the debate of the copyright amendment bill, we advised them how to make use of the rules and procedures, alongside a variety of possible strategies (ITV1920, 20 March 2019).

Table 19. Joint Statements of Post-Umbrella Professional Groups on Local Advocacy (2016–2019)

Date	Title	Platform
4 January 2016	'Stop Picking Fights! Give Us a Break!" (On Chief Executive's appointment of a chairman of the council of HKU)	Newspaper advertisement
4 August 2016	"Democratic professional groups" joint statement re political screening of candidates in legislative council elections"	Newspaper advertisement
8 November 2016	"Beijing destroys the Rule of Law, Hong Kong is a world city no more" (on the NPCSC interpretation of the Basic Law)	Newspaper advertisement
23 May 2018	"Joint Statement on Local Legislation for the National Anthem Law"	Internet circulation
3 June 2019	"8964 30th Anniversary Statement: Continue Our Fight for the Deceased and the Future"	Internet circulation
10 June 2019	Statement by the Joint Professional Groups: The People Have Spoken: Withdraw the Extradition Bill!	Internet circulation
18 June 2019	"Joint Statement on the Government Reluctance to Respond to Public Opinion" (on the calls for the withdrawal of the ELAB, de-characterisation of 6.12 incident as rioting, and the resignation of the Chief Executive) (in Chinese)	Internet circulation
22 July 2019	"Joint Statement on the Violent Event in Yuen Long" (in Chinese)	Internet Circulation
25 July 2019	"Joint Statement by the Professional Organisations to strongly condemn the excessive use of force by the police to disperse protesters on 7.21 in the area of Sheung Wan"	Internet Circulation

Source: Research based on archives of the website of PLG

Last but not the least, the PLG built solidarity with civil society when it became one of the mobilisers in anti-authoritarian protests. Examples included the 2016 bookseller case, in which Chinese state agents abducted five booksellers who allegedly published and sold books smearing top Chinese officials (Joseph and Hunt 2016) and the introduction of the ELAB in 2019. The mobilising role of the PLG was more comprehensive in the 2019 Anti-ELAB Movement. On 12 February 2019, the Hong Kong government introduced the ELAB, suggesting it as a remedy for transferring a homicide fugitive from Hong Kong to Taiwan, which had no extradition agreement with Hong Kong. However, the bill was unpopular as the proposal also allowed ad-hoc extradition to China, where the justice system was accused of abusing fair trials. As early as eight days after introducing the government's proposal, the PLG released a statement calling for the government to withdraw the bill (Progressive Lawyers Group 2019a). In addition to joining protests against the bill to demonstrate solidarity, the group actively engaged in conversations with journalists as well as public debates to express its disagreement with the provisions and air its alternative proposal, which would be only to permit extradition between Hong Kong and Taiwan (ITV1927, 23 September 2019). A few days before the third round of Anti-ELAB protests on 9 June 2019, in which more than a million citizens were estimated to have joined, PLG took the final chance to mobilise citizens to march against the bill. On the one hand, its convenor joined a series of videos titled "Stand Up on 9 June, Hong Kongers," with two barristers to elucidate the legal consequences of the proposed ELAB on Hong Kong's Rule of Law and judicial independence. It urged citizens to join the rally. On the other hand, PLG itself also released a video clip on YouTube explaining the "threats" of the bill. The video clip was regarded as a crucial tactic to widen the audience and support for the Anti-ELAB protest:

> In this critical moment, our most effective work would be our YouTube clip, which is entirely in English. It was a viral video, and after its release, many different organisations and correspondents contacted us as they watched the clip, interviewing us for opinions about the bill. After all, only a few people can clearly explain public affairs to expatriates in this city. It would be a big market to develop (ITV1927, 23 September 2019).

During the million people's march against the ELAB, which the Civil Human Rights Front (CHRF) organised in Hong Kong on 9 June and 16 June 2019, the convenors of the PLG were invited to speak at the stage of the rally, telling the crowd the fundamental flaws of the bill and calling for a broader mobilisation to push the government's withdrawal of the bill in the future. On 18 August 2019, a public assembly was held in Victoria Park: the organiser CHRF estimated 1.7 million citizens attended, while the police counted 128,000 (K. Cheng 2019b). The PLG gathered all former and current convenors to hold banners and join the assembly to demonstrate solidarity with peaceful protest. Through media reporting, the group expressed "their reasonable demands louder and clearer than ever to show their unyielding determination" to support the movement (Sing Tao Daily 18 August 2019). Moreover, PLG members also spoke at other public assemblies, mainly to explain to the attendants the legal knowledge related to public order policing, the rights of arrestees, and the limits of police powers (HK Hope China 2019a and 2019b). Like the lazy packs they published, PLG attempted to empower protestors, consolidate the bond between protest organisers and the progressive lawyers, and build resilience in the anti-authoritarian movement through these direct engagements.

Like the PLG, LLD also occasionally co-drafted civil society submissions of human rights shadow reports to the United Nations. Yet, LLD focused more on advancing the legal consciousness of social movement than mobilising for direct actions. LLD's approach was more responsive to providing legal discourse to empower political activism (ITV1922, 21 March 2019). It regarded advocating alternative legal discourse as a "weapon" in civil resistance:

> We provide an alternative to the mainstream legal discourse from the court. People will thus have resources to contemplate the law other than the court version and be able to diagnose the problems of the court's legal analysis. This is an unprecedented effort by the legal community. We become part of the movement (ITV1912, 4 March 2019).

The provision of legal discourse worked not only in the public's view but also with civil society organisations and activist groups behind the scenes. Some members of LLD brainstormed ideas and legal arguments with activists who were defendants in court trials. Grassroots groups and pro-democracy political parties also consulted LLD's members on various legal issues. On many occasions, the published commentaries of LLD, alongside its research archive, were adopted as discursive resources by civil groups and political parties, such as the joint statement against local legislation for the national anthem law, in which the government did not offer a genuine public consultation in advance (Law Lay Dream 2018b).

Besides providing legal discourse to civil society partners, LLD also held training seminars and workshops to transfer legal knowledge and skills to civil society workers, community organisers and citizens interested in law and court trials. Members of LLD were motivated to do so to get in touch with people who may have little knowledge of Hong Kong law, so that LLD could equip these active citizens with practical legal skills and ultimately to translate the law to a "vernacular" for the public (ITV1926, 30 March 2019). A capacity building workshop could also educate members of civil society through clarifying and contextualising the law in their corresponding fields. Hence, members of civil society would not be without a voice in law at all (ITV1945, 24 May 2019). LLD's first series of seminars was held in 2018, titled "Legal Knowledge 101: Seminars for Local Practice." It targeted NGO workers and community organisers and schooled them in the practical knowledge of the criminal law, personal injury, family law, tenancy and participation in public order activities. Ideally, service providers in civil society should be able to handle the law-related matters of their clients without depending on legal professionals. Another round of workshops was held in 2020. After the outbreak of the Anti-ELAB Movement, some citizens were eager to demonstrate solidarity with the movement by attending criminal trials against protestors accused of rioting and other criminal charges in protests. They stayed in the audience benches to document the trials, reported the trial processes on social media channels, and farewelled the sentenced protestors outside the courtroom to show solidarity (T. Wong 2020). Members of LLD thus saw the need to build capacities of those citizens to master their skills in documenting court hearings. LLD held a workshop titled "Workshop for Citizens Auditing Court Trials," teaching them legal proceedings in criminal justice, practical guidelines to follow up trials and practising court reporting with journalists. These workshops, which were promoted in LLD's social media platforms and independent media outlets, were essential to deepening popular legal education alongside consolidating their civil society network (ITV1801, 19 June 2020).

The last but not the least example of LLD's ties with civil society was their engagement with the "Citizens' Press Conference" during the Anti-ELAB Movement. It was an initiative by some protestors to counter the government line against protestors in the daily press conferences of the Hong Kong police (Sum 2019). It operated between 6 August 2019 and 30 June 2020, holding press meetings with guest speakers from different sectors of civil society organisations, protestors and victims of police abuse in the movement (Chung 2020). LLD was one of the groups invited to join the press conference twice. LLD first appeared on that platform on 19 August 2019, when one of its members criticised the police's alleged abuse of power by indiscriminatory stopping and searching passers-by after an Anti-ELAB protest on 18 August 2019 (*Inmediahk* 19 August 2019). On 22 May 2020, LLD was invited by the same platform again to comment on China's legislative proposal of the NSL (*Inmediahk* 22 May 2020). The LLD's representative disapproved of the Chinese authority imposing a national law on national security in Hong Kong since the act contravened Article 18(3) of the Basic Law: national laws being implemented should only be "confined to those relating to defence and foreign affairs as well as other matters outside the limits of the autonomy," whereas the substances of the national security law have been covered by Article 23 of the Basic Law already. LLD's collaboration with the Citizen's Press Conference successfully channeled the LLD's legal analysis from social media platforms to a wider public via media reporting and live streaming of the press conferences. LLD's physical presence in those events also demonstrated its solidarity with the anti-authoritarian movement.

Evaluation

A Realm of Middle Democracy between the Legal Profession, Civil Society and Democratic Movement

The PLG and LLD contributed to constructing a realm of "middle democracy" between lawyers, civil society organisers, political activists and the public. As explained in the introduction, "middle democracy" refers to a virtual sphere where professionals serve as an intermediary between citizens and democratic institutions (Dzur 2008, 130). To do so, PLG and LLD popularised legal education that promoted public awareness and commitment to the Rule of Law. The advocacy materials and strategies of the PLG and LLD complemented each other: PLG focused on mainstream media campaigns, while LLD concentrated on online social media platforms.

Regarding subject matter, the PLG disseminated legal knowledge creatively, publishing its opinions on various forms of authoritarian legal transplantation and providing a robust discourse on the liberal Rule of Law. LLD made more effort to comment on criminal trials against protestors and minor issues brought to courts. A member of LLD recollected that, by at least demonstrating a plurality of views within the legal profession, the PLG and LLD enriched public debates on the Rule of Law and widened the equal access to legal knowledge and discourse of every citizen (ITV1912, 4 March 2019). Furthermore, as noted by a member of the PLG, its organisational capacity allowed the PLG to produce various submissions and statements. Still, more importantly, its credibility made it popular with the media and the general public. Its credibility came from the professional identity of its barrister and solicitor members (ITV1945, 24 May 2019). The professional quality and legal expertise of PLG and LLD were essential in popularising their public legal education campaign. This was recognised by the fact that, in 2017, LLD won an "Annual Internet Citizen Award" given by a domestic foundation, for its active engagement in legal education and legal debates in the digital space (*Inmediahk* 2017).

The PLG and LLD also expanded the legal capital of civil society organisations by building solidarity networks and developing exchanges with local groups. Both engaged in internal legal trainings with activists, civil society workers and community organisers. They also worked with political parties and NGOs to draft bills and joint statements. Specifically, the PLG had strong connections with post-umbrella professional groups, sowing a solid basis for domestic and international advocacy. Positioning itself as part of the democratic movement in Hong Kong, the PLG repeatedly served as a mobiliser in anti-authoritarian protests and collaborator with protest organisers. For LLD, it stood firm to serve as a legal commentary group in the Internet. It supports activist groups and NGOs through discourse rather than direct mobilisation. Above all, the sharing of legal knowledge and discourse by the PLG and LLD was essential to consolidate what a democratic society is constituted by: promotion of and commitment to democratic norms, deliberative public engagement in policy debates, as well as mass mobilisation for social change or civil society defence.

Building Democratic Culture within the Profession

The civic engagement of the PLG and LLD also contributed to lawyers' political awakening and democratising professional legal culture in Hong Kong. As a founding member of LLD explained, one of its objectives is to "cultivate trainees and pupils with liberal legal values, to revive the spirit they had when entering law school" (ITV1801, 11 October 2018). He believed that new graduates in law would lose the enthusiasm to defend the Rule of Law once they entered the job market, which would shape them into becoming technocrats in the profession. LLD's advocacy and publications on political and legal analysis can thus serve as food for thought to the novices in the legal sector, encouraging them to pay more attention to public law and criminal law, which are less profitable in the local legal industry.

The political awakening of legal professionals also happened in the PLG, especially among the younger members. As recollected by one of the former convenors, a particular mission of the PLG was to cultivate a democratic culture among junior lawyers and law students to sustain and advance democratisation in Hong Kong (ITV1920, 20 March 2019). Through members-only workshops and their publications of statements and submissions, the PLG made efforts to nurture young lawyers' commitment to the PLG, and broadly the local democratic movement :

> From the organisational point of view, we need new blood to take over PLG. Thus, core members often try to know our members, figure out their views, and motivate them to engage in our work. In the long run, PLG will be more sustainable and vibrant (ITV1903, 30 January 2019).

Unlike previous largely apolitical pro bono provisions, the political agency of junior lawyers was awakened amid political crises and social movements. The PLG and LLD have provided new opportunities for liberal and activist-like solicitors and barristers to engage in political activism as legal professionals. In this sense, members of the PLG and LLD intersect legal professionalism and political activism when their expertise is instrumental to legal resistance. Quite often, the PLG heavily emphasised its professional identity while engaging in political mobilisation. For LLD, it went even further, claiming that its member's legal professional identity is less significant than its activist identity and citizenship when they engaged in public legal debate:

> We do not emphasise ourselves as professionals. If you agree with me, it is because you agree with my reasoning rather than trusting me as someone holding a practising certificate in law (ITV1912, 4 March 2019).

With less burden to stress a professional identity like the Bar or Law Society, LLD's strategy was to articulate the political elements in legal debate and legal analysis. It publications disagreed with the position of professional bodies that stress on political neturality. Instead, LLD believes that law and politics are inseparable. It preferred to include more political angles into the analysis of law and courts, especially on judicial culture:

> In a criminal trial against 13 activists who protested inside the Legislative Council Complex, opposing a government-led rural development project in 2017, the court stated that the political motivation of the convicted should not be considered in sentence, as the court does not engage in politics. I argue this approach ignores the reality that politically related crime is not an ordinary crime as the convicted acted out of public interest rather than a private one, or the convicted was exercising their human rights (ITV1922, 21 March 2019).

Such a view is distinctive from the professional language that neutralises the political nature of law. The law is often portrayed as administratively impartial and independent of any political ideology. In response, the PLG and LLD took steps to demythologise the neutrality of the law by enriching and amplifying the liberal and progressive voices in the legal profession for the sake of the Rule of Law, which is often conservatively interpreted by the Law Society and even the Bar:

> It is difficult to change the orientation of the Law Society, and no one can guarantee whether the Bar Council can still maintain its [less conservative] stance. Our organisation is thus essential as at least we can represent the liberal and progressive voices of the profession. After all, we still have much to do to consolidate the Rule of Law in Hong Kong, as such a core value is easy to uproot (ITV1903, 30 January 2019).

Many members of the PLG also engaged in political activism at the frontline to assist protestors in the Anti-ELAB Movement. The collective agency of the PLG empowered civil society and diffused a more vital ethos of political or activist lawyering in the profession to resist authoritarian governance. Their experience will be discussed in the next chapter.

Sustainability and Resilience

Organisational sustainability was a shared challenge to the PLG and LLD. Being a movement-driven and responsive platform, LLD lacked a systematic advocacy agenda. They could only rely on one or two members to take up the publication work:

> We don't consider promoting law reform through our commentaries; we don't have such a vision or detailed scheme. We are just reacting to the outbreak of a legal issue or a verdict (ITV1922, 21 March 2019).

> I found LLD has no goal, so we cannot foresee what the organisation will eventually become. We have no concrete plan of next step once activism or political advocacy no longer exist (ITV1912, 4 March 2019).

In April 2020, I interviewed one of the founding members of LLD again. She explained that sustaining LLD became more complicated when many members were qualified as lawyers, thus having less time to engage in LLD (ITV1912, 17 April 2020). Having a full-time job at law firms, these members were unable to audit court trials and to write reports as well as commentaries regularly.

For the PLG, although it recruited many early-career lawyers and law students, top leadership succession remained difficult. The main reason was that most members were too junior in the legal profession. Being overtly outspoken in the public domain may disrupt their career in the legal industry:

> Many of our core members are so young in the profession. Unless you are brave enough and affluent, once you make yourself known in public,

> you will be stereotyped and then lose your career future. Hence, most of our young solicitor members would not step up on behalf of the PLG but instead support us anonymously, such as writing commentary with pen names (ITV1930, 17 April 2019).

Such hesitation of the young PLG members can also be observed in the photo-taking session of its fourth annual dinner that I attended. After the inauguration of the new convenors and core members, the host called for a general photo-taking. Two photos were then taken. One photo included all the dinner attendants, but this was kept for records only. Another one was taken only with those who did not mind appearing on local and social media platforms. This arrangement was to protect those members who wanted to avoid being identified by the government, their law firms and clients. The threats of job security and the subsequent self-censorship among some members thus limited the pool of potential leaders in the PLG.

Conclusion

Lawyers are known for their eloquence in public debate and court trials, as well as their expertise in legal knowledge and skills. Many barristers and solicitors in Hong Kong have engaged in the democratic movement by either advancing the protection of constitutional rights in court or developing political careers to influence the establishment. Some lawyers devoted themselves to pro bono work for civil society by supporting different philanthropic organisations for vulnerable groups. This chapter's case studies of the PLG and LLD portray another model of the dynamics between lawyers, civil society, and the state.

To consolidate the popular Rule of Law culture against authoritarian legal ideology, the public legal education campaigns of the two groups were instrumental in challenging the top-down transplantation of Chinese authoritarian laws, norms and practices. Both the PLG and LLD engaged in various advocacy and training activities to empower civil society partners in the anti-authoritarian movement in Hong Kong. Moreover, the PLG and LLD built solidarity with lawyers who shared liberal and democratic values in their profession as well as citizenry lives. They took significant steps to democratise the professional legal culture as junior lawyers and law students became more active in mobilising peer lawyers at the grassroots level, in contrast to the dominance of senior barristers and solicitors in the leadership of professional bodies. The modelling effect of the PLG and LLD encouraged many lawyers to commit themselves to resisting authoritarian rule with their expertise and professional standing. This was proven in their works of legal assistance that backed political activism in Hong Kong, and will be further discussed in the next chapter.

References

Barrow, Amy. 2023. "Beyond the Courtroom: Lawyer Activism and Resistance in Hong Kong." In *Activism and Authoritarian Governance in Asia*, edited by Amy Barrow and Sara Fuller. Routledge.

Chan, Johannes M. M. 2018. "A Storm of Unprecedented Ferocity: The Shrinking Space of the Right to Political Participation, Peaceful Demonstration, and Judicial Independence in Hong Kong." *International Journal of Constitutional Law* 16 (2): 373–388.

Cheng, Kris. 2019b. "Organisers Say 1.7 Million Joined Hong Kong Pro-Democracy Rally Against Police Use of Force, as Protesters Reiterate 5 Demands." *Hong Kong Free Press*, August 18. Accessed April 7, 2021. https://hongkongfp.com/2019/08/18/breaking-organisers-say-1-7-million-joined-hong-kong-pro-democracy-rally-police-use-force-protesters-reiterate-5-demands.

Cheung, Tony. 2014. "Controversial Solicitor is No Lam to the Slaughter." *South China Morning Post*, June 20. Accessed March 21, 2021. https://www.scmp.com/news/hong-kong/article/1536410/controversial-solicitor-no-lam-slaughter.

Chief Executive of the Hong Kong Special Administrative Region and Another v. Yau Wai Ching and Others. 2016. HCMP 2819/2016.

Chung, Hiu-fung. 2020. "Changing Repertoires of Contention in Hong Kong: A Case Study on the Anti-Extradition Bill Movement." *China Perspectives* 3: 57–63.

Dezalay, Yves, and Bryant G. Garth. 2010. *Asian Legal Revivals: Lawyers in the Shadow of the Empire*. University of Chicago Press.

Dzur, Albert W. 2008. *Democratic Professionalism: Citizen Participation and the Reconstruction of Professional Ethics, Identity, and Practice*. Penn State University Press.

"Fǎ Mèng chéng yuán chū xí mín jiān jì zhě huì, fǎn bó jǐng suí yì sōu chá shì mín, kuā dà jìn rù sī rén dì fāng quán lì." 2019. *Inmediahk*, August 19. Accessed March 21, 2021. https://www.inmediahk.net/node/1066605.

"Fǎ Mèng huò wǎng luò gōng mín jiǎng, gōng zhòng fǎn sī fǎ lu jiè fēng bō." 2017. *Inmediahk*, December 12. Accessed October 31, 2024. https://www.inmediahk.net/%E5%AA%92%E9%AB%94/%E3%80%8C%E6%B3%95%E5%A4%A2%E3%80%8D%E7%8D%B2%E7%B6%B2%E7%B5%A1%E5%85%AC%E6%B0%91%E7%8D%8E-%E5%85%AC%E7%9C%BE%E5%8F%8D%E6%80%9D%E6%B3%95%E5%BE%8B%E7%95%8C%E9%A2%A8%E6%B3%A2 .

"Gǎng bǎn guó ān fǎ chā rù fù jiàn sān, Fǎ Mèng chéng yuán hōng wéi jī běn fǎ dì 18 tiáo." 2020. *Inmediahk*, May 22. Accessed March 21, 2021. https://www.inmediahk.net/node/1073686?fbclid=IwARojGI-AGQEMPohy7xF3cp9Xyol-HAPr_c69uWS2hrDsHZgAe1NdlQZ-3jJQ.

Griffiths, James, Helen Regan, Bex Wright, and Vanessa Yung. 2019. "Police Searched People Heading to the Protests." *CNN World*, June 11. Accessed April 7, 2021. https://cnn.it/3F55Boo.

Halliday, Terence C. 2005. "Legal Professions and Politics: Neocorporatist Variations on the Pluralist Theme of Liberal Democracies." In *Lawyers in Society: Comparative Theories*, edited by Richard L. Abel and Philip S. C. Lewis. Beard Books.

HK Hope China. 2019a. "Fǎ zhèng huì sī dà lu shī Lu Xī Yú tí gōng yīng duì làn bǔ làn quán de fǎ lu jǐn náng." YouTube, September 17. Accessed April 7, 2021. https://www.youtube.com/watch?v=SXdf2LyhBq4.

HK Hope China. 2019b. "Fǎ zhèng huì sī Lǐ Ān Rán dà lu shī jiào lù tóng xué zī bèi bǔ hòu rú hé yīng duì jǐng fāng de fǎ lu jǐn náng." YouTube, October 19. Accessed April 7, 2021. https://www.youtube.com/watch?v=irS7WFtloJk.

Hong Kong lawyers march in silence to condemn China's interpretation of Basic Law 2016, *The Strait Times*, November 8, Accessed March 21, 2021, https://www.straitstimes.com/asia/east-asia/hong-kong-lawyers-march-in-silence-to-condemn-chinas-interpretation-of-basic-law.

Hong Kong Lawyers March in Silence to Support Anti-Government Protesters. 2019. Channel News Asia, August 7. Accessed April 7, 2021. Archived on file with the author.

Jones, Carol. 2007. "Dissolving the People: Capitalism, Law and Democracy in Hong Kong." In *Fighting for Political Freedom: Comparative Studies of the Legal Complex and Political Change*, edited by Terence Halliday, Lucien Karpik, and Malcolm Feeley. Hart Publishing.

Joseph, Elizabeth, and Katie Hunt. 2016. "Missing Hong Kong Bookseller: I Was Kidnapped by Chinese 'Special Forces'." *CNN News*, June 16. Accessed August 29, 2022. https://edition.cnn.com/2016/06/16/asia/china-hong-kong-booksellers/index.html.

Kristine. 2018. "Fǎ Mèng: fēi cháng bù yī yàng de fǎ lu pǔ jí yùn dòng lù jìng" *Matters*, April 17. Accessed October 31, 2024. https://matters.town/a/g4ji4rscs15q.

Lam, Jeffie, and Julie Chu. 2014. "Solicitors Move for Vote of No Confidence in Lam Over White Paper Statements." *South China Morning Post*, June 21. Accessed March 21, 2021. https://www.scmp.com/news/hong-kong/article/1537182/solicitors-move-vote-no-confidence-lam-over-white-paper-statements.

Law Lay Dream. 2017. "[Fǎ Mèng jì shù wén] Zhěng lǐ 926 gōng mín guǎng chǎng àn (jí dōng běi àn) de fǎ lǐ yào diǎn." *Inmediahk*, August 21. Accessed April 4, 2021. https://www.inmediahk.net/node/1051548.

Law Lay Dream. 2018a. "[Fǎ Mèng kāi jiǎng] Fǎ lu zhī shí 101 x dì qū shí zhàn jiǎng zuò." Facebook. April 3. Accessed March 21, 2021. Archived on file with the author.

Law Lay Dream. 2018b. "Guó gē fǎ lián hé shēng míng." Facebook. May 22. Accessed March 21, 2021. Archived on file with the author.

Law Lay Dream. 2019a. "Fā mèng mèng huà." Facebook. July 2. Accessed April 4, 2021. Archived on file with the author.

Law Lay Dream. 2019b. "Wǒ di yī jiā jiù jiǎng rén huà: xì shī zhí yā DLLM." *Inmediahk.* July 23. Accessed April 4, 2021. https://www.inmediahk.net/%E6%94%BF%E7%B6%93/%E6%88%91%E5%93%8B%E4%BE%9D%E5%AE%B6%E5%B0%B1%E8%AC%9B%E4%BA%BA%E8%A9%B1-%E4%BF%82%E5%A4%B1%E8%81%B7%E5%91%80-dllm.

Law Lay Dream. 2019c. "[Face Check hēi jǐng] Tíng zhǐ rǎo luàn shì tīng, chū shì wěi rèn zhèng qī leng měng měng." *Inmediahk.* July 26. Accessed April 4, 2021. https://www.inmediahk.net/%E6%94%BF%E7%B6%93/%E3%80%90factcheck%E9%BB%91%E8%AD%A6%E3%80%91%E5%81%9C%E6%AD%A2%E6%93%BE%E4%BA%82%E8%A6%96%E8%81%BD%EF%BC%8C%E5%87%BA%E7%A4%BA%E5%A7%94%E4%BB%BB%E8%AD%89%E5%95%A6%E6%9F%92%E6%92%9A%E6%87%B5%E6%87%B5.

Law Lay Dream. 2019d. "Zǔ chà bàn gōng zuì' jū bǔ jì zhě? Di law 100% cuò leng shēn." *Tigerz-note.blogspot.com.* October 29. Accessed April 4, 2021. https://tigerz-note.blogspot.com/2019/10/law-100.html?m=0.

Law Lay Dream. 2020. "Zhì cái cán bào zhèng quán, fú hé guó jì fǎ." *Inmediahk.* May 30. Accessed April 4, 2021. https://www.inmediahk.net/node/1073962.

"Lián xiào fǎ lu xué shēng zhèng gǎi guān zhù zǔ shēng míng —— huí yīng dà lu shī gōng huì 10 yuè 8 rì zhī shēng míng." 2014. *Inmediahk.* October 13. Accessed March 21, 2021. https://www.inmediahk.net/node/1027225.

Ma, Ngok. 2020. "The Plebeian Moment and Its Traces: Post-Umbrella Movement Professional Groups in Hong Kong." In *Sunflowers and Umbrellas: Social Movements, Expressive Practices, and Political Culture in Taiwan and Hong Kong,* edited by Thomas Gold and Sebastian Veg. Institute of East Asian Studies of University of California.

Mo, Jojo Y. C. 2017. "The Copyright (Amendment) Bill 2014 in Hong Kong: A Blessing or a Curse?" *Statute Law Review* 38, no. 2: 211–225.

Ng, Joyce. 2014a. "Solicitors Vote to Unseat Law Society President Ambrose Lam." *South China Morning Post.* August 15. Accessed March 21, 2021. https://www.scmp.com/news/hong-kong/article/1573871/solicitors-pass-vote-no-confidence-law-society-chief-ambrose-lam.

Ng, Joyce. 2014b. "Law Society President Ambrose Lam Resigns After Historic No-Confidence Vote." *South China Morning Post.* August 19. Accessed

March 21, 2021. https://www.scmp.com/news/hong-kong/article/1576791/law-society-president-ambrose-lam-resigns-following-historic-no.

Ng, Julian, and Zoe Lai. 2015. "Professionals Get Political." *Varsity.* March 17. Accessed March 21, 2021. https://varsity.com.cuhk.edu.hk/index.php/2015/03/professionals-get-political/.

Progressive Lawyers Group. 2015. "Explainer: What Is Legal and What Is Not under Copyright (Amendment) Bill 2014." *Hong Kong Free Press.* December 12. Accessed April 7, 2021. https://hongkongfp.com/2015/12/12/explainer-what-is-legal-and-what-is-not-under-copyright-amendment-bill-2014/.

Progressive Lawyers Group. 2019a. "Statement of the Progressive Lawyers Group on the Government's Proposal to Amend Extradition Laws." Progressive Lawyers Group. February 20. Archived on file with the author.

Progressive Lawyers Group. 2019b. *The Hong Kong Rule of Law Report 2018.* Progressive Lawyers Group.

Progressive Lawyers Group. 2020. "Open Letter from 86 Groups: China – Scrap National Security Law to Save Hong Kong Freedoms." Progressive Lawyers Group. June 17. Archived on file with the author.

Sixtus Leung Chung Hang v. Chief Executive of the Hong Kong Special Administrative Region, Secretary for Justice. 2017. FAMV 10/2017; Yau Wai Ching v. Chief Executive of the Hong Kong Special Administrative Region, Secretary for Justice. 2017. FAMV 8/2017.

Steger, Isabella. 2016. "Beijing Is Determined to Keep Defiant, Pro-Independence Lawmakers Out of Hong Kong's Legislature." *Quartz.* October 19. Accessed March 21, 2021. https://qz.com/812500/hong-kongs-government-and-beijing-are-determined-to-kick-pro-independence-lawmakers-out-of-the-legislature.

Sum, Lok-kei. 2019. "Group of Extradition Bill Protesters Hold First Press Conference to Counter Hong Kong Government Line on Recent Demonstrations." *South China Morning Post.* August 6. Accessed March 21, 2021. https://www.scmp.com/news/hong-kong/politics/article/3021626/group-extradition-bill-protesters-hold-first-press.

Torode, Greg, and Anne Marie Roantree. 2019. "Hong Kong Lawyers Protest 'Polarising' Extradition Bill in Rare March." *Reuters.* June 6. Accessed April 7, 2021. https://reut.rs/3D6MulD.

"[Wéi yuán jí huì] fǎ zhèng huì sī : gǎng ào bàn jiě fàng jūn píng lùn fǎn xiū lì yùn dòng shè wéi fǎn jī běn fǎ." *Sing Tao Daily,* August 18. Accessed November 20, 2024. https://hk.news.yahoo.com/%E7%B6%AD%E5%9C%92%E9%9B%86%E6%9C%83-%E6%B3%95%E6%94%BF%E5%8C%AF%E6%80%9D-%E6%B8%AF%E6%BE%B3%E8%BE%A6%E8%A7%A3%E6%94%BE%E8%BB%8D%E8%A9%95%E8%AB%96%E5%8F%8D%E4%BF%AE%E4%BE%8B%E9%

81%8B%E5%8B%95%E6%B6%89%E9%81%95%E5%8F%8D-%E5%9F%BA%E6%9C%AC%E6%B3%95-080300368.html?guce_referrer=aHRocHM6Ly93d3cuZ29vZ2xlLmNvbS8&guce_referrer_sig=AQAAADHIQ8ZMZaS1tzqn6uRDOZ6goon7vzVXRome2S1oLiVO_VPAGdBmAx11rMPZIFwFeaygVLVy6erFvWQcuC-csLrbTHr46diIbW4JTvJLmQoMp3MlopkpyOdPm-otLn8JEEKfoSwRtMw_6pRSCOt4cLvZR3HlkCw3ATH2GsWyuEYdo&guccounter=2.

Wong, T. W. 2020. "Nǚ shēng tuì xià qián xiàn zhuǎn rèn fǎ tíng, 'páng tīng shī': péi bàn bèi bǔ shǒu zú, yán xù yùn dòng." *CitizenNews*. June 25. Accessed March 21, 2021. Archived on file with the author.

Young, Simon NM, and Richard Cullen. 2010. *Electing Hong Kong's Chief Executive*. Hong Kong University Press.

"[Zuì hòu fáng xiàn 3] Dà qí lì rì bù shì qí lì." 2015. *Stand News*, August 13. Accessed March 21, 2021. Archived on file with the author.

6. Defending Access to Justice in Social Movements

Abstract: This chapter investigates the development and operations of legal support networks in Hong Kong's social movements, focusing on the Anti-Extradition Law Amendment Bill (Anti-ELAB) protests. It highlights the critical role of cause lawyers in providing pro bono legal assistance to arrested protestors, countering authoritarian legal transplantation and colonial-era repressive laws. The chapter examines the evolution of legal assistance from individual initiatives to coordinated networks involving civil society, crowdfunding platforms, and professional legal teams. It also explores challenges such as police obstruction, financial sustainability, and internal coordination. These efforts safeguarded access to justice and fostered political awakening and professionalism among lawyers, consolidating a resilient front against authoritarian rule.

Keywords: Legal Support Networks, Cause Lawyers, Decentralisation, Protest Movements, Criminal Justice, Law Enforcement

Outside the police headquarters, dozens of parents, friends and lawyers of arrested protestors were waiting to get in. It was the night of 1 January 2020, after an anti-government protest featuring more than a million demonstrators was held in Hong Kong. The rally was part of the citywide movement against the introduction of the Extradition Law Amendment Bill (ELAB) in 2019. After this rally, 400 civilians were arrested. They were sent to police stations nearby, including the police headquarters. A barrister was helping both the arrested protestors waiting for bail and passers-by whose statements were being taken. She was there for more than five hours overnight.

It was a typical pro bono legal visit arranged by a legal support network for the Anti-ELAB Movement. The concept of a "legal support network" is derived from what Moustafa called a "judicial support network." A judicial support network concerns the organisational capacity for advocates to deliberate

Lai, Y. *Legal Resistance under Authoritarianism: The Struggle for the Rule of Law in Hong Kong.* Taylor & Francis Group, 2025
DOI: 10.5117/9789048558438_CH06

and strategise litigation campaigns, but it also focuses on the purpose of the network to safeguard judicial independence (Epp 1998; Moustafa 2014). It refers to institutions that "facilitate the expansion of judicial power by actively initiating litigation and supporting the independence of judicial institutions if they come under attack" (Ginsburg and Moustafa 2008; Moustafa 2007). I use the term legal support network instead. Although lawyers in Hong Kong are committed to serving the court, the civil society networks formed in those movements did not merely aim to safeguard judicial power from state intervention. Instead, they mainly focused on safeguarding the legal rights of clients in protest movements.

This chapter makes sense of such legal assistance for protestors. The Umbrella Movement of 2014 and the Anti-ELAB Movement of 2019 were ostensibly resistant to authoritarian legal transplantation by China. The Umbrella Movement strove to resist the decision of the National People's Congress Standing Committee (NPCSC) on a democratic backlash against Hong Kong in the future. The Anti-ELAB Movement was a citywide resistance against the indirect legal transplantation of the Chinese criminal justice system through a proposed extradition agreement between China and Hong Kong. In these movements, a legal support network was established and developed. Providing legal assistance for arrestees in protests serves as an essential form of legal resistance to authoritarian rule, where authoritarian legal transplants and the continuity of colonial legality work together to police mass protests.

China's authoritarian legal transplantation in Hong Kong is accompanied by the continuity of the colonial repressive legal regime. Strategies of authoritarian legal transplantation were effective because the state could suppress political opposition through criminal laws inherited from the British colonial administration. Therefore, the role of lawyers becomes significant in supporting activists, ranging from assisting arrestees inside police custody to defending them in court. In the case of post-colonial Hong Kong, the emergence of legal assistance for protestors evolved from individual practice to collective efforts, that was building a legal support network. Throughout the protest history in post-colonial Hong Kong, different pro bono legal visit teams were formed to support protestors. Such initiatives built collaboration between civil society and the legal profession, and strengthened the legal capital of Hong Kong's pro-democracy movement in terms of access to justice. Assisting protestors politicised the legal profession in Hong Kong, giving more direct experiences and witnesses of human rights violations and political injustice to the younger generation of the legal profession.

Resistance is a relational concept. It occurs when domination exists. Understanding how legal assistance has worked in Hong Kong also helps discover how the dominating state power reacted to political lawyering and legal support networks in resistant movements. The next section begins with examining the origin of legal assistance in Hong Kong's social movements.

Emergence of Legal Assistance in Hong Kong's Social Movements

During the 1960s, the Hong Kong government weaponised several transplanted laws to silence and repress dissents, including the Public Order Ordinance of 1967 (Cap.245), which charged protestors with offences of attending or organising unlawful assembly or rioting. Provisions on unlawful assembly and rioting in Hong Kong's Public Order Ordinance were ostensibly products of British colonial legal transplantation from Article 77 of the Penal Code of Nyasaland (*Xiāng Gǎng Tè Bié Xíng Zhèng Qū Sù Mò Jiā Tāo jí lìng bā rén* [2018] HKDC 225, para.89), which was a former British protectorate and now the Republic of Malawi (see chapter 1). After the transfer of sovereignty to China in 1997, the post-colonial government of Hong Kong continued to use such laws to arrest and prosecute pro-democracy activists, demonstrating a continuity of repression against political dissent. Establishing legal support networks for protestors, therefore, emerged as a strategy of lawyers to collectively defend the civil and legal rights of Hong Kong citizens against the application of such draconian laws.

Seeds of legal assistance for protestors can be found in lawyers assisting and defending activists in Hong Kong as early as in the 1970s. In 1979, 67 social workers and boat people went to the governor's residence to petition peacefully for resettlement in public housing. However, they were then arrested and charged with unlawful assembly under the Public Order Ordinance (Ng and Yiu 2018). Two barristers, Patrick Yu Shuk Siu and Henry Litton, defended them in court and appealed for their final sentences as pro bono lawyering. Another example was in 1997 when a group of student activists were arrested as they protested the World Bank and International Monetary Fund meeting in Hong Kong. A few pro bono lawyers and legal academics took the initiative to approach them, ensuring their legal support in criminal proceedings (ITV2001, 9 March 2020). However, these legal supports were individual efforts. It was not until 2005 that a legal support network of lawyers and activist groups emerged.

The emergence of legal support networks for activists was attributed to two factors. The first refers to the rise and expansion of contentious politics that embodied radical protests and thus led to subsequent mass arrests. In Hong Kong, there were times of peaceful mass mobilisations, such as the rally in support of the Tiananmen Student Movement in 1989 and the rally against an unpopular national security bill in 2003. These rallies remained generally peaceful, and the police did not arrest anyone. However, the dynamics between mass protest and public order policing changed in 2005, when more than a thousand protestors from different parts of the world, mainly South Korea, gathered to protest the sixth ministerial conference of the World Trade Organisation (WTO) in Hong Kong. The new situation further diffused political activism and radicalism in protests in the city (Cheng 2016). Protestors began to deploy more radical tactics in the Anti-ELAB protests, such as setting up barricades, directly disrupting traffic systems, throwing bricks and using Molotov cocktails. In return, the riot police also escalated the use of force to police protests and conducted mass arrests. The frequent mass arrests in protests during the Umbrella and Anti-ELAB Movements created enormous demands for defence lawyers. Therefore, a coordinating network became necessary to allocate legal staffing and resources efficiently.

The second factor is the institutional limitation of governmental legal assistance to citizens. The government-funded legal aid system is insufficient to support arrested protestors. The existing legal aid system and duty lawyer scheme in Hong Kong only support representation in court proceedings. Legal assistance and advice before trial representation, such as the stages of formal arrest and police interview, are not covered (DLA Piper and PILnet 2017; ITV2001, 9 March 2020). Seeing the institutional limits, some lawyers decided to form groups to provide pro bono legal assistance for protestors from the early stage of criminal proceeding, i.e., the arrest of protestors, to meet the legal needs that the government failed to provide.

The first legal support network was formed in 2005 contingently. As one of the founders of this first and foremost "legal support network" explained, the original purpose of forming a pro bono legal visit team was to support the arriving activists if they were barred from entry by the Immigration Department (ITV2001, 9 March 2020). The team, therefore, was just composed of a dozen lawyers at the beginning:

> In 2005, I looked for potential lawyers interested in helping protestors through my network only and then wrote their names down. In the end, we had around ten lawyers on standby, and this group later became the prototype of the pro bono legal visit team (ibid.).

Activists coming from abroad had been barred from meeting their lawyers in police stations for a few hours. After that, the team began to prepare for the potential arrests during the WTO protests (Hong Kong People's Alliance on WTO and Asian Human Rights Commission 2006). They assumed there would only be a small number of arrests. However, on the penultimate day of the WTO conference, a big clash between protestors and police took place, leading to the mass arrest of 900 protestors, who were later sent to different police stations for detention (Ho 2019). Recognising the unexpected demands for legal assistance in police stations, the team members expanded the network by recruiting their peers. After the mass arrest, the team had approximately 30 lawyers visited 18 police stations across the city, looking for the arrestees and accompanying them to make statements (ITV2001, 9 March 2020).

After this event, the pro bono legal visit team did not continue to operate. It was not until 2014 that a new legal support network was formed to prepare for the "Occupy Central with Love and Peace" (OCLP) campaign. This campaign was a mass sit-in as an act of civil disobedience to address the popular demand for universal suffrage in Hong Kong. It eventually developed into the Umbrella Movement, which was a 79-day occupation of major city hubs in Hong Kong, demanding a withdrawal of China's decision on a proposed screening methods for future Chief Executive elections in Hong Kong. The new network of pro bono legal visits teams was established before 1 July 2014, which was the day of an annual pro-democracy rally since 2003, as student activists called for a rehearsal of the occupation. As some of the anti-WTO legal team members had speculated on the need for pro bono lawyers in the possible mass arrests during the rehearsal, they had developed a more detailed plan to recruit lawyers and organise the structure of the support network. At the end of the sit-in rehearsal, 511 protestors were arrested in the dawn of 2 July. When they were sent to a general police station for detention, the legal support network sent a team of nearly 50 lawyers, including instructing solicitors and barristers, to provide legal support (ITV1930, 17 April 2019; ITV2001, 9 March 2020). The legal support network did not cease this time, as the occupation was forthcoming and expected to occur a few months later. The size of the legal team was doubled for the Umbrella Movement, and an Arrest Assistance Group (AAG) was formed by some lay people who also volunteered in the OCLP, serving as a call centre to mediate between the arrested protestors and the legal visit team. After the Umbrella Movement, some members of the AAG formed a civil society organisation called Civil Rights Observer (CRO) to sustain the service of legal assistance and human rights observation during protests.

The network continued to operate to support arrestees in a violent clash between activists and police during the Lunar New Year of 2016, as well as other single protest events (ITV2001, 9 March 2020).

The legal support network was further expanded when pro bono legal visit teams were multiplied by different groups of lawyers and civil society organisations in 2019. In previous practices, there was only one coordinating platform consisting of civil society groups and pro bono legal visit teams. Nevertheless, during the Anti-ELAB protests, at least three civil society groups worked closely with cause lawyers to develop pro bono legal visit teams, which were managed by the lawyers themselves, to assist arrested protestors. These groups were (i) the Civil Human Rights Front (CHRF), (ii) CRO, and (iii) Spark Alliance (SA), a crowdfunding platform close to localist activist groups. As early as May 2019, a group of lawyers had liaised with the CHRF on the need for forming a legal visit team in case mass protests were to break out during the reading and debate of the ELAB.[1] Hence, in early June, a hotline was established by the CHRF for protestors to contact lawyers for pro bono legal assistance in police detention. At the same time, CRO also formed a hotline for the same purpose.[2] After the violent clash between protestors and riot police outside the LegCo Complex on 12 June 2019, more hotlines were set up by different groups, including SA. Overall, the CHRF, CRO and SA became the best-known platforms providing protestors with legal assistance. As of December 2019, around 200 lawyers (including barristers, solicitors and law students) were ready for pro bono legal visits (*Commonwealth Magazine* 5 December 2019). In addition, some solicitor firms did not join the platforms but also coordinated with other activist groups to provide legal assistance on their own (ITV1912, 17 April 2020). These units all contributed to the process of social movement decentralisation, which is beneficial to movement sustainability, effective resource mobilisation, as well as the expansion of the legal support network for political activism in Hong Kong (Lai and Sing 2020).

Operating A Legal Support Network

The legal support network in Hong Kong's pro-democracy protests consisted of social movement organisations, civil society organisations and their respective pro bono legal visit teams. The legal visit teams were usually

1 My conversation with a member of the CHRF's secretariat in October 2019.

2 My observation in the CHRF since June 2019.

partitioned to a multitude of groups, which were composed of instructing solicitors and barristers. The partition was based on geographical allocation as the 2014 Umbrella Movment and the 2019 Anti-ELAB Movement were diffused across different districts in the city.

The legal support network in the Umbrella Movement and Anti-ELAB Movement operated similarly, but the network operation was more comprehensive in the Anti-ELAB Movement. During the Umbrella Movement, without crowdfunding platforms, a pro bono legal visit team was set up and coordinated with the AAG, which referred cases of protestors being arrested to the legal visit team (*Inmediahk* 19 November 2014). The AAG established two hotlines; one was called Legal Helpline SMS, and the other was Injury Report. Arrestees, victims of police use of excessive force and their family members could text for legal assistance. Once the AAG got the information about the arrestees, they would relay it to the coordinating group of the legal visit team, and the coordinators would distribute said information to different sub-groups for legal visits, corresponding to the geographical distance between lawyers available for legal visits and the respective police station. After legal visits, lawyers would report to the coordinators with the results, which were kept in a database for follow-up assistance. If the arrestees were charged later, the pro bono visit team could continue to assist them by helping them apply for legal aid, the duty lawyer scheme or asking team members to provide pro bono legal representation (ITV1912, 17 April 2020).

In the Anti-ELAB Movement, the operation of the legal support network became more comprehensive. This was because of the creation of new legal assistance hotlines by the CHRF, CRO and SA, and of the establishment of a new crowdfunding platform, namely "612 Humanitarian Relief Fund" (612HRF). It was launched by five trustees, including a Catholic cardinal Joseph Zen, two former pro-democracy lawmakers, a university professor and an activist Cantopop singer in Hong Kong (www.612fund.hk). Some of the trustees were experienced in public crowdfunding for supporting the pro-democracy movement and activists facing criminal trials in the past. This time, arrestees and their family members or friends had more options for legal visit teams, depending on their political orientation and perception towards different sponsoring organisations of the hotline. For example, the CHRF was a well-known social movement coalition for traditional pro-democracy parties and civil society organisations since 2002. In contrast, SA was formed by individuals sympathetic to localists and pro-independence activists. It provided legal assistance to arrested localist protestors and jailed activists who participated in the 2016 civil unrest (Spark Alliance 2017). Although SA had its crowdfunding platform, it also coordinated with the 612HRF such as sharing contact details for referral, as some localist protestors would want to seek legal assistance from groups holding a similar political and ideological orientation. Besides, many university student unions and school authorities also provided legal assistance hotlines, given the mass participation of university students in the movement (LIHKG 11 June 2019).

The operation of the legal support network can be divided into three stages. The first stage was legal visit at the police station. Lawyers engaged in this stage from meeting arresting protestors to applying for bail at the police station. Before a rally began, the CHRF, CRO and SA disseminated their legal assistance hotline on social media platforms, such as Facebook and Telegram, and sometimes distributed paper cards among rally participants in case they got arrested. During a rally, when protestors were arrested, their friends or family members would send information about the arrestees to established hotlines for referral. Once the information was received, the hotline operators would send a list of arrestees to lawyer members of the pro bono legal visit teams, which would then pair up instructing solicitors and barristers and assign them to visit police stations near their homes (ITV1910, 28 April 2020). In Hong Kong, barristers can only be directly instructed through solicitors. Thus, the coordinating teams had to ensure that each group for legal visits should have at least one instructing solicitor or a letter of proof from a law firm. When pro bono lawyers arrived at the police station, their first task was confirming the police station where the reported arrestees were detained. Lawyers needed to call or ask the reception desk at the police station to verify the names of the arrestees, as they may have been reallocated to other police stations for different reasons (ITV1907, 21 April 2020). Once the police confirmed the detainment of arrestees inside that police station, lawyers would request the police to meet the arrestees, advising them and accompanying them when making statements to the police and applying for bail (ITV1912, 17 April 2020). At this stage, crowdfunding platforms could provide loans for police bail, whereas the lawyers would leave their contact information to the arrestees to follow up.

The second stage was post-bail legal support. Usually, lawyers from different legal visit teams would contact the protestors with police bail for a post-bail conference. There were three ways of conducting a post-bail conference. Firstly, for arrestees who were just passers-by at the protest site, solicitors might call them to discuss the case and advise them. Secondly, for clients in general, an instructing solicitor and at least one instructed barrister would meet clients individually to follow up on their cases. If the client was charged for trial later, the 612 HRF could cover the fees of the post-bail conference and trial proceedings. Thirdly, some legal visit teams would organise a briefing for a group of arrestees, providing general legal information on the statutes and proceedings of criminal trials. Then, the arrestees could individually meet their respective lawyers who helped them at police stations (ITV2008, 8 June 2020). The only difference between the three approaches was that the last one would offer a general information sharing without going into any specific case details. It provided relevant knowledge and information on criminal proceedings to arrested protestors. In addition, crowdfunding platforms continued to cover the expenses of the legal visit teams in providing relevant legal support (612 Humanitarian Relief Fund 2020a,6).

The third stage commenced once arrestees were charged for criminal trials. They might either hire lawyers who visited and assisted them before or someone they preferred for criminal defence. The charged protestors, if eligible, were often asked by 612 HRF to apply for duty lawyers or legal aid as the first step, since many members of the legal visit teams were on the lists of duty lawyer schemes. Otherwise, clients could nominate their preferred barristers and law firms to take their cases in legal aid applications (ITV1912, 17 April 2020). Then, crowdfunding platforms such as 612HRF would cover the remaining costs of preparation for trial and legal representation. If the protestors were convicted, 612HRF would continue to accompany the defendants and their family members by providing legal and non-legal assistance with other civil society organisations, such as mental health support and prison visits. In the whole process, the crowdfunding platforms also received grant applications from hotline providers and the pro bono legal visit teams to sustain their operations (612 Humanitarian Relief Fund 2021). 612HRF, legal visit teams and the hotline providers periodically released reports to the public on their work to uphold accountability (Civil Human Rights Front 2019).

At each stage, crowdfunding platforms acted as a backbone to sustain NGO hotlines and legal visit teams, which both shared essential functions in assisting arrested protestors in the first stage. In the second and third stages, lawyers from the legal visit teams played a pivotal role as legal professionals who directly advised and defended their clients in court. The three principal actors constituted the leading legal support network, which continued to expand by connecting with other partners from civil society to provide non-legal support and public engagement in crowdfunding.

Challenges and Responses

Law firms' provision of pro bono legal services for political activists can be both selfless and self-interested. The act of pro bono lawyering is altruistic to the clients who cannot afford legal fees for settling disputes or criminal defence. However, as observed in the Anti-ELAB Movement and discussed with some members of the legal support network, providing pro bono legal services can be a competitive business among law firms and counsel to boost their popularity.

For activist or political lawyering, the challenges of providing legal support to clients are economic and political. As discussed in previous chapters, many law firms are attracted by the state's economic policies and the capital from mainland China and are inclined towards comprador professionalism. Assisting arrested protestors can be displeased by the political authorities, hence such service does not look like a worthy investment for lawyers from a career development perspective. This section identifies three challenges for pro bono legal visit teams in their support of protestors. They are economic and political challenges, and the economic challenge also caused issues of solidarity within the legal support network. While the legal support network found ways of overcoming the economic challenge, the political one was less easily remedied due to institutional constraints.

Economic Challenge: Unfavourable Occupation Structure

The first challenge to operating the legal support network related to the unfavourable occupation structure of the legal profession. The existing legal framework in Hong Kong requires all practising solicitors to have mandatory indemnity insurance, and the Law Society covers the insurance for all solicitor firms in Hong Kong with an amount of up to HKD 10 million per claim (DLA Piper and Hong Kong Association of Corporate Council 2018, 10). Unless a solicitor is granted exemption from the Law Society or they are in-house lawyers whereby the business firm covers the insurance, they cannot provide pro bono legal assistance without permission from their law firm (ibid.). Although barristers are self-employed, they must be instructed by solicitors under the same legal framework. It implies that non-profit organisations that would like to provide legal assistance for activists cannot employ in-house lawyers due to the huge cost of indemnity insurance. They can only work with solicitor firms to provide legal services. Also, due to the sensitive nature of pro bono legal service for arrested protestors, few law firms were willing to permit solicitors to pay visits to police stations during protests.

To overcome this challenge, the legal support network responded by mobilising lawyers through existing networks and providing economic incentives. Here, the Progressive Lawyers Group (PLG) played a significant role as a pool of human resources. As discussed in the previous chapter, the PLG consisted of practising lawyers, paralegals and law students. The PLG nurtured many law students and pupils who aspired to cause lawyering. Many PLG members joined different legal visit teams to support their administrative work (ITV2001, 9 March 2020).

To incentivise more barristers as well as solicitor firms to allow their employees to join the legal visit teams, crowdfunding platforms like 612HRF decided to subsidise legal fees for criminal defence related to the Anti-ELAB Movement (ITV1912, 17 April 2020). Those crowdfunding platforms sponsored fees not covered by legal aid or duty lawyer schemes. For example, 612HRF had a detailed funding scheme for legal fees in criminal proceedings, including case conferences, attending court hearings, application for bail at the High Court and legal visits at detention centres or prisons (612 Humanitarian Relief Fund 2020a, 5). As shared by one of my interviewees, even if she wanted to assist arrested protestors in the Umbrella Movement, she had to ensure that her law firm would be paid for the arrestees' criminal trials, as her boss was reluctant to do a pro bono case (ITV1930, 17 April 2019). With the funding scheme above, solicitors who wanted to commit themselves to the legal visit teams could bargain with their bosses, as law firms could still benefit from assisting these clients. However, the rate of the fees from crowdfunding platforms was lower than the government-sponsored legal aid (ITV1927, 23 September 2019).

612HRF also tried to attract junior barristers to defend protestors by introducing a "second counsel scheme." If criminal cases are transferred from magistrates to the district court in Hong Kong, defendants can apply for legal aid to cover legal fees for a defence counsel and a solicitor firm. However, the legal aid department usually sponsors one counsel only, and there were only a few qualified criminal barristers on the list of legal aid schemes. Hence, it may not be possible to assign a counsel who has established connections with the defendants at the stage of the pro bono legal visit. Therefore, 612HRF set up a funding scheme for defendants to appoint a second counsel to assist the legal team covered by the government legal aid, and 612HRF would pay for the second counsel at a lower rate than the market price.

This scheme had three advantages. Firstly, it helped defendants maintain relationships with trusted counsel whom the legal aid department does not sponsor. Secondly, it incentivised more junior counsel to defend protestors. Thirdly, junior counsel could accumulate more experience in criminal cases at the district court level. Thus, they could qualify sooner as a legal aid counsel (612 Humanitarian Relief Fund 2020b). Although these funding schemes from the crowdfunding platforms were below the market rate, they could still perform as economic incentives to lawyers who might not want to join legal visit teams due to concerns about their livelihood since it would be too costly for solicitors and barristers to do pro bono work for each protest case. In the end, several hundred law students, pupils of barristers, paralegals, solicitor trainees and barristers joined the legal support network during the Anti-ELAB Movement (ITV2001, 9 March 2020).

Economic Challenge: Competition and Coordination

Economic factor could also create relational challenges between pro bono legal visit teams. The emergence of multiple legal visit teams could accommodate arrested protestors from different sides of the political spectrum on the one hand but also engender tensions and clashes between the teams on the other. This was because, at the beginning of the Anti-ELAB Movement, different legal visit teams were in competitive relationships. Legal visits at police stations were pro bono work. However, all legal proceedings after the granting of police bail were paid by government legal aid, by the clients themselves or by crowdfunding platforms. Legal visits, as observed by some lawyers, could create a pool of potential clients for law firms and barristers, and they could earn money from the visited clients if the latter were going to face criminal trials later on (ITV1956, 26 September 2019; ITV2001, 9 Match 2020).

One example can shed light on the internal tensions among different legal visit teams at the beginning of the Anti-ELAB Movement. This example came from the first-hand experience of a barrister who visited his clients at a police station after one protest event during the Anti-ELAB Movement:

> When lawyers from two separate legal visit teams arrived at the police station where I was dealing with the police officers, they were arguing about who should take over the clients there. One said the parents of the arrestee called him at 15:13 and then called the other twelve minutes later. Thus, he who received the call earlier should meet the arrestee. Another lawyer disagreed and suggested that they ask the arrestee to meet them separately so he could choose which legal team he would want. When I heard this, I felt they were avaricious enough to grab clients out of dozens of young arrestees; they were just motivated by business, whereas some of these visited arrestees would be later prosecuted by the police and taken to court (ITV1910, 28 April 2020).

The disputes among different pro bono legal visit teams could be attributed to market competition and a lack of coordination. The former attribute refers to the potential economic benefits of being a pro bono lawyer in the legal support network. The latter means that, as explained by a counsel who witnessed the development of the legal support network, the legal support network was decentralised at the expense of central, effective coordination:

> Since the outbreak of the Anti-ELAB Movement, the core members of the new legal support network have attempted to coordinate systematically between the three major legal visit teams. However, when arrested protestors called several hotlines simultaneously, the legal teams would not know whether their counterpart should also be involved in legal visits. Thus, clients were snatched between different teams. Furthermore, the legal support network was an ad hoc product of the movement. Mutual trust could have been higher among the teams, and misunderstandings among different legal visit teams could have been diminished (ITV2001, 9 March 2020).

In the end, the relational challenges were mitigated by efforts from both within and outside the legal support network. After several clashes over the snatching of clients between the legal visit teams, they decided to coordinate by setting boundaries among the team members carrying out their services. They repeatedly asked protestors not to call different hotlines at the same time to avoid duplicate efforts as well (ITV1910, 28 April 2020). In fact, as Anti-ELAB protests lasted for almost seven months since its outbreak in June 2019, the demands for legal visits had never diminished when the law enforcement persisted the tactic of mass arrests. As a solicitor interviewee explained, too few law firms were specialised in public order events and human rights litigations in Hong Kong. Even if other law firms were interested in representing arrested protestors in court, they might not be able to do so given the quota limits of the duty lawyer scheme and government legal aid (ITV1956, 26 September 2019; ITV2001, 9 March 2020). Some members from the legal visit teams estimated that only 10 to 20 solicitor firms were involved in the legal support network during the Anti-ELAB Movement (ITV1912, 17 April 2020; ITV1907, 2002 and 2003, 21 April 2020). As a result, the small number of law firms and barristers committed to the legal support network eventually watered down internal conflicts among different legal visit teams.

Political Challenge

The last challenge for lawyers engaging in legal visit teams refers to the law enforcement's various obstruction tactics against the legal visit teams. These tactics were observed and documented by many of my interviewees who were members of different legal visit teams as early as during the Umbrella Movement in 2014. These tactics had a discouraging effect on lawyers in many ways.

Facing the protest waves during the Anti-ELAB Movement, the political authorities made it publicly clear that their top priority was "stopping violence and restoring order" (C. Choi 2019; Kuo 2019). The Chinese and Hong Kong governments heavily depended on local law enforcement to police protests. From August 2019, law enforcement began to employ the tactic of mass arrest in protests, targeting both militant protestors, peaceful and moderate demonstrators and sometimes passers-by at protest sites (National Democratic Institute and Georgetown Center for Asian Law 2020; Progressive Scholars Group 2020). Such massive-scale arbitrary arrests were purposive for creating a deterrent effect in the public, thus discouraging citizens from continuing their support and engagement in protest actions. As documented by Amnesty International, the Hong Kong police allegedly exercised excessive physical means to arrest protestors. The law enforcement was also accused of obstructing arrested protestors' access to lawyers in police detention. The latter tactic could be convenient for some police officers to abuse their power by using aggressive means and means with force against the detainees, forcing them to make statements without the presence of any legal professionals, who could monitor and stop police misconduct in the process of statement-making (Amnesty International 19 September 2019). These statements, therefore, could become evidence favourable to the prosecution when the cases were taken later to court, justifying a conviction of guilt and the subsequent sentences and achieving the goal of "stopping violence and restoring order."

Obstructive tactics such as delaying arrestees' access to counsel can be found as early as in the anti-WTO protest. Complaints by civil society organisations exposed that most of the detained protestors were not allowed to make phone calls to contact their counsel or family members, and police officers refused to allow visiting lawyers to meet the arrestees (Hong Kong People's Alliance on WTO and Asian Human Rights Commission 2006).

The first-hand experiences of my interviewees, who engaged in different legal visit teams in the Umbrella Movement and the Anti-ELAB Movement, further explained how these obstructive tactics were carried out inside police stations:

> The police officers abused their powers by delaying our meetings with arrested persons. When I visited Sun Uk Leng [the location of a detention centre], I could only meet my first client three hours after my request. Supposedly, a client should make a statement in the presence of a lawyer, but in many instances, they had made statements before our arrival and meeting (ITV1927, 23 September 2019).

> Often, the duty officer of a police station claimed that the names on our arrestees list were not listed in the system. One night at 10:45 pm, when we asked the duty officer to check our client's name, he said no such person had been detained there. We repeatedly asked him to double-check again and again. It was not until three am that he gave us our client's name, but the record showed that he had already made a cautioned statement and admitted [the charge] (ITV2004, 24 April 2020).

The delays of lawyers meeting clients by some police officers were common during the Anti-ELAB protests. As told by their clients, some legal visit lawyers found that police officers had asked them to make statements without a lawyer by using "carrot and stick" methods:

> My clients were told that they would only be able to meet a lawyer if they made a cautioned statement now. Sometimes, police officers would further pressure my clients by asking, "Aren't you going to make a cautioned statement? Everyone else here is going to." Furthermore, police officers would smear us by saying, "These lawyers are not pro bono lawyers; they just want to make money as they can get paid by accompanying you to make cautioned statements (ITV2006, 8 May 2020).

Ostensibly, these obstructions were aimed at barring arrestees' access to counsel on time while also trapping arrestees into making cautioned statements and taking photos without legal advice. This "evidence" would then be favourable to the prosecution:

> Some of my clients needed to be made aware of giving hints to police when not in our presence. For example, one of them was asked by a police officer whether he was arrested in Mong Kok [a district in Hong Kong]. He thought it was a fact that he got arrested in Mong Kok, so he told the police officer "yes." As a result, he admitted that he had been in that district, doing the prosecution a favour when preparing evidence and witnesses (ITV2006, 8 May 2020).

> Police officers likely wanted the arrestees to make cautioned statements as soon as possible and to be searched. Police officers would even ask the arrestees to take photos with their equipment before meeting lawyers, which was a surprise to the arrestees. Although we could challenge the admissibility of this evidence in court, judges could still accept them by discretion (ITV1957, 11 October 2019).

The police's alleged misconducts towards legal visits appeared to pressure the arrestees to admit their guilt and speed up prosecution processes. Nonetheless, existing regulatory mechanisms could not work speedily and effectively to check police power. The Police General Orders that regulate the police force are not part of the Hong Kong law but merely internal rules. Some of the chapters of the orders are even undisclosed to the public. Therefore, in the case of police officers obstructing legal visits, even if lawyers file complaints to the police, the corresponding police officers would not face criminal sanction or civil liability for violating the orders (ITV1910, 28 April 2020). The Complaints Against Police Office (CAPO) in Hong Kong is subject to the Commissioner of Police and is a unit under the Hong Kong police force (Hong Kong Police Force August 2015). In other words, the complaint mechanism is less effective as it is not independent of the law enforcement. Although there is a so-called Independent Police Complaints Council (IPCC), in which all members are appointed by the Chief Executive of Hong Kong, it can only review investigation reports from CAPO (Independent Police Complaints Council 10 January 2018). In short, the effectiveness and accountability of these institutions were in doubt when they were not independent bodies to oversee police misconduct.

Overall, the goal of the police's obstruction of providing legal assistance by the legal visit teams was twofold. Protections of the arrestees' right to access counsel and the right to acknowledge legal rights in detention were paralysed when arrestees could not meet their lawyers on time. Furthermore, the delaying tactics and non-cooperation by police were carried out as attrition against legal visit teams. The time it took to locate and then meet arrestees, sometimes even up to 10 hours, consumed lawyers' energy and resources, weakening their physical and psychological capacities to provide legal services (ITV1957, 11 October 2019).

The pro bono legal visit lawyers responded to government obstructive tactics in two ways. The first response referred to what a lawyer called an "ultra-cooperation movement." While activists promote non-cooperation, lawyers defend the establishment of the Rule of Law and are always good at cooperating with existing mechanisms. Hence, lawyers can maximise the potential of the limited and less effective complaint mechanisms of CAPO, IPCC or even the court for their clients. Although making complaints or taking legal action would be less cost-effective given the institutional constraints, they inevitably corner the public authorities to face the situation under public scrutiny:

> Although the immediate effect of the non-cooperation movement is limited, it could get in touch with the people who hold the authority at all. For the ultra-cooperation movement, you engage them in their institutions. A judge will be cornered to face the public allegation of police abuse of power in a civil claim against the Commissioner of Police, and he/she must respond to these allegations before the public (ITV1927, 23 September 2019).

In practice, 612HRF allows for the application of civil proceedings against alleged abuse of public power by affected parties. In contrast, some members of the pro bono legal visit teams also assisted protestors or civilians in filing lawsuits against law enforcement misconduct in court. As of May 2021, 612HRF has supported 15 civil proceedings for claims or judicial reviews against law enforcement (612 Humanitarian Relief Fund 2020b).

The second response was to promote popular legal education before protests, to which the PLG contributed. Popular legal education in criminal justice system was essential for protestors, who would be arrested and detained at police stations without any professional support from lawyers. Hence, PLG's "lazy packs" on various legal issues that emerged in protest policing became useful resources to disseminate basic knowledge to the public. In addition, some pro bono legal visit lawyers organised public talks to lecture on the rights of citizens in protests and police custody and to empower citizens in the face of police abuse of power. For instance, on 21 July 2019, three cause lawyers organised an on-site legal forum at the gathering site for a CHRF rally before the rally commenced.[3] This could be regarded as a preventive measure for individual protestors to know their rights lest police hold them in custody.

Nevertheless, these responses were limited in their effect when the state power continued to expand and intervene in due process during the Anti-ELAB Movement. Police officers could still force arrestees to make statements before anyone from the legal visit teams arrives. In contrast,

3 I observed the preparation of the legal forum near the fountain of Victoria Park in Hong Kong on 21 July 2019.

the Secretary for Justice in Hong Kong enjoys the power to intervene in private prosecutions against police officers by citizens and to call for the termination of such case hearings at any time. Worse still, throughout the Anti-ELAB Movement, mass arrests in protests and subsequent prosecutions did not cease, speeding up the expenses of crowdfunding platforms as well as exhausting resources from the legal community (ITV2005, 8 May 2020).

Sustaining Legal Support Networks: Political Commitment and Professionalism

The obstructions by police and the limited responses from lawyers, however, did not weaken the latter's commitment to continuing their legal assistance to protestors. The political will of resistance among those cause lawyers and commitment to professionalism were fundamental drivers of the sustainability and resilience of the legal visit teams and the legal support network, apart from material support. Some interviewees acknowledged that there was an opportunity cost when they engaged in pro bono legal visits and the subsequent criminal defence, as they would have less time to take up more profitable cases like civil proceedings:

> Taking up legal visits and protest cases would bring much less income to my firm than other cases. We can only get HKD6,000 for attending a half-day trial, and the rate does not include preparation time. On the contrary, I can get an hourly rate of HKD3,000 for commercial cases, say drafting a letter or civil litigation. I only chose to do it because I care about the Rule of Law. I must stand up and do something if I claim I care about it (ITV2008, 8 June 2020).

> If I am labelled as a counsel who specialises in protest-related cases, my business would be affected, as some law firms dislike counsel like me and turn to instruct someone else. I always struggle with whether I should keep a low profile by not taking up legal visits and defending protestors in the courtroom or continue to do so for Hong Kong's sake. In the end, I chose to continue. What motivates me to continue is the everyday injustice I see on the TV news. I want to do something substantive instead of blaming and yelling at home (ITV1957, 11 October 2019).

> Taking up protest-related cases would give me much less income because I would have to spend lots of time and energy tackling them. Moreover,

> I must thoroughly drill up on the cases as I feel I owe them (the protestors). If I could not perform due diligence when defending them in court, how could I defend the proud reputation of the Rule of Law? (ITV1910, 28 April 2020).

The atonement spoken of by the interviewee above revealed a sense of guilt that legal professionals felt from being unable to stop the passage of the extradition law at the frontline. The young protestors took militant action to paralyse the surroundings of the government headquarters on 12 June 2019 at the expense of their future, leading to the suspension and withdrawal of the unpopular bill. Therefore, the motivations for engaging in legal assistance were mixed. They included the lawyers' commitment to the Rule of Law, a sense of righteousness, and a sense of penance to defend protestors from repressive legal sanctions. These motivations were not based on an ethical code of the legal profession but on the political and moral consciousness of individual lawyers. While the legal support network provided economic incentives to lawyers, the main driver of sustaining the network was the political will and commitment of lawyers who pay a high opportunity cost to support political activism.

Legal visit teams succeeded in combining lawyers' political commitment and legal professionalism during the Anti-ELAB protests. Maintaining professionalism served as a key to consolidating the legal support network. On many occasions, lawyers chose to carry out "ultra-cooperation" only after the incidents of power abuse to minimise threats against clients' interests:

> Often, we do not confront police officers at police stations for our client's sake. We wanted to avoid provoking those officers who may retribute against the arrestees. Therefore, we had to maintain good manners there. After all, police officers also wanted to avoid being complained (ITV1927, 23 September 2019).

> We sometimes deliberated whether we should immediately file a complaint against a duty officer at a police station. Making a complaint is a subtle action, but we were concerned whether those police officers would treat our clients worse after the complaints. What we did was to document all misconducts and abuses experienced by our clients and consider civil claims afterwards (ITV2004, 24 April 2020).

These instances reflected that lawyering for protestors can be confrontational against state repression on the one hand, yet it does not compromise professionalism on the other. Legal visits for protestors demonstrated its dual nature: It was an act of political resistance by assisting arrested protestors who faced injustice and state repression on the one hand, and was a process of performing legal professionalism in contentious spaces, such as police stations, police detention centres and even the courts on the other.

Conclusion

In the post-colonial era of Hong Kong, legal assistance for protestors was performed by establishing and developing several legal visit teams that eventually formed a legal support network in civil society. It was an outcome in response to the limited supply of legal assistance to arrested protestors and the rising demands for legal visits and criminal defence amid the escalation of contentious politics in the city.

The strategy of legal assistance in protest settings, therefore, was both ideological and practical. It is ideological as those who engaged in it were cause lawyers who believe in the notion of Rule of Law that safeguards civil liberties and access to justice. They resisted authoritarian governance by the sovereign state that attempts to transplant a Chinese system of law and order over Hong Kong's Rule of Law. Legal assistance was a practical strategy as well, since it could not be performed without qualified lawyers, including their law firms, barrister chambers, and connections with civil society, such as crowdfunding platforms, to warrant access to lawyers, courts and overall, legal justice.

The contributions of legal assistance for protestors were two-fold. Firstly, it served as a bottom-up attempt to safeguard access to justice in authoritarian states. The establishment of legal support networks, formed by pro bono legal visit teams, civil society organisations and crowdfunding platforms, was both a safeguard of arrested protestors' right to access counsel and a concerted effort to check the state power that tries to manipulate due process in the early stage of criminal proceedings. Against the backdrop of the limited legal aid system and the repeated allegations of power abuse by law enforcement in protest events, the legal support network was a remedy. The provision of legal assistance ensured that the legal rights of arrestees were realised, and the violations of these rights were monitored and documented by on-site lawyers. In particular, the crowdfunding platforms in the legal support network were a significant source to pardon protestors who needed legal representatives to defend them but had limited financial support. The formation of legal support networks strengthened the legal capital as well as the resilience of Hong Kong's pro-democracy movement, and consolidated the bonding between the legal profession, at least the critical minority of cause lawyers, civil society, and political activism in resisting China's repressive rules in Hong Kong.

Another contribution was that the legal profession in Hong Kong leaned more towards democratic and progressive values under the development of a legal support network. The process of China's authoritarian legal transplantation eventually led to the emergence of resistance and contention by the legal community. Nevertheless, most of these contentions concentrated on the rhetorical and discursive aspects of the Rule of Law. Engaging in legal assistance, however, encountered the technical and practical aspects of the Rule of Law when lawyers directly experienced how police officers abused criminal proceedings that put their clients at peril. The need for resistance against the government's abuse of the Rule of Law and due process became more urgent and substantive. These experiences further led to the political awakening of the younger generation of lawyers to take further steps to resist authoritarian legal transplantation and legal repression. For instance, some cause lawyers in the Anti-ELAB Movement became convenors of the PLG in 2019 after realising the need to consolidate a liberal legal community in Hong Kong (*Inmediahk* 12 March 2020). Some lawyers from legal visit teams decided to run for the council election of the Law Society, hoping to address the police abuse of the legal system within the conservative solicitor leadership that embraced comprador professionalism in general (this will be discussed in chapter 8). The ties of the legal support network, activist lawyer groups and even members from the leadership of professional bodies became further strengthened.

The limitations of providing legal assistance for protestors should also be addressed here. The first limitation relates to the state's exercise of power to obstruct legal support networks. Many complaints and civil claims against the police force have been pending, whereas the Secretary for Justice intervened in a private prosecution against one police officer to terminate the hearing (B. Wong 2020). Moreover, six months after the outbreak of the Anti-ELAB protests, the police froze around HKD70 million in SA's bank account and arrested four people for money laundering. The arrest and freezing of assets created a citywide fear as many citizens had donated to this crowdfunding platform, and protestors worried about having fewer sources of financial support for legal proceedings (Saito and John 2019). In addition, 612HRF ceased operation in 2022, two years after the National Security Law (NSL) was enacted, after their trustees got arrested. They were alleged of colluding with foreign forces, a new crime under the NSL. It is unlikely that crowdfunding platforms or similar initiatives could continue to exist in the near future of Hong Kong.

The second limitation concerns the organisational sustainability of the legal support network. The legal constraints of indemnity insurance that discourage lawyering in non-profit organisations remain. Hence, activist lawyers could only continue their "missions" in law firms and chambers, which are inevitably business oriented. Clashes among legal visit teams over the snatching of potential clients were resolved during the Anti-ELAB Movement, yet it does not mean it will fade out permanently. Without legal reform of professional regulation and control, it is unlikely that Hong Kong's legal profession and civil society could further institutionalise activist or political lawyering. The case of Hong Kong is different from initiatives or organised efforts in other common law jurisdictions, such as the American Civil Liberties Union in the US or Liberty in the UK, which can hire lawyers to take up human rights litigations and criminal defence for activists.

Protest movements are eventful. Even if they last for a long period of time, it is unlikely for them to continue indefinitely. Finding sustainable strategies to resist China's authoritarian transplantation is thus an important task for lawyers in Hong Kong. One solution is to shift their battlefield from outside the establishment to within the establishment. Apart from the courtroom, legal professional bodies are contested space for liberal and activist lawyers to carry out resistance. In the following two chapters, I will turn my focus to the establishment of the legal professionals: the Bar and the Law Society, examining how liberal and activist lawyers in Hong Kong strategised leadership contestations to resist China's authoritarian agenda in Hong Kong.

References

"Bèi bǔ zhī yuán xiǎo zǔ jiù chōng jī lì fǎ huì shì jiàn shēng míng." 2014. *Inmediahk*, 19 November. Accessed 25 May 2021. https://www.inmediahk.net/node/1028691.

Cheng, Edmund W. 2016. "Street Politics in a Hybrid Regime: The Diffusion of Political Activism in Post-Colonial Hong Kong." *The China Quarterly* 226: 383–406.

Choi, Christy. 2019. "Hong Kong Protesters and Chinese Officials Hold Rival Press Conferences." *The Guardian*, August 6. Accessed June 19, 2021. https://www.theguardian.com/world/2019/aug/06/masked-hong-kongers-democracy-china-thugs.

Civil Human Rights Front. 2019. "Dài fā mín zhèn yì wù lu shī tuán gōng zuò jiǎn bào" *Facebook Page*, October 18. Accessed October 31, 2024.

Complaint Against Police Office. 2015. *Hong Kong Police Force*. August. Accessed June 24, 2021. https://www.police.gov.hk/info/doc/pledge/2016/html/CAPOENG.html.

"Dài fā: mín zhèn yì wù lu shī tuán." 2019. Facebook, October 18. Accessed June 3, 2021. https://www.facebook.com/story.php?story_fbid=2536809006366475&id=511608535553209&_rdr.

DLA Piper and Hong Kong Association of Corporate Council. 2018. *Pro Bono Legal Work in Hong Kong: A Guide for In-House Counsel*.

DLA Piper and PILnet (The Global Network for Public Interest Law). 2017. *This Way: Finding Community Legal Assistance in Hong Kong*.

Epp, Charles. 1998. *The Rights Revolution: Lawyers, Activists, and Supreme Courts in Comparative Perspective*. Chicago Press.

"Fǎn sòng zhōng yùn dòng de àn yè shǐ zhě 200 wèi rén quán lu shī: "Shuí De Shēn Tǐ Zhuàng Kuàng Huán Kě Yǐ, Shuí Jiù Chēng Xià Qù." 2019. *Commonwealth Magazine*, September 8. Accessed June 25, 2021. https://www.cw.com.tw/article/5096754.

Ginsburg, Tom, and Tamir Moustafa, eds. 2008. *Rule by Law: The Politics of Courts in Authoritarian Regimes*. Cambridge University Press.

Ho, Lawrence K. K. 2019. "Policing Transnational Protests in an Asian Context: The WTO Sixth Ministerial Conference in Hong Kong." *Contemporary Chinese Political Economy and Strategic Relations: An International Journal* 5 (1): 211–249.

Hong Kong: Arbitrary Arrests, Brutal Beatings and Torture in Police Detention Revealed. 2019. Amnesty International, September 19. Accessed June 19, 2021. https://www.amnesty.org/en/latest/press-release/2019/09/hong-kong-arbitrary-arrests-brutal-beatings-and-torture-in-police-detention-revealed/.

Hong Kong People's Alliance on WTO and Asian Human Rights Commission. 2006. "Briefing Report on Policing, Arrests and Detentions Regarding the WTO Protests." Submission to Legislative Council Panel on Security, CB(2) 1055/05-06(01).

"[Jǐn jí zhuàng kuàng fǎ lu zhī yuán diàn huà] Wǒ zhěng zuo zhāng A8 Size Māo Zhǐ Fāng Biàn Suí Shēn Xié Dài." 2019. LIHKG, June 11. Accessed May 25, 2021. https://lihkg.com/thread/1204851/page/1.

Kuo, Lily. 2019. "Second Death in Week as Xi Jinping Demands End to Hong Kong Violence." *The Guardian*, November 14. Accessed June 19, 2021. https://www.theguardian.com/world/2019/nov/14/second-death-in-hong-kong-protests-as-xi-demands-end-to-violence.

Lai, Yan-Ho, and Ming Sing. 2020. "Solidarity and Implications of a Leaderless Movement in Hong Kong: Its Strengths and Limitations." *Communist and Post-Communist Studies* 53 (4): 41–67.

Moustafa, Tamir. 2007. *The Struggle for Constitutional Power: Law, Politics, and Economic Reform in Egypt*. Cambridge University Press.

Moustafa, Tamir. 2014. “Law and Courts in Authoritarian Regimes.” *Annual Review of Law and Social Science* 10: 281–299.

National Democratic Institute and Georgetown Center for Asian Law. 2020. *The Promise of Democratization in Hong Kong: Discontent and Rule of Law Challenges.* April 23. Accessed September 21, 2021. https://www.ndi.org/publications/promise-democratization-hong-kong.

Ng, W. and W. T. You. 2018. “Tǐng Hù Kàng Zhēng 40 Nián, ‘Fēi Fǎ Jí Jié Zuì’ De Qián Shì Jīn Shēng.” *The News Lens,* April 18. Accessed May 19, 2021. Archived on file with the author.

Progressive Scholars Group. 2020. *Silencing Millions: Unchecked Violations of Internationally Recognized Human Rights by the Hong Kong Police Force.*

Saito, Mari, and Anne John. 2019. “Hong Kong Protesters Denounce Police Raid on Fund-Raising Platform.” Reuters, December 20. Accessed June 25, 2021. https://reut.rs/3n3mWQz.

Spark Alliance. 2017. “About” *Facebook Page.* Accessed October 31, 2024. https://www.facebook.com/sparkalliancehk/about .

612 Humanitarian Relief Fund. 2019. “Fund Facts.” Accessed June 16, 2021. https://612fund.hk/en/dummies.

612 Humanitarian Relief Fund. 2020a. *2019–2020 Annual Report.* Accessed June 16, 2021. https://static1.squarespace.com/static/5d53782d96f86e00015a4657/t/5f042321b7e1fd56c38ecce3/1594106754935/612-annual-report.pdf.

612 Humanitarian Relief Fund. 2020b. “Qū Yù Fǎ Yuàn Àn Jiàn ‘Dì Èr Wèi Dà Lu Shī’ Zī Zhù Jì Huá.” Google Doc, October 22. Accessed June 16, 2021. https://drive.google.com/file/d/1FJ3Cg04Xhp989OSw75_7FgZixKK2kneb/edit.

612 Humanitarian Relief Fund. 2021. “612 Rén Dào Zhī Yuán Jī Jīn Gōng Zuò Jiǎn Bào.” Google Doc. Accessed June 24, 2021. https://docs.google.com/spreadsheets/d/1U8U6174kRffycKjWcNALjKqzKNc03xxIPws2FzN1krI/edit#gid=1881645065.

“Two-Tier Police Complaints System.” 2018. *Independent Police Complaints Council,* January 10. Accessed June 24, 2021. https://www.ipcc.gov.hk/en/what_we_do/two_tier_police.html.

Wong, Brian. 2020. “Hong Kong Court Throws Out Two Private Prosecutions Tied to Social Unrest.” *South China Morning Post,* August 24. Accessed June 25, 2021. https://www.scmp.com/news/hong-kong/law-and-crime/article/3098628/hong-kong-justice-department-wins-court-approval-quash.

Xiāng Gǎng Tè Bié Xíng Zhèng Qū Sù Mò Jiā Tāo jí lìng bā rén. 2018. HKDC 225.

“[Zhuān fǎng] Gēng Tián Yī Nián, Fǎn Qián Xiàn Rèn Yì Wù Lu Shī, Chén Xìn Xīn Rèn Fǎ Zhèng Huì Sī Xīn Zhào Jí Rén.” 2020. *Inmediahk,* March 12. Accessed June 25, 2021. https://www.inmediahk.net/node/1071505?__cf_chl_captcha_tk__=606b633cea3800517281f7571f8b373fe34eab43-1624622163-0.

7. Leadership Contestation in the Bar

Abstract: This chapter examines the Hong Kong Bar Association's leadership contestation and evolving stance toward China's authoritarian legal transplantation. Focusing on the 2017 co-location controversy and the 2018 Bar Council election, it highlights a pivotal shift in the Bar's approach from moderate engagement with Chinese authorities to outspoken resistance. Under new leadership, the Bar adopted a confrontational stance, leveraging legal expertise to challenge policies undermining Hong Kong's Rule of Law. While this approach fostered solidarity with civil society, it also strained state-bar relations, curtailed mainland exchanges, and exposed internal divisions among barristers. By tracing these dynamics, the chapter reveals the Bar's critical role in defending professional autonomy and the Rule of Law within an increasingly restrictive political environment.

Keywords: Bar Association, Democratisation, Professional Autonomy, Public Education, Authoritarianism, Access to Justice

The Hong Kong Bar Association (the Bar) is a statutory professional body for barristers in Hong Kong and is represented by its council. As of January 2022, the Bar Council has regulated more than 1,600 barristers in Hong Kong, including senior counsel, who were titled the Queen's or King's counsel before the sovereignty transfer (Hong Kong Bar Association 2023). As a profession "based on individual integrity and a strong duty to the system of justice," the Bar has enjoyed a high reputation for preserving the Rule of Law for more than half a century in Hong Kong (Brennan 2000, xvii). As barristers are self-employed, they enjoy high occupational autonomy and economic independence. Thus, they have greater flexibility in speaking about public affairs without interference from law firms or employers. Throughout the history of Hong Kong, many junior and senior counsel have engaged in a variety of public affairs, such as serving the Bar Council, being appointed to government consultative committees, taking up pro bono legal service in communities and running for elections to become lawmakers.

Lai, Y. *Legal Resistance under Authoritarianism: The Struggle for the Rule of Law in Hong Kong.* Taylor & Francis Group, 2025
DOI: 10.5117/9789048558438_CH07

As highlighted by the chairman of the English Bar in the Bar's golden jubilee meeting in 1999, a bar association should promote the Rule of Law with public spirit through five duties: (1) the provision of independent and fearless advocates; (2) working for the community; (3) speaking out in protection of the Rule of Law; (4) working for the independence of the judiciary; and (5) ensuring the survival of the independent bar (Brennan 2000, xvii-xxiv). These duties are inevitably tied with political tensions when the state fails to comply with the Rule of Law, when the local community has increased needs for pro bono legal services due to the inadequate public budget, or when citizens attack judges because of undesirable court rulings. Simultaneously, the Hong Kong Bar, as a statutory body in Hong Kong, also has incentives to maintain good ties with Chinese and Hong Kong authorities and support the "One Country, Two Systems" formula, which fundamentally protects the continuity of the city's common law system that barristers are committed to defend.

This chapter examines why and how leadership contestation in the Bar became a form of resistance. The words and deeds of the Bar under the changing political opportunity structure sheds light on how lawyers defend their beliefs of the Rule of Law and professional autonomy within professional legal bodies. This chapter takes the controversy of "co-location arrangement" in 2017 as a critical event to explain the shifting state-bar relations in Hong Kong. Findings in this chapter illustrate that, before 2017, the Bar built official ties with the political authorities to advance the economic interests of its members in the mainland service market. However, the controversy of whether an express railway station in Hong Kong should set up a joint checkpoint for both Hong Kong and Chinese authorities in 2017, known as the "co-location arrangement," became a critical event for the change of the Bar's leadership. It led to a radical shift in the Bar's attitude towards the Chinese and Hong Kong authorities. Rather than merely commenting on the government's actions that they undermined the Rule of Law, as pro-democracy lawmakers and activists often did, the Bar became more critical and active against the state by using their professional knowledge and skills to engage in public advocacy and debates with the Chinese authorities.

Previous studies of Hong Kong's legal profession highlighted the emergence of divisions within the legal profession due to diverse positionings towards the non-democratic regime of the city, yet the description was too simplistic. Dezalay and Garth suggested that despite lawyers and the law faculty of the University of Hong Kong (HKU) being active since the 1990s in the pro-democracy movement during the political transition, a "new fraction of the legal elite and academia closely tied to business embedded in China" also emerged (Dezalay and Garth 2010, p.215). Carol Jones further classifies the lawyers into either "gentlemen lawyers" or "comprador-lawyers." Gentlemen lawyers are graduates of HKU and overseas law schools. They were elitist and became the majority in the Bar and judiciary in Hong Kong (Jones 2010, 117). Graduates who work in commercial law firms are seen as comprador lawyers (Jones 2010, 119). Jones argues that solicitors and the Law Society of Hong Kong (the Law Society) were less interested in liberal legal education and engagement in issues related to social and political issues than the Bar (Jones 2010, 123). However, this bifurcation is losing validity among Hong Kong's legal professionals today. As Lee discovered, there was also an increasing number of legal scholars becoming intellectual activists, such as Benny Yiu-ting Tai, and solicitors commenced to significantly engage in the democratic movement, promoting civil disobedience and bringing about social and political change (K. Lee 2017a, 89).

This book suggests that the Bar is not purely confrontational towards the state, and the Law Society cares more about than just the profit-making opportunities of solicitors. Scholars interested in the legal profession in Hong Kong tend to demonstrate a dichotomy between the Bar and the Law Society, such as labelling the Bar as a group of gentlemen lawyers whose only concern is their prestigious social status (Jones 2010, 118–120), or that the Bar solely portrays itself as a "defender of the Rule of Law" while the Law Society upholds its claim of "political neutrality" focusing on "legal technicality" (MY Lee 2017, 38). They may also only think that the Law Society wanted to align with the government's position on constitutional affairs to attain professional interests against the Bar (Sin 2001, 483). Both the Bar and the Law Society, however, are concerned with the economic issues of their members; both insist on claiming political neutrality and the importance of legal technicality in legal and constitutional disputes, and they both position themselves as defenders of the Rule of Law while sharing a common goal of advancing their professional interests. Any portrait of the dichotomy between the two bodies fails to explain the dynamics between the Bar, the Law Society, and the Hong Kong and Chinese authorities. Instead, it is more about the process of politicisation of the Bar and the Law Society. Such a process was reflected in leadership contestations in light of the awakening of the political agency of some lawyers in a particular political and social context inside and outside the legal profession, which is conceptualised as the political opportunity structure.

The concept of political opportunity structure is borrowed from social movement scholarship. In a minimal sense, this concept refers to "the degree to which groups are likely to be able to gain access to power and to manipulate the political system" (Elsinger 1973, 11). Components of a political opportunity structure range from the openness of institutional rules, the space of contention tolerated by the state to socioeconomic shifts in society over time; these components would affect the actual choice of activists in political contention (Meyer 2004, 5; Tilly 1995). At the same time, perceived "threats," such as systemic erosion of rights and state repressions, are equally important in explaining how social movements are generated and sustained (Goldstone and Tilly 2001; Almeida 2018; McAdam and Tarrow 2018). Here, the political opportunity structure refers to how lawyers perceived the chances to gain access to power in the Bar and the Law Society to resist China's legal encroachments, which constitute structural threats as ramifications of authoritarian legal transplantation. In addition, "political agency" is an analytical concept that explains the micro-foundation of collective action in attaining a political end (Elster 1986 and 1988; Little 1992). It refers to thoughts, intentional actions and emotions of individuals and groups that express their power in the political realm, and political agency can shape, reproduce and change existing structured conditions and relationships (Houghton 2011).

The controversy over the co-location arrangement of a new express railway in 2017 was a turning point for the relationship between the Bar and the political authorities in Hong Kong and China, while the 2019 Anti-Extradition Law Amendment Bill (ELAB) Movement served as a turning point for the rise of critical candidates in the Law Society elections. Both co-location proposal and the government's ELAB, which indicated as critical events in the process of authoritarian legal transplantation, were considered by the legal community and civil society as threats to the Rule of Law. These critical events twisted the political opportunity structure within the legal profession. Throughout these events, some barristers and solicitors captured those opportunities, attempting to push the Bar and the Law Society to be more progressive in defending Hong Kong's Rule of Law from China's legal transplantation via annual council elections.

As discussed in chapter 4, the Bar had long been eager to advance its ties with the Chinese government through material agreements and continuing dialogue, for the sake of advancing members' career opportunities in the mainland. Then, why would the Bar become more confrontational towards the Hong Kong and Chinese governments in the controversy over the "co-location arrangement"?

Leadership Contestation in the Bar of 2018

During the Umbrella Movement and the early years of the movement's aftermath, the Bar remained in a relatively moderate and balanced position towards constitutional controversies in Hong Kong. What twisted the official relationships and interactions between the Bar and the Chinese authorities was the controversy over the "co-location arrangement" beginning at the end of 2017. This event awakened some active barristers and led to a fierce leadership contestation in the Bar Council.

The controversy of the "co-location arrangement" refers to the agreement between the Hong Kong and mainland Chinese authorities to set up a joint checkpoint that co-locates their clearance facilities in the same terminal at the West Kowloon Station within Hong Kong's jurisdiction (G. Cheung 2020). In 2010, the Legislative Council (LegCo) approved a government budget to construct the Guangzhou-Shenzhen-Hong-Kong Express Rail Link (XRL). Seven years later, the Hong Kong government announced the proposal of a "co-location arrangement" inside the XRL at West Kowloon Station. In effect, the arrangement would allow Chinese personnel to enforce Chinese laws on clearance procedures in the station's mainland port area (Romanian Chamber of Commerce in Hong Kong 27 July 2017). However, this joint checkpoint plan proposal was allegedly inconsistent with the provisions of the Basic Law. Article 18(3) of the Basic Law disallows national laws to be implemented in the territory of Hong Kong except those enlisted in Annex III of the Basic Law or except when the National People's Congress Standing Committee (NPCSC) declares a state of emergency. However, the government insisted that the Basic Law did not clearly define the border of Hong Kong and that it would seek a resolution from the NPCSC to authorise the mainland port area as "falling outside of Hong Kong territory" (Tong 2017a).

Despite the inconsistency between the Basic Law provisions and the proposed co-location arrangement, the Bar had been silent on the controversy since the Hong Kong government's announcement on 25 July 2017. On 15 September 2017, local media reported that the Committee on Constitutional Affairs and Human Rights of the Bar had submitted a position paper for the council a month ago, claiming the co-location arrangement "may not comply with the Basic Law" and urging the government not to bypass the Basic Law and seek the NPCSC's resolution. However, after receiving the position paper, the Bar Council decided not to comment on the matter publicly. The next day, the Bar made a public statement to explain the council had considered it "inappropriate to comment on the relevant legal matters at this stage," stressed that the Bar had not decided on its position towards the co-location arrangement and denounced any disclosure of the Bar's internal material was "in breach of confidentiality" (Hong Kong Bar Association 17 September 2017).

After that, the Bar continued not to be explicitly critical of the co-location policy, as reflected by two relevant statements on 19 October 2017. The first statement consisted of three paragraphs only, urging the Hong Kong government to inform the public of more details for public discussion; the Bar "is monitoring the development closely and will publish its views if and when appropriate" (Hong Kong Bar Association 19 October 2017). The second statement, published as a six-page open letter with 29 pages of attachments, was directed against Dennis Kwok, a pro-democracy lawmaker elected by the legal sector. Before the statement, Kwok publicly commented on the Bar Council's reluctance to give any opinion on the co-location arrangement and suggested that the Bar Council had occasionally commented on constitutional issues undergoing judicial review (Kwok 2017). The Bar's statement rebuked Kwok's, stating its "connotation is untrue, unjustified and premised on factual inaccuracies and an unfairly skewed reading" of the Bar's previous press statements (Hong Kong Bar Association 29 October 2017). The Bar's light comment on the co-location arrangement and its heavy rebuttal of Kwok's comments on the Bar contrasted with each other. It implicated the Bar's embarrassment of positioning itself on the controversy.

On 27 December 2017, the NPCSC officially declared that the co-location arrangement complied with the Basic Law, and the NPCSC's decision could not be questioned; and domestic legislation of the decision should commence (E. Ng 2017a). The Bar finally responded by releasing a statement on the NPCSC decision one day after, heavily criticising the decision as "the most retrograde step to date in the implementation of the Basic Law" since the decision ceded a part of Hong Kong to the mainland Chinese law (Hong Kong Bar Association 28 December 2017).

Fuel was added to the ambiguous position of the Bar on the co-location arrangement when the chairmanship of the Bar Council was contested. Conventionally, every chairman of the Bar Council serves at least two years of office, although the election of the council is held annually. A few days before the NPCSC's decision, Philip Dykes, a former chairman of the Bar and a famous senior counsel for public law, announced his intention to run for the council election for the post of chairman at the end of 2017. His announcement was interpreted as a critical challenge to the incumbent Chairman, Paul Lam, who had only served one year of the chairmanship of the Bar and was criticised for just giving a minimal statement on the disputable co-location arrangement (Tong 2017b).

The unconventional contest of the 2018 Bar Council election was not attributed solely to the tightening legal environment amid authoritarian legal transplantation by China, as proven by the co-location arrangement.

Another attribute was the political awakening of barristers whose decided to contest against an incumbent, seen as underperforming in speaking out in defence of the Rule of Law and judicial independence in Hong Kong. As explained by a member of Dykes' campaign team, the decision to contest was made only a month before the election, and the motivation was attributed to the passive performance of the Bar in the co-location arrangement before the announcement of the NPCSC's decision:

> The co-location arrangement was an immediate cause. We felt Paul Lam (the Bar chairman) was shy about publishing statements on any matter. When the Bar refused to release a statement about co-location, some lawyers felt that the Bar behaved like a pro-government body. Hence, some senior counsel and junior barristers formed a group to discuss whether to contest the vacancies in the Bar Council. Finally, we decided to run for it (ITV1930, 17 April 2019).

Their determination to remove Paul Lam from the chairmanship sparked off internal division of the barrister community. The campaign team of Dykes was criticised as breaking the Bar's tradition and politicising the election within a professional body (ITV1930, 17 April 2019). For example, Winne Tam, a former Bar chairman who publicly supported Paul Lam's list in the contest, openly commented that the Bar Council's election had become over-politicised, implying that those barristers should be "professional" rather than "running a political campaign" or "using Facebook for media interviews" (*Ming Pao* 9 January 2018).

Although candidates on both sides agreed that the Bar Council should not be politicised, their choices of the positioning of the Bar, selections of issues concerned, and policy platforms have demonstrated a distinction between developing comprador professionalism and upholding a liberal and even confrontational approach to defending professional autonomy of the Bar. Two examples can explain their divergence.

The first example concerns their expectations towards the role of the Bar in society. Both teams agreed the Bar plays a significant role in defending the Rule of Law. Yet, in their first statement pronouncing the motivations behind running for the election, Dykes and his teammates explained the role of the Bar in the public domain. They suggested that the Bar should be willing to "speak out authoritatively and independently on important constitutional and legal issues," and the public also expected the Bar to express their legal opinions without any hesitation; they further expected the Bar to be "not only a profession but an honourable institution that stands for important principles and ideals" (Facebook Page of Philip Dykes' List – HKBA election 2018, 25 December 2017).

In contrast to Dykes' emphasis on the public-spirited vision of the Bar, Lam's team concentrated on the importance of the apolitical position of the Bar. They stressed the Bar should not be a "partisan spokesperson for any political force" and should be independent to "maintain and enhance its credibility" (W. Lee 2017). Making a solid voice on constitutional affairs in the public sphere and upholding an apolitical Bar Council are not mutually exclusive. However, when a sovereign factor, China, is involved in the constitutional debates, the Bar's vocal disagreement with political authority would engender confrontation and reaction from the Chinese authorities, impacting the state-Bar relations. A former Bar chairman opined that the non-partisan character of the Bar is more an implication of not acting as a "reserves team" of any of the political parties which "have for many years wrongly assumed that they could call upon the Bar to readily rally for their political acts from a "Rule of Law angle" (Shieh 2015). The notion of "political parties" were interpreted by some former members of the Bar Council as targeting the Civic Party, which was formed mainly by pro-democracy and liberal barristers and professionals in Hong Kong (ITV1918, 18 March 2019; ITV1929, 3 April 2019). Therefore, the contest between Dykes and Lam was also a fundamental choice in the position of the Bar towards the Chinese sovereign state.

The second example lies in the divergence between the two lists of candidates over economic policies for local barristers. Both lists paid attention to the career opportunities of junior barristers, but their solutions were pulled apart. For Dykes' list, they focused on expanding business opportunities in local settings, such as reviewing the remuneration systems in publicly funded work for barristers, reforming the practice of coverage and the entry requirement of barristers in legal aid services (Facebook page of Philip Dykes' List – HKBA election 2018 8 January 2018). Their rival did not oppose Dykes' proposals, but their solutions focused more on the creation and consolidation of business ties with the mainland. Lam and his team proposed more training and opportunities for arbitration, mediation and alternative dispute resolution work, which are the primary services to commercial firms in Hong Kong and mainland China. They also promised to multiply business networks with law firms and law associations in places within the Greater Bay Area and the Belt and Road Initiative (BRI) (Facebook page of Paul Lam and His Proposed Elected Members – HKBA Election 2018 16 January 2018). In short, Dykes' list concentrated on domestic remedies and public interest work, whereas Lam's list tends to improve the business development of barristers through external ties with Chinese economic initiatives.

In the end, on 19th January 2018, Dykes was elected as the Bar chairman at the council election, outweighing 109 votes than Lam; four other candidates on the Dykes' list were elected as council members as well (J. Lam 2018). The contest demonstrated the significance of the political agency of barristers perceiving an imminent threat to Hong Kong's Rule of Law by China. The introduction of the co-location arrangement, alongside the relatively passive response of the Bar under Lam's leadership, were new opportunities for liberal members of the legal profession to reshape the direction and ideological orientation of the Bar Council. The annual election publicised the campaign strategy of Dykes' team, and the contentious images were known by the media.

The return of Philip Dykes to the leadership of the Bar, alongside the rise of the "new blood" of liberal barristers in the Bar Council, was the result of the change of the political opportunity structure. When the Chinese authority expanded its intervention in Hong Kong's legal culture and practices and the NPCSC decided on the co-location arrangement, the incumbent Bar Council declined any pre-emptive initiative to address the co-location problems before the NPCSC's decision. That decision was regarded by the Bar as unconstitutional. Hence, liberal members of the barrister community took the opportunity to bridge the gap between the expansion of the states' transplantation of legal practice and the self-limiting position of the incumbent of the Bar Council to establish a new leadership of the Bar. The result of the contested election was a critical juncture for the Bar to reprioritise its mission in Hong Kong's legal profession and civil society. The position of the Bar in legal and constitutional controversies has long looked unfavourable to the political authorities, and the outcome of the Bar Council election in 2018 further intensified the tensions between the Bar and the state. The relationship between the Bar Council and its members has also been reshaped.

Marginalisation and Division

Unlike the previous leadership, the Bar under Dykes took a relatively more proactive role in public debates on certain politically sensitive controversies related to constitutional law and mainland-Hong-Kong relations. The governments and some veteran counsel then perceived the Bar Council as becoming further politicised, sowing seeds for the marginalisation of and division within the Bar.

Immediately after the 2018 election, a state-owned press criticised Philip Dykes as a "human rights lawyer serving particularly radical democrats, localists and advocates for Hong Kong independence," alongside a group of barristers who were "anti-China" and "disrupting Hong Kong." In the same article, Paul Lam was appreciated as a "professional and stable" Bar chairman who promoted exchange between Hong Kong and mainland China (*Ming Pao Instant News* 20 January 2018). The emerging dichotomy between Dykes and Lam reflected the state's suspicion of the Bar's political loyalty and whether it would support China's authoritarian project, including the NPCSC's controversial decision on the co-location arrangement. In fact, the Bar did not cease to comment on this matter but further published two submissions questioning the constitutionality of setting up a joint checkpoint inside the XRL station (Hong Kong Bar Association 12 March 2018).

The state-bar relations worsened, as reflected in mainland authorities' near-total termination of exchange activities with the Bar. While some of the council members, including the chairman, officially visited Guangxi and three cities in Guangdong for exchange in 2018, a proposed MoU with the Guangxi Lawyer Association was withdrawn at very late notice, and the deputy minister of the Shanghai Justice Bureau cancelled an official visit to the Bar at the last minute. The public and some of the Bar Council members regarded it as the Chinese government's disapproval of the new Bar Council (Mak 2018). Tensions escalated when objections were raised regarding two barristers continuing their teaching in public law at the joint programme of the Bar and Peking University in 2018, and Dykes was told by the university that he "must not come" to the graduation ceremony of the programme (Lum 2018). The Bar disagreed with the screening of instructors by Peking University and responded by pulling the joint programme indefinitely, except for the international arbitration course (*Stand News* 10 September 2018). After this incident, several mainland lawyers' associations visited Hong Kong for a BRI conference organised by the Law Society in September of that year, but unlike previously, only one made connections or requests to meet the Bar. Furthermore, the annual visit to Beijing by the Bar Council was not held either (Tam 2018, 5). The Guangdong Lawyers Association told the chairperson of the Bar's "China Standing Committee on Practice Development" that they decided not to resume contact with the Bar because they "could not have a trusting and mutually respectful relationship with the leadership of the Bar" (Tam 2018, 6). Last but not least, the All-China Lawyers' Association (ACLA) skipped sending an invitation to Bar Chairman Philip Dykes to attend the annual meeting of the Presidents of the Law Associations in Asia, which was hosted in Kunming in early 2019 (Dykes 2019b). Although a former member of the Bar Council insisted in my interview that there was never a "cut-off" of communication between the Bar and the Chinese authorities, the absence of public exchange activities since 2018 indicated China's attempt to isolate the Bar from any formal relationship-building (ITV1914, 6 March 2019).

A similar tactic of the Chinese government to "punish" disloyal collaborators by exclusion can also be found in the history of China's co-optation of Hong Kong elites. In 2003, after the mass protest against the national security bill, James Tien, the chairman of the Liberal Party, a pro-business party adjacent to the central authorities, decided not to support the legislation and resigned from the Executive Council. His move forced the government to postpone the bill, and he succeeded in winning two directly elected seats with another party cadre in the 2004 LegCo election (The Brookings Institution 15 September 2004). However, the Liberal Party lost all directly elected seats in the election just after four years, as their partners refused to mobilise votes for them and instead turned to other pro-China candidates (*The Standard* 10 September 2008). After that election, a news report revealed that China did not want to see Tien heading the party in the future and felt a more loyal figure should prevent Tien from rising to power again (*The Standard* 18 September 2008). What happened to Tien set a precedent for everyone who befriended and obeyed the Chinese authorities but later turned against them, including the Bar under Dykes' leadership since 2018.

The deterioration of the state-bar relations also stimulated internal tensions. Some senior counsel and veteran members of the Bar Council disapproved of the Bar being overtly politicised, losing mutual trust from political authorities as well as the spirit of "professionalism," thus damaging the prospects of the Bar per se. In the annual report of the Standing Committee on China Practice Development of 2018, Chairman Winnie Tam unreservedly expressed her discontent with the consequence of the "significant and unforeseen changes in leadership" of the Bar (Tam 2018b, 4). She commented that the new Bar Council lacked "continuity of any voice" that supported the work of the Standing Committee and suggested that the previous leadership was strong yet came to "an abrupt halt," implying that the new leadership was damaging the economic collaboration between the Bar and China (ibid.). The cessation of communication between the Bar and top authorities in China also worried some former members of the Bar Council:

> It is a terrible situation that the Bar loses contact and opportunities for exchange with higher education institutions and government agencies in the mainland...we have no idea whether members of the Bar Council would be welcome to revisit Beijing. Yet the Bar should prepare for that. It needs to restart the communication from ground zero (ITV1928, 3 April 2019).

Another former member of the Bar Council further pointed out the adverse consequences of suspending the joint programme on public law at Peking University:

> The halt of the programme at Peking University would be perceived as a "break-off" of the relationship by the authority.... Is self-isolating from the Chinese Communist Party (CCP) a positive signal to society? Many people may recognise the symbolic meaning of such positioning, but is it necessary? It is always better to avoid hostile relations rather than those relations [with the state] being broken off (ITV1918, 18 March 2019).

The tensions between the Bar and the government also led to a "downgrading" of the Bar's status in public consultations on government matters. Observed by a veteran barrister, the Bar Council no longer enjoyed a privileged position in presenting legal opinions at LegCo, indicating the government tended to marginalise the Bar less as a professional consultant than as moderate dissent in the realm of law:

> The bills committee for domestic legislation of the co-location arrangement did not specifically invite representatives from the legal profession to present legal opinions. Instead, when Philip Dykes, as the chairman of the Bar Council, requested to speak at the meeting, he was assigned to a session of public hearing with other groups. You may argue all groups, including the Bar, should have an equal position in consultation. Yet this arrangement is debatable if the Legislative Council needs more legal opinion rather than merely depending on its legal advisors (ITV1928, 3 April 2019).

The worries about the fading privileged relationship between the Bar and the political authorities, shared by some former members of the Bar Council, were also related to their criticism that the Bar was allegedly compromising its professionalism. In this sense, they disapproved of the Bar's confrontational approach in addressing its concerns in legal affairs, damaging the Bar's credibility as a profession in society. One interviewee addressed his concern over the composition of the members of the Bar Council in 2018 and 2019 because some of them were members of the Democratic Party, as well as elected members of the legal sector of the Election Committee for selecting the Chief Executive of Hong Kong (ITV1928, 3 April 2019). The Democratic Party was the oldest opposition party in Hong Kong. Also, the pro-democracy camp seized total seats in the legal sector of the Election

Committee in its election of 2016 (2016 Election Committee Subsector Elections 12 December 2016). In other words, his worries lie in the presence and influence of a specific political camp in the Bar Council. His view was also shared by other former members of the Bar Council who suspected the Bar of "double standards" in the public sphere since 2018:

> In January 2018, after the court sentence of a police sergeant charged with assault against a protestor in the 2014 Umbrella Movement and jailed for three months, pro-government groups protested against the judge, labelling her a "dog" and "moors," which is a demeaning word used against ethnic minorities in Hong Kong (CH Tai 2018). That evening, Philip Dykes' team immediately published a statement to express their "deep regret" at the "abusive remarks" against the magistrate, which "constitute unwarranted attacks" on the judicial independence of Hong Kong. In June 2018, after Edward Leung [a famous pro-independence activist in Hong Kong] was jailed for six years because of rioting, the judge's personal information was leaked, and she was widely insulted on electronic media by anti-Beijing groups calling her a "black widow" as her husband had passed away. However, the Bar remained silent for a few weeks regarding these personal attacks against the judge. Would the public perceive that many members of the Bar Council were close to Edward Leung, and thus they refused to speak out immediately against the public attack on the judge who tried Leung's case? (ITV1918, 18 March 2019).

His observation is a helpful lens through which to understand the rationale for the dissatisfaction of some senior members of the Bar towards the confrontational style of their new leadership. In this case, the Bar Council was regarded as holding double standards in defending judicial independence and the respect for judges due to the perceived dominant political orientation within its ranks. The decline of the state-bar relationship, the marginalisation of the Bar by the state and the perceived partisan image of the Bar Council, became setbacks for the Bar to maintain unity while continuing its critical approach against the government authorities.

Actions and Reactions of the Bar in the Anti-ELAB Movement

The Bar became more confrontational towards the political authorities in 2019. This is evident in the Bar's active role in resisting the Extradition Law Amendment Bill (ELAB) in 2019. Ever since the introduction of the bill by the government, the Bar had openly disagreed with the amendments by publishing statements and media interviews. Before the mass rally against the ELAB on 9 June 2019, which had an estimated turnout of more than 1 million demonstrators, the Bar released a bilingual Brief Guide to address the critical concerns of the bill's substance in a "Q and A" (Question and Answer) format. The Brief Guide was widely circulated and reprinted by local media, treating it as "the best Extradition Law Amendment Bill for Dummies" (*Stand News* 6 June 2019). After the outbreak of mass protests and violent crashes between protestors and the law enforcement, the Bar published a Summary Guide of its stance alongside the pros and cons of its proposal for the commission of inquiry (see chapter 4). The Bar's advocacy responded to the government's repeated objection to setting up a commission of inquiry (K. Cheng 2019a). This not only echoed the majority support for an independent investigation into police brutality of the Anti-ELAB Movement but also demonstrated the Bar's public spirit in defending, through its legal expertise, the Rule of Law that limits government power (Mang and Chow 2020; Pomfret and Jim 2019).

Furthermore, as discussed in chapter 6, the Bar chairman's open appreciation of the pro bono lawyers visiting and assisting arrested protestors in the Anti-ELAB Movement can also be seen as an endorsement of positively intersecting confrontation towards political authorities with lawyers' professionalism. To economically accommodate the massive demand for lawyers visiting arrested protestors in the Anti-ELAB protest, the Bar sent an internal memorandum to all members, stating that barristers could visit suspects in police stations or detention centres without the company of solicitors if those barristers had a letter of proof from solicitor firms (Low and Lum 2019). This memo could be read as an encouragement to many members of the Bar to visit and assist arrested protestors when there was an inadequate number of voluntary solicitors to accompany the legal visits. Besides the practical arrangement, in his public speech at the opening of the legal year 2020, Philip Dykes openly expressed his appreciation of the barristers who worked with solicitors to provide legal assistance at police stations and magistrate courts to people who were arrested for public order and other offences (Dykes 2020). He also reiterated his compliments to those lawyers in the earlier annual report to all members of the Bar (Dykes 2019b). While the state-sponsored media labelled those barristers and solicitors who assisted the protestors at court as "yellow ribbon lawyers," the Bar's vocal and substantial support for the professional practice of its members revealed its commitment to defend protestors' legal rights despite the state's antagonist attitude towards protestors.

Nevertheless, the confrontational positioning and tangible support for the Anti-ELAB Movement by the Bar had further widened the internal division of the barrister profession that had been happening since 2018. Such internal tension peaked amid the Anti-ELAB Movement of 2019 when a senior counsel resigned from his office as vice-chairman of the Bar Council. Between July and September 2019, the Bar published four statements disapproving of the storming of the LegCo Complex, the attack on civilians inside a metro station, protestors' obstructive tactics, and the "abuse of power" by police (see chapter 4). However, the Bar's position was challenged by its Vice-Chairman, Edwin Choy, who resigned from the Bar Council before opening his criticisms on 14 October 2019. He explained that his resignation came when the majority of members in the Bar Council disagreed with his opinion that the Bar should unequivocally denounce protest violence, including the protestors who committed serious crimes such as rioting, arson, and assault, as well as those who "provide a spine" on the those violent protestors. Choy further argued that the rioters in the protests would be led to believe that "they have secured allies from within" the Bar Council, which was in his view "shamefully silent on protest violence" (Choy 2019). Choy's opinion was also echoed by other senior counsel who saw the Bar Council as having become a politicised group rather than a professional body and that such a stance would undermine the integrity of the profession:

> The Bar's statement condemning police violence [dated 3 September 2019] crosses the boundary of a professional body...as you should not pass a judgment against the police without a trial....Once a professional body claims that those in power should be condemned as they have greater responsibility, the former becomes a political group....If the Bar takes sides, you lose the superiority, and your integrity will collapse (ITV1958, 1 November 2019).

In response to such criticisms, Philip Dykes, the chairman of the Bar told the media that all forms of violence attributed to either protestors or police were condemned in the Bar's public statements, and he asserted that people were "intelligent enough" to identify the wrongdoings happening during the social unrest (C. Lau 2019a). Later, Dykes sent a letter to all members of the Bar, stressing that political partisanship runs against the rules and regulations of the Bar, and reasserted that "there is nothing more corrosive to the Rule of Law than violence inflicted on members of the public by apparently unaccountable state agents" (Dykes 2019a). Three days after Choy's open letter was published, Lawrence Lok, another senior counsel and a member of the Bar Council, wrote to the media and rebuked Choy's opinion. While recognising that some protestors found "themselves on the wrong side of the law," Lok asserted that without protestors blocking entry into LegCo and engaging in violent conflict with the police on 12 June 2019, the passage of the extradition bill would not be halted. He further argued that condemning protestors would not solve the "root of the problem" that lies "in large part with those in government" and the police force, where none of the "lawbreakers in uniform" were made accountable (Lok 2019).

The resignation of Choy revealed to the public the full extent of the divisions in the Bar, and the debate between Choy and Lok indicated a fundamental divergence of the views on the role and positioning of the Bar. Choy's criticisms implied that the Bar Council had become partisan in the Anti-ELAB Movement when it refused to denounce violent protestors as much as condemning power abuse by police, losing sight of the severity of the criminal acts committed by the former and the cost of law and order in the social unrest. In contrast, Lok's arguments drew a more comprehensive picture of the movement, highlighting the lack of accountability of the government as well as the law enforcement in public order policing. He further argued that the government and the police should bear greater responsibility for the intensifying of the unrest; hence the Bar had played a proper role in its condemnation. While Choy stressed the Bar should be impartial in disapproving of violence from all sides, Lok highlighted the Bar's vision in defending the Rule of Law that limits the government rather than merely preserving law and order in society. In short, their views portrayed two visions of the Bar: one embraced a non-partisan position in social unrest to maintain the Bar's political neutrality and commitment to defending law and order, while the other aligned with the ideal of the Rule of Law that particularly limits the state that could abuse its power to damage the Rule of Law institutions.

Despite the orthodox criticisms from some senior counsel that the Bar had become politicised and partisan against the government, Dykes' leadership and the agenda of the Bar Council were repeatedly endorsed by its members in 2019 and 2020, as no one contested his chairmanship in the annual council election. Furthermore, the Bar Council did not cease to improve the livelihood issues for young barristers, despite the termination of contact between the Bar and the mainland authorities that provided market opportunities for members of the Bar. A new system of paid pupillage was introduced in 2018, whereby all pupil masters now had to pay their pupils a monthly stipend of HKD6,000. The Bar's rules governing supplementary occupations were also abolished by Dykes' leadership to help members develop their interests and employment opportunities (Dykes 2018). These reforms are economically beneficial to junior counsel and pupils as future barristers. They also provide, to a certain extent, a remedy for the narrowed market opportunities in the mainland due to the frosty relations with the mainland authorities.

Conclusion

This chapter explained why and how the Bar responded to China's authoritarian legal transplantation in Hong Kong, particularly in the aftermath of the 2014 Umbrella Movement. It further examined how the Bar's shifting of its positioning towards the state authorities positively and negatively impacted the professional legal culture and the state-bar relations in Hong Kong. Before the controversy of the co-location arrangement in 2017, the leadership of the Bar had adopted a policy of engagement with the Chinese authorities. Despite disagreements on legal and constitutional matters, the Bar and the state continued dialogue to secure economic opportunities and academic exchanges for Hong Kong barristers to develop a more robust network following the United Front. However, the weak response of the Bar to the proposed co-location arrangement in the XRL station led to a contest in the election of the Bar Council and the chairman was finally replaced. The new leadership became more outspoken against the legal discourse of the Hong Kong and Chinese governments. Using their professional legal knowledge and authority, they took a proactive approach in openly questioning the statecraft of legal transplantation. However, the critical position of the Bar was displeasing to the CCP, and most of the previous dialogue and exchanges in the mainland were terminated. At the same time, the confrontational position of the Bar towards the government also backfired within the profession, as seen in the division made public after the resignation of Edwin Choy from the Bar Council. Given the 2019 Anti-ELAB protests that deeply divided Hong Kong society, the divisive environment inevitably affected the Bar. Therefore, the response of the Bar to the movement eventually led to internal tensions among barristers. The Bar is supposed to unify the barrister profession, and an open division in the cabinet of the Bar Council was still a rare event in the legal history of Hong Kong.

The study of the Hong Kong Bar in this chapter demonstrates the changing relationship between the Bar and the sovereign state under the changing political opportunity structure. The political opportunity structure affects the choices made by political agents when components of the political opportunity structure change. In the case of the co-location arrangement, the space of contention between the state and the Bar did not diminish but grew. In contrast, the state's institutional openness was narrowed under authoritarian legal transplantation strategies. The state-driven threats to the Rule of Law alerted the barrister community, leading to which some of the active barristers to confront the statecraft and the conservativeness of the Bar's 2017 cabinet by electoral contest. In the case of the Anti-ELAB Movement, the space of contention was widened due to the cross-sectoral opposition to the bill in 2019. The support for the resistance movement by civil society, pro-democracy professionals and part of the legal profession gave confidence to the Bar to continue its critical position towards the Hong Kong government. The Bar's robust stance of calling for an independent commission of inquiry and its facilitation of pro bono legal visits lawyers to Anti-ELAB protesters strengthened its solidarity and ties with civil society and the space for contention against the state.

The Bar's attempts to defend the Rule of Law and consolidate resistance in society were essential. Its public statements served as a legal education for the public via media reporting and circulation and as discursive resources for the movement of resistance against the ELAB in 2019. Moreover, the Bar Council alongside its chairmanship did not suffer from any vote of no confidence in the annual general meetings in 2020 and 2021, implying that active members of the Bar did not disapprove their works. Another critical significance of leadership contestation in the Bar was the rise of solicitors in contesting the Law Society council elections since 2018. Inspired by the victory of liberal barristers taking over the Bar Council's leadership to revitalise the organised profession's public spirit, some solicitors with liberal backgrounds began to assemble and challenge the conservative and comprador-like incumbents of the council of the Law Society. Finally, they achieved a breakthrough in the 2020 council election. Their motivations and actions will be discussed in the next chapter.

References

Almeida, Paul D. 2018. "The Role of Threats in Collective Action." In *Wiley-Blackwell Companion to Social Movements*, edited by David A. Snow, Sarah A. Soule, Hanspeter Kriesi, and Holly J. McCammon. Blackwell.

Brennan QC, Daniel. 2000. "The Role of the Bar and the Rule of Law." In *Hong Kong Bar Association 50th Anniversary: 1949–1999*. Sweet and Maxwell Asia.

The Brookings Institution Center for Northeast Asian Policy Studies. 2004. "The 2004 Legislative Council Elections and Implications for U.S. Policy toward Hong Kong." [Transcript prepared from a tape recording], September 15.

Cheng, Kris. 2019a. "Beijing Deems Hong Kong Protests 'Colour Revolution,' Will Not Rule Out Intervention." *Hong Kong Free Press*, August 8. Accessed December 17, 2020. https://hongkongfp.com/2019/08/08/beijing-deems-hong-kong-protests-colour-revolution-will-not-rule-intervention/.

Cheung, G. 2020. "The Co-location Arrangement of the Guangzhou-Shenzhen-Hong Kong Express Rail Link." The Division of Public Policy, Institute for Public Policy, and Leadership and Public Policy Executive Education at the Hong Kong University of Science and Technology. Accessed January 29, 2021. Achieved on file with the author.

Choy, Edwin. 2019. "Hong Kong Bar Association Has Been Shamefully Silent on Protester Violence and Those Who Support It." *South China Morning Post*, October 14. Accessed January 29, 2021. https://www.scmp.com/comment/opinion/article/3032793/hong-kong-bar-association-has-been-shamefully-silent-protester.

"Dà gōng bào zhuān lán wèn Dài Qǐ Sī: rú qī jǐng pìn rèn dài biǎo lu shī, jiē bù jiē?." 2018. *Ming Pao Instant News*, January 20. Archived on file with the author.

"Dài Qǐ Sī jí liǎng dà zhuàng bèi jù fù běi dà, dà lu shī gōng huì zhí wěi: wú xiàn qī zàn tíng hé bàn sì kè chéng." 2018. *Stand News*, September 10. Accessed January 29, 2021. Archived on file with the author.

Dezalay, Yves, and Bryant G. Garth. 2010. *Asian Legal Revivals: Lawyers in the Shadow of the Empire*. University of Chicago Press.

Dykes SC, Philip. 2018. "Chairman's Report 2018." Hong Kong Bar Association, December 24. Accessed January 29, 2021. Archived on file with the author.

Dykes SC, Philip. 2019a. "Letter to Members." Hong Kong Bar Association, October 16. Accessed January 29, 2021. Archived on file with the author.

Dykes SC, Philip. 2019b. "Chairman's Report 2019." Hong Kong Bar Association, December 23. Accessed January 29, 2021. Archived on file with the author.

Dykes SC, Philip. 2020a. "Speech Given at the Opening of the Legal Year." Hong Kong Bar Association, January 13. Accessed January 26, 2021. Archived on file with the author.

"Election Results 2016." 2016. *2016 Election Committee Subsector Elections*, December 12. Accessed January 29, 2021. https://www.elections.gov.hk/ecss2016/eng/results_s2.html?1739137457162.

Elsinger, Peter K. 1973. "The Conditions of Protest Behaviour in American Cities." *American Political Science Review* 67 (1): 11–28.

Elster, Jon. 1986. "Three Challenges to Class." In *Analytical Marxism*, edited by John Roemer. Cambridge University Press.

Elster, Jon. 1988. "Marx, Marxism, and Rational Choice." In *Rationality and Revolution*, edited by Michael Taylor. Cambridge University Press.

Goldstone, Jack A., and Charles Tilly. 2001. "Threat (and Opportunity): Popular Action and State Response in the Dynamics of Contentious Action." In *Silence and Voice in the Study of Contentious Politics*, edited by Ronald R. Aminzade, Jack A. Goldstone, Doug McAdam, Elizabeth J. Perry, William H. Sewell, Sidney Tarrow, and Charles Tilly. Cambridge University Press.

"Government Announces Co-location Arrangement." 2017. *Romanian Chamber of Commerce in Hong Kong*, July 27. Accessed January 29, 2021. https://rochamhk.com/news/government-announces-co-location-arrangement/.

Hong Kong Bar Association. 2017a. *Statement of the Hong Kong Bar Association ("HKBA") in Response to News Reports Regarding HKBA's Stance on the Co-location Arrangement 2017*. September 17. Accessed January 29, 2021. Archived on file with the author.

Hong Kong Bar Association. 2017b. *Statement of the Hong Kong Bar Association ("HKBA") in Relation to the Co-location Arrangement 2017*. October 19. Accessed January 29, 2021. Archived on file with the author.

Hong Kong Bar Association. 2017c. *Hong Kong Bar Association's Open Letter to the Hon. Dennis Kwok in Response to an Article Published in Hong Kong Economic Journal on 21 September 2017*. October 29. Accessed January 29, 2021. Archived on file with the author.

Hong Kong Bar Association. 2017d. *Statement of the Hong Kong Bar Association on the Decision of the NPCSC of 27 December 2017 on the Co-operation Agreement between the Mainland and the SAR on the Establishment of the Port at the West Kowloon Station of the Guangdong-Shenzhen-Hong Kong Express Rail Link for Implementing Co-location Arrangement 2017*. December 28. Accessed January 29, 2021. Archived on file with the author.

Hong Kong Bar Association. 2018a. *Submission of the Hong Kong Bar Association in Respect of the Guangzhou-Shenzhen-Hong Kong Rail Link (Co-location) Bill (the "Bill")*. March 12. Accessed January 29, 2021. Archived on file with the author.

Hong Kong Bar Association. 2018b. *Further Submission of the Hong Kong Bar Association in Respect of the Guangzhou-Shenzhen-Hong Kong Express Rail Link (Co-location) Bill*. March 29. Accessed January 29, 2021. Archived on file with the author.

Hong Kong Bar Association. 2023. "About HKBA." Accessed September 19, 2023. https://www.hkba.org/content/about-us.

Houghton, David P. 2011. "Political Psychology." In *21st Century Political Science: A Reference Handbook*, edited by John T. Ishiyama and Marijke Breuning. SAGE Publications.

Jones, Carol. 2010. "Legal Education in Hong Kong: Producing the Producers." In *Legal Education in Asia: Globalization, Change and Contexts*, edited by Stacey Steele and Kathryn Taylor. Routledge.

"Kuk chief Lau may quit as infighting hits Liberal Party." 2008. *The Standard*, 10 September. P06.

Kwok, Dennis W.H. 2017. "Shè huì qī wàng de dà lu shī gōng huì." *Hong Kong Economic Journal*, September 21. A19.

Lam, Jeffie. 2018. "Philip Dykes Elected New Head of Hong Kong Bar Association in Upset Win." *South China Morning Post*, January 19. Accessed December 23, 2020. https://www.scmp.com/news/hong-kong/law-crime/article/2129589/philip-dykes-elected-new-head-hong-kong-bar-association.

Lau, Chris. 2019a. "Criminal Lawyer Edwin Choy Opens Up on Resignation from Hong Kong Bar Association, Saying His Outlook on Protest Violence Diverged Too Much from Others." *South China Morning Post*, October 15. Accessed January 29, 2021. https://www.scmp.com/news/hong-kong/law-and-crime/article/3032862/criminal-lawyer-edwin-choy-opens-resignation-hong-kong.

Lee, Karen M. Y. 2017a. "Lawyers and Hong Kong's Democracy Movement: From Electoral Politics to Civil Disobedience." *Asian Journal of Political Science* 25, no. 1: 89–108.

Lee, W.Y. 2017. "Dà Lù Shī Gōng Huì Gǎi Xuǎn, Lín Dìng Guó Jìng Zhú Lián Rèn: Zhī Yǒu Gēng Zì Zhǔ Cái Néng Gēng Qiáng Dà." *HK01*, December 27. Accessed January 29, 2021. https://www.hk01.com/社會新聞/144579/大律師公會改選-林定國競逐連任-只有更自主才能更強大.

Little, Daniel. 1992. "Jon Elster." In *New Horizons in Economic Thought: Appraisals of Leading Economists*, edited by Warren J. Samuels. Edward Elgar Publishing.

Lok, Lawrence. 2019. "Condemning Protest Violence in Hong Kong Won't Solve the Problem – Not When Police Are Part of the Problem." *South China Morning Post*, October 17. Accessed January 29, 2021. https://www.scmp.com/comment/opinion/article/3033142/condemning-protest-violence-hong-kong-wont-solve-problem-not-when.

Low, Zoe, and Alvin Lum. 2019. "Vice-Chairman Edwin Choy of Hong Kong Bar Association Resigns over Body's Stance on Anti-Government Protest Crisis." *South China Morning Post*, October 12. Accessed January 29, 2021. https://www.scmp.com/news/hong-kong/law-and-crime/article/3032680/vice-chairman-edwin-choy-hong-kong-bar-association.

Lum, Alvin. 2018. "Mainland Chinese University Bars Two Hong Kong Human Rights Lawyers from Teaching Regular Course There." *South China Morning Post*, August 27. Accessed January 29, 2021. https://www.scmp.com/news/hong-kong/politics/article/2161531/mainland-chinese-university-bars-two-hong-kong-human-rights.

Mak, A. 2018. "Report on Standing Committee on Greater China Affairs 2018." Hong Kong Bar Association, December. Accessed January 29, 2021. Archived on file with the author.

Mang, Carol, and Yanni Chow. 2020. "Exclusive: Support Dips for Hong Kong Democracy Protests as National Security Law Looms – Poll." *Reuters*, June 26. Accessed January 29, 2021. https://reut.rs/3wJecTa.

McAdam, Doug, and Sidney Tarrow. 2018. "The Political Context of Social Movements." In *Wiley-Blackwell Companion to Social Movements*, edited by David A. Snow, Sarah A. Soule, Hanspeter Kriesi, and Holly J. McCammon. Blackwell.

Meyer, David S. 2004. "Protest and Political Opportunities." *Annual Review of Sociology* 30 (1): 125–145.

Ng, Ellie. 2017a. "China's Top Legislature Approves Joint Checkpoint Plan; Says It Complies with Hong Kong Constitution." *Hong Kong Free Press*, December 27. Accessed December 23, 2020. https://hongkongfp.com/2017/12/27/chinas-top-legislature-approves-joint-checkpoint-plan-says-complies-hong-kong-constitution/.

"Paul Lam and His Proposed Elected Members – HKBA Election 2018, Moving Forward Together." 2018. Facebook, January 16. Accessed January 13, 2019. Archived on file with the author.

Philip Dykes' List – HKBA Election 2017, In Your Hands. 2018. "Election Platform: Bread and Butter Issues, Particularly for the Young Bar." Facebook, January 8. Archived on file with the author.

Philip Dykes' List – HKBA Election 2017, In Your Hands. 2018. "HKBA Election 2018 Joint Statement from Philip Dykes' List." Facebook, December 25. Archived on file with the author.

Pomfret, James, and Clare Jim. 2019. "Exclusive: Hong Kongers Support Protester Demands; Minority Wants Independence from China – Reuters Poll." *Reuters*, December 31. Accessed January 29, 2021. https://reut.rs/3D7GzNa.

Shieh SC, Paul. 2015. "Speech of the Chairman of the Hong Kong Bar Association at the Opening of the Legal Year 2015." Hong Kong Bar Association, January 12. Accessed January 29, 2021. Archived on file with the author.

Sin, Wai Man. 2001. "Law, Politics and Professional Projects: The Legal Profession in Hong Kong." *Social and Legal Studies* 10 (4): 483–504.

Tai, C.H. 2018. "Zhū Jīng Wěi zhī chí zhě tíng wài hǎn 'gǒu guān', 'mó luó chà'; Guō Róng Kēng : kě néng miǎo shì fǎ tíng." *CitizenNews*, January 2. Accessed January 29, 2021. Archived on file with the author.

Tam SC, Winnie. 2018. "Report of the Standing Committee on China Practice Development 2018." Hong Kong Bar Association, December 19. Accessed January 29, 2021. Archived on file with the author.

"Tán Yǔn Zhī Chì Gǎi Xuǎn 'Hǎo Duō Rén Qiáng Yìng Shǒu Duàn Līn Piào', Dài Qǐ Sī: Xiàn Zhāng Róng Jìng Zhēng, Bù Míng Fēn Liè Gōng Huì Zhǐ Kòng." 2018. *Ming Pao Daily News*, January 9. Accessed January 29, 2021. Archived on file with the author.

"Tien Rules Out Return as Liberal Leader." 2008. *The Standard*, September 18. P10.

Tilly, Charles. 1995. *Popular Contention in Great Britain 1758–1834*. Harvard University Press.

Tong, Elson. 2017a. "'Basic Law Doesn't Define Hong Kong's Borders': Justice Sec. Defends Mainland Rail Checkpoint." *Hong Kong Free Press*, July 25. Accessed January 29, 2021. https://hongkongfp.com/2017/07/25/basic-law-doesnt-define-hong-kongs-borders-justice-chief-defends-mainland-rail-checkpoint/.

Tong, Elson. 2017b. "Bar Council Chairman Paul Lam Seeks Re-Election amid Challenge from Rights Lawyer Philip Dykes." *Hong Kong Free Press*, December 28. Accessed December 23, 2020. https://hongkongfp.com/2017/12/28/bar-council-chairman-paul-lam-seeks-re-election-amid-challenge-rights-lawyer-philip-dykes/.

"[Zuì qiáng lǎn rén bāo] Dà lu shī gōng huì fā bù 'jiǎn yì zhǐ nán', jiě dá xiū dìng táo fàn tiáo lì 24 gè wèn tí." 2019. *Stand News*, June 6. Accessed January 24, 2021. Archived on file with the author.

8. Political Awakening in the Law Society's Elections

Abstract: This chapter examines the Law Society of Hong Kong's transition from a conservative, comprador-aligned institution to a contested space for liberal resistance catalysed by the Anti-Extradition Law Amendment Bill (Anti-ELAB) Movement. It explores how solicitors' political agency emerged through pro bono legal support for protestors and dissatisfaction with the Society's alignment with authoritarian legal transplantation. The chapter highlights the 2020 council election, where liberal candidates strategically overcame structural barriers, including proxy voting, to secure significant victories. These efforts signify a shift toward public-spiritedness and a redefinition of professional identity. By mobilising junior solicitors and leveraging public support, liberal lawyers challenged state co-optation, demonstrating the potential for transformation within Hong Kong's legal community under authoritarian pressures.

Keywords: Political Agency, Mobilisation, Legal Profession, Comprador lawyers, Democratisation, Authoritarianism

Whether legal professional bodies in Hong Kong have been tamed by the state draws our attention to the Law Society of Hong Kong (the Law Society). Registered in 1907, the Law Society serves as the only statutory professional body responsible for the licensing and discipline of solicitors in Hong Kong. In 2020, Melissa Pang, the President of the Law Society stressed in her speech that politically, the Law Society is "colour-blind" (R. Wong 2020). This statement implied that the Law Society should have no political affiliation or bias to political camps, in which they were classified with different colours. Does this statement reflect the reality of how the Law Society operates, or is it just a façade to cover the political character of this professional body?

Lai, Y. *Legal Resistance under Authoritarianism: The Struggle for the Rule of Law in Hong Kong.* Taylor & Francis Group, 2025
DOI: 10.5117/9789048558438_CH08

This chapter explains how the changing political opportunity structure reinforced and challenged the comprador professionalism of the Law Society. Liberal solicitors began to challenge the structure of comprador professionalism by exercising their political agency since 2018, and gained success in the 2020 council election of the Law Society. This chapter argues that the nature of the occupation, workplace culture of solicitors, their institutionalised professional interests and the voting method for council elections all reinforced a political opportunity structure that upheld comprador professionalism until 2019. The outbreak of the Anti-Extradition Law Amendment Bill (ELAB) Movement in 2019 reshuffled the constancy of the political opportunity structure of the Law Society and awakened some liberal lawyers' political agency. These lawyers chose to run for the council election in 2020 to influence the Law Society's trajectory to cultivate a more independent and critical voice in the organised solicitor community.

Structural Constraints of Leadership Contestation in the Law Society

Generally speaking, the client-oriented practice constituted a conservative professional legal culture that made many solicitors, including the Law Society, less eager to be politically outspoken to avoid offending or losing their corporate clients, of whom today are mainly from China (ITV1806, 2 December 2018). Moreover, against the tightening political environment after the Umbrella Movement, many solicitors had commercial concerns about airing their opinions in public (ITV1936, 30 April 2019). One interviewee, a solicitor in a local firm, explained that most solicitors in Hong Kong do not deal with contentious work, that is litigation in courts. Instead, they engage more in non-contentious work, such as preparing submissions for Initial Public Offering (IPO) applications in stock market, drafting wills or sales and purchase agreements. These tasks are less sensitive to the debate on the Rule of Law (ITV2006, 8 May 2020):

> Most of the solicitors do not need to enter the court in their lifetime. They don't need to care about the judges….They incline to be conservative, as they favour stability. A society of stability that allows them to make money and for their businesses to prosper….They also need to maintain relationships with Chinese state enterprises and companies in the mainland, thus they are unwilling to speak up against interventions by the Chinese Communist Party (CCP) (ITV2006, 8 May 2020).

Hence, many solicitors were less motivated to challenge the status quo of the Law Society. It also explained the lack of liberal and junior solicitors who are willing to contest the council elections of the Law Society. For instance, in the 2018 council election, although there were five vacancies open for contest, only two liberal solicitors, Eric Cheung (also a university law lecturer) and Kenneth Lam (a former student activist), ran for the election. Cheung and Lam and their support team seemingly could not recruit more solicitors to compete for all vacant seats in order to operate an intense election campaign. According to an interviewee who had recruited staffing for them:

> I helped them [the support team] recruit Jennifer [alias] to run for the election, but I did not help the campaign as I was busy then. One funny thing was that they wanted the electioneering to be low-key. Then I said I couldn't help as I was good at spinning public opinion (ITV1930, 17 April 2019).

Another member of the above campaign team also explained the difficulty in organising election campaigns within the Law Society:

> It is challenging to find a suitable candidate since many of us have much to do in our business. If you run for the council election, you only have four to five weeks for the campaign; thus, you need to conduct an intensive campaign to get in touch with your electorate, meeting them with diligence, like a political election. That was why we could have done better (ITV1936, 30 April 2019).

Their campaign in 2018 indicated that many solicitors were not interested in breaking the status quo inside or outside the profession. It also justifies why the voter turnout was so low in the council elections, as demonstrated in the following section. Their comprador-like professional legal culture discouraged them from active public engagement and support for liberal lawyers in influencing the establishment of the professional body representing their interests.

The more essential unfavourable condition for leadership contestation in the Law Society refers to the method of proxy votes. It played a pivotal role in achieving a favourable election result for the existing comprador-like leadership of the Law Society. According to the regulations of the Law Society, each member can select candidates to fill vacancies in the council by (1) voting in person at the annual general meeting (2) postal vote or (3) proxy vote (Article of Association of the Law Society, Article 15A(ii)). The significance of proxy votes can be found in the council elections in the past four years. As shown in tables 20—22, proxy votes were insignificant in warranting electoral victory before 2018. However, since 2018, when Cheung and Lam jointly ran for the council election, proxy votes were mobilised, and a majority of votes were shared among candidates favoured by the conservative camp. Candidates endorsed by Junius Ho, a pro-government lawmaker, got four seats out of five vacancies in 2018. For three elected candidates, more than 70 per cent of their total votes were proxy votes. The persistent victory of the conservative lawyers in council elections could be attributed to United Front Work and the mobilisation of the Liaison Office, which was discovered to have spread messages to solicitors asking them to vote for its preferred candidates on the eve of the 2019 council election. Eric Cheung posted these messages on his Facebook page (29 May 2019; also on *Stand News* 29 May 2019). In that election, those reported to have been supported by the Liaison Office won four seats, with proxy votes weighing around 70 per cent of their total votes (see tables 20—22).

Table 20. Election Results of Members of the Council of the Law Society of Hong Kong in 2017*

	Name of Candidate	No. of Postal Votes (% of Total Votes)	No. of Votes in Person (% of Total Votes)	No. of Proxy Votes (% of Total Votes)	Total Votes
1	Brock Denis Gareth	903 (79.56)	74 (6.52)	158 (13.92)	1135
2	Ho Kwan Yiu	83 (14.51)	43 (7.52)	446 (77.97)	572
3	Hung Wan Shun, Stephen	705 (51.88)	92 (6.77)	562 (41.35)	1359
4	Ma Wah Yan, Billy	797 (76.34)	62 (5.94)	185 (17.72)	1044
5	Rhoda Robert Christopher	880 (58.12)	83 (5.48)	551 (36.39)	1514
6	Ross Jonathan	782 (84.72)	47 (5.09)	94 (10.18)	923
7	Wong Pak Yan, Annie	321 (36.48)	50 (5.68)	509 (57.84)	880
8	Yeung Mo Sheung, Ann	184 (25.88)	55 (7.74)	472 (66.39)	711

* Elected candidates are in bold.
Source: Extract of Notice of the Law Society of Hong Kong's Annual General Meeting 2017

Table 21. Election Results of Members of the Council of the Law Society of Hong Kong in 2018*

	Name of Candidate	No. of Postal Votes (% of Total Votes)	No. of Votes in Person (% of Total Votes)	No. of Proxy Votes (% of Total Votes)	Total Votes
1#	Chan Tat Hin, Pierre	390 (19.53)	123 (6.16)	1484 (74.31)	1997
2^	Cheung Tat Ming, Eric	1363 (85.19)	102 (6.38)	135 (8.44)	1600
3	Daly Mark Douglas	1315 (87.03)	85 (5.63)	111 (7.35)	1511
4#	Gilchrist Brian William	1310 (73.84)	111 (6.26)	353 (19.90)	1774
5#	Lam Karen	390 (19.60)	120 (6.03)	1480 (74.37)	1990
6^	Lam Kenneth	1138 (87.14)	80 (6.16)	88 (6.74)	1306
7	Lintern-Smith Michael John	1212 (77.54)	108 (6.91)	243 (15.55)	1563
8	Millar John Charles Nicholas	258 (81.13)	42 (13.21)	18 (5.66)	318
9#	Wong Hau Yan	406 (20.36)	117 (5.87)	1471 (73.77)	1994

* Elected candidates are in bold.
\# Publicly recommended by solicitor member of the Legislative Council, Junius Ho
^ Teamed up in electioneering
Source: Extract of Notice of the Law Society of Hong Kong's Annual General Meeting 2018

Table 22. Election Results of Members of the Council of the Law Society of Hong Kong in 2019*

	Name of Candidate	No. of Postal Votes (% of Total Votes)	No. of Votes in Person (% of Total Votes)	No. of Proxy Votes (% of Total Votes)	Total Votes
1#	Cheng Calvin K.	478 (25.67)	75 (4.02)	1309 (70.30)	1862
2	Daly Mark Douglas	1618 (85.07)	143 (7.52)	141 (7.41)	1902
3#	Kan Yu Him Ronald	385 (22.32)	74 (4.29)	1266 (73.39)	1725
4#	Kong Yuk Foon Doreen	515 (27.35)	86 (4.57)	1282 (68.08)	1883
5	Lai Sau Cheong Simon	1365 (80.82)	143 (8.47)	181 (10.72)	1689
6	Liew Chin Chong	1348 (84.41)	123 (7.70)	126 (7.89)	1597
7#	Tong Man Lung (Roden)	477 (25.09)	92 (4.84)	1332 (70.07)	1901
8	Wong Louise Kam Faye	1395 (83.33)	140 (8.36)	139 (8.30)	1674
9#	Yu Kwok Kin	506 (28.09)	70 (3.89)	1225 (68.02)	1801

* Elected candidates are in bold.
\# Reported to have been endorsed by the Liaison Office
Source: Extract of Notice of the Law Society of Hong Kong's Annual General Meeting 2019

Proxy vote primarily benefited law firm partners, who collect proxy votes from their hired solicitors to secure the votes. Being pressured, either directly by the employers or indirectly by the workplace culture, most of the junior solicitors could only "cooperate" with their employers:

> Usually, your boss [a law firm partner] would collect the proxy of all their solicitor members in the firm, indicating voting for themselves or their favoured candidates….Every time the advent of the council election, they would enter each room to ask for a proxy, and then you would feel stressed….Some of my colleagues would submit their proxy forms, but I remember once a female colleague asked my boss whom she should vote in the proxy form, and then my boss instructed her to tick the boxes accordingly (ITV1935, 29 April 2019).

A veteran solicitor who previously served at some commissions of the Law Society agreed that the conservative position of the Law Society was attributed not to most of the support for conservatism but the method of proxy in an election that favoured the law firm partners:

> A lot of votes are done by proxy. Junior lawyers are pressured to give their proxy to a senior partner and bid for him…. By comparing it to the election of the legal sector representative for the Election Committee… if there is one person, one vote in the Law Society elections, and without proxy votes, [the liberal camp] would win (ITV1955, 9 September 2019).

As explained in chapter 1, "professionalism" can be merely a cover or rhetoric for legal professionals to institutionalise repressive power and justify professional control by the state (Ghai, Luckham and Snyder 1987, 649). Comprador professionalism is embedded in the solicitor community and largely materialised in the formation and consolidation of the conservative leadership of the Law Society, which has been supported by the rising demands for closer economic ties with the Chinese legal service market and the persistent majority of votes in council elections. Comprador professionalism is also state-adjacent as many leaders of the Law Society co-opt with the state's institutional and political control of the solicitor community, primarily via leadership contestation (Liu and Stern 2020). The following section explains how comprador professionalism was challenged by a group of liberal solicitors after 2019.

Leadership Contestation in the Law Society: the 2020 Council Election

Critical voices in the post-handover Law Society emerged in 2014 when members began to challenge the council's stance openly. As mentioned in chapter 5, in 2014, after the release of the State Council's White Paper on "One Country, Two Systems," Ambrose Lam, the president of the Law Society, publicly supported the document and appraised the "great" leadership of the Chinese Communist Party (CCP) in a radio programme. Lam's support angered some members of the Law Society, who later called an emergency general meeting to pass a majority vote of no confidence against Lam's presidency, and he resigned afterwards (Rose and Torode 2014). This incident proved that a robust bottom-up solicitor effort could change the council's line on comprador professionalism. However, members of the Law Society did not go further by contesting for the council election. Instead, they chose to form a new peer organisation for lawyers, which will be discussed in the following chapter.

Four years later, some liberal lawyers decided to contest for the seats in the council of the Law Society following the electoral victory liberalising the Bar Council election in 2018. Nevertheless, as the above tables show, the council elections in 2018 and 2019 did not threaten the conservative and comprador-like incumbent. The incumbent secured proxy votes from his colleagues, perpetuating the culture of self-censorship in law firms. However, the circumstance changed after the outbreak of the Anti-extradition Bill (Anti-ELAB) Movement, when a group of liberal solicitors decided to run for the council elections of the Law Society in 2020. The council election in that year was a landmark case of a bottom-up efforts of leadership contestation to the solicitor community in Hong Kong.

The 2020 Law Society Election: Reshuffling the Opportunity Structure

On 16 April 2020, one and a half months before the council election of the Law Society, three solicitors, Kenneth Lam, Janet Pang and Olga Choi, launched a Facebook page as their social media campaign platform, with a title expressing their intention to run for the upcoming council election of the Law Society (Facebook page of The Strong and Fearless Voices of Hong Kong Solicitors). Two weeks later, another three solicitors, Michelle Tsoi, Davyd Wong and George Chan, also launched a Facebook page to declare the same intention (Facebook Page of Law Society 2020–Independent and Firm Voices). Finally, both teams decided to work together. Five of them submitted nominations, and one withdrew to avoid confusion in voting (*Stand News*

6 May 2020). My interviews with some of the self-proclaimed "open-minded" lawyer candidates (or liberal candidates), alongside my observations of their meetings with the press, revealed that the 2019 Anti-ELAB Movement had significantly shaken the professional legal culture of solicitors in Hong Kong and awakened the legal consciousness and political agency of some liberal candidates (observation at a press meeting on 16 April 2020). The outbreak of the Anti-ELAB movement in 2019 not only changed the political and legal environment of Hong Kong but also reshuffled the dynamics between the council of the Law Society and its members in general. The new dynamics offered opportunities for liberal lawyers to contest leadership in the solicitor community.

Due to the repeated mass arrests in demonstrations and various protest actions during the Anti-ELAB Movement, some liberal lawyers and civil society organisations formed several pro bono legal visit teams to assist arrested protestors at police stations and follow up the cases and trials later (see chapter 6). Among more than a hundred solicitors and barristers from the legal visit teams, four of the original six liberal candidates were popularly known as part of the pro bono legal visit teams. They witnessed many forms of human rights violations allegedly committed by the law enforcement. Such experiences motivated these pro bono lawyers to realise the crises of the broader political and legal environment. They were also discontent with the state-adjacent position of the Law Society on the Anti-ELAB movement. Some of these lawyers commenced to consider contesting the leadership of the Law Society as they perceived contesting seats in the Law Society owns strategic values.

The liberal or open-minded candidates' decision of running for Law Society's council elections in 2020 could be attributed to several factors. The first attribute refers to the open-minded candidates' experience assisting arrestees in the Anti-ELAB Movement. These experiences included their witnesses about the denial of rights among arrestees and a sense of guilt. In many instances after the 2019 protests, some liberal candidates encountered obstruction by law enforcement when carrying out their duties as pro bono lawyers to assist the arrested protestors. They were, for example, made to wait for an unusual length of time to meet their clients, who had their statements taken by police officers without the presence of lawyers:

> Under Hong Kong's Basic Law and the Bill of Rights Ordinance, everyone is entitled to timely legal rights, and the rights should not be unreasonably protracted. Nevertheless, such legal rights have often been dragged out

> during our visits. While the rights of solicitors in providing legal services and the whole legal system were affected by such unfair treatment, we have not seen any response from the Law Society (Candidate A at the team's press meeting on 16 April 2020).

The silence of the Law Society, unlike the Bar's pronouncements against such abuses of legal rights, reinforced the liberal candidates' intention to stand against the incumbent of the Law Society. Their decision to contest the Law Society election also came from their encounters with protestors, whom the liberal candidates regarded as sacrificing themselves to protect their city. One liberal candidate felt indebted to the sufferings of protestors, who paid the price of physical injuries, career prospects and psychological pressures to resist the passage of the extradition law, especially when he met a client who was suspected of being beaten up by police officers inside a police station:

> When I saw him in the hospital, I asked whether he could stand with the injuries. He said he was not OK, but then he turned to me and said, "You guys must carry on." I was shocked by his words. Ordinary people try to protect the legal system regardless of the price they have to pay, If we do not defend it ourselves as part of the legal profession, how can we repay them [the protestors]? (Candidate B at the team's press meeting on 16 April 2020).

The treatment of arrested protestors also inspired them to go further than just being pro bono lawyers. The frustrations in providing legal assistance encouraged them to make changes in the Law Society, which could achieve a greater sense of commitment to the public-spiritedness of the legal profession in society. Activist lawyering in the Anti-ELAB Movement, therefore, inspired the liberal candidates to take a step further:

> As a pro bono lawyer, I have witnessed many injustices [towards the arrested protestors]. Would it be enough if we just kept complaining to the relevant bodies or representing the protestors in court? Certainly not. It may not change the circumstances and injustices..., that said, even when I cannot change the crux, I could step out of my comfort zone and join the Law Society Council election to maintain the spirit of the Rule of Law. At least we try to make a noise. The society will still have expectations on lawyers (Candidate C at the team's press meeting on 16 April 2020).

The second attribute was the liberal candidates' perceived threat when they connected their personal experience of lawyering with the broader legal and political contexts of Hong Kong. In the view of the liberal candidates, their frustrating experiences when carrying out their professional duties for protestors were contrasted with the public statements by the Law Society, which "overwhelmingly condemned violence by protestors":

> For example, when you see the President of the Law Society speaking at the opening of the legal year, interpreting the Rule of Law as just law and order that only focused on obedience to the law, her speech sounded like an echo of the government's call for 'stopping violence and restoring the order.' This interpretation is not shared by local lawyers, who are shaped by Hong Kong's legal education. We understand the Rule of Law as limiting government power and equality before the law, without exception to the police or the state (Candidate A at the team's press meeting on 16 April 2020).

In the eyes of the liberal candidates, the Law Society stood with the government and pro-establishment camp by staying silent or upholding a pro-government stance in many instances of legal rights abuses. For example, the liberal candidates disapproved of the Law Society's public statement that an independent investigation by a statutory commission of inquiry was unnecessary, contrary to popular demand. The liberal candidates thus saw that a change to the Law Society election was necessary and valuable.

The third attribute refers to the strategic value or perceived utility of contesting the council election of the Law Society. The utility consisted of instrumental and symbolic values. Instrumental value referred to the actual positive impact of entering the Law Society as an elected council member. The council of the Law Society consists of 20 members and each year, there must be an election of five seats, as the five members longest in office must retire; however, the retired council members are eligible for re-election (Article of Association of the Law Society, Article 15(a)). Therefore, even though the open-minded team would remain a minority in the council once elected, they could continue to stay there until they were obliged to resign. In the short run, more liberal council members could engender a more significant counterbalancing effect against the incumbent in deliberating the positioning of controversial legislation or practices of legal transplantation by the Chinese authority. After all, they could hold back or object to draft statements from the sub-committees by deliberation and bargaining in the council meetings (ITV2004, 25 September 2020). In the long run, winning a majority in the council election would keep the momentum in future, as they could, in theory, keep mobilising pro-democracy solicitors in future elections. If so, the conservative incumbent would eventually be replaced by liberal lawyers (ITV2006, 8 May 2020). This was also their vision of aligning the Law Society's commitment to defending the Rule of Law and lawyers' public spirit with the Bar:

> If we can successfully get more liberal voices in the [council of the] Law Society, once a controversial legislation like the extradition law is proposed, the Law Society and the Bar would be able to have "one voice" (ITV2006, 8 May 2020).

Symbolic value refers to the implications of winning seats in the Law Society council and the message to the public. In their view, success in gaining more seats in the committee would imply an endorsement of their interpretation of the Rule of Law. It could deliver a message to both the legal profession and the public that most of the members of the Law Society share the same understanding of the Rule of Law as the open-minded team, such as the importance of equality before the law and human rights, instead of merely obedience to the law (ITV2006, 8 May 2020).

The awakening of the political agency of those liberal candidates, as a subjective and intrinsic factor, was nevertheless insufficient to motivate them to take the risk of contesting the council election. Their motivation became more substantial when two external political opportunities were perceived and considered. The "endgame judgement" against the political and legal environment of Hong Kong served as a political opportunity, as well as a final push. It referred to the sense of threat and crisis perceived by the open-minded team. Seeing the increasing repression of protests by the local law enforcement and China's continuous transplantation of authoritarian legal ideology in Hong Kong, the liberal candidates believed the council election of the Law Society in 2020 would be the final opportunity for lawyers to speak up for the Rule of Law:

> Many people joined the "million people's march" on 9 June 2019 because they said that if they had not protested on that day, they would not know whether they still had the chance to do so after. Likewise, when you see how the Liaison Office in Hong Kong repeatedly rejects and represses the idea of the Rule of Law, then replaces it with a notion of rule by law, you never know whether you will still be able to speak publicly and loudly for your beliefs next year... It is now or never (ITV2006, 8 May 2020).

In other words, such endgame judgement was based on their interpretation of the severity of the Chinese authoritarian legal transplantation process in Hong Kong's legal system, expressed in the ideological intervention of the Liaison Office in 2019 and 2020. It was also a judgement that a new and rare opportunity to challenge the Law Society presented itself through council elections.

Another perceived opportunity was the liberal candidates' estimation of the potential of the liberal character of young solicitors. This belief was based on their observation of the electoral results of the legal sector in both Legislative Council (LegCo) and the Election Committee, in which pro-democracy lawyers repeatedly won by a majority of more than 3,000 votes. The victory could not simply lie in the support of the barrister community, which only numbers around 1,500 practitioners in Hong Kong. In addition, they also predicted that the pool of pro-democracy solicitors was expanded since many junior lawyers witnessed or engaged in acts of civil disobedience during the Umbrella Movement of 2014. One of the liberal candidates once met some young lawyers in 2016 who complained that the pro-democracy camp was "not radical enough" (ITV2004, 24 April 2020). Hence, they concluded that there was indeed solid support for pro-democracy and liberal lawyers, particularly from the younger generation of solicitors. They needed to avoid a quiet campaign whereby even solicitors were unaware of the council election (ITV2004, 24 April 2020).

Change of Campaign Strategies and Bottom-up Mobilisation

The liberal candidates leveraged a new political opportunity structure to design and operate an election campaign when the nominating stage was over. Unlike the contest in 2018, when candidates Cheung and Lam chose a low-key approach, the liberal candidates commenced an active campaign a month before the election to accelerate an "atmosphere of election" both within the profession as well as in public (ITV2004, 24 April 2020). As they explained:

> We want more people [solicitors] to know about and engage in the election ... We hope solicitors are aware that the Rule of Law is genuinely eroded, as reflected by the Anti-Extradition Movement, and that our campaign strategy will raise their awareness, and they will cast their votes [to us] (ITV2006, 8 May 2020).

To publicise their election campaign, the liberal candidates also took the initiative to meet the press, to publish statements and updates on their campaign activities, to hold meetings with members of the Law Society and to distribute platform flyers on the streets and their Facebook pages. Their election campaign targeted eligible voters and the public to raise public awareness of the Law Society election and to advertise the rival between the liberal team and their counterparts. Such strategies brought frequent media reports of the candidates' policy platform and political stances, such as their attitudes towards the Liaison Office's alleged intervention in Hong Kong's legal system and their call for setting up an independent commission of inquiry to investigate alleged police brutality in the Anti-ELAB Movement. After all, while candidates on both sides proposed various economic measures to secure solicitors' professional interests, their stances on controversial political and legal issues distinguished them. For instance, a newspaper reported a campaign advertisement featuring Cynthia Yen, one of the candidates in the conservative team, known as the self-claimed "professional team," in which two team members were endorsed by The Small and Medium Law Firms Association of Hong Kong (SAMLAW) in 2020 (also see chapter 3). The advertisement quoted Yen's comments on the proposed national security law (NSL) by the National People's Congress Standing Committee (NPCSC) "as a highly emotive and politically partisan issue" that might cause another round of "civil disturbance and violent social unrest" (Sha 2020) Moreover, SAMLAW sent two letters to its members, asking them to vote for fellow SAMLAW members Kung and Yen by appointing their president as their proxy (Chan and Lo 2020 a and b).

Fuel was added to the fire when a private email from Melissa Pang, the president of the Law Society, was leaked to the media on 8 May 2020. According to the news report, she sent an email to solicitors who received her donation of face masks, calling for the recipient's support for the five candidates from the conservative team. Pang declined to reply to the media enquiry (*Stand News* 8 May 2020). Cheung, a council member of the Law Society, posted the email on his Facebook page on 11 May 2020, expressing doubts about the president's impartiality in the council election. Three days later, Melissa Pang held a press conference at the headquarters of the Law Society, insisting her email was exercising her freedom of expression in a personal capacity (Lum and Lau 2020). The controversy did not cease. Some law firm partners, who claimed themselves to be from the mainland but had been in Hong Kong for 25 years, jointly posted to solicitors asking them to authorise Melissa Pang to cast votes for them in the council election for the sake of "defending the professional, rational and neutral image of solicitors and promoting the integration and development of the legal service markets in Hong Kong and the mainland."(*The Apple Daily,* 20 May 2020).

Apart from publicising the election to engender a supportive atmosphere for the candidates, the liberal team also mobilised support by highlighting the use of postal votes to counterbalance proxy votes' impact. As discussed previously, law firm partners have repeatedly used proxy votes to aggregate ballots for the incumbent of the Law Society. However, according to the Articles of Association of the Law Society, proxy votes can be countermanded by votes in person, and postal votes cannot be countermanded by proxy votes (Articles of Association of the Law Society, Article (15AA) (vii)). This means that even if a member gave a proxy vote to others before the annual general meeting (AGM), the proxy vote is invalidated if the member attends the AGM in person and casts a vote. The proxy vote will also be invalidated if the member sends a ballot to the Law Society by post three days before the AGM. Before the 2020 election, only a few solicitors would choose to post the ballot as early as possible, although it helps eliminate the effect of appointing their boss as a proxy:

> Once I got the ballot paper from the Law Society, I would send it back as early as possible. Thus, when my boss came to collect my proxy vote, I could tell him I had already sent a postal ballot. He could not ask me to vote twice (ITV1935, 29 April 2019).

Postal voting became essential for the liberal team to secure electoral support. They amplified the advantage of postal voting through propaganda, asking member solicitors to post their ballots. These could override proxy votes, and the proxies would not know their votes had been overridden. Their campaign poster on their Facebook page explicitly stated, "My boss collected my proxy! What should I do?" then explained the procedure of lodging a postal ballot (Facebook page of the Strong and Fearless Voices of Hong Kong Solicitors 24 May 2020). The suggestion was publicised to the solicitors and the general public, who realised how law firm partners secured their votes by proxy. The subtle tensions between the junior solicitors and the senior law firm partners were further exposed by the fact that the younger generation of solicitors could resist the domination of the senior colleagues in the Law Society by casting votes.

The tactical use of postal ballots effectively brought victory to the liberal candidates in the council election. On 28 May 2020, the liberal team won four out of five vacancies in the annual Law Society council election, with the fifth seat going to a candidate from the conservative team (Chong 2020). However, the elected member with the least votes only won by a small margin of less than 1 per cent; the significance of proxy votes was weakened by a sharp increase in postal votes. The victory of the elected candidates from the liberal team was attributed to postal ballots, which shared 88 per cent of their total votes (see table 23). This implies that members of the Law Society had a greater motivation to vote individually in 2020, against the backdrop of the Anti-ELAB Movement and the publicised electioneering of the liberal team. The voting motivation was cultivated by the changing political and legal environment in Hong Kong after the Anti-ELAB Movement and the active agency of the liberal candidates.

Table 23. Election Results of Members of the Council of the Law Society of Hong Kong in 2020*

Name of Candidate		No. of Postal Votes (% of Total Votes)	No. of Votes in Person (% of Total Votes)	No. of Proxy Votes (% of Total Votes)	Total Votes
1^	Chan George	2688 (88.25)	201 (6.60)	157 (5.15)	3046
2#	Ganesh Warren	1026 (33.06)	108 (3.48)	1969 (63.45)	3103
3#	Kung Olivia	904 (31.04)	108 (3.63)	1960 (65.95)	2972
4^	Lam Kenneth	2749 (88.42)	201 (6.47)	159 (5.11)	3109
5#	McConnell Simon	933 (31.40)	108 (3.63)	1931 (64.97)	2972
6^	Pang Janet	2730 (88.09)	210 (6.78)	159 (5.13)	3099
7#	Rhoda Robert	1011 (32.85)	104 (3.38)	1963 (63.77)	3078
8^	Tsoi Michelle	2727 (88.25)	210 (6.80)	153 (4.95)	3090
9^	Wong Davyd	2733 (88.05)	208 (6.70)	163 (5.25)	3104
10#	Yen Cynthia	897 (30.39)	101 (3.42)	1954 (66.19)	2952

* Elected Candidates are in bold.
# Teamed up in campaigning as a "professional team" and endorsed by the President of the Law Society in a personal capacity
^ Teamed up in campaigning as an "open-minded team."
Source: Chong 2020

The achievements of the liberal candidates in the council election were two-fold. First, although the turnout rate of the election was low, it broke the record of previous elections, implying the strategy of publicising the election campaign worked well, as the liberal lawyers expected. Second, the election proved the absolute advantage of postal votes in securing seats in the election. They threatened the incumbent proxy votes and could no longer be used as leverage. The 2020 council election became a trial for liberal lawyers to test the scope of support from solicitors after the citywide protests. In theory, their victory gave hope for another round of electoral victory in future elections.

The Aftermath: Performance of Liberal Lawyers in the Council

Could the elected liberal lawyers advance the position of the Law Society Council in terms of resisting authoritarian legal transplantation? As the liberal council members remained as a minority, one indicator would be the appearance of dissenting opinions from the liberal council members following the release of public statements by the committee. Immediately after the release of the NPCSC's decision on disqualifying four pro-democracy lawmakers on 11 November 2020 (see chapter 2), two liberal members of the council published a statement disapproving the decision as violating the Rule of Law and calling for the legal profession to speak up (Facebook page of the Strong and Fearless Voices of Hong Kong Solicitors 11 November 2020). Two days later, the Law Society released a statement in response to the NPCSC decision. Still, it only urged the government to clarify the legal basis of disqualification and the legality of the decision in empowering the executive government of Hong Kong to disqualify lawmakers in the future (Facebook page of the Strong and Fearless Voices of Hong Kong Solicitors 13 November 2020). The subtle tone of that statement was contrasted by a subsequent statement by seven council members, including the four new liberal solicitors. This latter statement made clear that the NPCSC's decision was "contrary to the Rule of Law, the principle of 'One Country, Two Systems,' the express provisions of Article 79 of the Basic Law, the constitutional rights and freedoms guaranteed by the Basic Law, as well as due process" (Cheung et al. 2020). The argument raised carried a much stronger tone than the Law Society's and served as a dissenting opinion.

Another instance could be found on 27 December 2020, when the four liberal new council members and a veteran member, Mark Daly, jointly released a statement in their capacity to express their "grave concern" that the *People's Daily* criticised a judge's decision on a bail application for Jimmy Lai, the founder of *Apple Daily*, while the bail application was under appeal. The statement urged a stop to any unfounded attacks against the judiciary in Hong Kong and called for the government to defend fair trial and the presumption of innocence in trials related to crimes of national security (Facebook page of the Strong and Fearless Voices of Hong Kong Solicitors 27 December 2020). The statement by the liberal lawyers was a response to both the shaky judicial independence in Hong Kong and the silence of the Law Society on the matter. At the same time, the Bar had sent an open letter to the secretary of justice concerning a similar pro-China media attack against judges in Hong Kong. The statement of the newly elected liberal members also indicated that, though present as a minority in the council, they persisted outspoken in defending the Rule of Law beyond the institutional constraints, attracting public attention to the critical voice from inside the Law Society.

Conclusion

Unlike the Bar, the solicitors in Hong Kong have long constituted a politically conservative or even apolitical outlook. This facilitated state co-optation through the provision of economic opportunities on the mainland. To consolidate the comprador-like practice of the Law Society Council, law firm partners tended to use the proxy system in voting to sustain the incumbents on the Council at the expense of its resilience in protecting the Rule of Law and judicial independence in Hong Kong. The repeated emphasis on law and order and the sympathetic attitude to the statecraft of authoritarian legal transplantation by the Law Society, as demonstrated in chapter 4, resulted from comprador professionalism.

This static structure was challenged when some liberal solicitors woke up to their political agency through their professional legal support in the Anti-ELAB Movement. Their decision to compete for seats in the Law Society council, backed by the sharp increase of postal votes that override the impact of proxies, revealed that the pillars sustaining comprador professionalism quivered under the mass protests of 2019. Therefore, the 2020 council election contest was a blatant case of how political agencies overcame unfavourable structures. Individual solicitors, whose experience, motivation and determination of resistance were enlightened by the events in the Anti-ELAB Movement, have broken through the existing political structure of the Law Society, and broadly the solicitor community.

The case of the 2020 Law Society election also sheds light on the usefulness and limitations of resisting authoritarian legal transplantation within the establishment. Together with the Bar, the Law Society is, after all, a statutory body endorsed by the state. The political authority delegates the powers of admitting and regulating the legal profession; hence, challenging the state carries a certain degree of risk of losing the autonomy and self-regulatory status of the organised profession if the state is intolerant of dissenting voices and is keen on reprisals. The new tactic of releasing alternative statements by the liberal members of the Law Society council indicated an obstacle to reaching a consensus on progressive pronouncements against the state. But at the same time, this tactic demonstrated the creativity and flexibility of the liberal council members to continue speaking for the Rule of Law through their publicity.

Despite the limitations of resisting within the establishment, the success of liberal council members could engender a modelling effect for junior solicitors, inspiring them to consider the meaning of lawyering and solicitor as a professional identity, and hence lead to the reshaping of the professional legal culture that transcends pursuits of merely profits and legal technicality for clients. More than providing professional services to clients or giving pro bono legal advice, engaging in the election of the Law Society council is a way to advance the public-spiritedness of lawyers. Here upholding legal professionalism and political lawyering were intersected: the politicisation of lawyers, which wass expressed in their awakening of political agency to make a change in the professional bodies, turned into a possible and practical way to defend the Rule of Law and professional autonomy when the political authorities were encroaching the legal system.

References

Chan, Maggie, and Loretta Lo. "SAMLAW Newsletter: AGM: Make Our Voice Heard in Law Society Council." *The Small and Medium Law Firms Association of Hong Kong*, May 7. Accessed December 17, 2020. https://www.samlaw.hk/index.php/lastnews/238-2020-05-08-samlaw-make-our-voices-heard-in-lawsociety-council.html.

Cheung, Eric. T. M., Kenneth Lam, Janet H. Y. Pang, Mark Daly, Davyd Wong, Jonathan Ross, and Michelle W. T. Tosi. 2020. "Statement on the Disqualification of Four Legislative Council Members." November 13. Google Drive. Accessed January 29, 2021. https://drive.google.com/file/d/1qrepplK-X0oe3QeY5NtxOswwv2AQ1JjY/view.

Chong, H. T. 2020. "[Lu Shī Huì Gǎi Xuǎn Jìng Zhēng Jī Liè] Yuē 6 Qiān Rén Tóu Piào Chuàng Xīn Gāo, Kāi Míng Pài 5 Xí Yíng 4 Xí, Zǒng Dé Piào Shuài Xiāng Chà Bù Dào 1%." *CitizenNews*, May 29. Accessed January 20, 2021. Archived on file with the author.

Ghai, Yash, Robin Luckham, and Francis Snyder, eds. 1987. *The Political Economy of Law: A Third World Reader.* Oxford University Press.

"Law Society 2020 – Independent and Firm Voices." 2020. Facebook. Accessed January 29, 2021. Archived on file with the author.

Liu, Lawrence J., and Rachel E. Stern. 2020. "State-Adjacent Professionals: How Chinese Lawyers Participate in Political Life." *The China Quarterly* 247: 793–813.

"[Lu Shī Huì Gǎi Xuǎn] Lu Shī Huì Huì Cháng Péng Yùn Xī Diàn Yóu Wéi Qīn Jiàn Zhì Hòu Xuǎn Rén Lā Piào, Lu Shī Zhì Yí Lì Yì Chōng Tū." 2020. *Stand News*, May 8. Accessed January 29, 2021. Archived on file with the author.

"[Lu Shī Huì Gǎi Xuǎn] Nèi Dì Lái Gǎng Lu Shī Tì Jiàn Zhì Pài Hòu Xuǎn Rén Lā Piào, Chàng Jiāng Shòu Quán Piào Jiāo Lu Shī Huì Huì Cháng Péng Yùn Xī." 2020. *The Apple Daily Breaking News*, May 20. Accessed January 29, 2021. Archived on file with the author.

"Lu Shī Huì Gǎi Xuǎn Wǔ Lǐ Shì Xí Wèi, Fǎn Xiū Lì Lu Shī Xié Diào Wǔ Rén Míng Dān, Jì Dài Rù Kāi Míng Shēng Yīn." 2020. *Stand News*, May 6. Accessed January 29, 2021. Archived on file with the author.

"Lu Shī Huì Yuè Dǐ Gǎi Xuǎn, Zhāng Dá Míng: Yǒu Lu Shī Shōu Zhōng Lián Bàn Lā Piào Xìn Xī." 2019. *Stand News*, May 29. Accessed December 23, 2020. Archived on file with the author.

Lum, Alvin, and Chris Lau. 2020. "Hong Kong Law Society Chief Defends Controversial Decision to Back Certain Candidates in Polarised Governing Council Election." *South China Morning Post*, May 14. Accessed January 29, 2021. https://www.scmp.com/news/hong-kong/law-and-crime/article/3084454/hong-kong-law-society-chief-defends-controversial..

"The Strong and Fearless Voices of Hong Kong Solicitors." 2020. Facebook. Accessed January 29, 2021. Archived on file with the author.

Sha, Pun Shan. 2020. "Lu shī huì gǎi xuǎn zhuān yè pài yán kūn yǐng : lu shī huì yīng bǎo chí fēi zhèng zhì xìng, fǎn rèn hé bào lì" *HK01*, May 26. Accessed October 31, 2024. https://www.hk01.com/%E6%94%BF%E6%83%85/477904/%E5%BE%8B%E5%B8%AB%E6%9C%83%E6%94%B9%E9%81%B8-%E5%B0%88%E6%A5%AD%E6%B4%BE%E5%9A%B4%E5%9D%A4%E7%A9%8E-%E5%BE%8B%E5%B8%AB%E6%9C%83%E6%87%89%E4%BF%9D%E6%8C%81%E9%9D%9E%E6%94%BF%E6%B2%BB%E6%80%A7-%E5%8F%8D%E4%BB%BB%E4%BD%95%E6%9A%B4%E5%8A%9B .

Wong, Rachel. 2020. "'Liberal' Voices Win Four Seats in Hong Kong's Law Society Council Election." *Hong Kong Free Press*, May 29. Accessed January 3, 2021. https://hongkongfp.com/2020/05/29/liberal-voices-win-four-seats-in-hong-kongs-law-society-council-election/.

9. Conclusion: Hong Kong's Struggle for the Rule of Law

Abstract: This chapter synthesises the findings of the monograph, exploring Hong Kong's transition from Rule of Law to "rule by law" under China's authoritarian legal transplantation. It highlights the erosion of judicial independence, civil liberties, and legal autonomy due to China's imposition of authoritarian legal norms. Despite systemic encroachment, Hong Kong's legal professionals employed strategies of legal resistance to defend the Rule of Law. These significant efforts are under stress tests due to China's introduction of a National Security Law in Hong Kong and shall be another subject of future research. The chapter situates Hong Kong's legal struggle within broader anti-authoritarian and decolonising discourses, emphasising the importance of both professional and political agency and civil resilience in countering autocratic legal projects.

Keywords: Authoritarian Legal Transplantation, Legal Resistance, Judicial Independence, National Security Law, Decolonisation, Rule of Law

A Battle between Rule of Law and "Rule by Law" in Hong Kong

The "One Country, Two Systems" framework in Hong Kong is inevitably full of tension. The market economy and the common law system of Hong Kong co-exist with the highly regulated economy and the socialist authoritarian legality of mainland China. Hong Kong is not an independent polity but rather a subnational jurisdiction under the sovereignty of the People's Republic of China (PRC). Therefore, the extent to which Hong Kong can uphold its enjoyment of civil liberties and self-government, including an independent judiciary and the Rule of Law, with a mother country that does not appreciate such liberal values, has always been questionable.

Scholars in interdisciplinary studies of the Rule of Law in Hong Kong often present a binary picture. Tam suggests that based on his empirical

---

Lai, Y. *Legal Resistance under Authoritarianism: The Struggle for the Rule of Law in Hong Kong.* Taylor & Francis Group, 2025
DOI: 10.5117/9789048558438_CH09

analysis of judicial review and cause lawyering in Hong Kong during the early period of the post-handover administration, the legal community, including lawyers and judges, can uphold the Rule of Law by safeguarding the enjoyment of human rights in the courtroom (2012). From a socio-cultural perspective, Jones speculates on the constraints of local lawyers if they want to defend the liberal values of the Rule of Law in the city, as the legal profession is facing the economic and political influence of the mainland Chinese authorities (2015). In his recent article, Tai also stresses that despite the solid liberal culture of the legal profession in Hong Kong, China's encroachment on the city's political and legal system has led to an "authoritarian Rule of Law" (2021).

This book follows the observations of Jones and Tai to deepen the study of the changing state-lawyer relations in post–2014 Hong Kong, of China's specific strategies for infringing on the legal system as well as the legal profession in Hong Kong, and the various forms of resistance to such moves by local lawyers and civil society. The main research questions of this book are (1) is the Rule of Law in Hong Kong at stake under the Chinese sovereign state? (2) If so, how have lawyers defended the Rule of Law in post-colonial Hong Kong? I answer these questions by introducing two concepts and applying them in examining the Chinese authoritarian encroachment in Hong Kong's legal system and the corresponding acts of resistance from legal professional bodies and activist lawyers in collaboration with civil society. The innovative concepts are "authoritarian legal transplantation" and "legal resistance." Authoritarian legal transplantation is a new concept developed from Alan Watson's idea of legal transplant. It indicates the transplantation or imposition of authoritarian legal norms, rules and practices from a jurisdiction with an authoritarian regime to another jurisdiction. In the context of this book, authoritarian legal transplantation refers to China's imposition of its authoritarian legal rules, norms and practices on its subnational territory, Hong Kong, where its political and legal systems are distinguished from the mainland one according to the constitutional document of the Basic Law of Hong Kong.

I use this concept to argue that the Rule of Law in Hong Kong has evolved incrementally towards authoritarian rule by law since its transfer of sovereignty to China. This is because of China's authoritarian legal transplantation in Hong Kong's legal system. Both governments of China and Hong Kong politicise the legal environment by directly intervening in the city's constitutional order and legal system. They do this by nurturing more pro-establishment lawyers to influence the legislature and civil society and absorbing the Hong Kong legal profession into the mainland legal service market, taming the local lawyers into subjugating the state's political project. Facilitated by the colonial legal legacy and China's United Front Work in the legal profession, the local legal profession has been further politicised than during colonial times. Consequently, Hong Kong's legal profession, including individual lawyers, law firms, and legal professional bodies, has become more adjacent to the authoritarian state's interests. More members of the legal profession have also been recruited and co-opted by the state to strengthen the implementation of authoritarian legal transplantation through their capacity as well as through the organisational resources of the Bar and the Law Society.

How could lawyers defend the Rule of Law in Hong Kong under the implementation of authoritarian legal transplantation? Findings from my fieldwork research between 2018 and 2020 reveal that Hong Kong lawyers, who exercised their political agency while carrying out their professional duty, is paramount in resisting the state's assault on the rule. To do so, lawyers had to go beyond a technical form of legal professionalism that concealed the tensions and dynamics between the state, professional bodies and individual lawyers. The idea of legal resistance, which comprises three strategies, is developed from my findings. These are how lawyers contested leadership in legal professional bodies to defend professional autonomy, how activist lawyers organised themselves to empower civil society's understanding of the Rule of Law, and finally, how cause lawyers provided legal assistance for protestors in pro-democracy, also known as anti-authoritarian movements. I argue that activist lawyers or cause lawyers in Hong Kong can defend the Rule of Law by strengthening the capacity of civil society to promote a legal culture and to defend its institutions against the project of authoritarian legal transplantation. Legal resistance was realised as a process of politicising the legal community, particularly young lawyers and law students, to commit themselves to liberal political ideals relevant to the Rule of Law, thus enhancing the resilience of the legal community and the rule in Hong Kong. Although the number of lawyers involved in the three approaches of legal resistance did not constitute a majority in the domestic legal profession, they became a critical minority in the legal community to resist authoritarian encroachment on the Rule of Law in the period between 2014 and 2020. The experiences in this period demonstrated that the awakening of lawyers' political agency is essential to upholding a genuine commitment to the rule eroded by the legal imposition and continuity of draconian laws and authoritarian legal transplantation in "post-umbrella" Hong Kong.

Authoritarian Legal Transplantation and the China Factor

In chapter 2, I explained the three motivations for China's transplantation of its authoritarian legal norms, rules and practices to Hong Kong. These motivations are nationalistic, political and economic. The Chinese authorities have a strong desire to institutionalise nationalism in Hong Kong in the name of decolonisation. Authoritarian legal transplantation, which commenced after the sovereignty transfer of Hong Kong, is part of the Chinese Communist Party's (CCP) project to "decolonise" Hong Kong from the British legacy and rebuild Hong Kong through nationalism. Authoritarian legal transplantation is a national state-building project after a colonial state-building project was established in Hong Kong under British rule. Besides, the CCP also aimed to expand direct political control in Hong Kong by weakening judicial autonomy and weaponising laws and courts to crack down on the opposition. Despite the preservation of some existing institutions in the Basic Law, China has begun to transplant its ideology and institutional practices in Hong Kong to consolidate its sovereignty and rule-by-law engineering in this subnational polity. As one of the major institutions in Hong Kong, the Rule of Law became a target of the national state-building project through authoritarian legal transplantation. Rather than removing the common law system and formally amending the Basic Law, China has transplanted the socialist authoritarian legal ideology and institutional practices to consolidate its control of Hong Kong's existing legal system. The project of authoritarian legal transplantation reached its climax in July 2020 when the Chinese authority introduced the national security law and the "Office for Safeguarding National Security", which operates under China's jurisdiction, to the legal system of Hong Kong. Last but not the least, authoritarian legal transplantation can also facilitate the Chinese government's scheme of infiltrating Hong Kong's legal community, which facilitates capital flow from the mainland to Hong Kong. To do so, the legal service market opportunities in the mainland is used as a lure to co-opt with some Hong Kong barristers and solicitors who behave as "comprador lawyers."

In chapters 2 and 3, I also demonstrated how China's authoritarian legal transplantation was carried out by adapting the China factor model to distinguish its direct and indirect mechanisms. As the sovereign state of Hong Kong, China is in a dominant position to encroach on Hong Kong's legal system without abolishing the constitutional arrangement of "One Country, Two Systems." Direct and indirect influencing mechanisms operationalise the China factor in four spheres: legal institutions, political elections, counter-mobilisation of pro-government lawyers and economic infiltration within the legal profession. Regarding a direct influencing mechanism, China combines its exercise of sovereign power with adapting pre-existing British institutions to weaken the normative foundation and practices of the Rule of Law in Hong Kong in five ways: (1) the National People's Congress Standing Committee's (NPCSC) interpretations of the Basic Law; (2) imposition of the NPCSC's binding decisions related to the provisions of the Basic Law; (3) indirect transplantation of laws in the mainland through the proposed extradition law amendment bill in Hong Kong; (4) direct transplantation or imposition of laws promulgated in China; (5) production of official legal discourse in favour of authoritarian rule over Hong Kong. These measures engender direct adverse effects on the judiciary and political opposition in Hong Kong as they weaken judicial independence, political freedoms and civic space, and at the same time strengthen the executive government to enjoy more extraordinary arbitrary powers. The autonomy of the courts to check and balance the executive power diminishes, and members of political and civil society have reduced capacities to challenge the political authorities.

Regarding indirect influencing mechanisms, China induces nationalistic and authoritarian legal ideology and shores its legitimacy in Hong Kong society by infiltrating and co-opting with the legal profession in Hong Kong through economic and political incentives. This refers to the United Front Work. This is illustrated by some lawyers being sponsored by the state to run for periodic elections as pro-government candidates or to form pro-government organisations in civil society as counter-mobilising forces against the pro-democracy movement in Hong Kong. The United Front Work can also be found in the economic opening policies of the legal service market in the mainland to consolidate economic and political ties with local law firms and legal professional bodies in Hong Kong. These pro-government lawyers and lawyer organisations are expected to endorse authoritarian legal ideology and produce illiberal legal norms in both the legislature and the public, reinforcing the effectiveness of authoritarian legal transplantation. However, the effectiveness of their performances varied in different domains. Economic integration of Hong Kong lawyers in the mainland market worked better than pro-government lawyers' engagement in elections and counter-mobilisation against pro-democracy lawyers.

The concept of authoritarian legal transplantation and its application in post-colonial Hong Kong provide two theoretical contributions to legal transplantation and politics in subnational governance. Firstly, it associates the study of legal transplant with the study of political regimes, ranging from liberal democratic and hybrid to authoritarian ones. As discussed in chapter 1, existing scholarship of legal transplants study the legal rules and norms of the original jurisdiction regardless of their democratic or autocratic nature. This book illustrates the significant role of the political regime, in this case authoritarianism, when examining the motives, processes and consequences of legal transplantation. While policies of legal transplantation often constitute modernisation in developing countries as part of the economic globalisation project, authoritarian legal transplantation is a process of autocratisation of the transplant jurisdiction. The political dimension of legal transplantation has been addressed in the study of law and colonialism. Hong Kong is not an exceptional case, given its history of British colonialism. No doubt, this book recognises that Hong Kong underwent the process of colonial legal transplantation under British rule as early as the mid-nineteenth century. Even so, the case study of post-colonial Hong Kong demonstrated that China operated the transplantation of authoritarian legal norms and practices through enforcing repressive legal rules, tightening control over the courts and teaching the ideology of law and order and rule by law in society. Therefore, this authoritarian project in Hong Kong aims to establish a political and legal order that centralises political power, weakens power-checking institutions like the courts, and legalises illiberal and anti-democratic norms in opposition to international human rights standards. These instances further affirm that post-handover Hong Kong is not a genuine beginning of decolonisation; rather, its sovereign state China decided to govern Hong Kong by consolidating authoritarian rule combined with the legacies of British colonialism.

To guarantee a well-functioning transplanted legal system, the political authorities engineer a holistic project that co-opts stakeholders of the legal system to consolidate the legal ideology and practices in the recipient jurisdiction. This book suggests authoritarian legal transplantation operates beyond black letter laws and statutes. It reaffirms that law, together with the discourse of the Rule of Law, is a socio-political product of state power. Tamanaha suggests that the production of law "is not simply state engineering, but an interplay with different forces within a particular setting of social interests, legal tradition, social norms that are all within broader social-cultural-economic-political surroundings" (2017, 198). His argument is realised in Hong Kong's case due to both the state and its collaborators in the legal community, including comprador lawyers, pro-government lawyers and sometimes legal professional bodies. These have fostered an authoritarian legal transplantation that strengthens the supremacy of the political sovereignty over safeguards of individual rights, treats laws and courts as instruments of political repression rather than rules that the powerful should abide, and infringes on the part of the legal profession to endorse and promote the transplantation of authoritarian legal norms and regulations.

Using the concept of authoritarian legal transplantation, this book also theorises how China regulates subnational governance today. As cited in chapter 1, many subnational regions have encountered challenges when handling tensions with their sovereign states. The responses of the sovereign state also differ, either by respecting the legal right of democratic rule in subnational regions, such as the UK towards Scotland, or by terminating the subnational regions' separate governing systems with coercive force, like India towards Kashmir, or by criminalising leading figures promoting national independence in the subnational areas, such as Spain towards Catalonia. In this book, the study of post-colonial Hong Kong and its relations with the sovereign state China reveals that China has chosen to diminish the autonomy of Hong Kong's common law institutions at the beginning of the sovereignty transfer. This observation can be found in the first and foremost interpretation by the NPCSC of the Basic Law in 1999, which, in effect, tamed the autonomy of the local courts to challenge the constitutionality of actions of the sovereign state. Instead of a direct crackdown by force or complete tolerance of achieving self-determination by subnational regions, China's convergence project in Hong Kong commenced when the Basic Law was finally drafted in 1990. While legal transplantation is often used between two independent jurisdictions, in this case, it also applies when explaining China's autocratisation of subnational governance in Hong Kong. This process is involuntary and known as "legal imposition." However, it is not linear, simply relying on the direct imposition of authoritarian rules and norms; it is also facilitated by recruiting legal elites and encroaching on the legal profession to promote the transplantation project and counter-mobilisation against the promotion of liberal values of the Rule of Law in Hong Kong society.

In this sense, this book also sheds light on our understanding of the future trajectory of China in global development, known as "Global China." The current design of the political, legal and economic systems of Hong Kong is not simply an architect of the Chinese authorities; it is based on the Joint Declaration between China and Britain in 1984, which was registered as an international treaty in the United Nations. The practice of authoritarian legal transplantation by China has been replacing the liberal and partially democratic norms with authoritarian and illiberal ones in Hong Kong's legal system, diminishing Hong Kong's autonomy, the Rule of Law and judicial independence that are promised in the Basic Law and the Joint Declaration.

As indicated at the beginning of the book, the study of China's sharp power, instead of the conventional notion of soft power, has become more popular among policy think tanks, academic institutions and national governments ever since China has been leveraging its economic capital to expand its influences in politics and culture beyond its territory. This includes the realms of international law, standards of international human rights, public health and economic development. Therefore, the case of Hong Kong here becomes an important lesson to those who are concerned by China's expansion of influence on the local development of the Rule of Law in its partner jurisdiction under the project of, for instance, the Belt and Road Initiative (BRI) and the Greater Bay Area, or how China influences the legal norms that are embedded in international and regional bodies, such as the United Nations and the World Bank.

Strengths and Limits of Legal Resistance under Authoritarianism

Chapters 5 to 8 of this book capture Hong Kong lawyers' strategies and tactics to resist authoritarian legal transplantation. In chapter 1, I hinted that the practice of legal resistance follows the theoretical insights in the scholarship of law and colonialism, who take an interactionist approach to explain the difficulties of implementing legal transplantation or imposition from one jurisdiction to another. When a legal system, which has been developed in a specific context, is transplanted to another context, where it is already "suffused with established indigenous cultural, social, economic, political and legal institutions," the legal system will function differently from the home jurisdiction and pose alternate impacts on society (Tamanaha 2017, 198). The reason is that the legal system is placed in a completely different social setting that may cause conflict, and the system is implemented without supporting social norms and legal culture that warrant well-functioning at home. The result of such legal transplantation would depend on the extent of adaptation between the transplanted laws and surrounding social arrangements over time (ibid). When there is strong resistance from society, the dysfunctional operation of the transplanted legal system could occur, thus putting political legitimacy and social stability at risk. It implies that the process of legal transplantation, the same as that of producing laws, is never linear and unidimensional. The state is not the sole player who imposes institutions on society without resistance. Therefore, the capacity of resistance from different social forces, usually legal system stakeholders, should not be excluded from the assessment. Herein lies the concept of legal resistance.

Legal resistance features the counterparts' response to authoritarian legal transplantation. The term "resistance" is often adopted to explain the orientation and tactics of individual and collective actors against unjust rules and structures. Lawyers organised resistance in these fields. They aimed at consolidating the Rule of Law and resisting encroachments under authoritarian rule by diffusing professional knowledge, legal skills, legal values and legal capital or networks. Resistance does not necessarily break professionalism as the tactics can be allowed within the boundaries of professional ethics and compatible with the professional identity as a lawyer. In short, the concept of legal resistance is an analytical device to examine the agency of lawyers against unfavourable structural conditions in law and politics. As I indicated in chapter 1, post-structuralist theories pay attention to the political agency of individuals to resist the political authority and the powerful in everyday life and their capacity to create new civic space as a contested site between ordinary citizens and state power (Arendt 2005; De Certeau 1984; Scott 1985). Lawyers' capacity to resist authoritarian legal transplantation in Hong Kong can be found in the legal professional bodies and mobilisation of cause lawyers. Lawyers' political agency and resilience can be found inside the establishment, including the statutory professional bodies, and outside the establishment, in the realms of civil society and social movement. Their common feature is that, unlike earlier pro-democracy lawyers who engaged in formal politics to promote the Rule of Law, the resistance is based on lawyers performing legal professionalism, including their visions and commitments to the rule, their provision of quality legal knowledge and skills same as with ordinary legal service.

"Professionalism," as Ghai et al expound, can be merely a facade for legal professionals to "monopolise the market rather than to fulfil their social responsibilities" or to "institutionalise repressive power" of many colonial states in history (Ghai, Luckham and Snyder 1987, 649). Working on my findings, I have improvised the concept of comprador professionalism, whereby some lawyers, with economic and political incentives, are willing to work with authoritarian governments to promote the political project of Rule by Law. In contrast, however, legal professionalism, if combined with the exercise of political agency by lawyers, can also serve as a meaningful and effective instrument to resist Rule by Law. To analyse lawyers' practices of legal professionalism as resistance in the professional sphere and civil society, including social movement events, I categorised three strategies: civil society empowerment, legal assistance for protestors and leadership contestation. Chapter 5 referred to activist lawyers forming civil society organisations to defend the Rule of Law by empowering civil society actors with legal knowledge and discourse. Chapter 6 explained how cause lawyers supported activists and protestors in the face of criminal arrests and prosecutions by providing legal assistance in criminal justice proceeding. Chapters 7 and 8 described how some Hong Kong lawyers engaged in elections of the Bar council and the Law Society council to resist the United Front work and defend professional autonomy of the legal community.

My findings from fieldwork between 2018 and 2020 illustrate that legal resistance in Hong Kong is controversial within the legal profession but more welcomed by civil society in response to the threats of the state's rule-by-law project. The strategy of leadership contestation indicates that lawyers' resistance was influential in legal professional bodies when pro-democracy lawyers had greater moral and discursive powers in the councils of the Bar and Law Society, as reflected in their dissenting opinions against authoritarian legal transplantation with their authoritative positions among barristers and solicitors. Resistance driven by legal professional bodies can also pressure the political authorities in the controversial imposition of legal rules and practices. It also indirectly increases the legitimacy of mass mobilisation in civil society. However, resistance through legal professional bodies is less sustainable in Hong Kong. The reasons are that legal professional bodies are, after all, part of the establishment by law, and the political authorities of both Hong Kong and China can reduce professional legal bodies' capacity to mobilise resistance by taking back their self-regulatory power and cutting official economic ties with them. When the Bar's tensions with the government escalated, some barristers worried about the adverse consequences of breaking off the relationship and saw the Bar council as over-politicised. In the case of Hong Kong between 2014 and 2020, the Bar was divided because of its confrontational attitudes towards the state and its sympathetic positioning towards citywide protests in 2019. The Law Society also remained adjacent to the state even though several liberal lawyers won seats in the council elections 2020, as the comprador lawyers continued to hold the majority. If lawyers in Hong Kong still have a desire to exercise resistance against the state's authoritarian project through the Bar or Law Society, perhaps one prerequisite is to unify the profession to reach a majority support on the professional bodies' relationship with the political authorities, legal profession and civil society, and their strategies of dealing with the Chinese authoritarian governance.

In terms of understanding how civil society empowerment worked in post-Umbrella Hong Kong, I study the contributions of two civil society organisations – the Progressive Lawyers Group (PLG) and Law Lay Dream (LLD). Founded by activist lawyers, their work included promoting popular legal education, developing a democratic culture within the legal profession and networking with civil society members. The lessons of the PLG and LLD between the Umbrella and the Anti-Extradition Law Amendment Bill (ELAB) Movements have demonstrated the significance of organised lawyers providing discursive resources of civil society's language of the Rule of Law and human rights and strengthening solidarity between activist lawyers and civil society. They constructed a realm of middle democracy between lawyers, civil society organisers, political activists and the general public, expanded the legal capital of civil society organisations, enriched rights-based legal discourse alternative to that of the government and legal professional bodies, exported such discourse to the grassroots, the youth, social movements and the international community and nurtured many cause lawyers in the younger generation of the legal profession to work with civil society organisations and social movement networks. Nevertheless, in the case of Hong Kong, civil society empowerment through organised activist lawyers also has its limitation, that is organisational sustainability. The junior profile of the PLG and LLD core members may have received less recognition from a legal profession that appreciates seniority. Members also must bear the risk of losing economic opportunities when being outspoken in political affairs. Suppose political confrontation between the state and civil society escalates. In that case, the PLG and LLD will inevitably face the dilemma between being more progressive and preserving their members' career futures to uphold the professional image of the organisations. One solution is to establish a collaboration between these activist lawyers' organisations and legal academia, which is expected to produce legal knowledge and transfer it to society for the common good. As previously mentioned, legal academics and research centres in local law schools have been active in educating the public and civil society, such as with the Rule of Law Education Project at the University of Hong Kong. As this book does not examine the role of law schools and legal academics in defending the Rule of Law, future research on the relationship between law schools, legal scholars, and civil society would enrich our understanding of the Hong Kong legal community's resistance to authoritarian legal engineering.

Legal assistance for protestors contributed lawyers' mobilisation process in anti-authoritarian movements by developing a legal support network with social movement organisations and crowdfunding platforms to provide legal visits, legal advice and legal representation for arrested and charged protestors. Legal assistance was a remedy for the limitation of the legal aid system in Hong Kong and a strategy of cause lawyers to play the role of rear-guard in social movements. This bottom-up strategy improved access to justice in Hong Kong's common law system. The legal support network in Hong Kong's anti-authoritarian protests aided arrested protestors in police custody and in preparation for criminal trials, empowering the arrestees in the criminal justice system, which is instrumentalised as an apparatus of political repression by the state.

Moreover, legal assistance in protest settings also contributed to speeding up the process of promoting a democratic ethos among the legal profession through collaboration with other civil society organisations to support direct resistance to the state. Junior lawyers or solicitors of corporate law firms earned on-ground opportunities to work with social movement organisations and networks when they provided legal assistance for arrested protestors. They gained direct experience in handling the law enforcement, opening their eyes to the problems in the criminal justice system and cultivating a greater sense of righteousness and willingness to do cause lawyering.

My study also reveals that, the legal support network for assistance encountered sustainability issues when the political authorities obstructed the operation of the legal support network. Undoubtedly, the less legal assistance for arrestees, the greater the benefits for the prosecution to take advantage in a criminal trial proceeding. Any legal support network that is dedicated to supporting protestors in criminal arrests and trials is ostensibly unfavoured by the governments. Unlike Halliday's notion of the legal complex in which judges own a stake, this network can only survive if financial and material resources are sustainable and if the ties between cause lawyers, social movement organisations, activist figures and individual citizens are further consolidated with creativity. One possible trajectory would be widening legal support networks to support citizens attending and documenting hearings of protest-related trials since 2019, which become an act of solidarity with the Anti-ELAB protestors (Lai 2021a, 82–83). Trial observations in countries where court systems are under-developed is a joint initiative by civil society or the legal community, such as the efforts of the Bar Human Rights Committee of England and Wales (2025). In Hong Kong, trial observations by voluntary citizens, who are honoured by civil society organisations and the press as "masters of trial auditing" (pang tīng shī), are still amateur. Still, those volunteers' real-time summaries and updates of protest-related court hearings have been widely circulated in a Telegram channel and have attracted more than 50,000 subscribers (Pang and Saito 2020). Without directly challenging the legitimacy of the criminal justice system and the state repression by laws and courts, activist lawyers can thus continue to engage in legal resistance by continuing to provide legal knowledge and training to trial observers to sustain solidarity and increase the transparency of the upcoming political trials in the long run.

Overall, the three strategies of legal resistance complement each other. Leadership contestation indicates the Bar and the Law Society's efforts of resisting authoritarian legal transplantation. They attempted to display professional autonomy and to remain independent professional bodies on one hand. Still, they could only demonstrate their commitments to the liberal Rule of Law and anti-authoritarianism to a limited extent due to pre-existing power structures. Both civil society empowerment and legal assistance for protestors took further steps to go beyond conventional understandings of professional autonomy and impartiality by connecting with civil society and different pro-democracy forces, as well as strengthening resistance against authoritarian legal transplantation by capacitating the legal resources of civil society and assisting arrested protestors' criminal arrests and subsequent criminal defence respectively. Their linkages with civil society and engagement with the legal support network for protestors also established a stronger tie between criminal defence counsel, activist lawyers and law firms to develop incentives to expand the critical minority of the legal profession in the time period between the Umbrella Movement and the Anti-ELAB Movement.

Legal resistance provides a framework for lawyers' engagement with the state-building process in the post-Umbrella era of Hong Kong. Whether the state rebuilding process can be implemented depends on the relationship and the power differentials between the state and stakeholders. The power differentials can be reflected in the existing power structure, the resilience of the parties, as well as the external environment, such as international relations. The state-building project implies structure-agency dynamics, whether the stakeholders exercise the agency constrained by the state-imposed and other structures to resist re-structuring institutionalised by the state. Experiences of Hong Kong lawyers engaging in resistance against authoritarian legal transplantation in this book have provided an example of the above insights.

Hong Kong's Legal Resistance: Both an Anti-authoritarian Resistance and a Decolonising Struggle?

In the beginning of this book, I contextualised China's authoritarian legal transplantation on Hong Kong with China's grand political project, i.e., empire-building that pretends as a building of a nation-state. Such an empire-building process is theoretically grounded on the analysis and discourse produced by Chinese state-sponsored scholars, including Jiang Shigong, that the Chinese Community Party today aims to enhance its legitimacy through reusing and reinventing the historical resources of the Qing Empire. Such adoption is evidenced by the communist rule in China's peripheral regions, such as Tibet, Xinjiang and Hong Kong: its "One Country, Two Systems" formula adheres to the peripheral rule of the Qing Empire, which eventually replaced its decentred governing structure with a system of assimilation and centralisation to the central government (Jiang 2008; Chen 2012; Carrico 2019; Hung 2022; Lai 2024a). Following this analysis, the process of authoritarian legal transplantation in Hong Kong is thus a process of consolidation of the communist rule in a former British colony.

How shall we understand the strategies and tactics of legal resistance in this broader context? No doubt, the main strategies of legal resistance, namely civil society empowerment, legal assistance for street protestors and leadership contestation in professional bodies, are both democratic and anti-authoritarian in nature. As explained above, these strategies promoted a democratic Rule of Law culture in civil society, legal community and legal professional bodies, and empowered anti-authoritarian movement by providing legal discourse, legal knowledge and professional assistance after street protests. Above all, the political agency of the activist lawyers had been strongly related to Hong Kong's democratisation movement ever since the sovereignty transfer to China. Legal resistance to authoritarian legal transplantation is thus an essential part of the broader democratic movement in Hong Kong.

Yet at the same time, we should also consider Hong Kong lawyers' resistance as a decolonising struggle. Ching-Kwan Lee, a sociologist on labour and social movement, recently authored a monograph that interprets Hong Kong's anti-authoritarian movement as a "decolonising struggle" (2025). Following the scholarly effort of interpreting Hong Kong as undergoing a process of "double colonisation" by the British and Chinese Communist powers (Choi 2014; Law 2014; A 2020), Lee argues that Hong Kong's decolonising struggle is a "liberation struggle against colonial domination in both political economic relations and collective cognition and subjectivity" (Lee 2025, 10). Lee's notion is complete opposite to the Chinese officials' narratives of Hong Kong's "decolonisation," which narrowly means Hong Kong's transfer from British colonial rule to the hands of the CCP. For instance, in 2015, a former Chinese official commented that Hong Kong's internal frictions were attributed to the absence of "decolonisation according to the law" (BBC News Chinese 20 September 2015). Another example can be found in 2022, when Chinese officials publicly called for Hong Kong to be decolonised by enhancing Hong Kong people's patriotism (Radio Free Asia, 2022). Yet this vision of "decolonisation" is not effectively facilitating liberation from domination in political economic relations, collective cognition and subjectivity. It is a notion of the CCP to exert greater ideological control and domination on the city's population with authoritarian patriotism and illiberal law and order, which is evidenced by the enforcement of a new national security law in Hong Kong since 2020.

In contrast, a genuine decolonisation would imply a liberation of the population from dominating power relations, including the political economy, the law, the collaborative power ties between colonisers and the power elites, alongside hegemonic knowledge. As Hong Kong scholar Wing-sang Law suggested, "decolonisation, meaning not only a change of political sovereignty but also a transformation of the society and culture that had sustained the colonial power relationship" (Law 2017, 236), the three strategies of legal resistance in this book can also be interpreted as decolonising strategies that challenge the sustained colonial power relationship in legal professional bodies, legal knowledge production and the criminal justice system that maintained "law and order."

Leadership contestation is a method of challenging the pre-existing power structure in legal professional bodies, which have been privileged by the political authorities to exert dominant control of the profession and, in return, as described by Ghai and his colleagues (1987), to endorse and legitimise the administration in Hong Kong with their professional hegemonic standing.

Civil society empowerment by the PLG and the LLD, which have made legal knowledge more available and accessible in public through the use of vernacular and popular language, also functioned as decentralising legal knowledge and discourse from the hegemonic legal community. Legal knowledge, especially the black letter law and case law, has been considered as the knowledge for insiders only, such as lawyers, legal scholars and judges. The technicality and nearly abstruse and unfathomable of the language of law also helped upholding the privilege of legal professionals in the market and the system of law. Nevertheless, activist lawyers' efforts in disseminating legal knowledge to the bottom not only empowered the target audience, but also indirectly loosened the exclusiveness of legal knowledge from the legal elites. As one of the LLD founders told journalists, they sought to challenge the aloof and hierarchical image often associated with legal professionals, and to cultivate a more egalitarian model for the exchange of legal perspectives in society: "The interpretation of law should not be the preserve of a select few; rather, it ought to be something accessible and comprehensible to all." (Lai 2017).

Providing legal assistance for anti-authoritarian protestors inevitably contests the criminal justice system in Hong Kong. As chapter 6 revealed, many pro bono lawyers witnessed power abuses by the law enforcement when interrogating arrested protestors and realised the repressive nature of the criminal justice system they are working with. Such system is inherited from the British colonial administration, which also introduced a number of draconian laws to suppress the dissent. In short, these frontline lawyers faced a legal system of double colonisation: the post-colonial Hong Kong authorities weaponised laws and courts that were at first established by the British colonial regime and then reinforced by the authoritarian regime under the Chinese sovereignty. Lawyers' professional support for street protestors in Hong Kong's social movement since 2005 is no doubt a challenge to the pre-existing power structure embedded in the criminal justice system.

In my interview with lawyers, none of them used words or notions such as "decolonisation" or "decolonising struggle" when elaborating their engagement in those strategies. However, their forms of resistance were inevitably interacting with the pre-existing power structures and orders that both the British and Chinese authorities have benefited from. as Lee highlighted,

> [D]ecolonizing politics in Hong Kong was fraught with uneven consciousness, meanings and visions of "decolonization...Regardless of, and perhaps exactly because of, its multivalence, (de)colonization and (de)coloniality were the keywords defining the political and discursive fields of contestation. Citizens' and Communist officials' understandings of these terms might be different from that of academics and intellectuals, but in their own mind and through their own action, all were engaged in a struggle with Hong Kong's (de)colonial order (2025, pp.129–130).

The temporal focus of this book stops at the end of the 2019 Anti-ELAB protests. Hong Kong lawyers' defence of the Rule of Law and their struggle against the Chinese authoritarian project is still ongoing. Defending the city's Rule of Law is inseparable from completing the city's decolonisation process. After all, defending the rule is part of the wider movement for the city's democratisation, which was promised by China as the best possible way of liberating from illiberal and authoritarian power relations that dominated Hong Kong for more than a century. Without a genuine democratisation, the population would not have an opportunity to determinate their political future by themselves. After the Anti-ELAB movement, China's introduction of a new national security law in Hong Kong marked a new era of consolidation of the Chinese autocratic rule. It made the bottom-up anti-authoritarian, or decolonising struggle, much more complicated. Yet, as I will discuss in the next section, resistance through the cracks could remain possible in the long run.

The Future of Hong Kong's Rule of Law in A "National Security" Era

The political and legal environment in Hong Kong has been in turmoil from July 2020 onwards. In May 2020, the National People's Congress (NPC) passed a decision to impose the "Law of the People's Republic of China on Safeguarding National Security in the Hong Kong Special Administrative Region" (national security law or NSL) and its enforcing agencies in Hong Kong. Although Article 23 of the Basic Law states that the Hong Kong government should legislate a national security law on its own, the NSL was a national law promulgated by the Standing Committee of the NPC on 30 June 2020. In other words, it is a direct legal transplantation of China into Hong Kong (also see chapters 2 and 4). As Pei highlighted, the imposition of the security law was a response by the central authorities to strike back against the Anti-ELAB Movement in 2019, which was perceived to be an attempt by local extremists to take over Hong Kong from China and therefore bust the bottom line of the sovereign state (Pei 2020).

The NSL is an instrument of autocratisation. The drafting process was untransparent, bypassing public consultation in Hong Kong. The offences under the law, including secession, subversion, terrorist acts and colluding with foreign forces, are vague and broadly defined, which do not comply with the conventional, narrow definition of crimes endangering national security or promoting terrorism (Kellogg and Lai 2021). The NSL also imposed new criminal proceedings that are allegedly violating due process rights, such as the removal of jury trial by the order of Secretary for Justice, designated national security judges by the Chief Executive, presumption against bail, as well as expanded police powers in national security investigation without judicial warrants (Wong, Kellogg and Lai 2021; Lai 2024b). Apart from this new act of authoritarian legal transplantation, the local authorities also revived the use of the sedition laws in the Crimes Ordinance, which was inherited from the British colonial rule, to prosecute political activists and civilians for their utterance of political speeches and pro-independence slogans (Lai 2023, 18).

As of January 2024, 286 individual citizens were arrested by the new National Security Department of the Hong Kong Police Force for committing offences under the law and the sedition provisions of the Crimes Ordinance. 156 of the arrestees were prosecuted, and sixty-eight were convicted. Moreover, five companies related to the pro-democracy newspaper *Apple Daily, the Stand News* and the Hong Kong Alliance in Support for Patriotic Democratic Movement in Hong Kong, in which all of them shut down in 2021, were also charged with security law offences and their properties were frozen (*ChinaFile* 2024). In addition, by February 2023, the police stated that its "reporting hotline" for crimes endangering national security had received more than 400,000 messages (Chen 2023). The mass reporting had created a chilling effect in schools, universities and among the public, and the whole social atmosphere has driven thousands of local families to leave Hong Kong and migrate to Western countries (Grierson 2021). The Hong Kong government's way of enforcing the NSL by arrests and prosecutions of pro-democracy figures, media moguls and student activists reflected that the law is an extension of authoritarian politics between China and Hong Kong.

As introduced in chapter 3, the state-recruited and state-co-opted lawyers had benefited from the new policies in post-national security law in Hong Kong. In March 2021, the NPC introduced an election overhaul of Hong Kong's electoral system to facilitate and consolidate the transplantation of the security law and the new national security regime under the imperative of "patriots administrating Hong Kong," implicating no genuine political opposition can run for elections in the future. Under the new electoral system, a candidate eligibility review committee is established to decide whether a candidate can run for election based on a background check by the national security institutions in Hong Kong as a way of prohibiting any pro-democracy figures from playing the new game (Lai 2021b). While personal voting has remained for the election of the legal sector in the functional constituency of the Legislative Council (LegCo), the new screening mechanism may bar any pro-democracy lawyers from being eligible candidates.

Also, for the new method of Election Committee subsector elections, personal voting is replaced by corporate voting in many professional sectors, including the legal one. Half of the members of the legal industry of the Election Committee are now composed of ex-officio members and those returned by nomination. At the same time, the remaining seats are elected by 30 corporate voters, including the Small and Medium Law Firms Association of Hong Kong (SAMLAW) and the Hong Kong Legal Exchange Foundation (HKLEF), which were examined in chapter 3 (C. Chau 2021a).

Nearly half of the corporate voters are lawyer associations either founded by mainland Chinese authorities and mainland businessmen or adjacent to members of the Chinese People's Political Consultative Conference (CPPCC) and pro-government lawmakers (*Ming Pao Daily* 15 April 2021). Although the Bar and the Law Society, the only statutory professional bodies in the legal profession, are also given one vote each in the Election Committee elections, their representativeness of the profession is diluted and thus diminished in the election dedicated to the legal community. The new composition of eligible corporate voters in the legal sector is seen as a further attempt by China to infringe on the legal profession and to unify the front of "patriots" among its politically obedient comprador lawyers, as individual lawyers are now unable to resist the state by casting a ballot.

The development of different forms of legal resistance also faces a profound challenge due to the threat of the NSL. While the Bar has performed confrontational professionalism since 2018, Paul Harris, the successor of Chairman Philip Dykes, has experienced various media attacks by pro-Beijing media outlets since the beginning of his chairmanship. He was criticised by the central authorities in Beijing for his party membership of the Liberal Democratic Party in the UK and his paper on self-determination in Tibet, which I also cited at the beginning of this book (C. Chau 2021b, Harris 2008). Harris could not even make a public statement in the ceremony of the opening of the legal year as he decided not to seek a second term and left Hong Kong at the end (Torode and Pomfret 2022). The criticisms also extended to the Bar, which was threatened with surrendering its regulatory power on barristers, leading in mid–2021 onwards to its total silence on local human rights violations under the security law. For the Law Society, although the liberal solicitors had won a significant number of seats in the 2020 council election, as explained in chapter 8, the electoral result in the following year was a complete setback to the liberal camp of the solicitor community, due to the government's repeated calls for the Law Society to be "apolitical," or otherwise the self-regulatory authority of the Law Society would be returned to the government (S. Cheng 2021). Such intimidation also expanded to individual candidates when solicitor Jonathan Ross, regarded as a liberal candidate in the 2021 council election, withdrew his candidacy due to suspected personal threats (Murdoch and Roantree 2021). Finally, all four liberal solicitor candidates lost the election, with a drop of almost a thousand votes for each candidate, compared to the result in 2020 (*The Standard* 24 August 2021).

Consequently, liberal solicitors fail to secure a majority in the Law Society Council, and confrontational professionalism becomes much less possible. In their speeches at the ceremony of the opening of the legal year, the new leaders of the Bar and the Law Society both avoided commenting on the national security law, which has been the most controversial development of the Rule of Law and judicial independence in Hong Kong (Chan 2022; Dawes 2022). Additionally, civil society empowerment and legal assistance also became more challenging to progress in 2021, when the PLG and the 612 Humanitarian Relief Fund (612HRF), which were the main drivers for the two forms of legal resistance, decided to disband in July and September 2021 respectively, under intense political pressure and potential criminalisation by the national security police (Stand News 4 July 2021; Lau 2021). Many human rights lawyers and liberal lawyers engaged in legal resistance also decided to leave Hong Kong for exile after receiving intimidation or assessing the risks of remaining in the city (Pomfret et al., 2022).

Does the post-national security law era of Hong Kong imply that legal resistance is unrealistic when it is now hard for lawyers to exercise their political agency to resist China's authoritarian project on Hong Kong? It would be too soon to draw such a conclusion. The first reason is that, while the legal institutions quickly become more authoritarian, Hong Kong has a long tradition of liberal culture in the legal profession and a history of resistance to the liberal values of the Rule of Law since the handover. It would be too early to claim the impositions of the NSL and the new electoral system have wiped out every aspect of the Rule of Law in the legal community. The awakened political agency of lawyers has its roots in such liberal tradition in Hong Kong. Although it is less practical for Hong Kong's activist lawyers to exercise political agency in direct resistance or confrontation against the authoritarian state nowadays, their political agency can still be played out by providing pro bono legal services to defendants charged under national security law or other political crimes. When the political authorities transfer the suppression of political opposition from parliamentary politics or street politics to the court, lawyers are paramount in providing legal information, knowledge, skills and representation to their clients and the public. Given there are more than a hundred security law defendants alongside thousands of defendants charged for their involvement in the Anti-ELAB protests, the demand for committed defence counsel, public legal education, and even training for voluntary citizens who audit and document court trials for public access, as discussed in chapters 5–8, would eventually rise, just as many human rights lawyers creatively continued their resistance in mainland China or other authoritarian regimes.

The geopolitical factors on Hong Kong's deterioration of the Rule of Law and legal resistance, though not studied in this book, should not be overlooked as well. Legal resistance requires the opening of civic space for activist lawyers and civil society actors to work together. External or international pressure plays an essential role in opening up more spaces from closed societies. One element of Hong Kong's legal system lies in its international reputation; it has been appreciated as a high degree of judicial independence and the Rule of Law. Many judges from Western common law jurisdictions, including the UK, Australia, Canada and New Zealand, were eager to preside in Hong Kong's Court of Final Appeal as non-permanent judges as a form of endorsement of the judiciary. Since the NSL was imposed in 2020, at least seven foreign judges, including two British judges presiding in the UK Supreme Court, decided to quit their jobs in Hong Kong's Court of Final Appeal. Such resignations signalled the change of some foreign judges towards Hong Kong's legal environment (Mahtani 2022). The wave of resignation went further in 2024, especially when one of the retired British judge Jonathan Sumption, after resigning from Hong Kong's Court of Final Appeal, made a public statement commending that:

> Hong Kong, once a vibrant and politically diverse community is slowly becoming a totalitarian state. The Rule of Law is profoundly compromised in any area about which the government feels strongly (Sumption 2024).

The resignations of foreign judges from Hong Kong's top judicial organ can be seen as a vote of no confidence to how laws and courts are instrumentalised for the state's authoritarian projects. Some international investors made similar decisions of departure as well. After the pandemic, both China and Hong Kong underwent a severe economic downturn. Many global investors decided to discontinue their businesses and relocate regional offices from China and Hong Kong, citing concerns on both the NSL implementation and the COVID-coping policies (Yiu and Wong 2023). While the Chinese authorities continue their efforts to exert greater influence in the United Nations, the latter's human rights bodies, including the United Nations Human Rights Committee and the United Nations Human Rights Council, repeatedly criticised Hong Kong's state of judicial independence and called for repealing both the NSL and sedition law (Lai 2022; Kaufman 2024). When government representatives and pro-government lawyers attempted to convince the global community of business groups and legal lawyers about the benefits of Hong Kong's judicial institutions after 2020, a transnational network of lawyers, including the International Bar Association, rebuked by criticising the use of the NSL as damaging Hong Kong's fair trial and due process (International Bar Association 2023). Both the Chinese and Hong Kong governments would eventually realise that as long as they continue to accelerate the pace of authoritarian legal transplantations, like introducing more security legislations and expanding the scope of criminal prosecutions on national security causes, the deterioration of their global images would be likely to persist, or even escalate.

The ongoing pressure from the global community may impact the decision of the political authorities to continue authoritarian legal transplantation. For example, in 2021, the Chinese government planned to transplant an "Anti-foreign Sanctions Law" to Hong Kong by promulgating its law as a national law applicable in Hong Kong (John and Murdoch 2021). However, the initiative was held off as news reports hinted that local business groups were hesitant about the enactment (Marlow 2021). The example indicated that sometimes the sovereign state would calculate the cost-benefits when advancing its authoritarian agenda in Hong Kong. Therefore, in the future, one important research direction of Hong Kong's legal politics and legal resistance could be to examine how international relations and geopolitics influence the authoritarian governance of China when carrying out their national security agenda in Hong Kong society, and whether the geopolitical dynamics between the Chinese and Hong Kong government and the Western liberal democratic counterparts would impact the remaining civic space and autonomy of the legal professionals, alongside the courts, in the city.

Furthermore, compared with Hong Kong's experiences of the post-Umbrella Movement crackdown by China, it is hard to tell whether the new security law regime can prevent the seeds of resistance from growing after the citywide Anti-ELAB protests. It is also important to remember that Hong Kong's legal resistance is only one part of the broader anti-authoritarian movement. The fate of legal resistance depends on the ongoing development of the broader struggle after all. In the aftermath of the Umbrella Movement, the Hong Kong government disbanded political parties, disqualified election candidates, and imprisoned vital figures of the Movement. The leadership of the Bar and the Law Society was also conservative until the co-location controversy in 2017. The overwhelming conservativeness in the professional sphere and the state suppression of civil society had accumulated many grievances, paving the way for the outbreak of the Anti-ELAB Movement in 2019. Only time will tell whether the crackdown on political opposition, civil society and political activism, alongside the encroachment of the legal profession, will lead to a more significant chilling effect in society and the legal profession or an escalation of grievance, conflicts and political awakening among individual lawyers in the future.

As Law highlighted in his book *Collaborative Colonial Power*, as long as the Hong Kong people are still eager to pursue Western liberal ideals that the British colonisers taught and denied to Hong Kong, such as the Rule of Law, democracy, human rights and liberty, such pursuit "could trigger demands for genuine decolonisation," and such pursuit of self-government "would threaten the psychic stability of the new paternal master, i.e., China" (2009, 174). The NSL does not constitutionally replace the Basic Law, which is embedded with promises of universal suffrage and human rights protections following international human rights treaties. Even the national security law has provisions that guarantee the application of the International Covenant on Civil and Political Rights (ICCPR), when the national security law is being enforced. Asking the ruling regime to fulfil its promises of self-government and safeguards of universal values could also serve as an incremental strategy for realising liberation from pre-existing power relations, and eventually a "genuine decolonisation." The political regime might be willing to repeal the constitutional and statutory safeguards of fundamental rights and self-government formally and robustly, but its cost would also be painful that such action could mark the end of "One Country, Two Systems," like how the CCP terminated Tibet's self-government in 1959.

The swift imposition of the national security law and the subsequent wave of political repression have instilled a profound sense of fear within Hong Kong. Yet it does not mean the city is silent like a graveyard. Civil society, the legal community and its institutions continue to endure significant stress tests. Civil groups are finding new ways of human rights defence. Local courts experiment striking a balance between safeguarding civil liberties and satisfying the executive government's political agenda when they adjudicate security law cases. Law schools are now tasked with studying and teaching the new law and its eco-system to future lawyers. Further research into Hong Kong's legal system, society, and political landscape becomes critically important. Future research agendas could, firstly, focus on the development of judicial politics through a detailed analysis of prosecution processes and court rulings in politically charged trials. Secondly, attention should be given to examining how locally based lawyers navigate and resist the state's autocratisation across various "contested sites," such as law schools, the Law Reform Commission, legal aid organisations, the legislature, and professional legal bodies. Lastly, the role of exiled Hong Kong lawyers within transnational legal networks demands close examination, particularly their contributions to the future of the Rule of Law in the city's national security era. Studying transnational or diasporic activist lawyering would provide valuable insights into the resilience of Hong Kong lawyers amid political crackdown, revealing Hong Kong future of anti-authoritarian as well as decolonising struggle in a new era.

References

An, Tu. 2020. *Nì quán lùn wǒ chéng.* Arcadia Press Ltd.

Arendt, Hannah. 2005. *The Promise of Politics.* Schocken Books.

Bar Human Rights Committee of England and Wales. 2025. "Trial Observations." February 21. Accessed March 31, 2025. https://barhumanrights.org.uk/category/trialobservations/ .

BBC News Chinese. 2015b. "Zhōng Guó zhì kù shǒu cháng Chén Zuǒěr: Xiāng Gǎng wú 'yī fǎ qù zhí mín huà' zhì nèi hào." September 20. Accessed November 16, 2024. https://www.bbc.com/zhongwen/trad/china/2015/09/150920_hong-kong_china_politics.

Carrico, K. 2019. "Seeing (Exactly) Like a State: Knowledge/Power in the Beijing–Hong Kong Relationship." *Hong Kong Studies* 2 (1): 1–17.

Chan, C. M. 2022. "Speech of Mr CM Chan, President of the Law Society of Hong Kong at the Ceremonial Opening of the Legal Year 2022." January 24. Accessed August 21, 2022. https://www.hklawsoc.org.hk/-/media/HKLS/Press-statement/EN/2022/20220124.pdf.

Chan, John K. C. 2012. *Zhōng Guó tiān zhāo zhǔ yì yǔ Xiāng Gǎng.* Oxford University Press.

Chau, Candice. 2021a. "Hong Kong Legal Sector Influence 'Diluted' in Election Committee under Election Revamp Plan, Says Lawmaker." *Hong Kong Free Press,* April 15. Accessed June 30, 2021. https://hongkongfp.com/2021/04/15/hong-kong-legal-sector-influence-diluted-in-election-committee-under-election-revamp-plan-says-lawmaker/.

Chau, Candice. 2021b. "Beijing Attacks Head of Hong Kong Bar Assoc. over 'Politicised' Comments on Peaceful Protest." *Hong Kong Free Press,* April 26. Accessed October 16, 2021. https://hongkongfp.com/2021/04/26/beijing-attacks-head-of-hong-kong-bar-assoc-over-politicised-comments-on-peaceful-protest/.

Chen, Zifei. 2023. "Hong Kong Police Got More Than 400,000 Tips Last Year on National Security Hotline." *Radio Free Asia,* February 15. Accessed January 29, 2024. https://www.rfa.org/english/news/china/china-hotline-02152023162702.html.

Cheng, Sara. 2021. "Hong Kong's Lam Tells Solicitors' Group to Stay Out of Politics." *Reuters,* August 17. Accessed October 16, 2021. https://reut.rs/3H6201Y.

Choi, Sam C. W. 2014. "Zài sī Zhōng Gang (5 of 5): Shì jiè de Xiāng Gǎng." *Liberty Times Net,* September 27. Accessed November 16, 2024. https://talk.ltn.com.tw/article/breakingnews/1116877.

Dawes, Victor. 2022. "Speech Given at the Opening of Legal Year 24 January 2022 by the Chairman of the Hong Kong Bar Association." January 24. Accessed August 21, 2022. Archived on file with the author.

De Certeau, Michel. 1984. *The Practice of Everyday Life*. University of California Press.

"Fǎ zhèng huì sī yuè qián jiě sàn, FB wú fǎ jìn rù, shí rì nèi bā zǔ zhī jiě sàn." 2021. *Stand News*, July 4. Accessed October 16, 2021. Archived on file with the author.

Ghai, Yash, Robin Luckham, and Francis Snyder, eds. 1987. *The Political Economy of Law: A Third World Reader*. Oxford University Press.

Grierson, Jamie. 2021. "UK Receives 34,000 Visa Requests from Hong Kong in Two Months." *The Guardian*, May 27. Accessed October 16, 2021. https://www.theguardian.com/world/2021/may/27/uk-receives-34000-visa-requests-from-hong-kong-in-two-months.

Harris, Paul. 2008. "Is Tibet Entitled to Self-Determination?" *China Digital Times*, April 26. Accessed October 16, 2021. https://chinadigitaltimes.net/2008/04/is-tibet-entitled-to-self-determination/.

Hung, Ho-fung. 2022. *City on the Edge: Hong Kong Under Chinese Rule*. Cambridge University Press.

International Bar Association. 2023. "IBAHRI Marks International Human Rights Day with Joint Statement Urging China to Respect Rights of Lawyers." December 14. Accessed January 29, 2024. https://www.ibanet.org/IBAHRI-marks-International-Human-Rights-Day-with-joint-statement-urging-China-to-respect-rights-of-lawyers.

Jiang, Shigong. 2008. *Zhōng Guó Xiāng Gǎng: Wén huà yǔ zhèng zhì de shì yě*. Oxford University Press.

John, Alun, and Scott Murdoch. 2021. "China's Planned Anti-Sanctions Law for Hong Kong Unsettles Financial Sector." *Reuters*, August 20. Accessed January 29, 2024. https://www.reuters.com/business/finance/chinas-planned-anti-sanctions-law-hong-kong-unsettles-financial-sector-2021-08-19/.

Jones, Carol. 2015. *Lost in China: Law, Culture and Identity in Post-1997 Hong Kong*. Cambridge University Press.

Kaufman, Arthur. 2024. "China Rallies Friends, Stifles Human Rights Criticisms at U.N. Universal Periodic Review." *China Digital Times*, January 26. Accessed January 29, 2024. https://chinadigitaltimes.net/2024/01/china-rallies-friends-stifles-human-rights-criticism-at-u-n-universal-periodic-review/

Kellogg, Thomas E., and Yan-ho Lai. 2021. *The Tong Ying-kit NSL Verdict: International and Comparative Law Analysis (A GCAL Briefing Paper)*. Center for Asian Law, Georgetown University, October 20. Accessed October 21, 2021. https://www.law.georgetown.edu/law-asia/wp-content/uploads/sites/31/2021/10/TongYing-KitVerdictGCAL.pdf.

Lai, Choi Yin. 2017. "Fǎ Mèng : fǎ lu bù yīng gāi yóu yī xiǎo cuō rén qù jiě shì (wǎng luò gōng mín jiǎng dé zhǔ zhuān fǎng zhī èr)" *Inmediahk*, December 1. Accessed October 31, 2024. https://www.inmediahk.net/%E5%AA%92%E9%AB%94/%E3%80%8C%E6%B3%95%E5%A4%A2%E3%80%8D%EF%B8%B0%E6%B

3%95%E5%BE%8B%E4%B8%8D%E6%87%89%E8%A9%B2%E7%94%B1%E4%B8%80%E5%B0%8F%E6%92%AE%E4%BA%BA%E5%8E%BB%E8%A7%A3%E9%87%8B%EF%BC%88%E7%B6%B2%E7%B5%A1%E5%85%AC%E6%B0%91%E7%8D%8E%E5%BE%97%E4%B8%BB%E5%B0%88%E8%A8%AA%E4%B9%8B%E4%BA%8C%EF%BC%89 .

Lai, Yan-ho. 2021a. "Solidarity and Resilience of Hong Kong's Anti-Authoritarian Movement: Lessons and Prospects". In *The May 18 Uprising Seoul Memorial Society 41st Anniversary Conference: After 5.18: Social Movements and Political Thoughts*, Seoul. The May 18 Uprising Seoul Memorial Society, Yonsei University.

Lai, Yan-ho. 2021b. "Ask the Experts: Has Democracy in Hong Kong Come to an End?" *LSE IDEAS: China Dialogues*, May 26. Accessed October 15, 2021. https://blogs.lse.ac.uk/cff/2021/05/26/ask-the-experts-has-democracy-in-hong-kong-come-to-an-end/.

Lai, Yan-ho. 2022. "UN Human Rights Committee Criticizes Rulings of Hong Kong's Top Court." *The Diplomat*. Accessed January 29, 2024. https://thediplomat.com/2022/07/un-human-rights-committee-criticizes-rulings-of-hong-kongs-top-court/.

Lai, Yan-ho. 2023. "Securitisation or Autocratisation? Hong Kong's Rule of Law Under the Shadow of China's Authoritarian Governance." *Journal of Asian and African Studies* 58 (1): 8–25.

Lai, Yan-ho. 2024a. *Resistance Through the Cracks: Understanding Hong Kong's Rule by Law and Resistance in the Courtroom in Comparative Perspective*. SpringHill Publishing.

Lai, Yan-ho. 2024b. "The Judiciary" in *Contemporary Hong Kong Government and Politics*, 3rd Edition, edited by Wai-man Lam, Percy Luen-tim Lui and Wilson Wong. Hong Kong University Press, Hong Kong.

Lau, Chris. 2021. "Hong Kong National Security Law: Protest Fund Facing Foreign Collusion Probe to Stop Taking Donations 'Until Further Notice.'" *South China Morning Post*, September 6. Accessed October 16. https://www.scmp.com/news/hong-kong/politics/article/3147752/hong-kong-national-security-law-protest-fund-facing-foreign.

Law, Wing Sang. 2009. *Collaborative Colonial Power: The Making of the Hong Kong Chinese*. Hong Kong University Press.

Law, Wing Sang. 2014. *Zhí mín jiā guó wài*. Oxford University Press.

Law, Wing Sang. 2017. "From a British to a Chinese Colony? Hong Kong Before and After the 1997 Handover." In *China Research Monograph 75*, edited by G. C. H. Luk. Institute of East Asian Studies, University of California, Berkeley.

Lee, Ching-kwan. 2025. *Forever Hong Kong: A Global City's Struggle for Decolonization*. Harvard University Press (forthcoming, summer 2025).

Mahtani, Shibani. 2022. "Britain Withdraws Its Judges from Hong Kong's Highest Court." *Washington Post*, March 30. Accessed January 29, 2024. https://www.washingtonpost.com/world/2022/03/30/hong-kong-uk-withdrawal-judges/.

Marlow, Iain. 2021. "China to Shelve Anti-Sanctions Law in Hong Kong, HK01 Says." *Bloomberg,* October 5. Accessed January 29, 2024. https://www.bloomberg.com/news/articles/2021-10-05/china-to-shelve-anti-sanctions-law-in-hong-kong-hk01-says?leadSource=uverify%20wall.

Murdoch, Scott, and Anne M. Roantree. 2021. "Candidate Pulls Out of Hong Kong Lawyers' Group Election Over Safety Fears." *Reuters,* August 21. Accessed October 16, 2021. https://reut.rs/3n5AISN.

Pang, Jessie, and Mari Saito. 2020. "Arrested Hong Kong Protesters Stuck in Limbo as Cases Grind Forward." *Reuters,* January 23. Accessed October 16, 2021. https://reut.rs/3H57Guy.

Pei, Minxin. 2020. "Investigation of a Death Long Feared: How China Decided to Impose Its National Security Law in Hong Kong." *China Leadership Monitor,* September 1. Accessed October 16. https://www.prcleader.org/post/investigation-of-a-death-long-feared-how-china-decided-to-impose-its-national-security-law-in-hong.

Pomfret, James, Greg Torode, Anne M. Roantree, and David Lague. 2022. "A Reuters Special Report: Lawyers Exit Hong Kong as They Face Campaign of Intimidation." *Reuters,* December 29. Accessed January 29, 2024. https://www.reuters.com/investigates/special-report/china-lawyers-crackdown-exodus/.

"'Professional' camp wins Law Society election." 2021. *The Standard*, August 24. Accessed October 16, 2021. https://www.thestandard.com.hk/breaking-news/section/4/179311/%22Professional%22-camp-wins-Law-Society-election.

Radio Free Asia. 2022. "Zhōng gòng guān yuán shǒu tí 'qù zhí huà', píng lùn: yù xiāo chú gǎng rén duì gǎng yīng zhèng fǔ huái niàn." December 5. Accessed November 16, 2024. https://www.rfa.org/cantonese/news/htm/hk-colony-12052022080900.html.

Scott, James C. 1985. *Weapons of the Weak: Everyday Forms of Peasant Resistance.* Yale University Press.

Sumption, John. 2024. "The Rule of Law in Hong Kong is in Grave Danger." *Financial Times,* June 10. Accessed November 19, 2024. https://www.ft.com/content/60c825be-b70a-4152-895f-f6127974570a.

Tai, Benny Y.T. 2021. "Authoritarian Rule of Law in Hong Kong." In *Democracy and Rule of Law in China's Shadow*, edited by Brain C. Jones. Hart Publishing..

Tam, Waikeung. 2012. *Legal Mobilization Under Authoritarianism: The Case of Post-Colonial Hong Kong.* Cambridge University Press.

Tamanaha, Brain Z. 2017. *A Realistic Theory of Law.* Cambridge University Press.

Torode, Greg, and John Pomfret. 2022. "Ex-chief of Hong Kong barristers says he left city after police interview." *Reuters*, March 2. Accessed August 21, 2022. https://www.reuters.com/world/china/ex-chief-hong-kong-barristers-says-he-left-city-after-police-interview-2022-03-02/.

"Tracking the Impact of Hong Kong's National Security Law." 2024. *ChinaFile*, updated January 5. Accessed January 29, 2024. https://www.chinafile.com/tracking-impact-of-hong-kongs-national-security-law.

Wong, Lydia, Thomas E. Kellogg, and Yan-ho Lai. 2021. *Hong Kong's National Security Law and the Right to Fair Trial: A GCAL Briefing Paper.* Center for Asian Law, Georgetown University Law Center. June 28. Accessed October 16, 2021. https://www.law.georgetown.edu/law-asia/wp-content/uploads/sites/31/2021/06/HongKongNSLRightToFairTrial.pdf.

"Xuǎn wěi huì jiě gòu: fǎ lu jiè 30 tuán tǐ xuǎn mín, yú 14 guān zhōng zī rén dà jiàn zhì děng; yuán 7400 rén yǒu piào tóu , Péng Yùn Xī: xīn míng dān yán shēn hé zī gé zhí yè zhě wài." 2021. *Ming Pao Daily*, 15 April. A01.

Yiu, Pak, and Echo Wong. 2023. "Multinationals turn away from Hong Kong for dispute resolution." *Nikkei Asia*, June 8. Accessed January 29, 2024. https://asia.nikkei.com/Spotlight/Hong-Kong-security-law/Multinationals-turn-away-from-Hong-Kong-for-dispute-resolution.

Appendix: List of the Interviewees

Table 24. Overview of the Interviews and Background of the Interviewees

Interview#	Interviewee	Date of Interview	Background
INTW1801	ITV1801	11/10/2018	Administrative staff of professional body
INTW1802	ITV1802	24/10/2018	Student of Postgraduate Certificate in Law (PCLL)
INTW1803	ITV1803	15/11/2018	Legal academic
INTW1804	ITV1804	22/11/2018	Barrister
INTW1805	ITV1805	29/11/2018	Senior Counsel; former member of LegCo and former chairman of the Hong Kong Bar Association (the Bar)
INTW1806	ITV1806	2/12/2018	Solicitor trainee
INTW1807	ITV1807	2/12/2018	Solicitor trainee
INTW1808	ITV1808	6/12/2018	Student of PCLL
INTW1901	ITV1901	18/1/2019	Paralegal
INTW1902	ITV1902	29/1/2019	Solicitor; founding member of Progressive Lawyers' Group (PLG)
INTW1903	ITV1903	30/1/2019	Barrister; one of the convenors of PLG
INTW1904	ITV1904	30/1/2019	Legal academic
INTW1905	ITV1905	31/1/2019	Barrister
INTW1906	ITV1906	20/2/2019	In-house lawyer; founding member of PLG
INTW1907	ITV1907	21/2/2019	Solicitor
INTW1908	ITV1908	22/2/2019	Barrister
INTW1909	ITV1909	26/2/2019	Former NGO worker; PhD student
INTW1910	ITV1910	27/2/2019	Barrister
INTW1911*	ITV1905	1/3/2019	Barrister
INTW1912	ITV1911	3/3/2019	Solicitor trainee
INTW1913	ITV1912	4/3/2019	Solicitor trainee
INTW1914	ITV1913	5/3/2019	Legal academic
INTW1915	ITV1914	6/3/2019	Legal academic
INTW1916	ITV1915	7/3/2019	Barrister; former unionist
INTW1917	ITV1916	12/3/2019	Senior Counsel
INTW1918	ITV1917	17/3/2019	Solicitor
INTW1919	ITV1918	18/3/2019	Senior Counsel; former chairman of the Bar
INTW1920	ITV1919	20/3/2019	NGO worker
INTW1921	ITV1920	20/3/2019	In-house lawyer; former convenor of PLG
INTW1922	ITV1921	21/3/2019	Legal academic
INTW1923	ITV1922	21/3/2019	Founder of Law Lay Dream (LLD); postgraduate student in law

Interview#	Interviewee	Date of Interview	Background
INTW1924	ITV1923	28/3/2019	Barrister; member of one of the committees in the Bar
INTW1925	ITV1924	28/3/2019	Barrister
INTW1926	ITV1925	29/3/2019	Legal academic
INTW1927	ITV1926	30/3/2019	Solicitor
INTW1928	ITV1927	30/3/2019	Barrister; one of the convenors of PLG
INTW1929	ITV1928	3/4/2019	Barrister; member of one of the committees in the Bar
INTW1930	ITV1929	16/4/2019	Activist
INTW1931	ITV1930	17/4/2019	Paralegal
INTW1932	ITV1931	23/4/2019	Activist
INTW1933	ITV1932	24/4/2019	Solicitor
INTW1934	ITV1933	26/4/2019	Solicitor
INTW1935	ITV1934	28/4/2019	Activist
INTW1936	ITV1935	29/4/2019	Solicitor
INTW1937	ITV1936	30/4/2019	Solicitor
INTW1938	ITV1937	6/5/2019	Legal academic
INTW1939	ITV1938	8/5/2019	NGO worker
INTW1940	ITV1939	9/5/2019	Solicitor; former member of LegCo
INTW1941	ITV1940	10/5/2019	Barrister
INTW1942	ITV1941	13/5/2019	Barrister
INTW1943	ITV1942	16/5/2019	Senior Counsel; former Chairman of the Bar
INTW1944	ITV1943	16/5/2019	Former solicitor; academic
INTW1945	ITV1944	17/5/2019	Barrister; former convenor of PLG
INTW1946*	ITV1933	20/5/2019	Solicitor
INTW1947	ITV1945	24/5/2019	Barrister
INTW1948	ITV1946	5/6/2019	Barrister; legal academic
INTW1949	ITV1947	5/6/2019	Legal academic
INTW1950	ITV1948	6/6/2019	Barrister
INTW1951	ITV1949	8/6/2019	Employed barrister
INTW1952+	ITV1950	10/6/2019	Solicitor
INTW1953+	ITV1951	22/6/2019	Legal academic
INTW1954+	ITV1952	15/7/2019	Employed barrister
INTW1955+	ITV1953	15/7/2019	Legal academic
INTW1956+	ITV1954	21/8/2019	Senior Counsel; former member of LegCo and former chairman of the Bar
INTW1957+	ITV1955	19/9/2019	Solicitor
INTW1958*+	ITV1927	23/9/2019	Barrister
INTW1959+	ITV1956	26/9/2019	Solicitor
INTW1960+	ITV1957	11/10/2019	Barrister
INTW1961+	ITV1958	1/11/2019	Senior Counsel
INTW2001*+	ITV1954	3/1/2020	Senior Counsel; former member of LegCo and former chairman of the Bar

Interview#	Interviewee	Date of Interview	Background
INTW2002+	ITV2001	9/3/2020	Barrister
INTW2003*+	ITV1912	17/4/2020	Solicitor trainee
INTW2004*+	ITV2002	21/4/2020	Solicitor trainee
	ITV2003	21/4/2020	Solicitor trainee
	ITV1907	21/4/2020	Solicitor
INTW2005+	ITV2004	24/4/2020	Solicitor
INTW2006+	ITV2001	27/4/2020	Barrister
INTW2007*+	ITV1910	28/4/2020	Barrister
INTW2008+	ITV2005	6/5/2020	Former judge
INTW2009+	ITV2006	8/5/2020	Solicitor
INTW2010+	ITV2007	14/5/2020	Legal academic
INTW2011+	ITV2008	8/6/2020	Solicitor
INTW2012*+	ITV1801	19/6/2020	Administrative staff of professional body
INTW2013+	ITV2009	10/7/2020	Journalist
INTW2014	ITV2010	11/8/2020	Local citizen filing lawsuit against commissioner of police
INTW2015	ITV1803	10/9/2020	Legal academic
INTW2016	ITV1925	3/10/2020	Legal academic
INTW2017	ITV2011	27/10/2020	Local citizen auditing court trials on public order cases

* Follow-up interviews
\+ Interviews since the outbreak of the Anti-ELAB Movement in Hong Kong

References

Adébísí, Folúkẹ́. 2023. *Decolonisation and Legal Knowledge: Reflections on Power and Possibility*. Bristol University Press.

Ahmed, Zahid Shahab, and Maria J. Stephan. 2010. "Fighting for the Rule of Law: Civil Resistance and the Lawyers' Movement in Pakistan." *Democratization* 17 (3): 492–513.

Albert, Eleanor. 2020. "China Appointed to Influential UN Human Rights Council Panel." *The Diplomat*, April 8. Accessed November 10, 2020. https://thediplomat.com/2020/04/china-appointed-to-influential-un-human-rights-council-panel/.

Allan, James. 1998. "Liberalism, Democracy and Hong Kong." *Hong Kong Law Journal* 28 (2): 156–168.

Almeida, Paul D. 2018. "The Role of Threats in Collective Action." In *Wiley-Blackwell Companion to Social Movements*, edited by David A. Snow, Sarah A. Soule, Hanspeter Kriesi, and Holly J. McCammon. Blackwell.

The American Chamber of Commerce in Hong Kong. 2019. "Press Release: Proposed Fugitive Offenders Ordinance." *The American Chamber of Commerce in Hong Kong*, May 30. Accessed August 13, 2020. https://www.amcham.org.hk/news/press-release-proposed-fugitive-offenders-ordinance.

An, Tu. 2020. *Nì quán lùn wǒ chéng*. Arcadia Press Ltd.

Arendt, Hannah. 2005. *The Promise of Politics*. Schocken Books.

Armstrong, James D. 1977. *Revolutionary Diplomacy: Chinese Foreign Policy and the United Front Doctrine*. University of California Press.

Arrangement between the National Development and Reform Commission and the Government of the Hong Kong Special Administrative Region for Advancing Hong Kong's Full Participation in and Contribution to the Belt and Road Initiative. 2017. HKSAR Government Press Release, December 14. Accessed December 10, 2020. https://gia.info.gov.hk/general/201712/14/P2017121400551_274123_1_1513236929437.pdf.

Bader, Julia, Jörn Grävingholt, and Antje Kästner. 2010. "Would Autocracies Promote Autocracy? A Political Economy Perspective on Regime-Type Export in Regional Neighbourhoods." *Contemporary Politics* 16 (1): 81–100.

Bar Human Rights Committee of England and Wales. 2025. "Trial Observations." February 21. Accessed March 31, 2025. https://barhumanrights.org.uk/category/trialobservations/ .

Barclay, Scott, and Anna-Maria Marshall. 2005. "Supporting a Cause, Developing a Movement, and Consolidating a Practice: Cause Lawyers and Sexual Orientation Litigation in Vermont." In *The Worlds Cause Lawyers Make: Structure and Agency in Legal Practice*, edited by Austin Sarat and Stuart A. Scheingold. Stanford University Press.

Barclay, Scott, and Susan S. Silbey. 2008. "Understanding Regime Change: Public Opinion, Legitimacy, and Legal Consciousness." In *The Oxford Handbook of Law and Politics*, edited by Gregory A. Caldeira, R. Daniel Kelemen, and Keith E. Whittington. Oxford University Press.

Barrow, Amy. 2023. "Beyond the Courtroom: Lawyer Activism and Resistance in Hong Kong." In *Activism and Authoritarian Governance in Asia*, edited by Amy Barrow and Sara Fuller. Routledge.

Bauhinia Foundation Research Centre. 2019. "Survey on Public Perceptions towards the Rule of Law in Hong Kong." December 18. Accessed July 9, 2020. http://www.bauhinia.org/index.php/english/research/106.

BBC News Chinese. 2015a. "Xiāng Gǎng Zhōng Lián Bàn Zhāng Xiǎo Míng: Tè Shǒu Dì Wèi Chāo Rán Yú Sān Quán." September 12. Accessed November 19, 2020. https://bbc.in/3c1JbQJ.

BBC News Chinese. 2015b. "Zhōng Guó zhì kù shǒu cháng Chén Zuǒěr: Xiāng Gǎng wú 'yī fǎ qù zhí mín huà' zhì nèi hào." September 20. Accessed November 16, 2024. https://www.bbc.com/zhongwen/trad/china/2015/09/150920_hong-kong_china_politics.

BBC News Chinese. 2020. "Dèng Xiǎo Píng Dào Lín Zhèng Yuè É: Xiāng Gǎng Sān Quán Fēn Lì Lùn Zhēng de Lái Lóng Qù Mài." September 2. Accessed November 19. https://bbc.in/3koLfqE.

"Bèi bǔ zhī yuán xiǎo zǔ jiù chōng jī lì fǎ huì shì jiàn shēng míng." 2014. *Inmediahk*, 19 November. Accessed 25 May 2021. https://www.inmediahk.net/node/1028691.

"Bèi tī bào fā xìn gōng lián huì yuán zhǐ shì tóu piào, èr líng líng bā lì fǎ huì xuǎn jǔ Zhèng Yào Táng chū miàn pèi piào chēng Liáng Měi Fēn." 2008. *Apple Daily*, August 27, A07.

"Bèi zhǐ yǔ dà lu shī gōng huì běi dà kè chéng 'nào shuāng bāo' zhì diào zhěng, Tán Yǔn Zhī chì Yú Ruò Wēi zī xùn cuò." 2018. *Ming Pao Instant News*, August 30. Accessed January 30, 2021. Archived on file with the author.

Benton, Lauren. 2002. *Law and Colonial Cultures: Legal Regimes in World History, 1400–1900*. Cambridge University Press.

Bisharat, George. 1998. "Attorneys for the People, Attorneys for the Land: The Emergence of Cause Lawyering in the Israeli-Occupied Territories." In *Cause Lawyering: Political Commitments and Professional Responsibilities*, edited by Austin Sarat and Stuart A. Scheingold. Oxford University Press.

Blackstone, Amy, Christopher Uggen, and Heather McLaughlin. 2009. "Legal Consciousness and Responses to Sexual Harassment." *Law and Society Review* 43 (3): 631–668.

Bourdieu, Pierre, and Abdelmalek Sayad. 2004. "Colonial Rule and Cultural Sabir." *Ethnography* 5 (4): 445–486.

Brennan QC, Daniel. 2000. "The Role of the Bar and the Rule of Law." In *Hong Kong Bar Association 50th Anniversary: 1949–1999*. Sweet and Maxwell Asia.

The Brookings Institution Center for Northeast Asian Policy Studies. 2004. "The 2004 Legislative Council Elections and Implications for U.S. Policy toward Hong Kong." [Transcript prepared from a tape recording], September 15.

Brown, Nathan J. 1995. "Law and Imperialism: Egypt in Comparative Perspective." *Law and Society Review* 29 (1): 103–125.

Bugarič, Bojan. 2014. "Protecting Democracy and the Rule of Law in the European Union: The Hungarian Challenge." *LSE 'Europe in Question' Discussion Paper Series*, no. 79.

Bush, Richard C. 2016. *Hong Kong in the Shadow of China: Living with the Leviathan*. Brookings Institute Press.

Butler, Daren, and Ece Toksabay. 2020. "Turkish Parliament Passes Disputed Bar Associations Law." *Reuters*, July 11. Accessed August 4, 2020. https://reut.rs/3D5Nqqf.

Cain, Maureen. 1974. "The Main Themes of Marx' and Engels' Sociology of Law." *British Journal of Law and Society* 1 (2): 136–148.

Cairnes, John E. 1887. *Some Leading Principles of Political Economy Newly Expounded*. Macmillan.

Cairns, John W. 2013. "Watson, Walton, and the History of Legal Transplants." *Georgia Journal of International and Comparative Law* 41: 637–96.

Carrico, K. 2019. "Seeing (Exactly) Like a State: Knowledge/Power in the Beijing–Hong Kong Relationship." *Hong Kong Studies* 2 (1): 1–17.

Castellucci, Ignazio. 2012. "Legal Hybridity in Hong Kong and Macau." *McGill Law Journal* 57 (4): 665–720.

Centre for Communication and Public Opinion Survey of the Chinese University of Hong Kong. 2017. "Press Release: Survey Result of Public Opinion and Political Development in Hong Kong." July 7. Accessed May 7, 2018. Archived on file with the author.

Chan, C. M. 2022. "Speech of Mr CM Chan, President of the Law Society of Hong Kong at the Ceremonial Opening of the Legal Year 2022." January 24. Accessed August 21, 2022. https://www.hklawsoc.org.hk/-/media/HKLS/Press-statement/EN/2022/20220124.pdf.

Chan, Cora, and Fiona de Londras. 2020. "Introduction: China's National Security in Hong Kong: A Challenge for Constitutionalism, Autonomy and the Rule of Law." In *China's National Security: Endangering Hong Kong's Rule of Law?*, edited by Cora Chan and Fiona de Londras. Hart Publishing.

Chan, Johannes M. M. 2007. "Basic Law and Constitutional Review: The First Decade." *Hong Kong Law Journal* 37 (2): 407–447.

Chan, Johannes M. M. 2015. "Human Rights, the Rule of Law and Democracy: Recent Experience of Hong Kong and China." *University of Hong Kong Faculty of Law Research Paper*, no. 2015/039. Accessed October 16, 2021. https://papers.ssrn.com/sol3/papers.cfm?abstract_id=2641332.

Chan, Johannes M. M. 2018. "A Storm of Unprecedented Ferocity: The Shrinking Space of the Right to Political Participation, Peaceful Demonstration, and Judicial Independence in Hong Kong." *International Journal of Constitutional Law* 16 (2): 373–388.

Chan, Johannes M. M. 2019. "A Shrinking Space: A Dynamic Relationship Between the Judiciary in a Liberal Society of Hong Kong and a Socialist-Leninist Sovereign State." *Current Legal Problems* 72 (1): 85–122.

Chan, Johannes M. M. 2020. "Reconciliation of the NPCSC's Power of Interpretation of the Basic Law with the Common Law in the HKSAR." *Hong Kong Law Journal* 50 (2): 657–684.

Chan, Johannes M. M., H. L. Fu, and Yash Ghai. 2000. *Hong Kong's Constitutional Debate: Conflict Over Interpretation*. Hong Kong University Press.

Chan, John K. C. 2012. *Zhōng Guó tiān zhāo zhǔ yì yǔ Xiāng Gǎng*. Oxford University Press.

Chan, Jun., Eric Y. H. Lai, and Tobias E. Kellogg. 2023. *The Hong Kong 2019 Protest Movement: A Data Analysis of Arrests and Prosecutions*. Center for Asian Law, Georgetown University Law Center, October. Accessed January 23, 2024. https://www.law.georgetown.edu/law-asia/wp-content/uploads/sites/31/2023/10/GCAL-HK-2019-ARREST-DATA-REPORT-FINAL-OCT-2023.pdf.

Chan, Kenneth K.L. 2023. "Open Society Contested: Liberal Universalism versus Autocratic Functionalism in Hong Kong." In *Open Society Unresolved: The Contemporary Relevance of a Contested Idea*, edited by Christof Royer and Liviu Matei. Central European University Press.

Chan, Maggie, and Loretta Lo. "SAMLAW Newsletter: AGM: Make Our Voice Heard in Law Society Council." *The Small and Medium Law Firms Association of Hong Kong*, May 7. Accessed December 17, 2020. https://www.samlaw.hk/index.php/lastnews/238-2020-05-08-samlaw-make-our-voices-heard-in-lawsociety-council.html.

Chan, Maggie. 2014. "Ài guó yǔ sī fǎ dú lì xū hé xié bìng cún." The Small and Medium Law Firms Association of Hong Kong, June 19. Accessed December 17, 2020. https://www.samlaw.hk/images/files/2014/2014-06-19譴責暴力維護法治_記者茶聚/香港中小型律師行協會愛國與司法獨立須和諧並存.pdf.

Chan, Maggie. 2016. "SAMLAW Statement Dated 16th October 2016." The Small and Medium Law Firms Association of Hong Kong, October 16. Accessed December 17, 2020. https://www.samlaw.hk/index.php/lastnews/162-re-samlaw-statement-dated-16th-october-2016.html.

Chanock, Martin. 1985. *Law, Custom, and Social Order: The Colonial Experience in Malawi and Zambia*. Cambridge University Press.

Chau, Candice. 2021a. "Hong Kong Legal Sector Influence 'Diluted' in Election Committee under Election Revamp Plan, Says Lawmaker." *Hong Kong Free Press,* April 15. Accessed June 30, 2021. https://hongkongfp.com/2021/04/15/hong-kong-legal-sector-influence-diluted-in-election-committee-under-election-revamp-plan-says-lawmaker/.

Chau, Candice. 2021b. "Beijing Attacks Head of Hong Kong Bar Assoc. over 'Politicised' Comments on Peaceful Protest." *Hong Kong Free Press,* April 26. Accessed October 16, 2021. https://hongkongfp.com/2021/04/26/beijing-attacks-head-of-hong-kong-bar-assoc-over-politicised-comments-on-peaceful-protest/.

Chau, Candice. 2021c. "Organiser of Mass Hong Kong Demos Civil Human Rights Front Disbands Citing 'Unprecedented Challenges.'" *Hong Kong Free Press,* August 15. Accessed September 2, 2021. https://hongkongfp.com/2021/08/15/breaking-organiser-of-mass-hong-kong-demos-civil-human-rights-front-disbands-citing-unprecedented-challenges/.

Chen, Albert H.Y. 2000. "The Court of Final Appeal's Ruling on the 'Illegal Migrant' Children Case: Congressional Supremacy and Judicial Review." In *Hong Kong's Constitutional Debate: Conflict Over Interpretation*, edited by J. M. M. Chan, H. L. Fu, and Y. Ghai. Hong Kong University Press.

Chen, Albert H.Y. 2019. "A Perfect Storm: Hong Kong-China Rendition of Fugitive Offenders, 2019." *Hong Kong Law Journal* 49 (2): 419–429.

Chen, Albert H.Y. 2020. "Hong Kong in China: The Project of 'One Country, Two Systems' and the Question of National Security." In *China's National Security: Endangering Hong Kong's Rule of Law?*, edited by Cora Chan and Fiona de Londras. Hart Publishing.

Chen, Jianfu. 2007. "The Transformation of Chinese Law: From Formal to Substantial." *Hong Kong Law Journal* 37 (2): 689–739.

Chen, Xunwu. 2016. "Positive Law and Natural Law: Han Feizi, Hobbes, and Habermas." *Journal of East-West Thought* 6 (1): 11–32.

Chen, Zifei. 2023. "Hong Kong Police Got More Than 400,000 Tips Last Year on National Security Hotline." *Radio Free Asia,* February 15. Accessed January 29, 2024. https://www.rfa.org/english/news/china/china-hotline-02152023162702.html.

Chen, Zimo. 2020. "HKMAO Backs HK Court Ruling That Anti-Mask Law Constitutional." *China Daily,* April 14. Accessed November 20, 2020. https://www.chinadaily.com.cn/a/202004/14/WS5e952291a3105d50a3d160b4.html.

Cheng, Edmund W. 2016. "Street Politics in a Hybrid Regime: The Diffusion of Political Activism in Post-Colonial Hong Kong." *The China Quarterly* 226: 383–406.

Cheng, Edmund W. 2020. "United Front Work and Mechanism of Countermobilization in Hong Kong." *The China Journal* 83: 1–33.

Cheng, Edmund W., and Samson Yuen. 2017. "How Hong Kong's Umbrella Movement Was Crushed and Pro-Democracy Activists Gradually Silenced." *The Conversation,* November 15. Accessed August 25, 2020. https://theconversation.com/how-hong-kong-umbrella-movement-was-crushed-and-pro-democracy-activists-gradually-silenced-84339.

Cheng, J. 2009. "The Story of a New Policy." *Hong Kong Journal.* Accessed November 18, 2020. Archived on file with the author.

Cheng, Joseph Y. S. 2009. "The Story of a New Policy." *Hong Kong Journal.* Accessed November 18, 2020. http://www.hkjournal.org/archive/2009_fall/1.htm.

Cheng, Joseph Y. S., ed. 2005. *The July 1 Protest Rally: Interpreting a Historic Event.* CityUHK Press.

Cheng, Kris. 2019a. "Beijing Deems Hong Kong Protests 'Colour Revolution,' Will Not Rule Out Intervention." *Hong Kong Free Press,* August 8. Accessed December 17, 2020. https://hongkongfp.com/2019/08/08/beijing-deems-hong-kong-protests-colour-revolution-will-not-rule-intervention/.

Cheng, Kris. 2019b. "Organisers Say 1.7 Million Joined Hong Kong Pro-Democracy Rally Against Police Use of Force, as Protesters Reiterate 5 Demands." *Hong Kong Free Press,* August 18. Accessed April 7, 2021. https://hongkongfp.com/2019/08/18/breaking-organisers-say-1-7-million-joined-hong-kong-pro-democracy-rally-police-use-force-protesters-reiterate-5-demands.

Cheng, Kris. 2019d. "Pro-Beijing Lawmaker Junius Ho Receives Honorary Degree from Chinese University after UK Degree Withdrawn." *Hong Kong Free Press,* December 6. Accessed December 23, 2020. https://hongkongfp.com/2019/12/06/pro-beijing-lawmaker-junius-ho-receives-honorary-degree-chinese-university-uk-degree-withdrawn/.

Cheng, Sara. 2021. "Hong Kong's Lam Tells Solicitors' Group to Stay Out of Politics." *Reuters,* August 17. Accessed October 16, 2021. https://reut.rs/3H62o1Y.

Cheng, Selina. 2020. "Senior Beijing official says only patriots should rule Hong Kong, "dissidents" must be ousted." *Hong Kong Free Press,* 17 November. Accessed 17 November 2020. https://hongkongfp.com/2020/11/17/senior-beijing-official-says-only-patriots-should-rule-hong-kong-dissidents-must-be-ousted/.

Cheung, Anthony B.L., and M. W. L. Wong. 2006. "Judicial Review and Policy Making in Hong Kong: Changing Interface Between the Legal and the Political." *Asia Pacific Journal of Public Administration* 28 (2): 117–141.

Cheung, Eric. T. M., Kenneth Lam, Janet H. Y. Pang, Mark Daly, Davyd Wong, Jonathan Ross, and Michelle W. T. Tosi. 2020. "Statement on the Disqualification of Four Legislative Council Members." November 13. Google Drive. Accessed January 29, 2021. https://drive.google.com/file/d/1qrepplK-Xooe3QeY5NtxOswwv2AQ1JjY/view.

Cheung, G. 2020. "The Co-location Arrangement of the Guangzhou-Shenzhen-Hong Kong Express Rail Link." The Division of Public Policy, Institute for Public

Policy, and Leadership and Public Policy Executive Education at the Hong Kong University of Science and Technology. Accessed January 29, 2021. Achieved on file with the author.

Cheung, Karen. 2017. "Anti-Occupy Figures Elected as Hong Kong Representatives in China's National Legislature." *Hong Kong Free Press,* December 19, updated March 31, 2020. Accessed November 20, 2020. https://hongkongfp.com/2017/12/19/anti-occupy-figures-elected-hong-kong-representatives-chinas-national-legislature/.

Cheung, Tony, and Chris Lau. 2020. "Hong Kong leader Carrie Lam sides with education chief on no "separation of powers" in city, defends move to delete phrase from textbooks." *South China Morning Post,* September 1. Accessed November 19, 2020. https://www.scmp.com/news/hong-kong/education/article/3099729/hong-kong-leader-carrie-lam-insists-there-no-separation.

Cheung, Tony, and Ernest Kao. 2017. "Hong Kong Leader Leung Chun-ying Admits Intervening in Probe into HK$50 Million Payment." *South China Morning Post,* May 16. Accessed December 23, 2020. https://www.scmp.com/news/hong-kong/politics/article/2094482/hong-kong-leader-cy-leung-admits-role-proposal-change-scope.

Cheung, Tony. 2014. "Controversial Solicitor is No Lam to the Slaughter." *South China Morning Post,* June 20. Accessed March 21, 2021. https://www.scmp.com/news/hong-kong/article/1536410/controversial-solicitor-no-lam-slaughter.

Cheung, Tony. 2017a. "Third Concern Group Set Up on Hong Kong's Controversial Border Plan for China Rail Line; Coalition Insists It Is Legal." *South China Morning Post,* August 8. Accessed November 22, 2020. https://www.scmp.com/news/hong-kong/politics/article/2105928/third-concern-group-set-hong-kongs-controversial-border-plan?utm_source=facebook.com&utm_medium=referral.

Chief Executive of the Hong Kong Special Administrative Region and Another v. Yau Wai Ching and Others. 2016. HCMP 2819/2016.

ChinaFile Editors. 2013. "Document 9: A ChinaFile Translation: How Much Is a Hardline Party Directive Shaping China's Current Political Climate?" *ChinaFile,* November 8. Accessed November 14, 2020. https://www.chinafile.com/document-9-chinafile-translation.

Chiu Luen Public Light Bus Company Limited v. Persons unlawfully occupying or remaining on the public highway namely, the westbound carriageway of Argyle Street between the junction of Tung Choi Street and Portland Street and/or other persons hindering or preventing the passing or repassing of Argyle Street. 2014. HCA2086/2014.

Chiu, Man-Chung. 2010. "Going Beyond Globalization and Localization: Articulating a Theory of Justice in Han-Chinese Culture." *Law and Critique* 21 (1): 93–100.

Choi, Christy. 2019. "Hong Kong Protesters and Chinese Officials Hold Rival Press Conferences." The Guardian, August 6. Accessed June 19, 2021. https://www.

theguardian.com/world/2019/aug/06/masked-hong-kongers-democracy-china-thugs.

Choi, S.C., and N. K. Lee. 2017. "Legalization of Politics: The Geopolitical Situations of Hong Kong and the Consolidation of Its Rule of Law in the Cold War." *Thoughts and Words Journal* 55: 187–225.

Choi, Sam C. W. 2014. "Zài sī Zhōng Gang (5 of 5): Shì jiè de Xiāng Gǎng." *Liberty Times Net,* September 27. Accessed November 16, 2024. https://talk.ltn.com.tw/article/breakingnews/1116877.

Chong, H. T. 2020. "[Lu Shī Huì Gǎi Xuǎn Jìng Zhēng Jī Liè] Yuē 6 Qiān Rén Tóu Piào Chuàng Xīn Gāo, Kāi Míng Pài 5 Xí Yíng 4 Xí, Zǒng Dé Piào Shuài Xiāng Chà Bù Dào 1%." *CitizenNews,* May 29. Accessed January 20, 2021. Archived on file with the author.

Chong, H.Y., and W.Y. Hui. 2007. "Zhōng yāng shòu yú xiāng gǎng tè qū duō shǎo quán, tè qū jiù yǒu duō shǎo quán! Wú bāng guó yān liǎo xiāng gǎng." *Apple Daily,* June 7. A01.

Chow, Lok Yiu. 2019. "Mǎ Ēn Guó Qù Xìn Lián Hé Guó Mì Shū Cháng Gào Zhuàng, Chì Měi Guó Zhǐ Shǐ Xiāng Gǎng Bào Luàn." *Inmediahk,* August 16. Accessed December 17, 2020. https://www.inmediahk.net/node/1066554.

Choy, Edwin. 2019. "Hong Kong Bar Association Has Been Shamefully Silent on Protester Violence and Those Who Support It." *South China Morning Post,* October 14. Accessed January 29, 2021. https://www.scmp.com/comment/opinion/article/3032793/hong-kong-bar-association-has-been-shamefully-silent-protester.

Chu Yee Wah v. Director of Environmental Protection. 2011.

Chua, Lynette J. 2019. "Legal Mobilization and Authoritarianism." *Annual Review of Law and Social Science* 15: 355–376.

Chua, Lynette J., and Mark F. Massoud. 2024. *Out of Place: Fieldwork and Positionality in Law and Society.* Cambridge University Press.

Chung, Hiu-fung. 2020. "Changing Repertoires of Contention in Hong Kong: A Case Study on the Anti-Extradition Bill Movement." *China Perspectives* 3: 57–63.

Civil Human Rights Front. 2019. "Dài fā mín zhèn yì wù lu shī tuán gōng zuò jiǎn bào" *Facebook Page,* October 18. Accessed October 31, 2024.

Civil Rights Observers. 2020a. *Brief Reports on National Security Law (July–August 2020).*

Civil Rights Observers. 2020b. *Brief Reports on National Security Law (September–November 2020).*

Code of Conduct 2020. The Hong Kong Bar Association. Last updated 4 June. Accessed January 12, 2021. https://www.hkba.org/content/code-conduct.

Cody, Stephen. 2020. "Dark Law: Legalistic Autocrats, Judicial Deference, and the Global Transformation of National Security." *University of Pennsylvania Journal of Law and Public Affairs* 6 (4): 643–686.

Comaroff, John L. 2001. "Colonialism, Culture, and the Law: A Foreword." *Law and Social Inquiry* 26 (2): 305–314.

Complaint Against Police Office. 2015. *Hong Kong Police Force.* August. Accessed June 24, 2021. https://www.police.gov.hk/info/doc/pledge/2016/html/CAPOENG.html.

"Comprador." 2021. *Encyclopaedia Britannica.* Accessed January 14, 2021. https://www.britannica.com/money/comprador.

Comprehensive Review of Legal Education and Training in Hong Kong: Final Report of the Consultants. 2018. Standing Committee on Legal Education and Training of the Hong Kong Special Administrative Region, April. Accessed January 27, 2021. https://www.sclet.gov.hk/eng/pdf/final2018.pdf.

"A Conversion with the Honourable Chief Justice Geoffrey Ma Tao-li." *GBM* 2020. International Bar Association, November 10. Accessed January 3, 2021. https://ibanet-org.zoom.us/rec/play/MF6R_RoimgwNrFX01KCsg85vYXE7CFnd5dhjwycPDq6P7hHWxpJgLgb5sZWcBUz_1Bqgzcsfb7GqzZQp.xj_4gEk-DPnS_ZFW?startTime=1604995208000&_x_zm_rtaid=NjgEmUyKTnm3yQKW8Mfm-Q.1605107701848.392f7b76476a21cabcade74076a67a57&_x_zm_rhtaid=848.

Court of Final Appeal of the HKSAR. 2001. "Zhōng shěn fǎ yuàn shǒu xí fǎ guān chū xí wǔ cān huì de yǎn cí quán wén." 26 October. Accessed 20 November 2024. https://www.hkcfa.hk/filemanager/speech/en/upload/17/CJ's%20Speech%20at%20a%20luncheon%20(26-10-2001)(Chinese%20only)tc.pdf.

Cownie, Fiona, and Anthony Bradney. 2013. "Socio-legal Studies: A Challenge to the Doctrinal Approach." In *Research Methods in Law,* edited by Dawn Watkins and Mandy Burton. Routledge.

Cummings, Scott L. 2011. "Introduction: What Good Are Lawyers?" In *The Paradox of Professionalism: Lawyers and the Possibility of Justice,* edited by Scott L. Cummings. Cambridge University Press.

"Dà gōng bào zhuān lán wèn Dài Qǐ Sī: rú qī jǐng pìn rèn dài biǎo lu shī, jiē bù jiē?." 2018. *Ming Pao Instant News,* January 20. Archived on file with the author.

"Dà lu shī gōng huì shí qián zhǔ xí quàn tuì, Yuán Guó Qiáng sǐ lài." 2008. *Apple Daily,* 18 January, A02.

"Dài fā: mín zhèn yì wù lu shī tuán." 2019. Facebook, October 18. Accessed June 3, 2021. https://www.facebook.com/story.php?story_fbid=2536809006366475&id=511608535553209&_rdr.

"Dài Qǐ Sī jí liǎng dà zhuàng bèi jù fù běi dà, dà lu shī gōng huì zhí wěi: wú xiàn qī zàn tíng hé bàn sì kè chéng." 2018. *Stand News,* September 10. Accessed January 29, 2021. Archived on file with the author.

Dai, Jianzhong. 2009. "On Several Problems in Legal Transplantation." *Journal of Politics and Law* 2 (3): 107–109.

Dawes, Victor. 2022. "Speech Given at the Opening of Legal Year 24 January 2022 by the Chairman of the Hong Kong Bar Association." January 24. Accessed August 21, 2022. Archived on file with the author.

De Certeau, Michel. 1984. *The Practice of Everyday Life.* University of California Press.

Dezalay, Yves, and Bryant G. Garth. 2010. *Asian Legal Revivals: Lawyers in the Shadow of the Empire.* University of Chicago Press.

Dezalay, Yves, and Bryant G. Garth. 2010. *Asian Legal Revivals: Lawyers in the Shadow of the Empire.* University of Chicago Press.

Diamond, Larry J, Marc F. Plattner, and Christopher Walker. 2016. *Authoritarian Goes Global: The Challenge to Democracy.* Johns Hopkins University Press.

Diamond, Larry J. 2016. *In Search of Democracy.* Routledge.

Diamond, Larry J. 2019. *Ill Winds: Saving Democracy from Russian Rage, Chinese Ambition and American Complacency.* Penguin Books.

Diamond, Larry, Marc F. Plattner, and Christopher Walker. 2016. *Authoritarian Goes Global: The Challenge to Democracy.* John Hopkins University Press.

Dicey, Albert V. 1915. *Introduction to the Study of the Law of the Constitution.* Liberty Classics.

The Director of Immigration v. Master Chong Fung Yuen. 2001. FACV26/2000.

DLA Piper and Hong Kong Association of Corporate Council. 2018. *Pro Bono Legal Work in Hong Kong: A Guide for In-House Counsel.*

DLA Piper and PILnet (The Global Network for Public Interest Law). 2017. *This Way: Finding Community Legal Assistance in Hong Kong.*

Donnelly, Tom. 2009. "Popular Constitutionalism, Civic Education, and the Stories We Tell Our Children." *The Yale Law Journal* 118 (5): 948–1001.

Dorfman, Zach. 2018. "The Disappeared." *Foreign Policy*, March 29. Accessed August 13, 2020. https://foreignpolicy.com/2018/03/29/the-disappeared-china-renditions-kidnapping/.

Drinoczi, Tamas, and Agnieszka Bień-Kacała. 2019. "Illiberal constitutionalism: The case of Hungary and Poland." *German Law Journal* 20 (8): 1140–1166.

"[Duǎn Piàn: Huí Yīng Shì Fǎ] Chēng Zhōng Yāng Èr Yuè Yǐ Kāi Shǐ Tǎo Lùn Shì Fǎ, Liáng Měi Fēn: Zhōng Yāng Gǎn Jué Wàng, Xiàn Yǐ Hǎo Kè Zhì (14:46)." 2016. *Ming Pao Instant News,* November 7. Accessed November 22, 2020. https://news.mingpao.com/ins/%E6%B8%AF%E8%81%9E/section/20250209/s00001.

"[Duǎn Piàn] [Fǎ Xué Jiāo Liú Jī Jīn Huì Qù Xìn Lián Hé Guó] Cù Chá Měi Guó Cān Yǔ Xiāng Gǎng Bào Luàn Qíng Kuàng, Mǎ Ēn Guó: Hěn Duō Biǎo Miàn Zhèng Jù Xiǎn Shì Měi Guó Bàn Yǎn Zhòng Yào Jiǎo Sè." 2019. YouTube, August 17. Accessed December 17, 2020. https://www.youtube.com/watch?v=H9j7TXtS8zs.

Dykes SC, Philip. 2018. "Chairman's Report 2018." Hong Kong Bar Association, December 24. Accessed January 29, 2021. Archived on file with the author.

Dykes SC, Philip. 2019a. "Letter to Members." Hong Kong Bar Association, October 16. Accessed January 29, 2021. Archived on file with the author.

Dykes SC, Philip. 2019b. "Chairman's Report 2019." Hong Kong Bar Association, December 23. Accessed January 29, 2021. Archived on file with the author.

Dykes SC, Philip. 2020a. "Speech Given at the Opening of the Legal Year." Hong Kong Bar Association, January 13. Accessed January 26, 2021. Archived on file with the author.

Dzur, Albert W. 2008. *Democratic Professionalism: Citizen Participation and the Reconstruction of Professional Ethics, Identity, and Practice*. Penn State University Press.

Dzur, Albert W. 2008. *Democratic Professionalism: Citizen Participation and the Reconstruction of Professional Ethics, Identity, and Practice*. Penn State University Press.

"Election Results 2016." 2016. *2016 Election Committee Subsector Elections*, December 12. Accessed January 29, 2021. https://www.elections.gov.hk/ecss2016/eng/results_s2.html?1739137457162.

Elsinger, Peter K. 1973. "The Conditions of Protest Behaviour in American Cities." *American Political Science Review* 67 (1): 11–28.

Elster, Jon. 1986. "Three Challenges to Class." In *Analytical Marxism*, edited by John Roemer. Cambridge University Press.

Elster, Jon. 1988. "Marx, Marxism, and Rational Choice." In *Rationality and Revolution*, edited by Michael Taylor. Cambridge University Press.

Eörsi, Gyula. 1979. *Comparative Civil (Private) Law*. Akadémiai Kiadó.

Epp, Charles. 1998. *The Rights Revolution: Lawyers, Activists, and Supreme Courts in Comparative Perspective*. Chicago Press.

The Essentials of the Common Law: Public Law Course Reports 2011–13. Peking University Rule of Law Research Centre and the Hong Kong Bar Association.

The Essentials of the Common Law: Public Law Course Reports 2014. Peking University Rule of Law Research Centre and the Hong Kong Bar Association.

The Essentials of the Common Law: Public Law Course Reports 2015. Peking University Rule of Law Research Centre and the Hong Kong Bar Association.

"Fǎ lu jiè: Wáng Guì Xun huò dà duī 'hóng' rén tí míng." 2012. *Apple Daily*, 13 August, A06.

"Fǎ Mèng chéng yuán chū xí mín jiān jì zhě huì, fǎn bó jǐng suí yì sōu chá shì mín, kuā dà jìn rù sī rén dì fāng quán lì." 2019. *Inmediahk*, August 19. Accessed March 21, 2021. https://www.inmediahk.net/node/1066605.

"Fǎ Mèng huò wǎng luò gōng mín jiǎng, gōng zhòng fǎn sī fǎ lu jiè fēng bō." 2017. Inmediahk, December 12. Accessed October 31, 2024. https://www.inmediahk.net/%E5%AA%92%E9%AB%94/%E3%80%8C%E6%B3%95%E5%A4%A2

%E3%80%8D%E7%8D%B2%E7%B6%B2%E7%B5%A1%E5%85%AC%E6%B0%91%E7%8D%8E-%E5%85%AC%E7%9C%BE%E5%8F%8D%E6%80%9D%E6%B3%95%E5%BE%8B%E7%95%8C%E9%A2%A8%E6%B3%A2 .
"Fǎ zhèng huì sī yuè qián jiě sàn, FB wú fǎ jìn rù, shí rì nèi bā zǔ zhī jiě sàn." 2021. *Stand News*, July 4. Accessed October 16, 2021. Archived on file with the author.
Fallon, Richard H., Jr. 1997. "'The Rule of Law' as a Concept in Constitutional Discourse." *Columbia Law Review* 97 (1): 1–56.
"Fǎn sòng zhōng yùn dòng de àn yè shǐ zhě 200 wèi rén quán lu shī: "Shuí De Shēn Tǐ Zhuàng Kuàng Huán Kě Yǐ, Shuí Jiù Chēng Xià Qù." 2019. *Commonwealth Magazine*, September 8. Accessed June 25, 2021. https://www.cw.com.tw/article/5096754.
Fanon, Frantz. 1963. *The Wretched of the Earth*. Grove Press.
Farran, Sue. 2013. "The 'Age of Empire': Again?" *The Law Teacher* 47 (3): 345–367.
Fitzpatrick, Peter. 1992. *The Mythology of Modern Law*. Routledge.
Fong, Brian C. H. 2016. "In-Between Liberal Authoritarianism and Electoral Authoritarianism: Hong Kong's Democratization under Chinese Sovereignty, 1997–2016." *Democratization* 24 (4): 724–750.
Fong, Brian C. H. 2017a. "One country, two nationalisms: Center-periphery relations between Mainland China and Hong Kong, 1997-2016." *Modern China* 43 (5): 523–556.
Fong, Brian C. H. 2017b. "The Rise of Localism in Hong Kong: Counter-Mobilization under the Hurricane of China Factor." *Mainland China Studies* 60 (1): 1–17.
Foreweaker, Joe. 1987. "Corporatist Strategies and the Transition to Democracy in Spain." *Comparative Politics* 20 (1): 57–72.
Foster, Nicholas H. D. 2007. "Comparative Commercial Law: Rules or Context?" In *Comparative Law: A Handbook*, edited by Esin Örücü and David Nelken. Hart Publishing.
Frankel, Ernst. 2017. *The Dual State: A Contribution to the Theory of Dictatorship*. Oxford University Press.
Frantz, Erica. 2018. *Authoritarianism: What Everyone Needs to Know*. Oxford University Press.
Freedom House. 2020. *Freedom in the World 2020: A Leaderless Struggle for Democracy*. Accessed July 31, 2020. https://freedomhouse.org/report/freedom-world/2020/leaderless-struggle-democracy.
Freidson, Eliot. 1983. "The Theory of Professions: State of the Art." In *The Sociology of the Professions: Lawyers, Doctors and Others*, edited by Robert Dingwall and Philip Lewis. The Macmillan Press.
Friedman, Milton. 1962. *Capitalism and Freedom*. University of Chicago Press.
Fu, Hualing, Carole J. Petersen, and Simon N. M. Young, eds. 2005. *National Security and Fundamental Freedoms: Hong Kong's Article 23 under Scrutiny*. Hong Kong University Press.

Fu, Hualing. 2018a. "Political Protest in High-Income Societies: The Case of Occupy Central Movement in Hong Kong." In *Law and Politics of the Taiwan Sunflower and Hong Kong Umbrella Movements*, edited by Brian C. Jones. Routledge.

Fu, Hualing. 2018b. "The July 9th (709) Crackdown on Human Rights Lawyers: Legal Advocacy in an Authoritarian State." *Journal of Contemporary China* 27 (112): 554–568.

Fugitive Offenders and Mutual Legal Assistance in Criminal Matters Legislation (Amendment) Bill 2019. 2019. Legislative Council of the Hong Kong Special Administrative Region of the People's Republic of China. Accessed November 22, 2020. https://www.legco.gov.hk/yr18-19/english/bills/b201903291.pdf.

Fukuyama, Francis. 2011. *The Origins of Political Order: From Pre-Human Times to the French Revolution*. Profile Books.

Fukuyama, Francis. 2014. *Political Order and Political Decay: From the Industrial Revolution to the Globalization of Democracy*. Profile Books.

"Gǎng bǎn guó ān fǎ chā rù fù jiàn sān, Fǎ Mèng chéng yuán hōng wéi jī běn fǎ dì 18 tiáo." 2020. *Inmediahk*, May 22. Accessed March 21, 2021. https://www.inmediahk.net/node/1073686?fbclid=IwAR0jGI-AGQEMP0hy7xF3cp9Xyol-HAPr_c69uWS2hrDsHZgAe1NdlQZ-3jJQ.

Garoupa, Nuno, and Anthony Ogus. 2006. "A Strategic Interpretation of Legal Transplants." *Journal of Legal Studies* 35: 339–363.

Geddes, Barbara, Joseph Wright, and Erica Frantz. 2014. "Autocratic Breakdown and Regime Transitions: A New Data Set." *Perspectives on Politics* 12 (2): 313–331.

Ghai, Yash, ed. 2013. *Practising Self-Government: A Comparative Study of Autonomous Regions*. Cambridge University Press.

Ghai, Yash, Robin Luckham, and Francis Snyder, eds. 1987. *The Political Economy of Law: A Third World Reader*. Oxford University Press.

Ghai, Yash, Robin Luckham, and Francis Snyder, eds. 1987. *The Political Economy of Law: A Third World Reader*. Oxford University Press.

Gilb, Corinne L. 1966. *Hidden Hierarchies: The Professions and Government*. Harper and Row.

Ginsburg, Tom, and Tamir Moustafa, eds. 2008. *Rule by Law: The Politics of Courts in Authoritarian Regimes*. Cambridge University Press.

Glick, Brian. 2017. "Two, Three Many Rosas! Rebellious Lawyers and Progressive Activist Organizations." *Clinical Law Review* 23: 611–634.

Gobe, Éric, and Lena Salaymeh. 2016. "Tunisia's 'Revolutionary' Lawyers: From Professional Autonomy to Political Mobilization." *Law and Social Inquiry* 41 (2): 311–345.

Gold, Thomas, and Sebastian Veg, eds. 2020. "Introduction." In *Sunflowers and Umbrellas: Social Movements, Expressive Practices, and Political Culture in Taiwan and Hong Kong*. Institute of East Asian Studies, Berkeley.

Goldstone, Jack A., and Charles Tilly. 2001. "Threat (and Opportunity): Popular Action and State Response in the Dynamics of Contentious Action." In *Silence and Voice in the Study of Contentious Politics*, edited by Ronald R. Aminzade, Jack A. Goldstone, Doug McAdam, Elizabeth J. Perry, William H. Sewell, Sidney Tarrow, and Charles Tilly. Cambridge University Press.

Goodstadt, Leo. F. 2005. *Uneasy Partners: The Conflict Between Public Interest and Private Profit in Hong Kong.* Hong Kong University Press.

"Government Announces Co-location Arrangement." 2017. *Romanian Chamber of Commerce in Hong Kong*, July 27. Accessed January 29, 2021. https://rochamhk.com/news/government-announces-co-location-arrangement/.

Gramsci, Antonio. 1971. *Selections from the Prison Notebooks.* Edited and translated by Quintin Hoare and Geoffrey Nowell Smith. Lawrence and Wishart.

Greater Bay Area. 2025. "Home Page. Accessed April 5, 2025. https://www.bayarea.gov.hk/en/home/index.html .

Grierson, Jamie. 2021. "UK Receives 34,000 Visa Requests from Hong Kong in Two Months." *The Guardian,* May 27. Accessed October 16, 2021. https://www.theguardian.com/world/2021/may/27/uk-receives-34000-visa-requests-from-hong-kong-in-two-months.

Griffiths, James, Helen Regan, Bex Wright, and Vanessa Yung. 2019. "Police Searched People Heading to the Protests." *CNN World*, June 11. Accessed April 7, 2021. https://cnn.it/3F55B0o.

Guinier, Lani, Michelle Fine, Jane Balin, Ann Barow, and Deborah L. Stachel. 1994. "Becoming Gentlemen: Women's Experiences at One Ivy League Law School." *University of Pennsylvania Law Review* 143 (1): 1–110.

Gutteridge, Harold C. 1949. *Comparative Law: An Introduction to the Comparative Method of Legal Study and Research*. Cambridge University Press.

Hajjar, Lisa. 2001. "From the Fight for Legal Rights to the Promotion of Human Rights: Israeli and Palestinian Cause Lawyers in the Trenches of Globalisation." In *Cause Lawyering and the State in a Global Era*, edited by Austin Sarat and Stuart A. Scheingold. Oxford University Press.

Halliday, Terence C. 2005. "Legal Professions and Politics: Neocorporatist Variations on the Pluralist Theme of Liberal Democracies." In *Lawyers in Society: Comparative Theories*, edited by Richard L. Abel and Philip S. C. Lewis. Beard Books.

Halliday, Terence C., Lucien Karpik, and Malcolm M. Feeley. 2007. "The Legal Complex in Struggles for Political Liberalism." In *Fighting for Political Freedom: Comparative Studies of the Legal Complex and Political Liberalism*, edited by Terence C. Halliday, Lucien Karpik, and Malcolm M. Feeley. Hart Publishing.

Halpérin, Jean-Louis. 2010. "Western Legal Transplants and India." *Jindal Global Law Review* 2 (1): 14–40.

Harris, Paul. 2008. “Is Tibet Entitled to Self-Determination?” *China Digital Times*, April 26. Accessed October 16, 2021. https://chinadigitaltimes.net/2008/04/is-tibet-entitled-to-self-determination/.

“Hé Jūn Yáo Lùn Lu Shī Huì Gǎi Xuǎn, Lǎo Bǎn Yǒu Quán Yào Yuán Gōng Shòu Quán Piào.” 2018. *Sing Tao Daily*, June 9. Accessed November 20, 2024. https://hk.news.yahoo.com/%E4%BD%95%E5%90%9B%E5%A0%AF%E8%AB%96%E5%BE%8B%E5%B8%AB%E6%9C%83%E6%94%B9%E9%81%B8-.

Hechter, Michael. 2001. *Containing Nationalism*. Oxford University Press.

Henry, Gary T., and Craig S. Gordon. 2003. “Driving Less for Better Air: Impacts of a Public Information Campaign.” *Journal of Policy Analysis and Management* 22 (1): 45–63.

Hilson, Chris. 2002. “New Social Movements: The Role of Legal Opportunity.” *Journal of European Public Policy* 9 (2): 238–255.

HK Hope China. 2019a. “Fǎ zhèng huì sī dà lu shī Lu Xī Yú tí gōng yīng duì làn bǔ làn quán de fǎ lu jǐn náng.” YouTube, September 17. Accessed April 7, 2021. https://www.youtube.com/watch?v=SXdf2LyhBq4.

HK Hope China. 2019b. “Fǎ zhèng huì sī Lǐ Ān Rán dà lu shī jiào lù tóng xué zī bèi bǔ hòu rú hé yīng duì jǐng fāng de fǎ lu jǐn náng.” YouTube, October 19. Accessed April 7, 2021. https://www.youtube.com/watch?v=irS7WFtloJk.

HKSAR Government Justice Department. 2020. “Justice Department Welcomes NPC Standing Committee’s Decision to Allow HK Law Practitioners to Work in Greater Bay Area.” *Xinhua Net*, August 12. Accessed December 10, 2020. http://en.people.cn/n3/2020/0812/c90000-9720726.html.

HKSAR v. Wong Cho Shing and others. 2017. DCCC980/2015.

HKTDC Research. 2019. “Legal Service Industry in Hong Kong.” Hong Kong Trade and Development Council, July 12. Accessed July 14, 2020. https://hkmb.hktdc.com/en.

HKTDC Research. 2019. “Legal Service Industry in Hong Kong.” Hong Kong Trade and Development Council, July 12. Accessed July 14, 2020. https://hkmb.hktdc.com/en.

HKTDC Research. 2020a. “Economic and trade information on China.” The Hong Kong Trade Development Council, March 16. Accessed November 24, 2020. https://hkmb.hktdc.com/en.

HKTDC Research. 2020b. “Legal Services Industry in Hong Kong.” Hong Kong Trade and Development Council, June 18. Accessed August 30, 2020. https://research.hktdc.com/en/article/MzEzODc5NTk5.

Ho, Denny K.L. 2004, “Citizenship as a Form of Governance: A Historical Overview.” In *Remaking Citizenship in Hong Kong: Community, Nation and the Global City*, edited by Agnes S. Ku and Ngai Pun. eReader version. Accessed October 11, 2021, from Amazon.com.

Ho, Kelly. 2020. "Hong Kong Education Bureau removes website slide on separation of powers as part of 'update.'" *Hong Kong Free Press*, September 2. Accessed November 19, 2020. https://hongkongfp.com/2020/09/02/hong-kong-education-bureau-justifies-removal-of-top-judges-slide-on-the-separation-of-powers-as-an-update/.

Ho, Lawrence K. K. 2019. "Policing Transnational Protests in an Asian Context: The WTO Sixth Ministerial Conference in Hong Kong." *Contemporary Chinese Political Economy and Strategic Relations: An International Journal* 5 (1): 211–249.

Hong Kong Bar Association. 2017a. *Statement of the Hong Kong Bar Association ("HKBA") in Response to News Reports Regarding HKBA's Stance on the Co-location Arrangement 2017*. September 17. Accessed January 29, 2021. Archived on file with the author.

Hong Kong Bar Association. 2017b. *Statement of the Hong Kong Bar Association ("HKBA") in Relation to the Co-location Arrangement 2017*. October 19. Accessed January 29, 2021. Archived on file with the author.

Hong Kong Bar Association. 2017c. *Hong Kong Bar Association's Open Letter to the Hon. Dennis Kwok in Response to an Article Published in Hong Kong Economic Journal on 21 September 2017*. October 29. Accessed January 29, 2021. Archived on file with the author.

Hong Kong Bar Association. 2017d. *Statement of the Hong Kong Bar Association on the Decision of the NPCSC of 27 December 2017 on the Co-operation Agreement between the Mainland and the SAR on the Establishment of the Port at the West Kowloon Station of the Guangdong-Shenzhen-Hong Kong Express Rail Link for Implementing Co-location Arrangement 2017*. December 28. Accessed January 29, 2021. Archived on file with the author.

Hong Kong Bar Association. 2018a. *Submission of the Hong Kong Bar Association in Respect of the Guangzhou-Shenzhen-Hong Kong Rail Link (Co-location) Bill (the "Bill")*. March 12. Accessed January 29, 2021. Archived on file with the author.

Hong Kong Bar Association. 2018b. *Further Submission of the Hong Kong Bar Association in Respect of the Guangzhou-Shenzhen-Hong Kong Express Rail Link (Co-location) Bill*. March 29. Accessed January 29, 2021. Archived on file with the author.

Hong Kong Bar Association. 2019. *A Brief Guide to Issues Arising from the Fugitive Offenders and Mutual Legal Assistance in Criminal Matters Legislation (Amendment) Bill 2019 ("The Bill")*. June 6. Accessed August 13, 2020. Archived on file with the author.

Hong Kong Bar Association. 2023. "About HKBA." Accessed September 19, 2023. https://www.hkba.org/content/about-us.

Hong Kong Institute of Asia-Pacific Studies of the Chinese University of Hong Kong. 2015. "Press Release on 'CUHK Releases Survey Findings on Views on Hong Kong's

Core Values.'" October 29. Accessed May 7, 2018. https://www.cpr.cuhk.edu.hk/en/press/cuhk-releases-survey-findings-on-views-on-hong-kongs-core-values/.

Hong Kong lawyers march in silence to condemn China's interpretation of Basic Law 2016, *The Strait Times*, November 8, Accessed March 21, 2021, https://www.straitstimes.com/asia/east-asia/hong-kong-lawyers-march-in-silence-to-condemn-chinas-interpretation-of-basic-law.

Hong Kong Lawyers March in Silence to Support Anti-Government Protesters. 2019. Channel News Asia, August 7. Accessed April 7, 2021. Archived on file with the author.

"Hong Kong Leader Carrie Lam Does Not Rule Out Reshuffle, Says Focus Is Restoring Order." 2019. *Channel News Asia,* December 10. Accessed January 26, 2021. Archived on file with the author.

Hong Kong People's Alliance on WTO and Asian Human Rights Commission. 2006. "Briefing Report on Policing, Arrests and Detentions Regarding the WTO Protests." Submission to Legislative Council Panel on Security, CB(2) 1055/05-06(01).

Hong Kong Public Opinion Research Institute. 2020a. "PORI Releases the Latest Social and Freedom Indicators." May 8. Accessed July 9, 2020. https://a2022.pori.hk/press-release-en/2020-07-21-pm.html?lang=en.

Hong Kong Public Opinion Research Institute. 2020b. "The Rule of Law, Fairness of the Judicial System, Impartiality of the Courts – Combined Charts." Accessed 13 August 2020. https://a2023.pori.hk/pop-poll/rule-law-indicators-en/g-combined.html?lang=en.

Hong Kong Public Opinion Research Institute. 2020c. "People's Ethnic Identity." Accessed 14 November 2020. https://www.pori.hk/pop-poll/ethnic-identity.

The Hong Kong Solicitors' Guide to Professional Conduct. 2013. The Law Society of Hong Kong. Accessed January 13, 2021. https://www.hklawsoc.org.hk/en/Support-Members/Professional-Support/Professional-Guide/The-hong-kong-solicitors-guide--to-professional-conduct--volume-1.

Hong Kong Special Administrative Region v. Mok Ka To. 2018.

Hong Kong Watch. 2019. *Outdated and Draconian: Hong Kong's Public Order Ordinance.* Accessed July 9, 2020. https://static1.squarespace.com/static/58ecfa82e3df284d3a13dd41/t/5d25c0676c3cb30001e74f6b/1562755179422/hkw+report_jul19+(3).pdf.

Hong Kong: Arbitrary Arrests, Brutal Beatings and Torture in Police Detention Revealed. 2019. Amnesty International, September 19. Accessed June 19, 2021. https://www.amnesty.org/en/latest/press-release/2019/09/hong-kong-arbitrary-arrests-brutal-beatings-and-torture-in-police-detention-revealed/.

Hoover Institute. 2018. *Chinese Influence and American Interests: Promoting Constructive Vigilance.* Stanford University. Accessed June 24, 2020. https://hvr.co/2YCbSkc.

Horlemann, Ralf. 2003. *Hong Kong's Transition to Chinese Rule: The Limits of Autonomy*. Routledge Curzon.

Houghton, David P. 2011. "Political Psychology." In *21st Century Political Science: A Reference Handbook*, edited by John T. Ishiyama and Marijke Breuning. SAGE Publications.

Huang, Zheping, and Huang Echo. 2016. "A brief history: Beijing's interpretations of Hong Kong's Basic Law, from 1999 to the present day". *Quartz*, November 6. Accessed November 15, 2020. https://qz.com/828713/a-brief-history-beijings-interpretations-of-hong-kongs-basic-law-from-1999-to-the-present-day.

Hui, Mary. 2019. "Everything You Need to Know About Hong Kong's Extradition Law." *Quartz*, June 11. Accessed August 13, 2020. https://qz.com/1635504/everything-you-need-to-know-about-hong-kongs-extradition-law.

Hung, Ching Tung. 2020. "Are Experiences Gained by Hong Kong in East-West Turbulences Being Squandered by China and the World?" In *Evaluation of the C. Y. Leung Administration*, edited by Joseph Y. S. Cheng, City University of Hong Kong Press.

Hung, Ho-fung. 2018. "Chinese State Capitalism in Hong Kong." In *Routledge Handbook of Contemporary Hong Kong*, edited by Tai-lok Lui, Stephen W. K. Chiu, and Ray Yep, Routledge.

Hung, Ho-fung. 2022. *City on the Edge: Hong Kong Under Chinese Rule*. Cambridge University Press.

Hung, Stephen. 2016. "Ceremonial Opening of the Legal Year 2016: Speech by Mr. Stephen Hung, President of the Law Society of Hong Kong." The Law Society of Hong Kong, January 11.

Hussain, Nasser. 2003. *The Jurisprudence of Emergency: Colonialism and the Rule of Law*. University of Michigan Press.

International Bar Association. 2023. "IBAHRI Marks International Human Rights Day with Joint Statement Urging China to Respect Rights of Lawyers." December 14. Accessed January 29, 2024. https://www.ibanet.org/IBAHRI-marks-International-Human-Rights-Day-with-joint-statement-urging-China-to-respect-rights-of-lawyers.

Ip, Eric C. 2019. *Hybrid Constitutionalism: The Politics of Constitutional Review in the Chinese Special Administrative Regions*. Cambridge University Press.

Jackson, Nicole J. 2010. "The Role of External Factors in Advancing Non-Liberal Democratic Forms of Political Rule: A Case Study of Russia's Influence on Central Asian Regimes." *Contemporary Politics* 16 (1): 101–118.

"Jiàn zhì pài wǔ yì yuan dēng lu shī huì guān fāng kān wù fēng miàn, bèi zhì yí yòng gōng jiā zī yuán zhèng zhì xuān chuán." 2016. *Stand News*, November 18. Accessed November 22, 2022. Archived on file with the author.

Jiang, Shigong. 2008. *Zhōng Guó Xiāng Gǎng: Wén huà yǔ zhèng zhì de shì yě.* Oxford University Press.

Jiang, Shigong. 2015. "'Hé Píng Gé Mìng' Zhōng de Sī Fǎ Guǎn Xiá Quán: Cóng 'Mǎ Wéi Kūn Àn' Hé 'Wú Jiā Líng Àn' Tán Xiāng Gǎng Xiàn Zhèng Zhì Xù Zhuǎn Xíng Zhōng de Sī Fǎ Zhǔ Quán Zhī Zhēng." In *Xiāng Gǎng Jī Běn Fǎ Miàn Miàn Guān*, edited by Albert H. Y. Chen and Zou Pingxue. Joint Publishing.

"[Jǐn jí zhuàng kuàng fǎ lu zhī yuán diàn huà] Wǒ zhěng zuo zhāng A8 Size Māo Zhǐ Fāng Biàn Suí Shēn Xié Dài." 2019. LIHKG, June 11. Accessed May 25, 2021. https://lihkg.com/thread/1204851/page/1.

John, Alun, and Scott Murdoch. 2021. "China's Planned Anti-Sanctions Law for Hong Kong Unsettles Financial Sector." *Reuters*, August 20. Accessed January 29, 2024. https://www.reuters.com/business/finance/chinas-planned-anti-sanctions-law-hong-kong-unsettles-financial-sector-2021-08-19/.

Jones, Carol. 1999. "Politics Postponed: Law as a Substitute for Politics in Hong Kong and China." In *Law, Capitalism and Power in Asia: The Rule of Law and Legal Institutions*, edited by Kanishka Jayasuriya, Routledge.

Jones, Carol. 1999. "Politics Postponed: Law as a Substitute for Politics in Hong Kong and China." In *Law, Capitalism and Power in Asia: The Rule of Law and Legal Institutions*, edited by Kanishka Jayasuriya. Routledge.

Jones, Carol. 2007. "Dissolving the People: Capitalism, Law and Democracy in Hong Kong." In *Fighting for Political Freedom: Comparative Studies of the Legal Complex and Political Change*, edited by Terence Halliday, Lucien Karpik, and Malcolm Feeley. Hart Publishing.

Jones, Carol. 2010. "Legal Education in Hong Kong: Producing the Producers." In *Legal Education in Asia: Globalization, Change and Contexts*, edited by Stacey Steele and Kathryn Taylor. Routledge.

Jones, Carol. 2015. *Lost in China: Law, Culture and Identity in Post-1997 Hong Kong.* Cambridge University Press.

Jones, Carol. 2015. *Lost in China: Law, Culture and Identity in Post-1997 Hong Kong.* Cambridge University Press.

Jones, Lynn C. 2001. "Career Activism by Lawyers: Consequences for the Person, the Legal Profession, and Social Movements." In *Legal Professions: Work, Structure and Organization*, edited by Jerry Van Hoy. Emerald Publishing Limited.

Joseph, Elizabeth, and Katie Hunt. 2016. "Missing Hong Kong Bookseller: I Was Kidnapped by Chinese 'Special Forces'." CNN News, June 16. Accessed August 29, 2022. https://edition.cnn.com/2016/06/16/asia/china-hong-kong-booksellers/index.html.

Kapai, Puja. 2011. "Principled Approach Towards Judicial Review: Lessons from *W v Registrar of Marriages*." *Hong Kong Law Journal* 41 (1): 49–74.

Karpik, Lucien, and Terence C. Halliday. 2011. "The Legal Complex." *Annual Review of Law and Social Science* 7: 217–236.

Katuna, Barret, and Elizabeth Holzer. 2016. "Unobtrusively Stretching Law: Legal Education, Activism, and Reclaiming Title IX." *Social Movement Studies* 15 (1): 80–96.

Kaufman, Arthur. 2024. "China Rallies Friends, Stifles Human Rights Criticisms at U.N. Universal Periodic Review." *China Digital Times,* January 26. Accessed January 29, 2024. https://chinadigitaltimes.net/2024/01/china-rallies-friends-stifles-human-rights-criticism-at-u-n-universal-periodic-review/

Kellogg, Thomas E., and Yan-ho Lai. 2021. The Tong Ying-kit NSL Verdict: International and Comparative Law Analysis (A GCAL Briefing Paper). Center for Asian Law, Georgetown University, October 20. Accessed October 21, 2021. https://www.law.georgetown.edu/law-asia/wp-content/uploads/sites/31/2021/10/TongYingKitVerdictGCAL.pdf.

Khamzayeva, Anar A. 2012. *Resilience of Authoritarianism and Its Projection onto International Politics: The Case of Russia.* Doctoral dissertation, Department of Political Science, LUISS Guido Carli, Italy.

Killingray, David. 1986. "The Maintenance of Law and Order in British Colonial Africa." *African Affairs* 85 (340): 411–437.

King, Ambrose Y. C. 1975. "Administrative Absorption of Politics in Hong Kong: Emphasis on the Grass Roots Level." *Asian Survey* 15, no. 5: 422–439.

Klug, Heinz. 2001. "Legal Advocacy, Global Engagement: The Impact of Land Claims Advocacy on the Recognition of Property Rights in the South African Constitution." In *Cause Lawyering and the State in a Global Era*, edited by Austin Sarat and Stuart A. Scheingold. Oxford University Press.

Kong, Karen. 2012. "Adjudicating Social Welfare Rights in Hong Kong." *International Journal of Constitutional Law* 10 (2): 588–599.

Krebs, Judith R. 2000. "One Country, Three Systems? Judicial Review in Macau after Ng Ka Ling." *Pacific Rim Law and Policy Journal* 10 (1): 111–146.

Kristine. 2018. "Fǎ Mèng: fēi cháng bù yī yàng de fǎ lu pǔ jí yùn dòng lù jìng" Matters, April 17. Accessed October 31, 2024. https://matters.town/a/g4ji4rscs15q.

Ku, Agnes S. 2004. "Negotiating the Space of Civil Autonomy in Hong Kong: Power, Discourses and Dramaturgical Representations." *The China Quarterly* 179: 647–664.

Kuan, Hsin-chi. 1991. "Power Dependence and Democratic Transition: The Case of Hong Kong." *The China Quarterly* 128: 774–793.

Kuan, Hsin-chi. 1997. "Support for the Rule of Law in Hong Kong." *Hong Kong Law Journal* 27 (2): 187–205.

"Kuk chief Lau may quit as infighting hits Liberal Party." 2008. *The Standard,* 10 September. P06.

Kuo, Lily. 2019. "Second Death in Week as Xi Jinping Demands End to Hong Kong Violence." *The Guardian*, November 14. Accessed June 19, 2021. https://www.theguardian.com/world/2019/nov/14/second-death-in-hong-kong-protests-as-xi-demands-end-to-violence.

Kwok Wing Hang and others v. Chief Executive in Council and Secretary for Justice. 2019. HCAL2945/2019.

Kwok, Dennis W.H. 2017. "Shè huì qī wàng de dà lu shī gōng huì." *Hong Kong Economic Journal*, September 21. A19.

Kwong, Bruce K. K. 2010. *Patron-Client Politics and Elections in Hong Kong*. Routledge.

Kwong, Ying-ho. 2015. "Chì Sè Fēng Bào Xià de Fǎ Lǜ Jiè: Wǒ Chéng Fǎ Lǜ Jīng Yīng de Shí Dài Shǐ Mìng." In *Xiāng Gǎng Gé Xīn Lùn: Gé Xīn Bǎo Gāng, Mín Zhǔ Zì Zhì, Yǒng Xù Zì Zhì, Wèi Xiāng Gǎng Qián Tú Ér Zhàn*, edited by Brian C.H. Fong. Azothbooks.

Lague, David, James Pomfret, and Greg Torode. 2019. "How Murder, Kidnappings and Miscalculation Set Off Hong Kong's Revolt." *Reuters*, December 20. Accessed November 22, 2020. https://reut.rs/3qvORep.

Lai, Choi Yin. 2017. "Fǎ Mèng : fǎ lu bù yīng gāi yóu yī xiǎo cuō rén qù jiě shì (wǎng luò gōng mín jiǎng dé zhǔ zhuān fǎng zhī èr)" Inmediahk, December 1. Accessed October 31, 2024. https://www.inmediahk.net/%E5%AA%92%E9%AB%94/%E3%80%8C%E6%B3%95%E5%A4%A2%E3%80%8D%EF%B8%B0%E6%B3%95%E5%BE%8B%E4%B8%8D%E6%87%89%E8%A9%B2%E7%94%B1%E4%B8%80%E5%B0%8F%E6%92%AE%E4%BA%BA%E5%8E%BB%E8%A7%A3%E9%87%8B%EF%BC%88%E7%B6%B2%E7%B5%A1%E5%85%AC%E6%B0%91%E7%8D%8E%E5%BE%97%E4%B8%BB%E5%B0%88%E8%A8%AA%E4%B9%8B%E4%BA%8C%EF%BC%89 .

Lai, Yan-Ho, and Ming Sing. 2020. "Solidarity and Implications of a Leaderless Movement in Hong Kong: Its Strengths and Limitations." *Communist and Post-Communist Studies* 53 (4): 41–67.

Lai, Yan-ho. 2019. "Lady Justice or the Golden Calf? The 'China Factor' in Hong Kong's Legal System." *Social Transformations in Chinese Societies* 15 (2): 178–196.

Lai, Yan-ho. 2021a. "Solidarity and Resilience of Hong Kong's Anti-Authoritarian Movement: Lessons and Prospects". In *The May 18 Uprising Seoul Memorial Society 41st Anniversary Conference: After 5.18: Social Movements and Political Thoughts*, Seoul. The May 18 Uprising Seoul Memorial Society, Yonsei University.

Lai, Yan-ho. 2021b. "Ask the Experts: Has Democracy in Hong Kong Come to an End?" *LSE IDEAS: China Dialogues*, May 26. Accessed October 15, 2021. https://blogs.lse.ac.uk/cff/2021/05/26/ask-the-experts-has-democracy-in-hong-kong-come-to-an-end/.

Lai, Yan-ho. 2021c. *Pò Jiě Xiāng Gǎng de Wēi Quán Fǎ Zhì: Sǎn Hòu yǔ Fǎn Sòng Zhōng Yǐ Lái de Mín Zhǔ Yùn Dòng*. Showwe.

Lai, Yan-ho. 2022. "UN Human Rights Committee Criticizes Rulings of Hong Kong's Top Court." *The Diplomat*. Accessed January 29, 2024. https://thediplomat.com/2022/07/un-human-rights-committee-criticizes-rulings-of-hong-kongs-top-court/.

Lai, Yan-ho. 2023. "Securitisation or Autocratisation? Hong Kong's Rule of Law Under the Shadow of China." *Journal of Asian and African Studies* 58 (1): 8–25.

Lai, Yan-ho. 2023. "Securitisation or Autocratisation? Hong Kong's Rule of Law Under the Shadow of China's Authoritarian Governance." *Journal of Asian and African Studies* 58 (1): 8–25.

Lai, Yan-ho. 2024a. *Resistance Through the Cracks: Understanding Hong Kong's Rule by Law and Resistance in the Courtroom in Comparative Perspective*. SpringHill Publishing.

Lai, Yan-ho. 2024b. "The Judiciary" in *Contemporary Hong Kong Government and Politics*, 3rd Edition, edited by Wai-man Lam, Percy Luen-tim Lui and Wilson Wong. Hong Kong University Press, Hong Kong.

Lai, Yan-ho. 2024c. "Not Just About the Law: Reflections on *A Report on the National Security Regime in Hong Kong* (2024)." *Taiwan Human Rights Journal* 7 (4): 89–110.

Lam, Jeffie, and Julie Chu. 2014. "Solicitors Move for Vote of No Confidence in Lam Over White Paper Statements." *South China Morning Post*, June 21. Accessed March 21, 2021. https://www.scmp.com/news/hong-kong/article/1537182/solicitors-move-vote-no-confidence-lam-over-white-paper-statements.

Lam, Jeffie. 2018. "Philip Dykes Elected New Head of Hong Kong Bar Association in Upset Win." *South China Morning Post*, January 19. Accessed December 23, 2020. https://www.scmp.com/news/hong-kong/law-crime/article/2129589/philip-dykes-elected-new-head-hong-kong-bar-association.

Lam, Kay C. Y. 2020. "Besides DQ, What Was Overlooked in NPCSC Decision." *HK Columns* (trans.). *CitizenNews*, November 16. Accessed November 17, 2020. Archived on file with the author.

Lam, L. C., K. L. Chan, H. Y. Fung, and K.H. Cheung. 2016. "[Tè shǒu xuǎn zhàn] Zhōng jí jīn zhǔ pù guāng: qí xīn jī jīn yōng èr qiān wàn xiàn jīn chǔ bèi 2016." *HK01*, May 6. Accessed December 17, 2020. https://www.hk01.com/%E7%A4%BE%E6%9C%83%E6%96%B0%E8%81%9E/19657/%E7%89%B9%E9%A6%96%E9%81%B8%E6%88%B0-%E7%B5%82%E6%A5%B5%E9%87%91%E4%B8%BB%E6%9B%9D%E5%85%89-%E9%BD-%8A%E5%BF%83%E5%9F%BA%E9%87%91-%E6%93%81%E4%BA%8C%E5%8D%83%E8%90%AC%E7%8F%BE%E9%87%91%E5%84%B2%E5%82%99.

Lam, Wai-man, and Kay C. Y Lam. 2013. "China's United Front Work in Civil Society: The Case of Hong Kong." *International Journal of China Studies* 4, no. 3: 301–325.

Lam, Wai-man. 2020. "Belief in the Rule of Law and Its Resilience in the Hong Kong Political Identity." In *China's National Security: Endangering Hong Kong's Rule of Law?*, edited by Cora Chan and Fiona de Londras. Hart Publishing.

Lau, Chris. 2019a. "Criminal Lawyer Edwin Choy Opens Up on Resignation from Hong Kong Bar Association, Saying His Outlook on Protest Violence Diverged Too Much from Others." *South China Morning Post*, October 15. Accessed January 29, 2021. https://www.scmp.com/news/hong-kong/law-and-crime/article/3032862/criminal-lawyer-edwin-choy-opens-resignation-hong-kong.

Lau, Chris. 2021. "Hong Kong National Security Law: Protest Fund Facing Foreign Collusion Probe to Stop Taking Donations 'Until Further Notice.'" *South China Morning Post*, September 6. Accessed October 16. https://www.scmp.com/news/hong-kong/politics/article/3147752/hong-kong-national-security-law-protest-fund-facing-foreign.

Lau, Siu-kai, and Hsin-chi Kuan. 2002. "Between Liberal Autocracy and Democracy: Democratic Legitimacy in Hong Kong." *Democratization* 9 (4): 58–76.

Lau, Siu-kai. 1987. *Decolonization Without Independence: The Unfinished Political Reforms of the Hong Kong Government*. Institute of Social Studies, Chinese University of Hong Kong.

Law Lay Dream. 2017. "[Fǎ Mèng jì shù wén] Zhěng lǐ 926 gōng mín guǎng cháng àn (jí dōng běi àn) de fǎ lǐ yào diǎn." *Inmediahk*, August 21. Accessed April 4, 2021. https://www.inmediahk.net/node/1051548.

Law Lay Dream. 2018a. "[Fǎ Mèng kāi jiǎng] Fǎ lu zhī shí 101×dì qū shí zhàn jiǎng zuò." Facebook. April 3. Accessed March 21, 2021. Archived on file with the author.

Law Lay Dream. 2018b. "Guó gē fǎ lián hé shēng míng." Facebook. May 22. Accessed March 21, 2021. Archived on file with the author.

Law Lay Dream. 2019a. "Fā mèng mèng huà." Facebook. July 2. Accessed April 4, 2021. Archived on file with the author.

Law Lay Dream. 2019b. "Wǒ di yī jiā jiù jiǎng rén huà: xì shī zhí yā DLLM." *Inmediahk*. July 23. Accessed April 4, 2021. https://www.inmediahk.net/%E6%94%BF%E7%B6%93/%E6%88%91%E5%93%8B%E4%BE%9D%E5%AE%B6%E5%B0%B1%E8%AC%9B%E4%BA%BA%E8%A9%B1-%E4%BF%82%E5%A4%B1%E8%81%B7%E5%91%80-dllm.

Law Lay Dream. 2019c. "[Face Check hēi jǐng] Tíng zhǐ rǎo luàn shì tīng, chū shì wěi rèn zhèng qī leng měng měng." Inmediahk. July 26. Accessed April 4, 2021. https://www.inmediahk.net/%E6%94%BF%E7%B6%93/%E3%80%90factcheck%E9%BB%91%E8%AD%A6%E3%80%91%E5%81%9C%E6%AD%A2%E6%93%BE%E4%BA%82%E8%A6%96%E8%81%BD%EF%BC%8C%E5%87%BA%E7%A4%BA%E5%A7%94%E4%BB%BB%E8%AD%89%E5%95%A6%E6%9F%92%E6%92%9A%E6%87%B5%E6%87%B5.

Law Lay Dream. 2019d. "Zǔ chà bàn gōng zuì' jū bǔ jì zhě? Di law 100% cuò leng shēn." Tigerz-note.blogspot.com. October 29. Accessed April 4, 2021. https://tigerz-note.blogspot.com/2019/10/law-100.html?m=0.

Law Lay Dream. 2020. "Zhì cái cán bào zhèng quán, fú hé guó jì fǎ." Inmediahk. May 30. Accessed April 4, 2021. https://www.inmediahk.net/node/1073962.

"Law Society 2020 – Independent and Firm Voices." 2020. Facebook. Accessed January 29, 2021. Archived on file with the author.

The Law Society of Hong Kong Annual Reports 1998–2019. The Law Society of Hong Kong.

The Law Society of Hong Kong. 2020a. "Statement by the Law Society of Hong Kong on Proposals for the Law Society Examination and the Common Entrance Examination under Rule 7(a) of the Trainee Solicitors Rules Cap. 159J." The Law Society of Hong Kong, May 29. Accessed January 27, 2021. https://www.hklawsoc.org.hk/-/media/HKLS/Press-statement/EN/2020/20200529a_EN.pdf?rev=e7bc550a8050413ea915cc090266b6ac&hash=7D698030615D85637A14D015D1F0BB44.

Law, Wing Sang. 2009. *Collaborative Colonial Power: The Making of the Hong Kong Chinese*. Hong Kong University Press.

Law, Wing Sang. 2014. *Zhí mín jiā guó wài*. Oxford University Press.

Law, Wing Sang. 2017. "From a British to a Chinese Colony? Hong Kong Before and After the 1997 Handover." In *China Research Monograph 75*, edited by G. C. H. Luk. Institute of East Asian Studies, University of California, Berkeley.

Leachman, Gwendolyn. 2013. "Legal Framing." In *Studies in Law, Politics, and Society*, edited by Austin Sarat. Emerald Group Publishing.

Lee, Ching-kwan. 2017. *The Spectre of Global China: Politics, Labour and Foreign Investment in Africa*. University of Chicago Press.

Lee, Ching-kwan. 2025. *Forever Hong Kong: A Global City's Struggle for Decolonization*. Harvard University Press (forthcoming, summer 2025).

Lee, Ching-kwan. 2025. *Forever Hong Kong: A Global City's Struggle for Decolonization*. Harvard University Press (forthcoming, summer 2025).

Lee, Chun-yi, and Chun-yan Yu. 2020. "Diǎn Míng Zhuī Jī Fǎ Guān, 'Sān Quán Zhòng Zài Pèi Hé,' Jiàn Zhì Lì Liáng Rú Hé Zhòng Sù Xiāng Gǎng Fǎ Zhì Guān?" *Initium Media*, 17 September 17. Accessed February 17, 2022. https://theinitium.com/article/20200917-hongkong-judicial-judges-discourse-turning-point/.

Lee, Francis L. F. 2018. "Changing Political Economy of the Hong Kong Media." *China Perspectives* 3: 9–18.

Lee, Francis L. F., and Chi-kit Chan. 2023. "Legalization of Press Control Under Democratic Backsliding: The Case of Post-National Security Law Hong Kong." *Media, Culture and Society* 45 (5): 916–31.

Lee, Francis L. F., and Joseph M. Chan. 2018. *Media and Protest Logics in the Digital Era: The Umbrella Movement in Hong Kong*. Oxford University Press.

Lee, Karen M. Y. 2017a. "Lawyers and Hong Kong's Democracy Movement: From Electoral Politics to Civil Disobedience." *Asian Journal of Political Science* 25, no. 1: 89–108.

Lee, Karen M. Y. 2017b. "Lawyers as an Interest Group in Hong Kong's Democracy Movement." In *Interest Groups and the New Democracy Movement in Hong Kong*, edited by Sonny Shiu-Hing Lo. Routledge.

Lee, Karen M. Y., and Yan Lam Lo. 2020a. "Are Legal Values Gendered? Gender Differences in Support for Judicial Independence in Hong Kong." *International Journal of Law, Crime and Justice* 62. Accessed September 1, 2021. https://doi.org/10.1016/j.ijlcj.2020.100391.

Lee, Karen M. Y., and Yan Lam Lo. 2020b. "Contesting Visions of Hong Kong's Rule of Law and Young People's Political Discontent." *Social and Legal Studies* 29 (6): 858–80.

Lee, Martin. 2018. "Wǒ shì fǒu yǐ bèi tǒng zhàn liǎo?" *Apple Daily*, January 10. Accessed January 29, 2021. Archived on file with the author.

Lee, W. Y. 2018. "[Dà wān qū zhuān fǎng] Guō Róng Kēng chàng chéng lì wān qū zhòng cái zhōng xīn, zhù nián qīng lu shī zēng zhí yè jīng yàn." *HK01*, May 16. Accessed December 10, 2020. https://www.hk01.com/%E6%94%BF%E6%83%85/186302/%E5%A4%A7%E7%81%A3%E5%8D%80%E5%B0%88%E8%A8%AA-%E9%83%AD%E6%A6%AE%E9%8F%97%E5%80%A1%E6%88%90%E7%AB%8B%E7%81%A3%E5%8D%80%E4%BB%B2%E8%A3%81%E4%B8%AD%E5%BF%83-%E5%8A%A9%E5%B9%B4%E8%BC%95%E5%BE%8B%E5%B8%AB%E5%A2%9E%E5%9F%B7%E6%A5%AD%E7%B6%93%E9%A9%97.

Lee, W.Y. 2017. "Dà Lù Shī Gōng Huì Gǎi Xuǎn, Lín Dìng Guó Jìng Zhú Lián Rèn: Zhī Yǒu Gēng Zì Zhǔ Cái Néng Gēng Qiáng Dà." *HK01*, December 27. Accessed January 29, 2021. https://www.hk01.com/社會新聞/144579/大律師公會改選-林定國競逐連任-只有更自主才能更強大.

Legislative Council of the HKSAR. 2011. *LCQ6: Regarding the Judicial Review of Hong Kong-Zhuhai-Macao Bridge*, June 8. https://www.info.gov.hk/gia/general/201106/08/P201106080155.htm.

Levitsky, Steven, and Lucan A. Way. 2010. *Competitive Authoritarianism: Hybrid Regimes After the Cold War.* Cambridge University Press.

Li, Ling. 2019. "Political-Legal Order and the Curious Double Character of China's Courts." *Asian Journal of Law and Society* 6 (1): 19–39.

Li, Raymond. 2013. "Seven Subjects Off Limits for Teaching, Chinese Universities Told." *South China Morning Post*, May 10. Accessed November 14, 2020. https://www.scmp.com/news/china/article/1234453/seven-subjects-limits-teaching-chinese-universities-told.

"Lián xiào fǎ lu xué shēng zhèng gǎi guān zhù zǔ shēng míng —— huí yīng dà lu shī gōng huì 10 yuè 8 rì zhī shēng míng." 2014. Inmediahk. October 13. Accessed March 21, 2021. https://www.inmediahk.net/node/1027225.

Lino, Dylan. 2018. "The Rule of Law and the Rule of Empire: A. V. Dicey in Imperial Context." *The Modern Law Review* 81 (5): 739–764.

Linz, Juan J., and Alfred Stepan. 1996. *Problems of Democratic Transition and Consolidation: Southern Europe, South America, and Post-Communist Europe.* The Johns Hopkins University Press.

Linz, Juan J., and Alfred Stepan. 1996. *Problems of Democratic Transition and Consolidation—Southern Europe, South America, and Post-Communist Europe.* The Johns Hopkins University Press.

Little, Daniel. 1992. "Jon Elster." In *New Horizons in Economic Thought: Appraisals of Leading Economists*, edited by Warren J. Samuels. Edward Elgar Publishing.

Liu, Lawrence J., and Rachel E. Stern. 2020. "State-Adjacent Professionals: How Chinese Lawyers Participate in Political Life." *The China Quarterly* 247: 793–813.

Liu, Sida, and Anson Au. 2020. "The Gateway to Global China: Hong Kong and the Future of Chinese Law Firms." *Wisconsin International Law Journal* 37 (2): 308–349.

Liu, Sida, and Anson Au. 2020. "The Gateway to Global China: Hong Kong and the Future of Chinese Law Firms." *Wisconsin International Law Journal* 37, no. 2: 308–349.

Liu, Sida, and Terence C. Halliday. 2011. "Political Liberalism and Political Embeddedness: Understanding Politics in the Work of Chinese Criminal Defense Lawyers." *Law and Society Review* 45 (4): 831–865.

Liu, Sida. 2015. "Law's Social Forms: A Powerless Approach to the Sociology of Law." *Law and Social Inquiry* 40 (1): 1–28.

Liu, Zunfa. 2017. "Zhè Shì Fǎ Zhì de È Lì." *Nán Fāng Zhōu Mò*, February 23. Accessed November 20, 2020. http://www.infzm.com/content/123087.

Lo, Sunny S.H. 2008. *The Dynamics of Beijing-Hong Kong Relations: A Model for Taiwan?* Hong Kong University Press.

Loh, Christine. 2018. *Underground Front: The Chinese Communist Party in Hong Kong, Second Edition*. Hong Kong University Press.

Lok, Lawrence. 2019. "Condemning Protest Violence in Hong Kong Won't Solve the Problem – Not When Police Are Part of the Problem." *South China Morning Post*, October 17. Accessed January 29, 2021. https://www.scmp.com/comment/opinion/article/3033142/condemning-protest-violence-hong-kong-wont-solve-problem-not-when.

Low, Zoe, and Alvin Lum. 2019. "Vice-Chairman Edwin Choy of Hong Kong Bar Association Resigns over Body's Stance on Anti-Government Protest Crisis." *South China Morning Post*, October 12. Accessed January 29, 2021. https://www.scmp.com/news/hong-kong/law-and-crime/article/3032680/vice-chairman-edwin-choy-hong-kong-bar-association.

"[Lu Shī Huì Gǎi Xuǎn] Lu Shī Huì Huì Cháng Péng Yùn Xī Diàn Yóu Wéi Qīn Jiàn Zhì Hòu Xuǎn Rén Lā Piào, Lu Shī Zhì Yí Lì Yì Chōng Tū." 2020. *Stand News*, May 8. Accessed January 29, 2021. Archived on file with the author.

"[Lu Shī Huì Gǎi Xuǎn] Nèi Dì Lái Gǎng Lu Shī Tì Jiàn Zhì Pài Hòu Xuǎn Rén Lā Piào, Chàng Jiāng Shòu Quán Piào Jiāo Lu Shī Huì Huì Cháng Péng Yùn Xī." 2020. *The Apple Daily Breaking News*, May 20. Accessed January 29, 2021. Archived on file with the author.

"Lu Shī Huì Gǎi Xuǎn Wǔ Lǐ Shì Xí Wèi, Fǎn Xiū Lì Lu Shī Xié Diào Wǔ Rén Míng Dān, Jì Dài Rù Kāi Míng Shēng Yīn." 2020. *Stand News*, May 6. Accessed January 29, 2021. Archived on file with the author.

"Lu shī huì huì cháng dāng yuè zhèng xié rě zhì yí." 2013. *Ming Pao Daily News*, 15 January, A02.

"Lu Shī Huì Yuè Dǐ Gǎi Xuǎn, Zhāng Dá Míng: Yǒu Lu Shī Shōu Zhōng Lián Bàn Lā Piào Xìn Xī." 2019. *Stand News*, May 29. Accessed December 23, 2020. Archived on file with the author.

Lui, Tai-lok, and Brian C. H. Fong. 2014. "Editorial." *China Perspectives*, Special Feature 2014 (1): 3–4.

Lui, Tai-lok. 2020. "The Unfinished Chapter of Hong Kong's Long Political Transition." *Critique of Anthropology* 40 (2): 270–276.

Lum, Alvin, and Chris Lau. 2020. "Hong Kong Law Society Chief Defends Controversial Decision to Back Certain Candidates in Polarised Governing Council Election." *South China Morning Post*, May 14. Accessed January 29, 2021. https://www.scmp.com/news/hong-kong/law-and-crime/article/3084454/hong-kong-law-society-chief-defends-controversial..

Lum, Alvin. 2017. "Zhèng gǎi zī xún zāo fù hé, dà lu shī gōng huì zēng 'zǒu wèi' huí yīng." *CitizenNews*, September 16. Accessed January 29, 2021. Archived on file with the author.

Lum, Alvin. 2018. "Mainland Chinese University Bars Two Hong Kong Human Rights Lawyers from Teaching Regular Course There." *South China Morning Post*, August 27. Accessed January 29, 2021. https://www.scmp.com/news/hong-kong/politics/article/2161531/mainland-chinese-university-bars-two-hong-kong-human-rights.

Lum, Alvin. 2019. "British University Strips Pro-Beijing Lawmaker Junius Ho of Honorary Degree over Remarks during Hong Kong Protests." *South China Morning Post*, October 29. Accessed December 23, 2020. https://www.scmp.com/news/hong-kong/politics/article/3035297/british-university-strips-pro-beijing-lawmaker-junius-ho.

Lum, Alvin. 2021. "Zài zuì huài de shí dài bān huí xiāng gang——Xià Bó Yì (Paul Harris)." *CitizenNews*, January 30. Accessed January 31, 2021. Archived on file with the author.

Luo, Huining. 2020. "Xiāng Gǎng Wéi Hù Guó Jiā Ān Quán Zhì Dù Bù Gòu Wán Shàn, Xū Jìn Kuài Zhì Dìng Fǎ Lǜ (Quán Wén)." HK01, April 15. Accessed September 27, 2021. https://www.hk01.com/%E6%94%BF%E6%83%85/461078.

Ma, Geoffrey. 2014. "Chief Justice's Speech at Ceremonial Opening of the Legal Year 2014." January 13. Accessed 19 November 2020. https://www.info.gov.hk/gia/general/201401/13/P201401130352.htm.

Ma, Ngok. 2005. "Civil Society in Self-Defense: The Struggle Against National Security Legislation in Hong Kong." *Journal of Contemporary China* 14 (44): 465–482.

Ma, Ngok. 2005. "Civil Society in Self-Defense: The Struggle against National Security Legislation in Hong Kong." *Journal of Contemporary China* 14, no. 44: 465–482.

Ma, Ngok. 2007. *Political Development of Hong Kong: State, Political Society and Civil Society.* Hong Kong University Press.

Ma, Ngok. 2017. "The China Factor in Hong Kong Elections: 1991 to 2016." *China Perspectives* (3): 17–26.

Ma, Ngok. 2020. "The Plebeian Moment and Its Traces: Post-Umbrella Movement Professional Groups in Hong Kong." In *Sunflowers and Umbrellas: Social Movements, Expressive Practices, and Political Culture in Taiwan and Hong Kong,* edited by Thomas Gold and Sebastian Veg. Institute of East Asian Studies of University of California.

Magnusson, Eva, and Jeanne Marecek. 2015. *Doing Interview-Based Qualitative Research: A Learner's Guide.* Cambridge University Press.

Mahtani, Shibani. 2022. "Britain Withdraws Its Judges from Hong Kong's Highest Court." *Washington Post,* March 30. Accessed January 29, 2024. https://www.washingtonpost.com/world/2022/03/30/hong-kong-uk-withdrawal-judges/.

Mai, Jun, and William Zheng. 2019. "China's Communist Party Elite Wrap Up Meeting with Pledge to Safeguard National Security in Hong Kong." *South China Morning Post,* November 1. Accessed November 18, 2020. https://www.scmp.com/news/china/politics/article/3035818/chinas-communist-party-elite-wrap-meeting-pledge-safeguard.

Mainland and Hong Kong Close Economic Partnership Arrangement 2003. Trade and Industry Department of the Government of Hong Kong Special Administrative Region, June 29. Accessed December 8, 2020. https://www.tid.gov.hk/english/cepa/files/main_e.pdf.

Mainland and Hong Kong Close Economic Partnership Arrangement 2020. Trade and Industry Department of the Government of Hong Kong Special Administrative Region. Accessed 8 December 2020. https://www.tid.gov.hk/english/cepa/index.html.

Mainland and Hong Kong Closer Economic Partnership Arrangement: Agreement on Economic and Technical Cooperation (Ecotech Agreement) 2017. Trade and Industry Department of the Government of Hong Kong Special Administrative Region, June 28. Accessed December 8, 2020. https://www.tid.gov.hk/english/cepa/legaltext/files/cepa15_main.pdf.

Mak, A. 2018. "Report on Standing Committee on Greater China Affairs 2018." Hong Kong Bar Association, December. Accessed January 29, 2021. Archived on file with the author.

Maldonado-Torres, Nelson. 2007. "On the Coloniality of Being: Contributions to the Development of a Concept." *Cultural Studies* 21 (2–3): 240–270.

Mang, Carol, and Yanni Chow. 2020. "Exclusive: Support Dips for Hong Kong Democracy Protests as National Security Law Looms – Poll." *Reuters*, June 26. Accessed January 29, 2021. https://reut.rs/3wJecTa.

Markesinis, Basil S. 2000. "Our Debt to Europe: Past, Present and Future." In *The Coming Together of the Common Law in the Courtroom and Classroom: The Story of the Last Thirty-Five Years*, edited by Basil S. Markesinis. Hart Publishing.

Marlow, Iain. 2021. "China to Shelve Anti-Sanctions Law in Hong Kong, HK01 Says." *Bloomberg*, October 5. Accessed January 29, 2024. https://www.bloomberg.com/news/articles/2021-10-05/china-to-shelve-anti-sanctions-law-in-hong-kong-hk01-says?leadSource=uverify%20wall.

Marsden, Simon. 2006. "Regional Autonomy, Judicial Criticism, and the 2005 Interpretation: Judicial Independence in Hong Kong Compromised Again." *Hong Kong Law Journal* 36 (1): 117–142.

Marshall, Anna-Maria, and Daniel C. Hale. 2014. "Cause Lawyering." *Annual Review of Law and Social Science* 10: 301–320.

Marshall, Anna-Maria. 2001. "A Spectrum in Oppositional Consciousness: Sexual Harassment Plaintiffs and Their Lawyers." In *Oppositional Consciousness*, edited by Jane J. Mansbridge and Aldon Morris. University of Chicago Press.

Marx, Karl, and Friedrich Engels. 1848. *Manifesto of the Communist Party* (*The Communist Manifesto*). Accessed November 6, 2020. https://www.marxists.org/archive/marx/works/1848/communist-manifesto/.

Mattei, Ugo, and Laura Nader. 2008. *Plunder: When the Rule of Law Is Illegal.* Wiley-Blackwell.

Mattei, Ugo, Teemu Ruskola, and Antonio Gidi. 2009. *Schlesinger's Comparative Law*, 7th ed. Foundation Press.

McAdam, Doug, and Sidney Tarrow. 2018. "The Political Context of Social Movements." In *Wiley-Blackwell Companion to Social Movements*, edited by David A. Snow, Sarah A. Soule, Hanspeter Kriesi, and Holly J. McCammon. Blackwell.

McBarnet, Doreen. 2002. "Transnational Transactions: Legal Work, Cross-Border Commerce and Global Regulation." In *Transnational Legal Processes: Globalisation and Power Disparities*, edited by Michael Likosky. Butterworths.

McCann, Michael, and Helena Silverstein. 1998. "Rethinking Law's 'Allurements': A Relational Analysis of Social Movement Lawyers in the United States." In *Cause*

Lawyering: Political Commitments and Professional Responsibilities, edited by Austin Sarat and Stuart A. Scheingold. Oxford University Press.

McCann, Michael. 2004. "Law and Social Movements." In *The Blackwell Companion to Law and Society*, edited by Austin Sarat. Blackwell Publishing.

McDermott, John. 1997. "The 'Rule of Law' in Hong Kong after 1997." *Loyola of Los Angeles International and Comparative Law Review* 19 (2): 263–292.

McMorrow, Judith, Sida Liu, and Benjamin Van Rooij. 2017. "Lawyer Discipline in an Authoritarian Regime: Empirical Insights from Zhejiang Province, China." *Georgetown Journal of Legal Ethics* 30 (Spring): 267–300.

Meick, Ethan. 2019. "Hong Kong's Proposed Extradition Bill Could Extend Beijing's Coercive Reach: Risks for the United States." *U.S.-China Economic and Security Review Commission*, May 7. Accessed August 13, 2020. https://www.uscc.gov/research/hong-kongs-proposed-extradition-bill-could-extend-beijings-coercive-reach-risks-united.

Meili, Stephen. 1998. "Cause Lawyers and Social Movements: A Comparative Perspective on Democratic Change in Argentina and Brazil." In *Cause Lawyering: Political Commitments and Professional Responsibilities*, edited by Austin Sarat and Stuart A. Scheingold. Oxford University Press.

Meili, Stephen. 2001. "Latin American Cause Lawyering Networks." In *Cause Lawyering and the State in a Global Era*, edited by Austin Sarat and Stuart A. Scheingold. Oxford University Press.

Menski, Werner F. 2006. *Comparative Law in a Global Context*, 2nd ed. Cambridge University Press.

Merry, Sally E. 1995. "Resistance and the Cultural Power of Law." *Law and Society Review* 29 (1): 11–26.

Merry, Sally E. 2000. *Colonizing Hawaii: The Cultural Power of Law. Princeton University Press.*

Merry, Sally E. 2010. "What Is Legal Culture? An Anthropological Perspective." *Journal of Comparative Law* 5 (44): 48–52.

Merton, Robert K. 1972. "Insiders and Outsiders: A Chapter in the Sociology of Knowledge." *American Journal of Sociology* 78 (1): 9–47.

Mertus, Julie. 2011. "From Legal Transplants to Transformative Justice: Human Rights and the Promise of Transnational Civil Society." *American University International Law Review* 14 (5): 1335–1389.

Mertz, Elizabeth. 2007. *The Language of Law School: Learning to 'Think Like a Lawyer'*. Oxford University Press.

Meyer, David S. 2004. "Protest and Political Opportunities." *Annual Review of Sociology* 30 (1): 125–145.

Mignolo, Walter D., and Catherine E. Walsh. 2018. *On Decoloniality: Concepts, Analytics and Praxis*. Duke University Press.

Milhaupt, Curtis J., and Katharina Pistor. 2008. *Law and Capitalism: What Corporate Crises Reveal About Legal Systems and Economic Development Around the World.* Chicago University Press.

Miller, Jonathan M. 2003. "A Typology of Legal Transplants: Using Sociology, Legal History, and Argentine Examples to Explain the Transplant Process." *American Journal of Comparative Law* 51 (4): 839–885.

Minutes of Hong Kong Legislative Council. 1967. *Official Report of Proceedings,* November 1.

Mo, Jojo Y. C. 2017. "The Copyright (Amendment) Bill 2014 in Hong Kong: A Blessing or a Curse?" *Statute Law Review* 38, no. 2: 211–225.

Mommsen, Wolfgang J. 1992. "Introduction." In *European Expansion and Law: The Encounter of European and Indigenous Law in 19th- and 20th-Century Africa and Asia,* edited by Wolfgang J. Mommsen and Jaap A. de Moor. Berg Publishers.

Moustafa, Tamir. 2007. *The Struggle for Constitutional Power: Law, Politics, and Economic Reform in Egypt.* Cambridge University Press.

Moustafa, Tamir. 2014. "Law and Courts in Authoritarian Regimes." *Annual Review of Law and Social Science* 10: 281–299.

Müller-Chen, Markus, Christoph Müller, and Corinne W. Lüchinger. 2015. *Comparative Private Law.* Dike.

Munn, Christopher. 2009. *Anglo-China: Chinese People and British Rule in Hong Kong, 1841–1880.* Hong Kong University Press.

Munn, Christopher. 2017. "'Our Best Trump Card': A Brief History of Deportation in Hong Kong 1857–1955." In *Civil Unrest and Governance in Hong Kong: Law and Order from Historical and Cultural Perspectives,* edited by John D. Wong and Michael H.K. Ng. Routledge.

Murdoch, Scott, and Anne M. Roantree. 2021. "Candidate Pulls Out of Hong Kong Lawyers' Group Election Over Safety Fears." *Reuters,* August 21. Accessed October 16, 2021. https://reut.rs/3n5AISN.

National Democratic Institute and Georgetown Center for Asian Law. 2020. *The Promise of Democratization in Hong Kong: Discontent and Rule of Law Challenges.* April 23. Accessed September 21, 2021. https://www.ndi.org/publications/promise-democratization-hong-kong.

National Endowment for Democracy. 2017. *Sharp Power: Rising Authoritarian Influence.* Accessed June 24, 2020. https://www.ned.org/wp-content/uploads/2017/12/Sharp-Power-Rising-Authoritarian-Influence-Full-Report.pdf.

Nelkin, David. 2001. "Towards a Sociology of Legal Adaptation." In *Adapting Legal Culture,* edited by David Nelkin and Johannes Feest. Hart Publishing.

Ng, Ellie. 2017a. "China's Top Legislature Approves Joint Checkpoint Plan; Says It Complies with Hong Kong Constitution." *Hong Kong Free Press,* December 27. Accessed December 23, 2020. https://hongkongfp.com/2017/12/27/

chinas-top-legislature-approves-joint-checkpoint-plan-says-complies-hong-kong-constitution/.

Ng, Joyce. 2014a. "Solicitors Vote to Unseat Law Society President Ambrose Lam." *South China Morning Post.* August 15. Accessed March 21, 2021. https://www.scmp.com/news/hong-kong/article/1573871/solicitors-pass-vote-no-confidence-law-society-chief-ambrose-lam.

Ng, Joyce. 2014b. "Law Society President Ambrose Lam Resigns After Historic No-Confidence Vote." *South China Morning Post.* August 19. Accessed March 21, 2021. https://www.scmp.com/news/hong-kong/article/1576791/law-society-president-ambrose-lam-resigns-following-historic-no.

Ng, Julian, and Zoe Lai. 2015. "Professionals Get Political." *Varsity.* March 17. Accessed March 21, 2021. https://varsity.com.cuhk.edu.hk/index.php/2015/03/professionals-get-political/.

Ng, Kang-Chung. 2020. "Hong Kong Lawyers Can Soon Earn Qualification to Practise in Greater Bay Area under New Pilot Scheme." *South China Morning Post,* October 22. Accessed December 10, 2020. https://www.scmp.com/news/hong-kong/politics/article/3106710/hong-kong-lawyers-can-soon-earn-qualification-practise.

Ng, Michael H.K. 2016. "Rule of Law in Hong Kong History Demythologised: Student Umbrella Movement of 1919." *Hong Kong Law Journal* 46 (3): 829–848.

Ng, Michael H.K. 2017. "When Silence Speaks: Press Censorship and Rule of Law in British Hong Kong (1850s–1940s)." *Law and Literature* 29 (3): 425–56.

Ng, W. and W. T. You. 2018. "Tǐng Hù Kàng Zhēng 40 Nián, 'Fēi Fǎ Jí Jié Zuì' De Qián Shì Jīn Shēng." *The News Lens,* April 18. Accessed May 19, 2021. Archived on file with the author.

Norton-Kyshe, James William. 1971. *The History of the Laws and Courts of Hong Kong from the Earliest Period to 1898,* 2 vols. Vetch and Lee.

O'Donnell, Guillermo A. 2004. "Why the Rule of Law Matters." *Journal of Democracy* 15 (4): 32–46.

Ogbonnaya, John O., and Chioma V. Iteshi. 2016. "The Jurisprudential Issues Arising from Legal Transplant: An Appraisal." *Journal of Law, Policy and Globalization* 50: 1–12.

One Country, Two Systems Index 2020. Path of Democracy. Hong Kong.

Pang, Jessie, and Mari Saito. 2020. "Arrested Hong Kong Protesters Stuck in Limbo as Cases Grind Forward." *Reuters,* January 23. Accessed October 16, 2021. https://reut.rs/3H57Guy.

Pang, Jessie, and Sarah Wu. 2020. "Hong Kong Leader Rejects Protesters' Call for Independent Police Probe." *Reuters,* May 15. Accessed January 24, 2021. https://reut.rs/3ododIQ.

Pang, Laikwan. 2020. *The Appearing Demos: Hong Kong During and After the Umbrella Movement.* University of Michigan Press.

Patten, Chris. 1996. *Hong Kong, Transition: The 1996 Policy Address*. Government Printer.

"Paul Lam and His Proposed Elected Members – HKBA Election 2018, Moving Forward Together." 2018. Facebook, January 16. Accessed January 13, 2019. Archived on file with the author.

Pedriana, Nicholas, and Robin Stryker. 1997. "Political Culture Wars 1960s Style: Equal Opportunity Employment-Affirmative Action and the Philadelphia Plan." *American Journal of Sociology* 103 (3): 633–691.

Pedriana, Nicholas. 2006. "From Protective to Equal Treatment: Legal Framing Processes and Transformation of the Women's Movement in the 1960s." American Journal of Sociology 111 (6): 1718–1761.

Pei, Minxin. 2020. "Investigation of a Death Long Feared: How China Decided to Impose Its National Security Law in Hong Kong." *China Leadership Monitor*, September 1. Accessed October 16. https://www.prcleader.org/post/investigation-of-a-death-long-feared-how-china-decided-to-impose-its-national-security-law-in-hong.

Philip Dykes' List – HKBA Election 2017, In Your Hands. 2018. "Election Platform: Bread and Butter Issues, Particularly for the Young Bar." Facebook, January 8. Archived on file with the author.

Philip Dykes' List – HKBA Election 2017, In Your Hands. 2018. "HKBA Election 2018 Joint Statement from Philip Dykes' List." Facebook, December 25. Archived on file with the author.

Pils, Eva. 2014. *China's Human Rights Lawyers: Advocacy and Resistance*. Routledge.

Pirie, Fernanda. 2013. *The Anthropology of Law*. Oxford University Press.

Pomfret, James, and Clare Jim. 2019. "Exclusive: Hong Kongers Support Protester Demands; Minority Wants Independence from China – Reuters Poll." *Reuters*, December 31. Accessed January 29, 2021. https://reut.rs/3D7GzNa.

Pomfret, James, and Jessie Pang. 2019. "Hong Kong Extradition Bill a 'Terrible Blow' to Rule of Law: Patten." *Reuters*, June 6. Accessed November 21, 2020. https://reut.rs/3bYSTTW.

Pomfret, James, Greg Torode, Anne M. Roantree, and David Lague. 2022. "A Reuters Special Report: Lawyers Exit Hong Kong as They Face Campaign of Intimidation." *Reuters*, December 29. Accessed January 29, 2024. https://www.reuters.com/investigates/special-report/china-lawyers-crackdown-exodus/.

Pomfret, James. 2019. "EU Lodges Formal Diplomatic Note Against Contentious Hong Kong Extradition Bill." *Reuters*, May 24. Accessed August 13, 2020. https://reut.rs/3c6xxEo.

Poon, C. H. 2020. "Legal Service Industry in Hong Kong." *Hong Kong Trade Development Council*, June 18. Accessed December 10, 2020. https://research.hktdc.com/en/article/MzEzODc5NTk5.

"'Professional' camp wins Law Society election." 2021. *The Standard*, August 24. Accessed October 16, 2021. https://www.thestandard.com.hk/breaking-news/section/4/179311/%22Professional%22-camp-wins-Law-Society-election.

Progressive Lawyers Group. 2015. "Explainer: What Is Legal and What Is Not under Copyright (Amendment) Bill 2014." *Hong Kong Free Press*. December 12. Accessed April 7, 2021. https://hongkongfp.com/2015/12/12/explainer-what-is-legal-and-what-is-not-under-copyright-amendment-bill-2014/.

Progressive Lawyers Group. 2019a. "Statement of the Progressive Lawyers Group on the Government's Proposal to Amend Extradition Laws." Progressive Lawyers Group. February 20. Archived on file with the author.

Progressive Lawyers Group. 2019b. *The Hong Kong Rule of Law Report 2018*. Progressive Lawyers Group.

Progressive Lawyers Group. 2020. "Open Letter from 86 Groups: China – Scrap National Security Law to Save Hong Kong Freedoms." Progressive Lawyers Group. June 17. Archived on file with the author.

Progressive Scholars Group. 2020. *Silencing Millions: Unchecked Violations of Internationally Recognized Human Rights by the Hong Kong Police Force*.

Radio Free Asia. 2022. "Zhōng gòng guān yuán shǒu tí 'qù zhí huà', píng lùn: yù xiāo chú gǎng rén duì gǎng yīng zhèng fǔ huái niàn." December 5. Accessed November 16, 2024. https://www.rfa.org/cantonese/news/htm/hk-colony-12052022080900.html.

Rajah, Jothie. 2012. *Authoritarian Rule of Law: Legislation, Discourse and Legitimacy in Singapore*. Cambridge University Press.

Rajah, Jothie. 2024. "Normalising Authoritarianism: Authoritarian Rule of Law in Singapore and Hong Kong." In *The Palgrave Handbook of Political Norms in Southeast Asia*, edited by Gaëlle Facal, Elise L. Micheaux, and Astrid Norén-Nilsson. Springer Nature Singapore.

Raz, Joseph. 1994. *Ethics in the Public Domain*. Oxford University Press.

"Restrictions Eased for Qualified Hong Kong and Macau Lawyers Practicing in Mainland China." 2013. *China Briefing*, August 20. Accessed December 10, 2020. https://www.china-briefing.com/news/restrictions-eased-for-qualified-hong-kong-macau-lawyers-practicing-in-mainland-china/.

Richardson, Sophie. 2020. "China's Influence on the Global Human Rights System: Assessing China's Growing Role in the World." *Human Rights Watch*, September 14. Accessed November 10, 2020. https://www.hrw.org/news/2020/09/14/chinas-influence-global-human-rights-system.

Rifkind, Malcolm. 2019. "There Is No 'Loophole' in Hong Kong's Current Extradition Law. Rather, It Provides a Necessary Firewall to Protect the Legal System." *South China Morning Post*, June 4. Accessed August 13, 2020. https://www.scmp.com/comment/opinion/article/3012853/there-no-loophole-hong-kongs-current-extradition-law-rather-it.

"Róng Hǎi En duó xīn dōng yì xí, xī huán qì zī qì nǚ dà sheng." 2016. *Apple Daily Breaking News*, September 5. Accessed January 13, 2019. Archived on file with the author.

Rostain, Tanina. 2008. "Professional Power: Lawyers and the Constitution of Professional Authority." In *The Blackwell Companion to Law and Society*, edited by Austin Sarat. Blackwell.

Saito, Mari, and Anne John. 2019. "Hong Kong Protesters Denounce Police Raid on Fund-Raising Platform." Reuters, December 20. Accessed June 25, 2021. https://reut.rs/3n3mWQz.

Sarat, Austin, and Stuart A. Scheingold. 1998. "Cause Lawyering and the Reproduction of Professional Authority: An Introduction." In *Cause Lawyering: Political Commitments and Professional Responsibilities*, edited by Austin Sarat and Stuart A. Scheingold. Oxford University Press.

Sarat, Austin, and Stuart A. Scheingold. 2001. "State Transformation, Globalisation, and the Possibilities of Cause Lawyering." In *Cause Lawyering and the State in a Global Era*, edited by Austin Sarat and Stuart A. Scheingold. Oxford University Press.

Sarat, Austin, and Stuart A. Scheingold. 2006. "What Cause Lawyers Do For, and To, Social Movements: An Introduction." In *Cause Lawyers and Social Movements*, edited by Austin Sarat and Stuart A. Scheingold. Stanford University Press.

Schauer, Frederick. 2000. "The Politics and Incentives of Legal Transplantation." *CID Working Paper Series* 2000.44, Harvard University.

Scheingold, Stuart A., and Austin Sarat, eds. 2004. *Something to Believe In: Politics, Professionalism and Cause Lawyering*. Stanford University Press.

Schmidhauser, John R. 1989. "Power, Legal Imperialism, and Dependency." *Law and Society Review* 23 (5): 857–878.

Schmitter, Philippe C., and Terry Lynn Karl. 1991. "What Democracy Is....and Is Not." *Journal of Democracy* 2 (3): 3–16.

Schwab, Klaus, ed. 2019. The Global Competitiveness Report 2019. World Economic Forum. Accessed July 9, 2020. https://www3.weforum.org/docs/WEF_TheGlobalCompetitivenessReport2019.pdf.

Scott, James C. 1985. *Weapons of the Weak: Everyday Forms of Peasant Resistance*. Yale University Press.

Secretary for Justice v. Law Man Chung. 2020. CAAR4/2019.

Sha, Pun Shan. 2020. "Lu shī huì gǎi xuǎn zhuān yè pài yán kūn yǐng : lu shī huì yīng bǎo chí fēi zhèng zhì xìng, fǎn rèn hé bào lì" HK01, May 26. Accessed October 31, 2024. https://www.hk01.com/%E6%94%BF%E6%83%85/477904/%E5%BE%8B%E5%B8%AB%E6%9C%83%E6%94%B9%E9%81%B8-%E5%B0%88%E6%A5%AD%E6%B4%BE%E5%9A%B4%E5%9D%A4%E7%A9%8E-%E5%BE%8B%E5%B8%AB%E6%9C%83%E6%87%89%E4%BF%9D%

E6%8C%81%E9%9D%9E%E6%94%BF%E6%B2%BB%E6%80%A7-%E5%8F%8D%E4%BB%BB%E4%BD%95%E6%9A%B4%E5%8A%9B .

Shafqat, Sahar. 2018. "Civil Society and the Lawyers' Movement of Pakistan." *Law and Social Inquiry* 43 (3): 889–914.

Sherr, Avrom, and Julian Webb. 1989. "Law Students, the External Market, and Socialization: Do We Make Them Turn to the City?" *Journal of Law and Society* 16 (2): 225–249.

Shieh SC, Paul. 2015. "Speech of the Chairman of the Hong Kong Bar Association at the Opening of the Legal Year 2015." Hong Kong Bar Association, January 12. Accessed January 29, 2021. Archived on file with the author.

Siems, Mathias M. 2018. *Comparative Law*. 2nd ed. Cambridge University Press.

Sin, Wai Man. 2001. "Law, Politics and Professional Projects: The Legal Profession in Hong Kong." *Social and Legal Studies* 10 (4): 483–504.

Siu, Jasmine. 2019. "Body Folded in Suitcase: Gruesome Details Emerge of Hong Kong Man's Killing of Pregnant Girlfriend in Taiwan." *South China Morning Post*, April 13. Accessed November 21, 2020. https://www.scmp.com/news/hong-kong/law-and-crime/article/3005990/body-folded-suitcase-gruesome-details-emerge-hong-kong.

612 Humanitarian Relief Fund. 2019. "Fund Facts." Accessed June 16, 2021. https://612fund.hk/en/dummies.

612 Humanitarian Relief Fund. 2020a. *2019–2020 Annual Report*. Accessed June 16, 2021. https://static1.squarespace.com/static/5d53782d96f86e00015a4657/t/5f042321b7e1fd56c38ecce3/1594106754935/612-annual-report.pdf.

612 Humanitarian Relief Fund. 2020b. "Qū Yù Fǎ Yuàn Àn Jiàn 'Dì Èr Wèi Dà Lu Shī' Zī Zhù Jì Huá." Google Doc, October 22. Accessed June 16, 2021. https://drive.google.com/file/d/1FJ3Cg04Xhp989OSw75_7FgZixKK2kneb/edit.

612 Humanitarian Relief Fund. 2021. "612 Rén Dào Zhī Yuán Jī Jīn Gōng Zuò Jiǎn Bào." Google Doc. Accessed June 24, 2021. https://docs.google.com/spreadsheets/d/1U8U6174kRffycKjWcNALjKqzKNc03xxIPws2FzN1krI/edit#gid=1881645065.

Sixtus Leung Chung Hang v. Chief Executive of the Hong Kong Special Administrative Region, Secretary for Justice. 2017. FAMV 10/2017; Yau Wai Ching v. Chief Executive of the Hong Kong Special Administrative Region, Secretary for Justice. 2017. FAMV 8/2017.

The Small and Medium Law Firms Association of Hong Kong. 2014a. "Methods for Selecting the Chief Executive in 2017." April 25. Accessed December 17, 2020. https://www.samlaw.hk/index.php/lastnews/89-2017.html.

The Small and Medium Law Firms Association of Hong Kong. 2014b. "Press release: Free "Anti-Occupy Central" helpline starts talking calls tomorrow." August 31. Accessed December 17, 2020. https://www.samlaw.hk/images/

files/2014/2014-08-31Anti-Occupy_Central_Helpline_Press_Releases/SAMLA-WAnti-Occupy_Central_Helpline_Press_Releases_with_signature.pdf.

The Small and Medium Law Firms Association of Hong Kong. 2025. "Home Page". Accessed April 5, 2025. https://www.samlaw.hk .

So, Peter. 2014. "Judges Don't Need to Be Patriots, Says Former Top Judge Andrew Li." *South China Morning Post*, August 15. Accessed November 20, 2020. https://www.scmp.com/news/hong-kong/article/1573867/judges-dont-need-be-patriots-andrew-li.

Solomon, Peter H., Jr. 2010. "Authoritarian Legality and Informal Practices: Judges, Lawyers, and the State in Russia and China." *Communist and Post-Communist Studies* 43 (4): 351–362.

Spalding, Rose J. 2003. "State Power and Its Limits: Corporatism in Mexico." *Comparative Political Studies* 14 (2): 139–161.

Spamann, Holger S. 2009. "Contemporary Legal Transplants: Legal Families and the Diffusion of (Corporate) Law." *BYU Law Review* 2009 (6): 1813–1878.

Spark Alliance. 2017. "About" Facebook Page. Accessed October 31, 2024. https://www.facebook.com/sparkalliancehk/about .

The State Council of the People's Republic of China. 2014. *White Paper on the Practice of the "One Country, Two Systems" Policy in the Hong Kong Special Administrative Region*. June 10. Accessed November 18, 2020. https://english.www.gov.cn/archive/white_paper/2014/08/23/content_281474982986578.htm.

Steger, Isabella. 2016. "Beijing Is Determined to Keep Defiant, Pro-Independence Lawmakers Out of Hong Kong's Legislature." *Quartz*. October 19. Accessed March 21, 2021. https://qz.com/812500/hong-kongs-government-and-beijing-are-determined-to-kick-pro-independence-lawmakers-out-of-the-legislature.

Stern, Rachel E. 2017. "Activist Lawyers in Post-Tiananmen China." *Law and Social Inquiry* 42 (1): 234–251.

Stern, Rachel E., and Lawrence J. Liu. 2020. "The Good Lawyer: State-Led Professional Socialization in Contemporary China." *Law and Social Inquiry* 45 (1): 26–48.

Stoler, Ann L., and Frederick Cooper. 1997. "Between Metropole and Colony: Rethinking a Research Agenda." In *Tensions of Empire: Colonial Cultures in a Bourgeois World*, edited by Frederick Cooper and Ann L. Stoler. University of California Press.

Stone, Alan. 1985. "The Place of Law in the Marxian Structure-Superstructure Archetype." *Law and Society Review* 19 (1): 39–68.

Stott, Clifford, Lawrence Ho, Matt Radburn, Ying Tung Chan, Arabella Kyprianides, and Patricio S. Morales. 2020. "Patterns of 'Disorder' During the 2019 Protests in Hong Kong: Policing, Social Identity, Intergroup Dynamics, and Radicalization." *Policing* 14 (4): 814–835.

Stromseth, Jane E., David Wippman, and Rosa Brooks. 2006. *Can Might Make Rights? Building the Rule of Law After Military Interventions*. Cambridge University Press.

Sum, Lok-kei, and Xinqi Su. 2019. "Pro-Beijing Lawmaker Junius Ho Defends White-Clad Mob That Attacked Civilians in Hong Kong MTR Station, Says They Can Be 'Pardoned for Defending Their Home'." *South China Morning Post*, July 22. Accessed December 23, 2020. https://www.scmp.com/news/hong-kong/politics/article/3019621/pro-beijing-lawmaker-junius-ho-defends-white-clad-mob.

Sum, Lok-kei. 2019. "Group of Extradition Bill Protesters Hold First Press Conference to Counter Hong Kong Government Line on Recent Demonstrations." *South China Morning Post.* August 6. Accessed March 21, 2021. https://www.scmp.com/news/hong-kong/politics/article/3021626/group-extradition-bill-protesters-hold-first-press.

Sumption, John. 2024. "The Rule of Law in Hong Kong is in Grave Danger." *Financial Times*, June 10. Accessed November 19, 2024. https://www.ft.com/content/60c825be-b70a-4152-895f-f6127974570a.

"The Strong and Fearless Voices of Hong Kong Solicitors." 2020. Facebook. Accessed January 29, 2021. Archived on file with the author.

Tai, Benny Y.T. 2007. "Developing an Index of the Rule of Law: Sharing the Experience of Hong Kong." *Asian Journal of Comparative Law* 2 (1): 1–19.

Tai, Benny Y.T. 2012. "The judiciary" In *Contemporary Hong Kong Government and Politics: Expanded Second Edition*, edited by Wai-man Lam, Percy L.T. Lui, and Wilson Wong. Hong Kong University Press.

Tai, Benny Y.T. 2015. *Report on rule of law and Legal Culture in Hong Kong.*

Tai, Benny Y.T. 2021. "Authoritarian Rule of Law in Hong Kong." In *Democracy and Rule of Law in China's Shadow*, edited by Brain C. Jones. Hart Publishing..

Tai, Benny Y.T. 2021. "Authoritarian Rule of Law in Hong Kong." In *Democracy and Rule of Law in China's Shadow*, edited by Brian C. Jones. Hart Publishing.

Tai, C.H. 2018. "Zhū Jīng Wěi zhī chí zhě tíng wài hǎn 'gǒu guān', 'mó luó chà'; Guō Róng Kēng : kě néng miǎo shì fǎ tíng." *CitizenNews*, January 2. Accessed January 29, 2021. Archived on file with the author.

Tam SC, Winnie. 2016. "Speech of the Chairman of the Hong Kong Bar Association Winnie Tam SC, at the Opening of the Legal Year." The Hong Kong Bar Association, January 11. Accessed January 29, 2021. Archived on file with the author.

Tam SC, Winnie. 2017. "Report on Committee on China Practice Development 2017." The Hong Kong Bar Association, December. Accessed January 29, 2021. Archived on file with the author.

Tam SC, Winnie. 2018. "Report of the Standing Committee on China Practice Development 2018." Hong Kong Bar Association, December 19. Accessed January 29, 2021. Archived on file with the author.

Tam, Waikeung. 2010. "Political Transition and the Rise of Cause Lawyering: The Case of Hong Kong." *Law and Social Inquiry* 35 (3): 663–687.

Tam, Waikeung. 2012. *Legal Mobilization under Authoritarianism: The Case of Post-Colonial Hong Kong*. Cambridge University Press.

Tamanaha, Brain Z. 2017. *A Realistic Theory of Law*. Cambridge University Press.

Tamanaha, Brian Z. 2004. *On the Rule of Law: History, Politics, Theory*. Cambridge University Press.

Tamanaha, Brian Z. 2007. "A Concise Guide to the Rule of Law." *Legal Studies Research Paper Series*, Paper 07–2282.

Tamanaha, Brian Z. 2012. "The History and Elements of the Rule of Law." *Singapore Journal of Legal Studies*: 232–247.

Tamanaha, Brian Z. 2017. *A Realistic Theory of Law*. Cambridge University Press.

"Tán Yǔn Zhī Chì Gǎi Xuǎn 'Hǎo Duō Rén Qiáng Yìng Shǒu Duàn Līn Piào', Dài Qǐ Sī: Xiàn Zhāng Róng Jìng Zhēng, Bù Míng Fēn Liè Gōng Huì Zhǐ Kòng." 2018. *Ming Pao Daily News*, January 9. Accessed January 29, 2021. Archived on file with the author.

Terwindt, Carolijn. 2019. *When Protest Becomes Crime: Politics and Law in Liberal Democracies*. Pluto Press.

Teubner, Gunther. 1998. "Legal Irritants: Good Faith in British Law or How Unifying Law Ends up in New Divergences." *Modern Law Review* 61 (1): 11–32.

"Tien Rules Out Return as Liberal Leader." 2008. *The Standard*, September 18. P10.

Tilly, Charles. 1984. "Social Movements and National Politics." In *Statemaking and Social Movements: Essays in History and Theory*, edited by Charles Bright and Susan Harding. University of Michigan Press.

Tilly, Charles. 1995. *Popular Contention in Great Britain 1758–1834*. Harvard University Press.

Ting, Victor. 2019. "As Hong Kong Protests Rage On, Barristers Hit Back at Beijing's Comments on the City's Judiciary and Its Responsibilities." *South China Morning Post*, November 9. Accessed November 20, 2020. https://www.scmp.com/news/hong-kong/politics/article/3037054/hong-kong-protests-rage-barristers-hit-back-beijings.

Tong, Elson. 2017a. "'Basic Law Doesn't Define Hong Kong's Borders': Justice Sec. Defends Mainland Rail Checkpoint." *Hong Kong Free Press*, July 25. Accessed January 29, 2021. https://hongkongfp.com/2017/07/25/basic-law-doesnt-define-hong-kongs-borders-justice-chief-defends-mainland-rail-checkpoint/.

Tong, Elson. 2017b. "Bar Council Chairman Paul Lam Seeks Re-Election amid Challenge from Rights Lawyer Philip Dykes." Hong Kong Free Press, December 28. Accessed December 23, 2020. https://hongkongfp.com/2017/12/28/bar-council-chairman-paul-lam-seeks-re-election-amid-challenge-rights-lawyer-philip-dykes/.

Torode, Greg, and Anne Marie Roantree. 2019. "Hong Kong Lawyers Protest 'Polarising' Extradition Bill in Rare March." Reuters. June 6. Accessed April 7, 2021. https://reut.rs/3D6MulD.

Torode, Greg, and James Pomfret. 2019. "Exclusive: Hong Kong Judges See Risks in Proposed Extradition Changes." *Reuters*, May 29. Accessed December 23, 2020. https://www.reuters.com/article/us-hongkong-politics-extradition-judges-idUSKCN1SZ09U/.

Torode, Greg, and James Pomfret. 2020. "Hong Kong Judges Battle Beijing over Rule of Law as Pandemic Chills Protests." *Reuters*, April 14. Accessed December 23, 2020. https://www.reuters.com/investigates/special-report/hongkong-politics-judiciary/.

Torode, Greg, and John Pomfret. 2022. "Ex-chief of Hong Kong barristers says he left city after police interview." *Reuters*, March 2. Accessed August 21, 2022. https://www.reuters.com/world/china/ex-chief-hong-kong-barristers-says-he-left-city-after-police-interview-2022-03-02/.

"Tracking the Impact of Hong Kong's National Security Law." 2024. ChinaFile, updated January 5. Accessed January 29, 2024. https://www.chinafile.com/tracking-impact-of-hong-kongs-national-security-law.

Trevaskes, Susan. 2019. "Socialist Law." In *Afterlives of Chinese Communism: Political Concepts from Mao to Xi*, edited by Christian Sorace, Ivan Franceschini, and Nicholas Loubere. ANU Press and Verso Books.

Tsang, Emily, and Tony Cheung. 2017. "Opposition Ramps Up Bid to Impeach Hong Kong Leader for Intervening in Fee Probe." *South China Morning Post*, May 19. Accessed December 23, 2020. https://www.scmp.com/news/hong-kong/politics/article/2094923/lawmaker-holden-chow-quits-ugl-investigation-panel-wake-cy.

Tsang, Steve. 2004. *A Modern History of Hong Kong*. Hong Kong University Press.

Tso, Kelvin K. S. 2012. "Fundamental Political and Constitutional Norms: Hong Kong and Macau Compared." *Australian Journal of Asian Law* 13 (1): 25–47.

Turk, Austin T. 1976. "Law as a Weapon in Social Conflict." *Social Problems* 23 (3): 276–291.

Turner, Bertram. 2006. "Competing Global Players in Rural Morocco: Upgrading Legal Arenas." *The Journal of Legal Pluralism and Unofficial Law* 48 (3): 101–139.

"Two-Tier Police Complaints System." 2018. *Independent Police Complaints Council*, January 10. Accessed June 24, 2021. https://www.ipcc.gov.hk/en/what_we_do/two_tier_police.html.

Unger, Jonathan, and Anita Chan. 1995. "China, Corporatism, and the East Asian Model." *The Australian Journal of Chinese Affairs* 33: 29–53.

Unger, Roberto M. 2015. *The Critical Legal Studies Movement: Another Time, A Greater Task*. Verso.

United Nations. 1994. "No. 23392. China and United Kingdom of Great Britain and Northern Ireland: Joint Declaration on the Question of Hong Kong (with Annexes). Signed at Beijing on 19th December 1984." *Treaties and International Agreements Registered or Filed and Recorded with the Secretariat of the United Nations* 1399.

Vago, Steven, Adie Nelson, Veronica Nelson and Steven E. Barkan. 2017. *Law and Society*. 11th ed. Routledge.

Vallejos Evangeline Banao, also known as Vallejos, Evangeline B. and Daniel Domingo L. v. Commissioner of Registration and Registration of Persons Tribunal. 2013. FACV19/2012.

Wacks, Raymond. 1989. *The Future of the Law in Hong Kong*. Oxford University Press.

Wang, Chenguang. 2013. "Legal Transplantation and Legal Development in Transitional China." *World Bank Legal Review* 4: 161–178.

Wang, Ping. 2017. "Rénmín rìbào hǎiwài bǎn fǎng xiānggǎng fǎlǜ zhuānjiā: Jǐngchá bèi zhòngpàn chōngjī xiānggǎng fǎzhì." *Rénmín Rìbào Hǎiwài Bǎn*, February 21. Accessed November 20, 2020. https://www.thepaper.cn/newsDetail_forward_1623166.

Watson, Alan. 1993. *Legal Transplant: An Approach to Comparative Law*. 2nd ed. The University of Georgia Press.

Watson, Alan. 1996. "Aspects of Reception of Law." *The American Journal of Comparative Law* 44 (2): 335–351.

Weber, Max. 1946. *Politics as a Vocation*. Oxford University Press. Accessed July 29, 2020. https://archive.org/details/weber_max_1864_1920_politics_as_a_vocation/page/n1/mode/2up.

Weber, Max. 1978. *Economy and Society*. Edited by Guenther Roth and Claus Wittich. University of California Press.

"[Wéi yuán jí huì] fǎ zhèng huì sī : gǎng ào bàn jiě fàng jūn píng lùn fǎn xiū lì yùn dòng shè wéi fǎn jī běn fǎ." *Sing Tao Daily*, August 18. Accessed November 20, 2024. https://hk.news.yahoo.com/%E7%B6%AD%E5%9C%92%E9%9B%86%E6%9C%83-%E6%B3%95%E6%94%BF%E5%8C%AF%E6%80%9D-%E6%B8%AF%E6%BE%B3%E8%BE%A6%E8%A7%A3%E6%94%BE%E8%BB%8D%E8%A9%95%E8%AB%96%E5%8F%8D%E4%BF%AE%E4%BE%8B%E9%81%8B%E5%8B%95%E6%B6%89%E9%81%95%E5%8F%8D-%E5%9F%BA%E6%9C%AC%E6%B3%95-080300368.html?guce_referrer=aHR0cHM6Ly93d3cuZ29vZ2xlLmNvbS8&guce_referrer_sig=AQAAADHIQ8ZMZaS1tzqn6uRDOZ6goon7vzVXRome2S10LiVO_VPAGdBmAx11rMPZIFwFeaygVLVy6erFvWQcuC-csLrbTHr46diIbW4JTvJLmQoMp3MlopkpyOdPm-otLn8JEEKfoSwRtMw_6pRSCOt4cLvZR3HlkCw3ATH2GsWyuEYdo&guccounter=2.

Whiting, Susan H. 2017. "Authoritarian 'Rule of Law' and Regime Legitimacy." *Comparative Political Studies* 50 (14): 1907–1940.

Wiarda, Howard J. 1997. *Corporatism and Comparative Politics: The Other Great 'Ism'*. M.E. Sharpe.

Wiener, Martin J. 2012. "Some Difficulties of Colonial Judging: The Bahamas 1886–93." In *Judges and Judging in the History of the Common Law and Civil Law: From Antiquity to Modern Times*, edited by Paul Brand and Joshua Getzler. Cambridge University Press.

Wilson, Joshua C. 2011. "Sustaining the State: Legal Consciousness and the Construction of Legality in Competing Abortion Activists' Narratives." *Law and Social Inquiry* 36 (2): 455–483.

Wilson, Sophia. 2017. "Cause Lawyering in Revolutionary Ukraine." *Journal of Law and Courts* 5 (2): 267–288.

Winn, Jane K. and Tang-chi Yeh. 1995. "Advocating Democracy: The Role of Lawyers in Taiwan's Political Transformation." *Law and Social Inquiry* 20 (2): 561–599.

Wong, Brian. 2020. "Hong Kong Court Throws Out Two Private Prosecutions Tied to Social Unrest." *South China Morning Post*, August 24. Accessed June 25, 2021. https://www.scmp.com/news/hong-kong/law-and-crime/article/3098628/hong-kong-justice-department-wins-court-approval-quash.

Wong, John D. 2020. "Protests, Politics and Challenges to Hong Kong's Rule of Law." *Harvard Political Review*, March 2. Accessed August 30, 2020. https://harvardpolitics.com/world/protests-politics-and-challenges-to-hong-kongs-rule-of-law.

Wong, John D. 2022. "Constructing the Legitimacy of Governance in Hong Kong: 'Prosperity and Stability' and 'Democracy and Freedom.'" *The Journal of Asian Studies*, First View. Accessed February 17, 2022. https://doi.org/10.1017/S0021911821002230.

Wong, Lydia, Thomas E. Kellogg, and Yan-ho Lai. 2021. *Hong Kong's National Security Law and the Right to Fair Trial: A GCAL Briefing Paper.* Center for Asian Law, Georgetown University Law Center. June 28. Accessed October 16, 2021. https://www.law.georgetown.edu/law-asia/wp-content/uploads/sites/31/2021/06/HongKongNSLRightToFairTrial.pdf.

Wong, Max W. L. 2011. "Social Control and Political Order: Decolonisation and the Use of Emergency Regulations in Hong Kong." *Hong Kong Law Journal* 41 (2): 449–480.

Wong, Max W. L. 2017. *Re-Ordering Hong Kong: Decolonisation and the Hong Kong Bill of Rights Ordinance.* Wildy, Simmonds and Hill Publishing.

Wong, Rachel. 2020. "'Liberal' Voices Win Four Seats in Hong Kong's Law Society Council Election." *Hong Kong Free Press*, May 29. Accessed January 3, 2021. https://hongkongfp.com/2020/05/29/liberal-voices-win-four-seats-in-hong-kongs-law-society-council-election/.

Wong, Stan H.W., Ngok. Ma, and Wai-man Lam. 2018. "Immigrants as Voters in Electoral Autocracies: The Case of Mainland Chinese Immigrants in Hong Kong." *Journal of East Asian Studies* 18 (1): 67–95.

Wong, T. W. 2020. "Nǚ shēng tuì xià qián xiàn zhuǎn rèn fǎ tíng, 'páng tīng shī': péi bàn bèi bǔ shǒu zú, yán xù yùn dòng." *CitizenNews*. June 25. Accessed March 21, 2021. Archived on file with the author.

The World Bank. 2019. *Worldwide Governance Indicators*. Accessed July 31, 2020. https://databank.worldbank.org/databases/rule-of-law.

World Economic Forum. 2019. *The Global Competitiveness Report*. Accessed 31 July 2020. https://www3.weforum.org/docs/WEF_TheGlobalCompetitivenessReport2019.pdf.

World Justice Project. 2019. *The WJP Rule of Law Index 2019*. Accessed July 9, 2020. https://worldjusticeproject.org/rule-of-law-index/.

Wu, Jieh-min, and Mei Liao. 2015. "From Unification-Independence Divide to the China Factor: How Changing Political Identity Influences Voting Behavior." *Taiwan She Hui Xue* 29: 89–132.

Wu, Jieh-min. 2016. "The China Factor in Taiwan: Impact and Response." In *Handbook of Modern Taiwan Politics and Society*, edited by Gunter Schubert. Routledge.

"Xiāng gǎng dà lu shī gōng huì zhǔ xí chū rèn zhèng xié wěi yuán yǐn qǐ zhì yí." 2008. *Radio Free Asia*, January 6. Accessed January 29, 2021. https://www.rfa.org/cantonese/news/hongkong_politics_beijing-20080116.html.

Xiāng Gǎng Tè Bié Xíng Zhèng Qū Sù Mò Jiā Tāo jí lìng bā rén. 2018. HKDC 225.

"Xiè Wěi Jùn Zhōng Rèn Shì 'Xī Huán Qì Zī'." 2012. *Apple Daily*, December 31, A03.

Xinhua News Agency. 2019. "Quánguó réndà chángwěihuì fǎgōngwěi fāyánrén jiù xiānggǎng fǎyuàn yǒuguān sīfǎ fùhé ànpànjué fābiǎo tánhuà." November 19. Accessed November 20, 2019. https://www.gov.cn/xinwen/2019-11/19/content_5453345.htm.

"Xuǎn wěi huì jiě gòu: fǎ lu jiè 30 tuán tǐ xuǎn mín, yú 14 guān zhōng zī rén dà jiàn zhì děng; yuán 7400 rén yǒu piào tóu , Péng Yùn Xī: xīn míng dān yán shēn hé zī gé zhí yè zhě wài." 2021. *Ming Pao Daily*, 15 April. A01.

Yam, Julius, and Po Jen Yap. 2023. "Legalism and Strategic Judicial Decision-Making in Hong Kong." *Hong Kong Law Journal* 53 (1): 207–224.

Yang, Shen. 2019. "In the Name of the Law: Legal Frames and the Ending of the Occupy Movement in Hong Kong." *Law and Social Inquiry* 44, no. 2: 468–490.

Yap, Po Jen. 2007. "Constitutional Review under the Basic Law: The Rise, Retreat and Resurgence of Judicial Power in Hong Kong." *Hong Kong Law Journal* 37 (2): 449–474.

Yazdiha, Haj. 2014. "Law as Movement Strategy: How the Islamophobia Movement Institutionalizes Fear through Legislation." *Social Movement Studies* 13 (2): 267–274.

Yep, Ray. 2007. "Links with the Mainland." In *Contemporary Hong Kong Politics*, edited by Wai-Man Lam, Percy L. T. Lui, and Wilson Wong. Hong Kong University Press.

Yiu, Pak, and Echo Wong. 2023. "Multinationals turn away from Hong Kong for dispute resolution." *Nikkei Asia*, June 8. Accessed January 29, 2024. https://asia.nikkei.com/Spotlight/Hong-Kong-security-law/Multinationals-turn-away-from-Hong-Kong-for-dispute-resolution.

Young, Simon NM, and Richard Cullen. 2010. *Electing Hong Kong's Chief Executive.* Hong Kong University Press.

Yuen, Chris. 2016a. "Incoming Lawmaker Junius Ho Thanks China Liaison Office and Others for Support." *Hong Kong Free Press*, September 5. Accessed November 22, 2020. https://hongkongfp.com/2016/09/05/incoming-lawmaker-junius-ho-thanks-china-liaison-office-others-support/.

Yuen, Chris. 2016b. "Over 44,000 sign petitions against Youngspiration's Yau Wai-ching amid "Chee-na" oath fallout." *Hong Kong Free Press*, October 14. Accessed December 17, 2020. https://hongkongfp.com/2016/10/14/over-44000-sign-petition-against-youngspirations-yau-wai-ching-amid-chee-na-oath-fallout/.

Yuen, Samson, and Edmund W. Cheng. 2020. "Between High Autonomy and Sovereign Control in a Subnational Island Jurisdiction: The Paradox of Hong Kong under 'One Country, Two Systems.'" *Island Studies Journal* 15 (1): 131–150.

Zēng, Zhāo Míng. 2014. "Qí Lù Pái Huái de Zhōng Guó Mèng: Mín Zú Guó Jiā Huò Tiān Xià Dì Guó?" *Reflexion* 25: 25–47.

Zhang, Dejiang. 2017. "Shùlì guójiā guānniàn shì jīběnfǎ shíshī hé xīn yàoqiú (quánwén)." *Ta Kung Pao*, May 27. Accessed September 27, 2021. http://www.takungpao.com.hk/hongkong/text/2017/0527/84870.html.

Zhang, Dejiang. 2017. "Zhōngyāng hé xiānggǎng shì shòuquán hé bèishòuquán guānxì, qiángdiào bù róng yǐ gāodù zìzhì wéi míng duìkàng zhōngyāng quánlì." *Ming Pao Instant News*, May 27. Accessed November 19, 2020. Archived on file with the author.

Zhou, Ling. 2011. "The Independent Director System and Its Legal Transplant into China." *Journal of Comparative Law* 6 (2): 262–291.

Zhu, Han. 2019. "Beijing's 'Rule of Law' Strategy for Governing Hong Kong: Legalisation without Democratisation." *The China Perspective* 2019 (1): 23–33.

"[Zhuān fǎng] Gēng Tián Yī Nián, Fǎn Qián Xiàn Rèn Yì Wù Lu Shī, Chén Xìn Xīn Rèn Fǎ Zhèng Huì Sī Xīn Zhào Jí Rén." 2020. *Inmediahk*, March 12. Accessed June 25, 2021. https://www.inmediahk.net/node/1071505?__cf_chl_captcha_tk__=606b633cea3800517281f7571f8b373fe34eab43-1624622163-0.

Zhuang, Shaohong. 2005. "Legal Transplantation in the People's Republic of China: A Reply to Alan Watson." *European Journal of Law Reform* 7 (1&2): 215–236.

"[Zuì hòu fáng xiàn 3] Dà qí lì rì bù shì qí lì." 2015. *Stand News*, August 13. Accessed March 21, 2021. Archived on file with the author.

"[Zuì qiáng lǎn rén bāo] Dà lu shī gōng huì fā bù 'jiǎn yì zhǐ nán', jiě dá xiū dìng táo fàn tiáo lì 24 gè wèn tí." 2019. *Stand News*, June 6. Accessed January 24, 2021. Archived on file with the author.

Index